Research Skills for
Policy and Development

Edited by Alan Thomas and Giles Mohan

Research Skills for
Policy and Development
How to find out *fast*

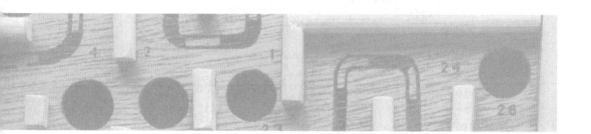

The Open University

in association with

SAGE Publications
Los Angeles • London • New Delhi • Singapore

 SAGE Publications Ltd
1 Oliver's Yard
55 City Road
London EC1Y 1SP

SAGE Publications Inc.
2455 Teller Road
Thousand Oaks, California 91320

SAGE Publications India Pvt Ltd
B 1/I 1 Mohan Cooperative Industrial Area
Mathura Road, New Delhi 110 044
India

SAGE Publications Asia-Pacific Pte Ltd
33 Pekin Street #02-01
Far East Square
Singapore 048763

Library of Congress Control Number: 2006936079

British Library Cataloguing in Publication data

A catalogue record for this book is available from the British Library

ISBN 978-1-4129-4563-9
ISBN 978-1-4129-4564-6 (pbk)

Typeset by C&M Digitals (P) Ltd, Chennai, India
Printed in Great Britain by The Alden Press, Witney
Printed on paper from sustainable resources

Contents

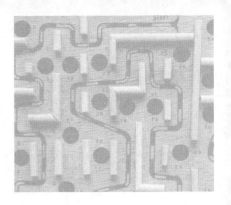

Contributors

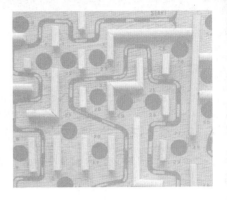

Dina Abbott is a senior lecturer in Geography and Development Studies at the University of Derby. Her primary research interest is urban gendered poverty, especially Mumbai. She is currently involved with women's urban agricultural projects in Banjul, The Gambia. She also has a long association with the Development Policy and Practice Department, The Open University for which she has both taught and carried out various research-related activities, recently on issues of Development Management.

Stephanie Barrientos is a Research Fellow at the Institute of Development Studies, Sussex. Her main research interests are in gender, work and global production, and ethical and fair trade. She has published widely on women's employment in agribusiness and global value chains, and on the impact of ethical and fair trade on workers and small producers.

Christine Blackmore is Senior Lecturer in Environment and Development Systems in the Open University's Systems Department. She focuses on environmental decision making in the context of sustainable development, learning systems and communities of practice in both teaching and research. Before joining the Open University in 1986 Christine worked in Africa for 5 years (Nigeria, Lesotho, Sierra Leone).

Joanna Chataway is Professor in the Development Policy and Practice Department at the Open University. As an academic and consultant she works on issues of innovation in the life sciences, institutional development and science and technology policy.

Joseph Hanlon is a Senior Lecturer in Development and Conflict Resolution at the Open University, but he considers himself more a journalist than an academic. He is author or editor of 14 books on southern Africa and on civil war, most recently *On Your Bike, the Development Dilemma in Mozambique* (Oxford, James Currey, 2007). He was policy advisor to the Jubilee 2000 campaign to cancel poor country debt and writes extensively about debt and aid.

Ray Ison is Professor of Systems and Director of the Open Systems Research Group at the Open University. His research specialisations include: development and evaluation of systemic, participatory and process-based environmental decision making; natural resource management; organisational change and R&D methodologies; social learning in the context of integrated catchment management and sustainable use of water. Ray also has much experience of designing and developing learner centred, experiential and open learning systems and models. Prior to joining the Open University in 1994 he worked in Australia at the Universities of Sydney and Western Sydney (Hawkesbury).

Hazel Johnson is Senior Lecturer in Development Studies at the Open University, has written widely for the undergraduate and postgraduate courses in development, and is a core member of the Global Programme in Development Management team, of which she has also been Programme Director. She has a background in Sociology and Development Studies, and has carried out research in food production and markets, and on social learning and institutional change.

Sue Mayer gained a PhD in Veterinary cell biology from Bristol University in 1987. Since then she has lectured at Bristol University, worked for the RSPCA and spent 5 years as Director of Science for Greenpeace UK. In January 1998 she became a founder of GeneWatch UK, a not-for-profit organisation that monitors developments in genetics from a public interest perspective.

Linda Mayoux is an independent consultant. She has done extensive research on gender and micro-enterprise development, co-operatives and micro-finance. One of her current interests is the development of participatory methods for gender analysis of micro-finance programmes.

Chandan Mukherjee is Professor of Quantitative Methods and Director, at the Centre for Development Studies, Trivandrum, India, a research institute. He has been teaching statistics for 25 years, at post graduate level and above, to students with varied disciplinary backgrounds.

Giles Mohan is a Senior Lecturer in Development Studies at the Open University. He has researched questions of local governance and participation in Africa and the dynamics of diasporic communities. He has published extensively in human geography and development studies journals.

Jill Mordaunt is Senior Lecturer in Social Enterprise at the Open University where she was extensively involved in the development of specialist courses for public and non-profit organisations. She has research interests in the role of institutional funding in shaping non-profit activity and more recently her main work has focused on issues of organisational failure, turnaround and recovery in public and non-profit organisations. She is currently evaluating the impact of consultancy interventions on organisational development.

Bridget O'Laughlin is Reader in Population and Development at the Institute of Social Studies in the Hague. From 1979–1992, she worked at Eduardo Mondlane University in Mozambique. She continues to focus her research on Southern Africa and particularly on Mozambique. Her current interests are the politics of AIDS and the consequences of the restructuring of migrant labour for gender relations in Southern Africa.

Stephen Potter joined the Open University in 1977 working on a number of transport research projects and also on an urban studies and a statistical sources course. In 1984 he left the Open University to be a freelance researcher and also worked with Dial-a-Ride in London. He rejoined the Open University in 1987 and is now the University's Professor of Transport Strategy (design.open.ac.uk/people/people. htm).

Chris Roche is currently International Programme Director for Oxfam Australia. Previously he headed up Oxfam Great Britain's Programme Policy Team and before that worked for 10 years with the international NGO consortium ACORD. He has conducted research on Impact Assessment methods, on NGOs in West Africa, and on an Atlas of Social Protest in the UK.

Ramya Subrahmanian is a Research Fellow at the Institute of Development Studies, University of Sussex, where she does research and teaches on gender issues in development and social policy, with a particular emphasis on elementary education and child labour. She is the co-editor (with Naila Kabeer) of 'Institutions, Relations and Outcomes: A Framework and Case Studies for Gender-Aware Planning' (Kali for Women, 1999 and Zed Books, 2000) and (with Naila Kabeer and Geetha B Nambissan) of 'Child Labour and the Right to Education in South Asia: Needs versus Rights?' (Sage 2003). Her doctoral research focused on schooling processes in two villages in Southern India, and other subsequent research has focused on education exclusion in India and South Africa.

Alan Thomas is a Visiting Professor both at the Centre for Development Studies, Swansea and at the Open University, where he was a co-founder of the University's Development Policy and Practice group and a core member of the team working on the Global Programme in Development Management. He takes an action-oriented, case study approach to his research, where his main interests are learning and knowledge sharing in development policy and management, co-operative development mainly in the UK and Europe, non-profit management and the role of NGOs in sustainable development and environmental policy, globally and particularly in Southern Africa.

Philip Woodhouse is Senior Lecturer in Environment and Rural Development at the Institute for Development Policy and Management (IDPM), University of Manchester. He is a member of the Society and Environment Research Group, and has been engaged in research on land and water management in Africa for over 20 years, particularly in Mozambique, South Africa, and francophone West Africa, and more recently in Latin America.

Marc Wuyts is Professor in Statistics and Development Economics at the Institute of Social Studies, The Hague, and teaches and writes about data analysis, statistics and econometrics. His research focuses on the macroeconomics of development and policies for poverty reduction and socioeconomic security, with specific emphasis on Mozambique and Tanzania.

Acknowledgements

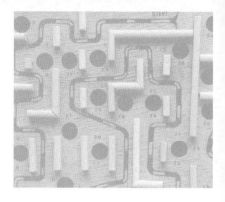

Grateful acknowledgement is made to the following sources for permission to reproduce material in this book:

Figures
Figure 2.1: Kersten, S.M.M. 1995, 'In search of dialogue: vegetation management in Western NSW, Australia', PhD Thesis, University of Sydney, © 1995 by Stephany Kersten; *Figure 2.5:* Reprinted from *Agricultural Systems*, no. 49, Macadam, R., Van Asch, R., Hedley, B., Pitt, E. and Carroll, P., 'A case study in development planning using a systems learning approach generating a master plan for the livestock sector in Nepal', Copyright 1995, with kind permission from Elsevier Science Ltd, The Boulevard, Langford Lane, Kidlington, OX5 1GB, UK; *Figure 2.6:* Uphoff, N. 1986, *Local Institutional Development: an Analytical Sourcebook with Cases*, Kumarian Press; *Figure 8.1:* Welbourn, A. 1991, 'RRA and the anaysis', figure 1, *RRA Notes*, no. 14, International Institute for Environment and Development; *Figure 8.3:* Mayoux, L. and ANANDI (2005) 'Participatory Action Learning System (PALS): impact assessment for civil society development and grassroots-based advocacy in Anandi, India', *Journal of International Development*, vol. 17, no. 2, pp. 211–42. © John Wiley & Sons Ltd; *Figure 12.1:* adapted from Goetz, A. 1996, 'Understanding gendered institutional structures and practices', Institute of Development Studies, by permission of the author; *Figure 12.2:* Howes, M. and Roche, C. 'A participatory appraisal of ACORD', *PLA Notes*, Institute of Development Studies, by permission of the author.

Tables
Table 10.1: Collier, P., Radwan, S. and Wangwe, S. 1986, *Labour and Poverty in Rural Tanzania: Ujamaa and Rural Development in the United Republic of Tanzania*, Clarendon Press, by permission of Oxford University Press; *Table 10.2: Tanzania: the Informal Sector*, pp. 2–5, 1991, The Planning Commission and the Ministry of Labour Youth Development, Tanzania; *Table 12.2:* adapted from Goetz, A. 1996, 'Understanding gendered institutional structures and practices', Institute of Development Studies, by permission of the author.

Introduction

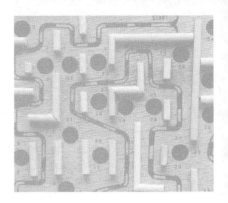

Alan Thomas

This book is about research to inform policy and public action. It is aimed at development managers and others who are involved in policy investigation. Those doing academic research on policy-related issues should also find it useful, although it is not specifically addressed to them. The collection is an updated version of Thomas, Chataway and Wuyts (1998), which was more squarely aimed at people involved in international development. But sales of that original text exceeded this target audience and we found people from diverse geographical and professional backgrounds using it. It was also written at a time when the Internet was taking off, but it had not become the mainstay of communication that it is today. So, we decided a new book was in order that appealed to this broader market of busy people involved in multiple forms of public action, but with a broader (and bewildering) array of information at their fingertips.

When we talk of development managers, we use it in a broad sense that includes, but goes beyond, those working in *international* development. We understand development to incorporate what observers term 'intentional' and 'immanent' development, whereby the former is concerned with 'willed' development policy and action and the latter is concerned with underlying processes of development (Cowen and Shenton, 1996). *Intentional* development emerged over the past two centuries, largely as a means of managing those 'surplus populations' that had either been excluded from or 'adversely incorporated' into processes of *immanent* capitalist development. For much of this time the 'development doctrine purported to put this relative surplus population to work within the integument of the nation' (Cowen and Shenton, 1996, p.153). As we know this faith in the redistributive state has given way to a plurality of public and private agents pursuing actions to protect and include the disadvantaged. From this perspective development is a resolutely global phenomenon and its management involves an increasingly wide array of people and organisations who will at some point have to undertake investigations for policy and public action. So, this book is relevant for those working in community groups, non-governmental organisations, social movements, and central and local governments in both the global North and South, as well as internationally.

Policy investigation differs from 'pure' research in that its results are meant to have immediate, practical application. Ideally, perhaps, it will provide information to help design and implement policies that will achieve their objectives effectively and contribute to the achievement of broad development goals. However, there is an immediate issue in that development is a hugely contested concept. It is about *alternative* paths of social and economic transformation. While there is a broad global consensus on the Millennium Development Goals (Maxwell, 2005), particularly the first MDG, with its target of halving the number of people living on less than a dollar day by 2015, there can be radical disagreement on how to achieve them. Arguably, also, the focus on numerical targets such as reductions in income-based poverty obscures bigger differences over what constitutes a desirable, 'developed' society. Research for development is thus often used to back up particular policy options within political debates. Policy investigation, in being designed to be 'useful', may be aimed to inform policy-makers who are already fixed in their positions or to provide ammunition for campaigners for change. In either case it is open to accusations of 'bias', and it is important to be able to defend against such criticisms.

Since the first edition of this book there has been an explosion of interest in 'evidence-based policy' (EBP) (see Mayer's chapter in this volume). This is partly a result of the emphasis placed by the Blair administrations in the UK since 1997 on 'what works', the idea being that a modernising government should utilise rational decision-making based on the best evidence available, rather than promote policies based on ideology. A great deal of work has been undertaken on the applicability of such an approach to development, notably by the 'Research and Policy in Development' (RAPID) programme of the Overseas Development Institute (ODI). Sutcliffe and Court (2005), in a paper on the relevance of evidence-based policy-making in developing countries, define EBP as 'a discourse or set of methods which informs the policy process, rather than aiming to directly affect the eventual goals of the policy', and argue that: 'Better utilisation of evidence in policy and practice can help save lives, reduce poverty and improve development performance in developing countries' (p. iii).

One might criticise the EBP approach for accepting the *status quo*. Surely it is legitimate also to utilise research evidence to challenge assumptions underlying the goals of policy, especially where these act to entrench injustice by denying the feasibility of any alternatives. We argue that it is crucial to acknowledge the role of investigation in building up arguments for alternative policy goals, as well as in working out the details of how best to achieve an agreed policy goal. It is better for policy to be based on a realistic assessment of evidence *as well as* on values or ideology, rather than on ideology alone. For a salutary warning, consider the following report of a conversation with an aide of George W. Bush:

> The aide said that guys like me were 'in what we call the reality-based community,' which he defined as people who 'believe that solutions emerge from your judicious study of discernible reality'. I nodded and murmured something about enlightenment principles and empiricism. He cut me off. 'That's not the way the world really works anymore', he continued. 'We're an empire now, and when we act, we create our own

reality. And while you're studying that reality – judiciously, as you will – we'll act again, creating other new realities, which you can study too, and that's how things will sort out. We're history's actors . . . and you, all of you, will be left to just study what we do'.

(Suskind, R., 'Without a Doubt', *New York Times*, 17 Oct. 2004)

We see, then, that research for development is undertaken in a context shaped by power relations and differences over values. But, more than this, it is often at least partly *about* such matters. This makes it extremely difficult, if not impossible, to separate normative issues about what exactly constitute development principles from the research itself. There are particular ethical issues involved in all social research, but research in the name of development carries an expectation of improvement of some kind. In addition, such research often touches on matters of extreme personal sensitivity or involving trauma, such as those related to people's experience of poverty or HIV/AIDS, corruption, religion or the effects of violence. Given the normative differences over development policy noted above, and the uncertainty over the outcomes of any development policy, we argue there is a strong imperative to uphold development principles within the conduct of the research itself. This point is elaborated further below.

The first edition of this book had the title *Finding out Fast*. Policy decisions are often required quickly, with incomplete data or with limited resources with which to obtain information. Hence, those involved in or learning about development policy need ideas and guidance on how to find out, evaluate and use relevant information *fast*.

However, some people suggested that the title was wrong, too slick or risked lending credibility to the idea that substantive research is generally an unnecessary waste of resources. The very idea of 'finding out' could sound as though the problem under investigation is more or less well understood and all that is needed is to 'fill in the boxes' with data. It could also imply that the investigator is extracting information from a situation without any involvement from those actually living or working in it.

As for finding out *fast*, the book could easily appear to be promoting speed in relation to policy research as a good thing in itself. If rapid research is good, then more considered investigations may appear a luxury. It is already all too common to engage consultants to spend a very limited time investigating 'the field' at such a late stage in the policy development process that hardly any changes can be made to the proposed policy, whatever their findings. One critic suggested that the only useful book on the subject would be a polemic against the 'rapid rural appraisal' (RRA) movement, pointing out that even the leading proponent of this approach, Robert Chambers, had doubts about some of the ways it is used: 'the word "rapid" ... has been used to legitimate brash and biased rural development tourism' (Chambers, 1994a, p. 1441). In fact the idea of '*rapid* rural appraisal' has largely been superseded by '*participative* rural appraisal' (PRA) and most recently by 'participative learning and action' (PLA – see chapters 7 and 8). This probably confirms that speed as such is less important than issues about who is involved and how the results of research for development are used.

The focus of the book, then, is on *policy investigation:* research which is required to inform policy or is meant to influence policy. This may mean 'finding out fast', although a better emphasis is on timeliness rather than speed as such. There are real dangers in certain methods being open to misuse and in the need for action becoming an excuse for not allocating adequate resources to analysis and investigation. Nevertheless, speed is often required and delay is itself a policy decision. Whether you are implementing policy or trying to influence the actions of others, the other agencies involved will certainly not wait for your convenience. Thus, the need to act as the situation or a politically imposed timetable demands may limit the applicability of standard research methods which have self-imposed requirements for sample size, statistical confidence or corroboration of evidence. It is a reality for many development managers that investigations have to be done quickly – or if not, then to a timetable dictated by events outside their control.

This book aims to help readers faced with the need to develop policy or make decisions quickly, about public action or their agency's input into the policy process. Typically, there are incomplete data and limited resources with which to undertake an investigation. However, this is not a handbook extolling the virtues of a specific bag of tools which supposedly provides answers to all policy questions in as short a space of time as may happen to be available. Rather, the book both explains and critically reviews the use of a variety of methods for policy investigation, in the belief that methods aimed at practically useful results can still be rigorous and that, if those results are required fast, that need not mean sloppy.

The aims of the book can be summarised as follows:

1 to help development managers to become competent investigators (not necessarily fully expert researchers), in the context of development as public action involving multiple agencies and of policy as process;
2 for readers to understand how to use research better (including commissioning and evaluating research);
3 for readers to develop sufficient skills to enable them to do some of their own investigation, at least to a point that allows them to appreciate the research done by others;
4 to make clear the importance of attempting to uphold developmental principles within the conduct of policy investigations;
5 to introduce a range of generic analytical and investigative skills at a conceptual level, with emphasis on how the appropriateness of different methods derives from the needs of different contexts. Some practical examples are provided;
6 for each such skill area introduced, to present a checklist of points to bear in mind when using it or assessing an investigation which uses it.

The rest of this Introduction is in four sections. The first explores the context of policy investigations and shows the relevance of ideas about development management, with the aid of some illustrative examples. Section 2 looks more closely at how such investigation differs from pure research, including both the *dangers of* assuming that policy investigation can ignore the tenets of academic research and the *need for* some special features in one's approach when undertaking investigations aimed at informing or influencing policy. Section 3 explains the general approach taken to investigation in the book, with some additional points on investigation when it is specifically aimed at informing development policy and public action. The final section sets out how the rest of the book is organised.

1 Policy investigations and development management • • •

Here are a number of examples where policy is developing and choices have to be made (some of which appear as more detailed cases in later chapters). In each case there was an investigation, aimed at informing policy directly, at improving the quality of policy decisions, or at backing up a case being made for a change in policy. Although the examples are deliberately chosen to illustrate the enormous variety of situations where there is a need for research to inform development policy, it is instructive to look for points of commonality between the various examples.

Example A   Gathering information for project design

A large international development agency has already undertaken a preliminary design for an integrated rural development project. 'It aimed to provide heavily subsidised credit to small-scale farmers so that they would adopt a tobacco fertiliser package. Credit was to be delivered through a newly instituted co-operative society. Rural roads construction would enable farmers to market crops more easily. Nutrition education and kitchen gardens would be developed for women'. The agency then puts together a project design team consisting of an anthropologist, an economist, a food scientist, two road engineers and an expert on finance. They are to provide information on the local communities, on the costs of road construction, on appropriate varieties of vegetable, etc. This information is required for the detailed design of the project so that its implementation can be agreed by the national government and the required disbursement of aid funds can be confirmed by the agency's headquarters.

(taken from Staudt, 1991, pp. 46–47)

Example B   Routine information or investigating causes?

In Britain for many years, transport policy has consisted mainly of attempts by the Department for Transport, on the one hand, and various local authorities on the other, to build roads to cope with the continuously rising demand for travel by car. Information has been routinely collected on trip lengths, types of destinations and frequency of trips, etc. so that trends in demand can be estimated. However, it has recently been suggested that policy should not just cope with demand but should attempt to affect travellers' behaviour; perhaps policy should be designed deliberately to shape or even reduce demand in order to reduce congestion and pollution (especially carbon dioxide emissions), while maintaining accessibility and improving quality of life. This would imply the need not just for routine information gathering but for investigation of why people make the journeys they do and what controllable factors are likely to have an effect on demand. It also calls for much more integrated policy responses. However, while the need for an integrated approach which tackles the causes of traffic problems in their widest sense has been acknowledged, information lags behind by still focusing on the level of outcomes rather than causes.

(See Chapter 1 for more on this example.)

Example C   Investigation to involve stakeholders in policy

The term 'Participatory Poverty Assessment' (PPA) refers to a particular type of organised investigation which has been carried out in many countries from the early 1990s. They bring together the widespread acceptance of the importance and usefulness of participatory research techniques with the need for information on the extent and causes of poverty to inform poverty reduction strategies (especially the Poverty Reduction Strategy Papers – PRSPs – which the governments of developing countries are often effectively required to produce by the World Bank and other donor agencies).

PPAs achieved their greatest recognition when the World Bank used a major study of poverty worldwide, entitled 'Voices of the Poor', that combined information from PPAs in many countries to inform its World Development Report 2000/01 on *Attacking Poverty*. In that study, Narayan *et al.* (2000, p. 15) provides the following definition:

> A PPA is an iterative, participatory research process that seeks to understand poverty from the perspective of a range of stakeholders, and to involve them directly in planning follow-up action. The most important ... are poor men and women. PPAs also include decisionmakers from all levels of government, civil

(Continued)

(Continued)

society and the local elite, thereby uncovering different interests and perspectives and increasing local capacity and commitment to follow-up action. PPAs seek to understand poverty in its local social, institutional and political context. Since PPAs address national policy, microlevel data are collected from a large number of communities in order to discern patterns across social groups and geographic areas, and across location and social group specificities.

(See Chapter 7 for more on the particular example of the Uganda PPA.)

Example D   Research aimed at influencing policy

The idea of Community Animal Health Workers (CAHWs) is similar to the well known 'barefoot doctors' in China, but applied to veterinary services. Where financial constraints or remoteness restrict access to professionals, local people, themselves livestock keepers, are trained to provide basic services of diagnosis, treatment and prevention of animal diseases. From the mid-1980s, the UK-based NGO ITDG (now called Practical Action) promoted this idea in Kenya. As a result, with the help of some government field veterinarians, a number of NGOs set up decentralised animal health programmes on this basis and produced good evidence that they were very successful. However, the approach was (and remains) illegal, and was opposed by the veterinary profession, with threats to expel any professional veterinarians involved. More recently, following a multi-stakeholder consultation, a study was carried out by government, university and external experts, with the aim of informing a new policy framework to legalise decentralised animal health services using CAHWs, although this has not yet been implemented.

(Source: Court and Young, 2003, Case Study 43. See Example 11.2, Chapter 11 for more on this example.)

Some of the points in common between the four examples are as follows:

1 The contexts of Examples A, C and D are in developing countries. As contexts for research, they may be characterised by factors such as incompleteness of information, huge uncertainties surrounding everything from day-to-day livelihoods to the functioning of government bureaucracies, and a sense of aiming at a 'moving target' as developmental and other changes to the subjects of research take place even while the researcher is trying to investigate them. In some cases these factors take on an extreme

form, as when research on development is done in conditions of crisis or violent conflict. A moment's reflection, however, shows that these factors also apply to policy oriented research in countries like the UK which are referred to as 'developed'. Researchers in Example B are equally certain to be bedevilled by *uncertainty, incomplete information* and *constant change in what is being researched.* These are certainly characteristics of development contexts, but in the sense that development can occur anywhere, not only in poor countries.

2 Rather than being concerned solely with improving their own positions, the agencies involved in each case are *intervening in social processes* in order to try to work towards broad social (or environmental) *goals external to the agencies themselves.*

In Example A, the agency's project is presumably intended to improve the livelihoods of the small farmers, while in Example B the possible change to transport policy would clearly be designed to change people's behaviour in a way which is not occurring voluntarily but which would be intended to improve their quality of life. In Example C, under pressure from international donors, Southern governments utilise participatory investigative techniques to inform policy to reduce poverty. Example D sees an international non-governmental organisation (NGO) based in the North attempting to influence the policy of a Southern government in the name of improving rural livelihoods.

3 In each case *multiple agencies* are involved, including several other organisations and groups as well as the agency undertaking the investigation.

The relationship between them can be of different kinds. In Example A the project team is seeking support from its agency's headquarters and from the government of the country concerned, as well as having to deal with local community groups and interests. In Example B the Department of Transport and the various local authorities are said to be working together, although there may be some differences of interest between particular local needs and considerations of overall effects at national level. In Example C, the point is to involve a range of stakeholders at the same time as producing information on the situation of poor people. The NGOs involved in Example D find themselves opposed to some extent to the national government, although in alliance with certain local interests.

4 The decisions which may be informed by particular investigations are always part of the continuing development of policy so that it is best to think of *policy as process.*

This means that not only is policy designed to change a given situation but, as noted in 1 above, the situation is changing anyway and giving rise to changing pressures for changes in policy. The fact that policy is constantly developing in this way makes it useful to think of policy as itself a process.

The alternative view, of policy as prescription, is not appropriate in development contexts. It is never the case that an agency simply comes to a 'green field' situation, finds out what is needed, and prescribes and implements policies designed on that basis. In Example A the agency is undertaking an investigation as part of its own process of designing a project. More generally, agencies tend to have policies already operating, as with the policy of building roads to meet demand in Example B. Example C actually involves a designed process relating a continuous cycle of investigation to a policy cycle. And if a particular agency is indeed new to a situation – as with the NGOs in Example D back in the late 1980s – then there are generally other agencies already involved which are carrying out policies. This means you cannot assume things will remain static for as long as it takes to do whatever investigation is deemed necessary. The situation may change as the policies of the other agencies involved impact upon it.

Similarly, once an investigation is complete, an agency's policies may be informed by it for some time, as may the actions of others, but both the policies and the actions of all concerned will continue to change and develop as events unfold and one reacts to another.

5 The social goals being aimed at are subject to *value-based conflicts*.

It is clear in Example D that the NGOs' goals with respect to improving rural livelihoods in remote areas may conflict with certain views of the integrity of the veterinarian profession and the regulatory principles of the national bureaucracy. In Example C, involving stakeholders in one organised investigation using 'participatory' principles may be construed as an attempt to forestall likely differences between interest groups over priorities in national poverty policy. In Example B, saving energy and reducing pollution nationally may conflict with improving accessibility in a particular location. As for Example A, what the agency headquarters or its national staff sees as a good rural development project may differ from the priorities of the particular government concerned, while what different groups in the community want may be different again. It is not just that different interests clash, but views as to what constitute desirable social and development goals differ according to what weight is given to different values, as for example when improved material welfare may be obtained at the expense of freedom of choice.

The above commonalities between the examples may be summarised by pointing out that they all involve *development management* (Thomas, 1996a), where development is seen in terms of *public action* (Drèze and Sen, 1989; Wuyts, Mackintosh and Hewitt, 1992). Boxes 1 and 2 give definitions of these terms, for reference.

Note here that so far the points made about these examples relate to the notion of development management as a set of tools for managing development interventions (management *of* development). Policy investigation then becomes one of the tools for ensuring that development is 'done' effectively and efficiently. However, as discussed elsewhere (Thomas, 1999), while such tools are very important, this is an over-instrumental view of development. Development management is also a normative concept ('management *for* development') involving building developmental values into the management of all activities. As we will see, this can include incorporating particular values (such as participation in Example C) into policy investigation itself. This means that contestation over values is not just a question of how research results are utilised but also involves debate about how policy investigation should be carried out.

Box 1 Development management

... development management [is] the management of deliberate efforts at progress on the part of one of a number of agencies, the management of intervention in the process of social change in the context of conflicts of goals, values and interests. (... in this view, development management is a process or an activity that can take place anywhere, not just in developing countries.)

(Thomas, 1996, p. 106)

... we can [also] define development management as management undertaken with a development orientation, rather than management of the development process or the management of development interventions or tasks. ... [T]his view of development management: 'management *for* development' ... implies a style of management in which any and every activity is undertaken in such a way as to enhance development. ... it implies considering how [tasks] are done, not just getting immediate results.

(Thomas, 1999, pp. 10, 13)

Box 2 Public action

Public action is not ... just a question of public delivery and state initiative. It is also ... a matter of participation by the public in the process of social change.

(Drèze and Sen, 1989, p. 259)

By *public action* we mean purposive collective action, whether for collective private ends or for public ends (however defined). ... [A] wide definition of public action ... include[s] ... the actions, not only of states and organisations which claim to seek to promote the public good or assist the disadvantaged, but also clubs of the powerful who seek to influence the public sphere for their own ends.

(Mackintosh, 1992, p. 5)

There are some final points to note about the above examples. First, *who* is doing the research is a political question which affects how the research can be done and how the results are likely to be utilised. The investigator cannot think of herself or himself as standing apart from what is being investigated or think of the investigation as an exercise in objectivity to be kept separate from policy actions. It does matter whether the investigator is male or female, or is perceived as an agent of a powerful agency, and so on. In particular, the *investigator's relationship with the agencies* involved is an important part of the context. This relationship can be of various kinds. In Example A the investigators will be trying to influence their own agency (and an outside agency – the government) without having direct power to implement. In Example D, the NGO carrying out the investigations used research results both to inform and implement their own policies directly and at the same time to attempt to influence government policy. Other possibilities are: carrying out a consultancy for one of a number of agencies; representing a specific interest group trying to influence another, perhaps more powerful, agency; and so on.

In each case the investigations to be carried out are not only action- or policy-oriented but are themselves part of the process of policy development and public action, not separate activities. In Example A, the way the investigation is carried out will lead to certain expectations on the part of those being investigated. Example C, as noted already, involved investigation designed to have direct implications in terms of empowerment and potentially also local development activities designed by the research subjects as a result of their involvement, in addition to the more indirect implications of results being used to inform national poverty reduction strategy. In general, *investigations are part of the policy process*. However, such investigation is equally demanding of rigour as other academic research.

Box 3 summarises the above discussion in the form of a suggested framework for placing in context the type of investigations covered in this book.

Box 3   The context of policy investigations

Investigations aimed at informing or influencing policy or public action can be usefully viewed in the following framework:

1 The situations under investigation involve *uncertainty, incomplete information and 'moving targets'.*
2 The agencies involved are *intervening in social processes.*
3 They are aiming at *goals external to the agencies themselves.*
4 This means development as public action involving *multiple agencies.*
5 Such situations are best understood in terms of *policy as process.*
6 Development goals tend to be subject to *value-based conflicts.*
7 Developmental *values may also be built in to investigations*, in how they are conducted.
8 The *investigator's relationship with the agencies* has to be considered.
9 Finally, one should see *investigations as part of the policy process.*

2 Policy investigation: pitfalls and special features • • •

As pointed out at the very beginning of this Introduction, policy investigation is specifically aimed at producing research results that will have an immediate practical effect. Research for the ODI's 'RAPID' programme, mentioned already, comes to one simple conclusion on what is needed for research to influence policy, namely: 'whether research provided a solution to a problem' (Court and Young, 2003, p. viii). As noted above, the research results also have to be timely, if not necessarily produced 'fast'.

However, these ideas should not be adopted uncritically. This section discusses some of the pitfalls that can arise and the special features of policy investigation required in order to avoid them. I will divide the problems into dangers of a problem-solving approach and dangers of (over) rapid research. In each case the same examples (A to D, outlined above) are used to provide illustrations. In fact you may already have noticed some of the dangers which I am about to bring out when the examples were being discussed above.

2.1 Dangers of a problem–solving approach

We agree that, if research is to have any policy impact, its results must solve a practical problem. However, there are dangers in simply adopting a problem-solving approach (Box 4 summarises these).

1 'Problem-solving' sounds very much as though one knows in advance what is to be 'solved'. In other words, the problem under investigation is conceptualized in advance. But *conceptualisation should not remain fixed* or contrary evidence may be ignored.

   In Example A, it appears that the outline of the project is already fixed so that the investigation is simply to find out things like which vegetable varieties are appropriate. 'Provid[ing] information on the local communities' sounds more open-ended, but this formulation fails to make explicit what underlying assumptions may have been made about the nature of social relations in these communities. As far as gender relations are concerned, some assumptions are clearly implied by the fact that the project appears to be designed with a built-in women's element, including nutrition education and vegetable gardens. While this assumption may be well founded, thinking of the investigation in terms of simply 'solving' the 'problem' of how to design a project in detail may mitigate against looking for evidence that could either confirm or cast doubt on the underlying way in which aspects of the problem, such as the pattern of gender relations, have been conceptualised.

2 'Problem-solving' seems to imply that the form of the problem is already known, so that one knows which boxes have to be filled in with data. This may be appropriate for administration but *'filling in the boxes' is not sufficient to inform development interventions*, which are aimed at assisting a process of change in a positive direction.

Thus, in Example B we see how continuing to fill in boxes with data about trip lengths, etc. will build up data series over time which are consistent in form from year to year, and thus help to administer a road-building programme. However, once it is decided to use policy to manage demand, that is, to try to change the direction of development, then simply finding out is not sufficient. There is a need to build up a picture of motivations and interlocking causes, and in such a case there is likely to be conflicting evidence needing to be weighed up so that the notion of problem-solving may lead to over-simplification.

3 The notion of *gathering or extracting information can imply no involvement* from those in the situation.

   Again, the idea of 'provid[ing] information on the local communities' in Example A seems to imply observing or measuring them from outside. Quite apart from the dubious ethics of such an approach, the fact that people in any situation have their own aims and aspirations and will react to a policy initiative accordingly, makes it important for such an investigation to be interactive if not fully participative. In fact it will be argued in several chapters of this book that investigations always involve the people in the situation under investigation in some way, whether the methods are labelled participative or not, and the question is on what terms they are involved.

4 Providing a solution to a problem may imply *bias towards the interests of policy-makers or those sponsoring the research.*

   In order to influence a particular policy, the problem being solved by research has to be one of immediate political importance to those making or implementing that policy. Thus, in Example C, although the point is for the voices of poor people to be heard, the researchers who facilitate discussion and interpret what is said may be tempted to emphasise points which they know will fit with the political priorities of government decision makers and donor agencies. Example D demonstrated the other side of this problem. Here, although the research pointed to the solution of a problem for certain remote rural dwellers, it was not a problem of importance to government and the 'solution' conflicted with other powerful interests.

Box 4   Dangers of a problem solving approach

1 'Problem-solving' implies the conceptualisation of the problem under investigation is fixed.
2 'Filling in the boxes' with data is not sufficient to inform development interventions.
3 'Gathering' or 'extracting' information can imply no involvement from those in the situation.
4 Solving policy-makers' problems may imply bias towards their interests or those sponsoring the research.

2.2 Dangers of (over) rapid research

We have also noted how research results must be timely in order to inform or influence policy. But there are dangers in assuming that doing research quickly is a good thing in itself (see Box 5 for a summary of these):

1 The fact that teams of professional researchers can be assembled and paid to produce reports in very short spaces of time means *'proper' research can appear a luxury* and resources may not be made available. In the case in Example A, for example, Staudt (1991, p. 46) describes how only 10 working days were specified for the project in the researchers' contracts, of which two were allocated to visit 'the field'.

   The existence of known and labelled rapid research techniques may encourage the idea that research can be done extremely quickly, although this may be less of a problem now that the idea of 'rapid' rural appraisal (RRA) has mostly given way to 'participative' rural appraisal (PRA) or 'participative learning and action' (PLA). In fact, as you will see in Chapters 7 and 8, many of the techniques used in these approaches, although not as time-consuming as traditional anthropological research, still require considerable time and resources if they are to be carried out rigorously.

2 Research thought to be shallow can be rubbished.

   NGOs and other interest groups lobbying to change official policies of governments or intergovernmental agencies, such as the World Bank, can all too easily run into this type of criticism, especially as they often have to react quickly to policy changes announced by those official agencies. Even when not actually done over a short period, research to support campaigns by such groups may have to make do with very limited resources. This makes it all the more important to show clearly the rigorous basis of investigation on which alternatives put forward are based – an important part of the NGOs' strategy in Example D which may eventually be bearing fruit after a long time.

3 Certain specific rapid research techniques may be used unthinkingly, in an over-standard way, including the advance definition of problems from outside.

   Here I am reminded of the possibly apocryphal tale in which a research team arrives in a remote village, to be greeted by an old woman who makes it known through their interpreter that she expects them to interview her as she is a 'key informant'. It is not only that 'participatory' or other techniques can become over-standardised. In general the availability of standard techniques can all too readily combine with the tendency to define problems from outside, as in the first of the dangers of a 'problem-solving' approach explained above, viz. that of fixing one's conceptualisation of a situation in advance. This is certainly an issue in Example C. In this view, the use of standard techniques for participatory poverty assessment is unlikely to bring out certain types of findings, such as those that threaten local power structures. In order to counter this criticism, one would have to demonstrate clearly that the techniques used were chosen as appropriate after an open-ended appraisal of the overall situation and that there was a real possibility of a conflictual result from the investigation.

4 Having to complete an investigation quickly may mean *effort may be channelled into what is easier to investigate* – towards topics which are less challenging or towards people who are easier to reach and to communicate with. This can all too easily lead to a bias against those who are poor and powerless, which often includes women, those in remote or inaccessible areas, children and old people. It may mean not broaching issues of social differentiation and power relations, and failing to challenge assumptions – particularly if that might be politically difficult as well as requiring more time to build up evidence. In Example D, the NGOs clearly avoided this danger – but failed to achieve a policy change for many years.

In Example A, it appeared that an assumption of the preliminary project design was that the project should concentrate on those farming between 5 acres and 20 acres of land. It was therefore not expected that time should be spent finding out about the majority – women farmers with plots much smaller than 5 acres and with menfolk migrating for wage employment elsewhere – or to investigate the likely effects of the proposed project on them. It would have been particularly difficult and time-consuming to investigate the absent men.

5 The combination of limited resources (especially time) with the expectation that rapid research includes some kind of direct field observation involving outsiders can mean that other research methods such as *literature study and the analysis of secondary data may be squeezed out.*

It is all too easy to assume that there is no prior knowledge of a particular case. However, there are often relevant studies either by academics or by other agencies lying unread. Perhaps the fact that certain methods of field observation and interviewing are called 'rapid research', combined with the apparent uncertainty of getting results from a literature study or from the analysis of incomplete data, make the latter appear rather risky undertakings when there is a fixed and very limited timescale.

Box 5 Dangers of (over) rapid research

1 'Proper' research can appear a luxury.
2 Research which appears shallow can be rubbished.
3 Certain specific rapid research techniques may be used unthinkingly.
4 Effort may be channelled into what is easier to investigate.
5 Literature study and analysis of secondary data may be squeezed out.

Thus, although the context may require investigation to be done to a timescale outside one's control, one has to be aware of the dangers of assuming that research done quickly is necessarily the best research. In particular, the necessity for rigour is if anything intensified when the policy context requires results to be obtained fast.

2.3 Avoiding the pitfalls

The difficulties of policy investigation are substantial and cannot be wished away. If such investigation is to succeed in influencing development policy or informing public action generally, it does have to try to be relevant to a problem which someone in power needs answering. More often than not, it also has to be done with limited human and financial resources as well as to a timescale which is outside one's control. The special features of policy investigation are those which allow it to meet these constraints while avoiding the pitfalls.

Examples A and D both show how such constraints can operate. In Example A, the researchers were contracted for 10 days only, presumably because the agency had limited resources available for this part of the project development process. In Example C, a relative lack of resources and differences in how the problem was conceptualised meant there was no policy change for a very long time, despite apparently overwhelming evidence. Generally, any agency faced with the need for evidence, whether to strengthen its own project design or to make a case to another agency, has to decide how much of its resources should be committed. This implies weighing up the benefit to be obtained from the likely results of an investigation against the cost of the resources needed to obtain them, which could otherwise be put to use elsewhere.

If financial resources are the main constraint, then there is a choice as to how fast a piece of research should be done. If resources are extremely limited, there is a lot to be said for a concentrated effort giving some results quickly, perhaps at least an interesting reconceptualisation. Taking a long time over an investigation may lead to expectations that the work will have been extremely detailed when resources were not available for that. On the other hand, it may be worth spreading small amounts of available time over a longer period if that is the way to get access to a number of very busy people, to obtain various documents as they are suggested by the unfolding investigation, and to fit in visits to different locations.

Whether or not a policy investigation is actually done fast, it is likely to be done to meet someone else's deadline. This may be short and suddenly imposed. For example, when challenging a decision, the opposition case has to be put forward at the time if implementation is to be prevented, so that evidence for that case may have to be prepared almost immediately. In other cases, the deadline may be known well in advance. In Example C, the PPA process is supposed to be designed to fit in with government policy timetables. If the results of a piece of evaluative research are to be used to argue for the continuation of a certain project then the case has to be put at the right time to fit in with the budget cycle. Although there should be enough notice to set up monitoring or other investigations in good time, there will always be limited resources, those who will undertake the evaluation will have other responsibilities, and the research work may well end up having to be done fast. Though not an evaluation, the investigation in Example A seems to have been rather like this.

One should also realise that coming up with some results when required does not have to be the end of the investigative process. The need for ideas and evidence to input to a particular policy discussion or decision is not the end of the matter. Just as the development and implementation of policy is an ongoing process so too investigation is a parallel process which informs both specific interventions and reviews of policy. Thus, in Example B, I can envisage particular investigations needing to be done quickly for a particular meeting or decision, while debate over the future direction of transport policy continues, informed by the cumulative results from such investigations and in turn informing the way such investigations are carried out, over an indefinite period.

There is of course an apparent conflict between having to meet deadlines imposed by policy timetables and being able to back up your findings with firm evidence. The need for rigour cannot be emphasised too much. Readers who are also development managers are likely to have pressures on them to act quickly and may have begun this book in the hope that it will enable them to act even more quickly and on a secure basis. However, problem-solving in a timely fashion does not mean you can necessarily do everything you would like in as short a time as is available. One answer to this problem is to recognise that in policy investigation *rigour implies selectivity* about the object of study. The need for rigour implies using the time available to challenge the most basic assumptions or to look for evidence in the areas of greatest uncertainty. There is no point in a broad search for all kinds of data if lack of time means none of it can be cross-checked.

To summarise this section, we note two tensions which in general any policy-oriented investigation has to resolve. First, although ultra-rapidity is not necessarily required, certainly any such investigation has to meet deadlines set by others or by limitations of resources, rather than to suit the ideal requirements of particular research methods. Maintaining rigour in this context implies selectivity about the aspects to be focused on within the set timescale; given that investigation is itself an ongoing process, other aspects may be investigated later if necessary. Second, while avoiding bias and prior assumptions that may fix how an issue is conceptualised from outside, policy investigations must still provide relevant answers to problems of immediate political importance to policy-makers and other powerful stakeholders.

3 The approach to investigation in this book • • •

Although development policy and public action are the context, the book will be focused on skills and methods for investigation rather than on the policy process itself. This section explains the general approach taken to investigation, before going on to some additional points specific to investigation for policy and public action. Many of the following points come directly from some of the arguments made above.

3.1 General points about investigation

1 *Investigation* is considered to be a more fruitful notion than that of information gathering. Investigation evokes the image of a detective rather than a note-taker. It implies asking about how and why things happen as well as about what has happened. It may be necessary to spend time checking the answers to a set series of questions, but investigation implies going beyond this, worrying about loose ends and following up leads.

2 *Rigour* is always crucial in any investigation. This is equally the case whether one is undertaking academic research or working in the practical context of development policy. Rigour means being able to show that one has enough evidence to justify one's conclusions, that the evidence has been obtained properly and that contrary evidence has been sought but either not found or found to be relatively unconvincing.

3 Investigation means *conceptualising and reconceptualising*, not just gathering information to fit pre-defined categories. A good analogy is with the way a journalist finds a 'story' through which to tell the results of an investigation. One may start off expecting to build up a particular story but end up finding that the facts do not fit and tell a rather different story.

   A journalist is, of course, generally an 'outsider'. Investigative development managers may also be 'insiders' in being part of one of the agencies closely involved in a given situation. However, outsider or insider, the important thing is not only to be prepared to reconceptualise but to be aware of your own assumptions and actively to look out for evidence that may contradict them.

4 This willingness to reconceptualise implies a *two-way relationship between ideas and evidence*. Ideas come from theory, though not necessarily grand theory. In turn different theoretical perspectives relate to competing systems of values. Ideas in this sense are what make up your conceptualisation of a problem or situation. Evidence is in the form of data about that problem or situation. Ideas are what lead you to search for particular kinds of evidence, but the evidence may also lead you to change your ideas, despite the implied challenge to underlying values.

5 In addition to confronting ideas with evidence it is also useful to think in terms of *confronting one set of ideas with another*. This can also be thought of as pitting one theory against another to see which gives the best explanations in the circumstances under investigation. One set of ideas will mean searching for certain related kinds of evidence while another set of ideas may lead to finding different evidence.

6 *Investigation should be 'uneasy'*. There must always be the possibility of finding out what you didn't know, not just reinforcing prejudices. This implies following up odd pieces of data that don't fit in with your prevailing mode of explanation, rather than ignoring them and concentrating only on data that conform to expectations.

7 *It is often necessary to 'step back'* and find a different way of looking at a problem before being able to make progress. This is really another way of saying you should

be prepared to reconceptualise. However, the point is that you cannot be constantly changing your ideas; generally speaking, you work on the basis of a particular theory or conceptualisation for a while. The idea of 'stepping back' is to build in review points to ensure that you have a chance of looking at things differently before assuming too readily that your ideas are correct.

8 Finally, *communication of results* is a necessary part of any investigation. There is more to this point than just the observation that research results are useless unless made known to others. Communication of results should be thought of from the outset as part of the process of investigation. This means, for example, that the question of who or what the results are for should inform the way in which the research is designed and also have a bearing on what is regarded as sufficient evidence.

A general question about investigation which has only been hinted at so far is how the *validity of research* is to be judged. Some of the language used above ('the image of a detective', 'finding that the facts do not fit', 'the best explanations') might fit with the notion of a search for objectivity – the realist conception that there is an underlying truth which research aims progressively to discover by building up knowledge. However, some of the other language used ('a "story" through which to tell the results', 'another set of ideas may lead to finding different evidence', 'who ... the results are for should ... have a bearing on what is regarded as sufficient evidence') fits with a quite different notion, the social constructionist conception of the possible simultaneous validity of different accounts or constructions of human interactions based on different perspectives, interests and values. In this notion, what makes a good piece of research is its utility, which is necessarily judged from a particular perspective.

Indeed, there is a tension between these two positions throughout the book. The Conclusion returns to it with a fuller discussion, but it is perhaps not a question that can be fully resolved. Certainly investigation can never be separated from questions of values.

3.2 Investigation for development policy and public action

This book's focus on investigative methods is in the context of investigating questions of concern for development policy and public action, not just for academic research. We noted in Section 1 that such questions are subject to value-based conflicts over what constitute desirable social and development goals. Thus, the above tension about how to judge the validity and usefulness of a piece of research is particularly acute in the case of *investigation for policy and action*.

Policy investigation is also something which necessarily takes place in a particular institutional context. Investigation is not done for its own sake, but with the aim of informing or influencing the actions of one's own or another agency. Here are some additional points about investigation in this context that also form part of the book's approach.

1   *Conceptualisation should include a consideration of agency.* This means how things are made to happen as well as which agencies are involved. It is not just a matter of who has commissioned the research and who needs to know the results and to take part in implementation. Questions of who is concerned, which organisations and groups are engaged in doing what, which interests are implicated by different policy options, and what values underlie them, should be part and parcel of how you conceive of a development problem or issue throughout an investigation.

2   *The institutional setting can be a trap.* One can be caught in a particular (often narrow) way of thinking which may be strongly related to the perspectives and values of the particular institutions which have set up the investigation in this way. The nature of a trap is that you cannot find the way out from inside, so it is hard to say what you should be looking for in order to escape. However, it can help a lot to make a point of soliciting views from sources outside your agency and those with which you habitually work, or to look for literature written from different points of view or data collected for different purposes.

3   *'Stepping back' and reconceptualising may endanger one's position* even while being essential to rigorous investigation. Looking at things from different perspectives can cause problems at all kinds of levels. It might imply questioning your personal values and perhaps uncovering hidden biases and prejudices. It might create more overt political problems, not only within your agency by questioning the basis of its policies, but in terms of relationships to other agencies with important positions in the situation under investigation.

4   The character of *available data reflects the previous history of public action* in a society. In other words, previous policies in the public arena determine what data were routinely collected. If a new agency becomes involved with a different perspective, or if you change your ideas on an issue, it is likely that information relevant to the new way of thinking will not be so readily available. This should not in itself be a reason for eschewing new ideas, though it might limit the extent of a new investigation that can be carried out in a limited time. However, the very fact of the limitations of data and the reasons for those limitations may in themselves be evidence to be fed back into the overall picture.

5   *Investigations can themselves be interventions.* It is important to consider not only the cases where investigation informs or influences intervention by a powerful agency into a situation. There is also the case where the actual carrying out of an investigation directly affects the situation and should be considered among the interrelated actions of a number of agencies in an ongoing process of change. Arguably, the latter is always the case to some extent.

6   *Communicating results involves questions of rights and responsibilities.* When investigations are aimed at public action they are intended to lead to changes which will affect those whose situation was investigated. Hence, communicating the results involves questions of who should be involved, who has a right to the information,

who will be responsible for acting on it, and so on. As noted above, this is not a consideration only for the end of an investigation but should inform the way an issue is conceptualised throughout.

7 *Developmental values should be built into policy investigation.* Such values are, of course, subject to contestation. This underlines the importance of research *ethics* in such investigation. For example, values such as respect for research subjects carry added weight because the research subjects may also be potential beneficiaries of the development policies which are informed by the research. However, as we will see in Chapter 8, building developmental values such as participation into policy research is not straightforward. It poses difficult questions about power relations between researcher and researched, and between both of these and the sponsors of the research and those promulgating development policies informed by it.

The tension between different ways of judging policy-oriented investigations suggests that it seems vain to search for complete objectivity, particularly when the subject of investigation includes policies which may be based on competing values. However, it seems dangerous to judge investigations simply by reference to utility. Is research successful because it has helped the implementation of certain policies or halted others? Alternatively, is it successful simply because it helped empower the research subjects? Whose utility, whose interests, are to take precedence? How in that case can one avoid bias in the direction of those, necessarily powerful, who are able to commission research?

Difficulties like these have led to the centrality of the idea of 'challenge' in the book. Whichever view is taken, it seems important for ideas to be open – or for biases to be acknowledged – so that they can be challenged as rigorously as possible. It may not be feasible to achieve objectivity or to agree on the perspective from which to judge utility, but a challenging form of investigation should at least avoid incoherent explanations or advocating policies which fail to achieve their own aims.

4 Organisation of the book • • •

It is the relationship of investigative methods to the policy and public action context which is intended to make this book more than just another research methods book.

The central part of the book is organised in terms of investigative methods. These are designed to cover the main generic skills required for carrying out an investigation. Three general methods each have a section: 'thinking with documents'; 'thinking with people'; and 'bringing in data'. These central sections on skills or methods follow an opening section on the conceptualisation of investigations in relation to policy questions.

Thus the sections are as follows:

I Conceptualising policy-related investigation

The first section looks at how areas for investigation which relate to questions of policy and public action can be conceptualised. The first chapter uses examples of policy change to explore how different policy contexts make it appropriate to formulate different kinds of research questions and use different methods. The second discusses boundaries and boundary-setting as an important part of conceptualising areas for investigation. The third uses the analogy of how a journalist formulates a 'story' to consider how the need for results to make an impact affects how an issue is conceptualised from the beginning. Finally, Chapter 4 considers how the need for communicating results throughout an investigation also affects how it is conceptualised.

II Thinking with documents

Literature study is to be treated as an investigative method in its own right, not just a preliminary. A general chapter on how to 'do' a literature study is followed by one on the interpretation of institutional discourses as evidenced in reports, publicity materials and so on. The title of this section refers to 'documents' (rather than the first edition's 'thinking with paper') to emphasise the importance of electronic documents found on the internet as well as paper documents.

III Thinking with people

'Fieldwork' includes an enormous range of specific methods, including PLA, organisational assessment, semi-structured interviews, the use of oral testimony, and so on. The title of this section is 'Thinking with people', indicating that carrying out investigations using evidence gained from interacting with people at first hand is always a two-way process, whether or not a particular method is labelled 'participative'.

Development managers may need different sorts of skills to think with people and organisations in different situations and contexts, even if they don't always do the fieldwork themselves. Hence, this section will cover generic skills at three levels: an appreciation of what is involved in good research design and particularly interviewing, both with individuals and groups; the development of judgement and an appreciation of rigour in order to commission, interpret and evaluate fieldwork carried out by others; and an understanding of the relationship between investigations about people and organisations and the way results of investigations involve and implicate the same people and organisations.

Of the chapters in this section, Chapter 7 compares the two main methods of using people as informants, namely structured survey and semi-structured interview, discusses how rigour can be achieved in each case and introduces some concerns about research which is specifically labelled 'participative'. Chapter 8 follows this with a more detailed account of 'participative' research methods and considers both the potential for such methods to be empowering and their limitations. Chapter 9 gives a personal reflection on some practical and ethical difficulties in a case of researching poverty.

IV Bringing in data

The title of this section recognises how, when data is used in policy investigation it is almost always in addition to qualitative information. Our approach meshes with the recent emphasis on combining qualitative and quantitative research methods (Holland and Campbell, 2005; Kanbur, 2002) but prefers to assume that the best research necessarily has aspects of both rather than separating methods on the basis of a qualitative-quantitative distinction.

The title of Chapter 10 ('Thinking with quantitative data') echoes that of the previous two sections, to indicate that in all cases the concepts brought to the investigation challenge and are challenged by the evidence, whether the evidence comes direct from people or from data. It covers the analysis of secondary quantitative data, developing the basic skill of numerical literacy. Chapter 11 deals with critical issues in the use of data, particularly the case where research results are to be used for advocacy and the stringent requirements for rigour which this places on the investigation. Chapter 12 brings in organisational data, looking at investigating organisations and their 'footprints', to inform either change in the organisation itself or public action in an arena where the 'footprints' are found. Chapter 13 applies the concept of challenge to the use of case studies which combine quantitative and qualitative data as different forms of evidence.

Finally, there is a Conclusion which discusses questions of personal effectiveness and integrity. It points out some of the differences between the chapter authors, and returns to the questions about how to judge the worth of a policy investigation introduced briefly in Section 4 of this Introduction, before concluding by emphasising yet again the importance of the idea of challenge and 'trying not to get it wrong'.

PART I

Conceptualising policy-related investigation

Information needs and policy change

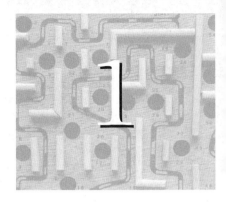

Stephen Potter and Ramya Subrahmanian

It is a very simple idea that different types of policy measures require different types of information and different skills to gather this information. If a policy of water supply involves building dams and reservoirs, then to do this requires hydrologists and engineers, with a policy administrative system that provides the resources to implement their work. Their information requirements will include measurements of water flow, pressures, and dimensions of structures, and they will ask questions about the capacity, cost, safety, etc. of alternative configurations. But if the policy requires the elimination of leaks from pipes in cities, then different engineering skills and information are required. No knowledge or information on dams or reservoirs is needed. Instead, engineers who are skilled in leak detection and measurement, technologies to repair pipes *in situ* and systems of water distribution management and monitoring are called for.

Behind this is a general point about research, which applies particularly strongly to policy-oriented investigation. Different policies require different research questions to be asked in order to obtain results that will usefully inform those policies. When the policy changes, the core question at the centre of related policy investigations also changes and it is frequently necessary to change the method by which those investigations are carried out. Furthermore, there can also be a need to change the sort of information gathered.

The first section of this chapter, particularly Figure 1.1, Table 1.1 and Figure 1.2, explores this relationship between the nature of an investigation and consequent information needs. This section is developed from material used in research training courses at the UK Open and Brunel Universities by a team including the first author of this chapter.

In the following two sections we present two case studies of situations where a change in policy has led to a need for changes in the sorts of understanding, skills and types of information required. They are intentionally contrasting. Lessons are then drawn in the final section from what they have in common as well as from the contrasts.

1.1 Changed question: changed investigation • • •

Figure 1.1 is intended to help students or policy investigators focus upon a research topic and project aim. Once a project aim is established, a sequence should be initiated that structures how the research is carried out. The aim of a research project can often be articulated in terms of a key question: for example, 'What role could renewable energy technologies play in developing economies'?

The formulation of a focused project aim then leads on to developing questions that need to be answered to achieve the overall project aim. In the above example this is likely to involve specifying the type of renewable energy technologies considered and the functions they would serve in developing economies. From such a consideration should emerge a clear idea of the sort of information that is needed to answer these questions. This then raises the issue of how this information can be obtained.

For clarity, the sequence is presented linearly in Figure 1.1, but in practice the situation is always more iterative. Obtaining information and understanding may lead to a revision of the project aim or constraints on information availability could lead to a less ambitious project or a different methodology.

It is important to distinguish different types of research question. One useful way is to think in terms of three dimensions on which to differentiate between types of question:

1 Is the question about the *field* of policy (including those affected by policy or for whom policy is made) or is it a question about policy itself?
2 Is the question a *normative* or an *evaluative* one ('How should...?'; 'What is the best way to...?'; 'How well does X compare with Y?') or is it a *descriptive* or an *explanatory* one (about what is happening and how to explain it)?
3 Particularly in the case of descriptive/explanatory questions about the field of policy, is it a 'What?' question, a 'How?' question, a 'Why?' question or a 'What if?' question?

The first two of these dimensions, taken together, give rise to a matrix of four types of question, examples of which are shown in Table 1.1.

In the straightforward case where those undertaking an investigation are able to implement policy themselves or report to those with the power to do so, it is questions of the type in the top left box of Table 1.1 that need answering in order to decide directly which policies to implement. Answering such questions directly ('How well does such-and-such a policy work compared with the alternatives?', 'What is the best education policy?', etc.) requires a mixture of evidence and subjective judgement.

In order for a policy investigation to help a decision-maker or development manager to answer such a question, it is often helpful to separate out the evidence from the judgement. Gathering evidence generally involves asking questions aimed at describing or explaining what happens in the field of policy, i.e. questions of the type in the bottom right box of Table 1.1.

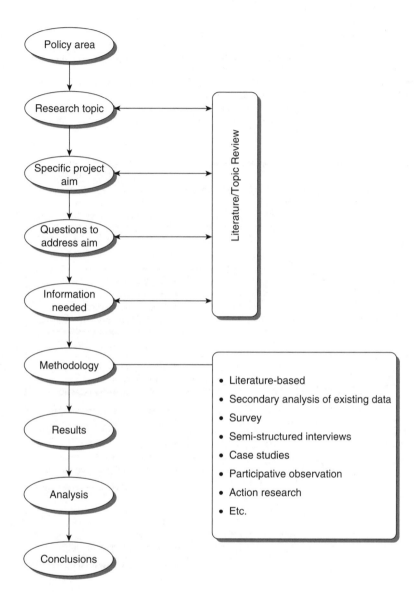

FIGURE 1.1 Sequence for focusing a research project

Although the other two boxes of Table 1.1 do not come into this straightforward picture, they can also provide important aspects of a broader investigation into policy. In the bottom left box, questions ask directly what people *should* do and are close to the 'What if?' questions in the bottom right box. In the top right box the questions treat

TABLE 1.1   *Examples of four types of research question*

	Normative/evaluative questions	Descriptive/explanatory questions
Questions about policy itself	Should this policy be adopted? How well does policy P work? What is the best transport policy?	Which agencies are stakeholders in this policy? How did policy Q come about? Is there the capacity to implement the policy?
Questions about the field of policy	How should people react to this new policy? What is the best way to live in given circumstances?	What do people grow? How is cultivation organised? Why do people grow the particular crops they do? What if more water were available?

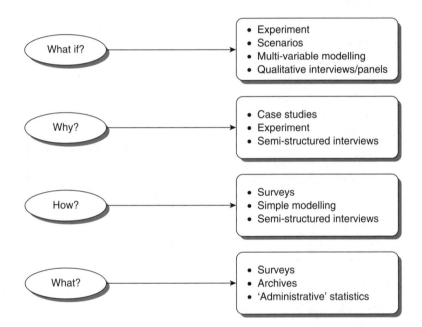

FIGURE 1.2   Descriptive and explanatory research questions and methodologies of investigation

policy almost as an object itself, tracing its context, its history, the interests and organisations that shape it, and so on. At the very least, investigating questions in this box gives a broad background and helps to give a better understanding of the policy.

In practice, the 'field' of policy includes beneficiaries who do not simply react to the impact of policy or generate demands as predictable responses to certain causal factors, but act independently and indeed implement 'policies' of their own. The strong movement towards different forms of participative research is one recognition of this. Whether research is carried out in an overtly participative way or not, it has to be recognised that the boundary between policy (and those agencies that make policy) and the field of policy is at best fuzzy and at worst a construct which may hinder rather than help investigation.

Nevertheless, much research undertaken or commissioned by development managers is aimed at gathering evidence about what we have called the field of policy. This can often be quite similar to research undertaken by postgraduate students, many of whose topics would not have been sponsored without some policy relevance envisaged for the results. We have already noted how research questions about the *field* of policy differ considerably amongst themselves according to whether they begin with the words 'What', 'How', 'Why' or 'What if'. These differences reflect whether the investigation's core interest concerns:

(a) description and basic data gathering (typically involving questions beginning with the word 'What' or the phrase 'How many' (for example: What is the pattern of energy demand in a particular country?);
(b) an analysis of how something happens (for example, explaining how electricity demand arises from the domestic, commercial and industrial sectors);
(c) an understanding of causality (for example, the nature of the relationship between electricity demand and economic activity in the commercial sector);
(d) being able to predict what will happen if causal factors change (for example, if electricity tariffs were altered, how would the pattern of demand alter?).

These categories are, of course, somewhat artificial and, in practice, a project may encompass a range across this spectrum. But this is a useful way of thinking about how deep an understanding is needed of what causes an end result, and if an important part of the project is to intervene in the system to change that end result. As an investigation shifts across the spectrum from descriptive 'What?' and 'How?' questions to contemplate the 'Why?' and 'What if?' questions, the sort of information that is needed changes and the methods of investigation change as well.

Broadly, this shift involves a change from the gathering of basic factual information and 'hard' statistical methodologies through to information and methods that allow an understanding of systems and involve 'softer' qualitative information as well as modelling methods. This is broadly summarised in Figure 1.2.

These considerations of identifying the nature of the questions being asked and what sorts of information and methods of investigation are needed apply as much to policy and public action as they do to a postgraduate student's project. Indeed, even though research students may take some convincing on the matter, this is more difficult than in a PhD or Masters project. A student can relatively easily shift to a different methodology, but entire professions with specialist skills and methodologies have built up around key areas of policy-making. Departmental structures have been assembled around these methodologies, skills and professions. So what happens when there is a shift in policy that requires new or different skills? What happens if a policy shifts to become the domain of a new government department or, horror upon horrors, requires close co-ordination between previously separate departmental empires? Do institutional structures represent a significant barrier to developing new policy directions? Is the problem even acknowledged?

Increasingly, public policy is requiring a shift across the investigative spectrum towards a deeper understanding of systems, rather than taking the systems for granted and responding to their outputs. This shift arises for a number of reasons, not least the increasing uncertainty in which policy-making takes place. A common type of change, explored in the two case studies in this chapter, is from a relatively stable policy environment of reacting to demand and administering established public services, towards a *developmental* policy involving active intervention and trying to manage demand in order to achieve development goals. The consequences of this shift in the level of understanding needed are rarely appreciated. If a student submitted a thesis claiming to understand how a system would react to possible external changes without using a research method that provided an understanding of that system, the chances are he or she would fail. Yet today, in many policy areas, initiatives to influence and change systems are under way, serviced by only the barest information of the 'How much?' variety. It is just as well that such policy programmes do not have to be submitted to a university examination panel!

1.2 UK transport policy • • •

Recent changes in UK transport policy provide a good example of research method and data implications when there is a change in the core policy rationale requiring a systems understanding (systems approaches are discussed in more detail in Chapter 2). The system generating the overall demand for travel is a complicated one. Figure 1.3 is a representation of this system and some of the links involved. This is not a proper systems diagram, but is simply here to show some of the elements involved and three key levels that are present in this system.

The first level is towards the edge of this diagram (coloured cream). Here there are a number of non-transport factors that have a strong determining influence of the amount and nature of travel. There are three groups of these: Income and lifestyle factors are to the top right; economic factors (such as the price of fuel) to the top left and geographical factors to the bottom left (e.g. living in rural areas means that you have to go further to the shops). These root 'causes' produce the second level transport results/effects in the centre (coloured light orange), including the number and length of

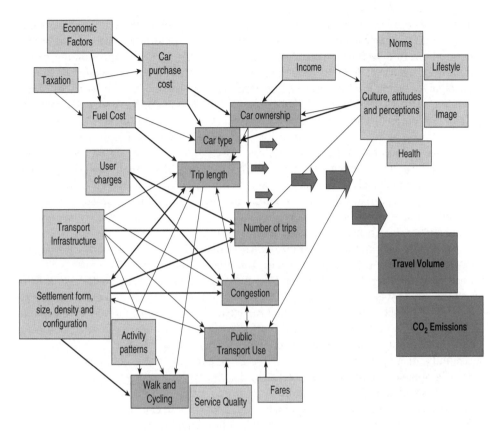

FIGURE 1.3   Factors generating travel demands

trips by different forms of transport. Together this leads to the third level output of total travel volume and any other related consequences. The diagram includes CO_2 emissions, as transport's contribution to emissions causing global warming is now a hot topic.

In terms of information needs, these three levels of the travel generating system involve different sorts of data. The lowest, third, or output, level is measured largely with information about 'What' and 'How much'. Moving up to the second level gets into more complexity, splitting 'What' data by travel method, but also requiring some explanatory 'How' information regarding the interplay between these second level factors. Moving to the primary level involves not only the complexity of a wide number of structural factors influencing travel, but also requires information exploring issues of what is causing the 'how' relationships at the second level – i.e. questions of 'Why' and also 'What if' these underlying causal factors change or are affected by policy interventions.

In the last decade, transport policy has sought to shift up the levels in the travel demand system. Until the early 1990s, the approach to transport planning in Britain, and most other nations, had been to respond to changing travel demands – i.e. the final third level output from the travel demand system. Predominantly this involved providing increased road capacity, together with the progressive trimming of rail and bus services, with some exceptions due to 'social need' (e.g. subsidising local bus, rail and ferry services, particularly in rural areas). The way in which these services have been provided, particularly whether by the state or the private sector, has been the subject of numerous reforms. These have culminated in the privatisation in the 1980s and 1990s of bus and rail services (and the more recent virtual renationalisation of rail infrastructure following major failures in the privatised rail industry). However, these reforms have been within the context of a policy approach that took changes in travel demand for granted. Policy was essentially built around the third level output of the system – i.e. the final orange output box in Figure 1.3 with selected incursions into some bits of the second level.

A policy built around the final outputs of a system can be serviced by relatively straightforward information that simply measures those outputs in terms of demand for travel infrastructure and services ('What?' or 'How much?'). Examples of such data include traffic counts, traffic speed surveys, parking supply figures, road capacity and public transport supply. Such a policy approach has little need for understanding about how this demand arises up at the second and first levels of the system. Demand is taken for granted, it is measured using various output indicators and the policy response is to accommodate any measured and anticipated changes. Only in large cities, particularly London, has this 'system output' approach been rendered impossible by the sheer volume of traffic concentrated into a relatively small area. Even so, the general desire was, until the 1990s, to provide as much road capacity as possible and the sort of data gathered was still related to third level outputs.

This demand-led transport policy has now lost its credibility. Part of this was, from the 1990s, the recognition that transport is a key environmental problem area, in particular transport's emissions of carbon dioxide (CO_2), the key gas contributing to global warming. Following ratification of the 1997 Kyoto climate change conference, the UK, along with most developed nations, has a legally-binding obligation to reduce CO_2 emissions. The UK's target is to reduce emissions to below 1990 levels by 2008–12. The transport sector is the fastest-growing source of CO_2 emissions. CO_2 emissions from transport have risen from 80 million tonnes of carbon in 1970 to 130 million tonnes in 2000 and are continuing to rise. Current projections, contained in the 2004 Transport Policy White Paper (Department for Transport, 2004a, p. 23) are for road transport emissions to rise to 15% above 1990 levels by 2010 (possibly returning to about 1990 levels by 2025).

Despite the rise in transport emissions, the UK is set to meet its Kyoto obligation as emissions from the domestic, industry and commercial sectors are declining. Thus, for the moment at least, the pressure is off the transport sector, but the UK cannot indefinitely rely on other energy sectors cutting their emissions to permit those from transport to continue growing into the indefinite future. In the longer term the situation becomes more challenging. Successive reports of the Intergovernmental Panel on

Climate Change (for example, Houghton *et al.*, 1990 and Watson *et al.*, 2001) indicate that a 60% cut on 1990 CO_2 emissions is needed to mitigate the effects of climate change. Failing to get transport to take its fair share in cutting CO_2 emissions may work in the short term, but creates a worsening crisis for future generations.

However, although concerns about the environmental impacts of transport are growing in importance, a more entrenched and economically powerful factor for the re-evaluation of Britain's road-building policy has been the inability of road-building to reduce traffic congestion. It was the publication, in 1989, of government road traffic forecasts that brought home the reality that accommodating predicted traffic growth was impossible. The 1991 update of the road traffic forecasts predicted an increase of between 72% and 121% in road traffic over the period 1990 to 2025.

In 1991, a key piece of research, *Transport: the new realism* (Goodwin *et al.*, 1991), showed there is no way that Britain could physically, economically or socially accom-modate the Department of Transport's forecasts for a 100% or more increase in traffic. In 1992, the Institution of Highways and Transportation noted that road congestion is likely 'to occur in more areas for longer periods of the day', with 'an increasing likeli-hood of urban gridlock' (IHT, 1992, p. 5).

A number of significant government-commissioned reports in 1994 left the ratio-nale for a major road-building/upgrading programme in tatters. The Royal Commission on Environmental Pollution's transport report indicated the need for radical measures to manage the demand for transport if environmental objectives were to be taken seri-ously. This was closely followed by the SACTRA (Standing Advisory Committee on Trunk Road Assessment) report (1994) on the methods to justify and assess new road schemes, indicating the role that new roads play in actually generating more traffic, which led to serious doubts over the way roads are financially justified. This situation was summarised by Goodwin (1994), who argued that transport policy's 'New Realism' was entering a second phase. The first phase was the gradual (if grudging) acceptance that for major towns and cities demand management has to be the core rationale for transport policy. The second phase involves the realisation that demand restraint is inevitable for trunk roads and motorways also. Quoting British Road Federation research, Goodwin showed that even a road-building programme of an uncontemplated vastness (beyond what Britain's economy could sustain) would fail to stop congestion getting worse. As a policy response, road-building will always fail; demand management is the only direction possible for transport policy at all levels.

There has thus, since the early 1990s, been a gradual policy acceptance that, rather than simply building new roads and widening existing ones, policies to manage the demand for motorised travel are required. Demand needs to be shifted away from cars to public transport, walking and cycling. This changing ethos was initially reflected in the Conservative administration's 1995 Transport Green Paper (Department of Transport, 1995), but much more strongly in the New Labour government policies in the 1998 Transport White Paper (DETR, 1998) and the 2004 Transport White Paper (Department for Transport, 2004a).

The 1990s saw the government cut roadbuilding programmes and increasing fuel duty on petrol and diesel. The latter was abandoned following the fuel duty protests in 2000, with no effective policy to replace it. Some roadbuilding recommenced (but with the idea that this should be tolled to manage demand). Of particular significance was the success of the London congestion charge, introduced in 2003, which reduced traffic in central London by 20% and congestion by 30% (TfL, 2004). This led to the emergence of proposals for a national road pricing scheme. In July 2004, UK Transport Secretary, Alistair Darling, announced that replacing road fuel duty and vehicle excise duty (VED) with some form of widespread road user charging was envisaged (Department for Transport, 2004b). Since then, UK plans for national road user congestion charging have been firming up, with plans for in-vehicle instrumentation for all cars within 10–15 years, preceded by a series of regional pilot projects (Potter and Parkhurst, 2005). The question is not of 'if' national road user charging will be introduced, but 'how' and 'when'.

In practice the shift towards demand management transport policies has been far from straightforward. There has been considerable political and other resistance, policy effectiveness has been patchy (traffic growth has continued and congestion worsened), and the economic and social impacts unclear. Developing policies to manage transport demand requires considerable understanding of how that demand for travel arises at the second and first levels of the transport system. This involves answering explanatory questions about the field of policy (the bottom right box in Table 1.1). With such an understanding, the uncertainties arising from intervening in the complexities of the first level of the travel generating system could be more easily accommodated. At this first level, there are strong structural changes in British society and economy that have led to the historical rise in mobility, and traffic in particular. It is a self-reinforcing process that has for several decades increased the amount of travel that people undertake. This is a process that is far from complete, as projections for future levels of traffic and travel indicate.

1.2.1 Information needs for demand-management transport policies

Understanding the key factors behind the generation of demand for travel becomes increasingly important when transport policies shift from just reacting to demand towards developmental goals.

There is now a need both to manage second level traffic demands (e.g. vehicle occupancy, method of transport used) and the first level factors that affect the generation of these demands (e.g. land use planning – such as where the workplace, shops and social facilities are, compared with where people live). Some first level factors in Figure 1.3, like income and economic growth, are more independent, with others being more amenable to policy influence. For example, central and local government have strong control over the provision of transport infrastructure (roads, rail lines or cyclepaths) and can exert influence over settlement patterns through land use planning. Transport taxation can affect part, but not all, of the costs of travelling.

Managing the demand for traffic growth requires an understanding of what are the key components of change and the underlying causal factors. To put this in terms of types of research questions, in order to answer the normative policy question 'What is the best way to manage traffic demand in order to achieve goals of accessibility and mobility?' we need first to ask some descriptive and explanatory questions about the field of policy, i.e. the traffic itself: 'How and why does demand for traffic grow?'. Moving up and exploring the higher levels of the travel generating system would permit an identification of where transport demand management policies can be most effectively applied. Without such an understanding, policy will be merely tinkering with symptoms and not causes. Equally, it is important to identify where policy can and cannot make a difference – i.e. what traffic-generating elements need to be accepted and which are amenable to policy influence. It is also important to identify where other areas of policy have significant indirect transport effects (e.g. changes in schools admission procedures or patterns of health care leading to changed transport demands). It is now accepted that planning and land use policies need closer integration with transport policies, but the boundary has not extended to include other key policy areas such as health, education, welfare or fiscal policies.

Ideally, in this case, 'finding out fast' would imply having new generic information to hand that can provide quick answers to changing policy needs. However, managing transport demands is a new and very uncertain field, and comprehensive information on the nature of demand is not available. The information needs of the old demand-led, transport policies were relatively simple, relating to the third level outputs of the travel system. These involved statistics measuring demand, for example, traffic numbers, flows, origins and destinations, vehicle types, etc. How this demand was generated was not of particular importance. Thus, before the policy change, finding out meant looking up and interpreting data supplied by established information systems.

Policies seeking to manage traffic growth require the development of a package of co-ordinated policy measures and integration with other areas of urban policy intervention (e.g. land use planning, employment policies, health, education and welfare provision). Once policy shifts from responding to demand to seeking to manage demand, there is a need for information to understand interplay and causes not merely statistics of measurement. Rather than seeking factual information on 'How much?', transport planning now needs to answer questions beginning with the words 'How' and 'Why' and contemplate 'What if?' (e.g. 'How does demand arise, why does it arise and what if changes are made?'). Finding out now implies special investigation on particular topics, since the standard statistics are in the wrong form for answering the new questions.

As noted at the beginning of this chapter, as you proceed across the investigative spectrum there is a shift away from hard 'scientific' type approaches towards softer, more socially based methodologies. This requires the use of techniques and measurements that have previously been on the fringes of transport policies. These are behavioural methodologies that can assess the public understanding and acceptance of demand management measures and the effects of different combinations of measures, over time and in different places and circumstances. Equally, there is a need for the transport modelling methodologies that have emerged to be modified, at the same time as a more complete and dynamic understanding of travel and traffic generation is sought.

This sort of understanding needs to be rapidly assimilated if traffic growth demand management is to have any chance of success. The danger is that the new demand management approach is being serviced by information system of yesterday's policies. Policy has shifted up to the second and first levels of the travel generating system, but information (and professional expertise) is largely stuck at the third (output) level. The shift in transport policy requires additional skills, understanding and additional information systems. If policy development and investigations have sought to answer questions about level one and two of the travel system using statistics designed to understand only level three of that system, then perhaps it is not surprising that there have been big problems with the design and effectiveness of the resultant transport policies.

1.3 Policy shifts in primary education in India • • •

The case of transport policy in Britain illustrates the complexity of relationships between the institutions which make public policy, and the people for whom policy is designed. In particular, it highlights the extent to which planning for public policy need not be just an issue of *reaction* to expressed demands, but can involve *intervening* in order to manage demand to try to achieve developmental goals. This involves understanding the *dynamics* of 'demand' and its causes, in terms of the changing needs and interests of users. This is true of most public service sectors across different national contexts. To illustrate this point we will be looking at education policy in India, and assessing the shift in information required, prompted by changing directions in policy goals.

Changes in policy take multiple forms, arise from a variety of contexts, and are influenced by different actors. Often policy changes are evolutionary, and involve making shifts and adjustments rather than effecting disruptions with the past. These shifts could be in terms of restructuring a particular intervention in a sector to include new constituencies, and/or putting into place new mechanisms for intervention. The National Policy on Education (NPE), introduced in India in 1986, is an example of an evolutionary policy shift triggered by several factors: a change in political leadership, bringing with it a renewed focus on the importance of education for modernisation and development; a recognition within government that national education achievements have not matched projected goals over years of planning; a renewed international focus on education, particularly primary education and women's education, spearheaded by the World Bank and strongly influenced by its ideological framework and financial support; and finally, the activism of social movements including the anti-child labour campaigns, literacy campaigns and organisations of the women's movement. The interplay of these different factors over a period of time saw the birth of a new policy approach to education, which was built on the lessons of the past, but with elements that emphasised new ways of doing things.

The NPE was produced through a lengthy consultative period, and based on a comprehensive sector review prepared by the Department of Education. The review identified several symptoms of systemic failure: low enrolment rates, with disparities across social groups based on gender, caste, ethnicity and geographical location; high discontinuation rates; low academic achievement rates; and overall high rates of illiteracy. These symptoms were exacerbated by the low levels of resource allocation, averaging 3% of the GNP, with declining expenditure on primary education, insufficient infrastructure to meet the needs of sections of the population, particularly in rural areas, high rates of teacher absenteeism, and overall poor management of schools, particularly in terms of monitoring and evaluation. The review, published in 1985, was followed by the NPE in 1986, and then by a Programme of Action in 1992 and a revised policy statement on Education for All, in 1993. These documents present a consolidated policy discourse on education, which represent some significant changes in the approach to education planning.

Particularly significant shifts are the explicit commitment to equality, empowerment and a proactive role for government. The NPE accords priority to the 'removal of disparities and equalising educational opportunity by attending to specific needs of those who have been denied equality so far', with a particular emphasis on using education to empower women. The NPE also envisages a 'positive interventionist role' for the education system, viewing it as a vehicle through which the government can act as a catalyst for social change. Given the entrenched social and economic inequality in India, it is a significant policy commitment. The innovation or shift in policy discourse can be identified both in the explicitness of these statements and in their location as a central statement of public policy goals.

That the NPE set the basic framework for subsequent interventions is demonstrated in the Sarva Shiksha Abhiyan (SSA) programme for Universal Elementary Education, launched by the Ministry of Human Resources Development in 2001–02. The SSA describes itself as an 'umbrella programme' defining the framework for the implementation of elementary education policy based on lessons from the decade of the 1990s, which saw several different programmes aimed at universalising education through reaching out to different target populations. Below we focus on two programmes – Mahila Samakhya and the District Primary Education Programme (DPEP) – from which considerable lessons were learned. While the DPEP as a distinct programme does not exist any more, having been subsumed into the wider SSA, the lessons provided by it are instructive for the kinds of shifts in intervention that were set in motion since the NPE was developed as a policy (vision) statement.

In this section we look at the types of information needed, the mode of investigation required, and the research questions that require answers, in order for this new policy approach to be effective.

At the broadest level, we can ask normative or evaluative questions about the changing policy itself in its context. For example: How should more specific programmes be developed from the new policy approach? Is the new approach 'better' than the old?

Before thinking about research questions, however, we should check there really is something substantial to investigate. To what extent can alterations in policy language be considered to constitute a policy shift? In assessing the evidence here, there are two points that need to be borne in mind (which apply to the transport policy case study as well).

1   Policy documents are general statements of intention, and do not serve as a guarantee of implementation or action, even where they use progressive terminology and promise radical change. On their own, they tell us little about how changes will be put into practice, and provide little indication of the 'real' nature of the change that is likely to be experienced. For example, using intangible concepts like 'equality' and 'empowerment' to describe policy goals may provide an important conceptual framework, but these terms are likely to remain relatively meaningless unless they inform the design of programmes, and become values shared by policy actors including planners, programme implementors and users. In the history of education planning in India, there have been numerous commissions, reviews and reports identifying most of the problems cited in the NPE policy documents. The universalisation of education has always been the priority or goal cited in policy documents, including those of the five-year plans produced by the country's centralised Planning Commission. The NPE documents provide little insight into why, despite earlier policies, outcomes have not matched expectations or goals.

2   Policy documents are often political documents, but disguise from their public the politics of the decision-making process that precedes and influences their formulation. Policy documents often use neutral terminology that does not indicate the nature of the decision-making process, or illuminate the reasons why some strategies are included and not others. While experienced observers of policy processes may be able to identify the critical influences on policy options (either in terms of influential individuals such as politicians, or agencies like the World Bank), the general public would have little insight into the politics of policy formulation.

Because policies tend to represent a generalised outline of desired 'ends', research that seeks to evaluate the impact and/or inform the direction of policy change needs to be based on more concrete events in the policy process. Grindle (1980) identifies implementation as the critical stage where public policy is executed after the goals and objectives have been designed, and resources are allocated. Specific programmes then become the means through which policy goals are delivered. Research focusing on programmes can often provide insightful snapshots of policy, capturing the dynamics of policy change at the meso or micro levels, and demonstrating how categories of analysis developed on paper are converted into action. In the case of education policy in India, new programmes have been designed and established in selected districts of the country; they highlight the shifts made in the NPE from merely addressing shortfalls in education provision to creating a climate for innovation. These programmes focus on both adult and primary education, and two are discussed in a little detail below.

1.3.1 Innovative programmes in India

The Mahila Samakhya programme, launched in 1989 by the Government of India with donor assistance, was born out of the consultative process of the NPE. Aimed at adult women in poor communities in selected states and districts in India, the programme is based on a reconceptualisation of education 'as a process of ongoing collective action and reflection which would empower women' (Government of India, 1995), using process-based methods of raising consciousness and awareness. Education, in the formal sense of literacy and numeracy, is not imposed on the target group, women. The principles of the programme stress that the pace and the priorities of the programme are to be determined by the women and communicated through their facilitators to the programme offices at district and state level. The programme is based on a reversal of traditional programme hierarchy, empowering the users to make decisions, while programme staff are viewed as facilitators. Significantly, Mahila Samakhya was not designed as a resource-intensive programme, but focuses on sustainability through building people's organisations at the village and community levels.

The District Primary Education Programme (DPEP), officially launched in 1992 with principal financial assistance coming from the World Bank, and now incorporated into the wider Universal Elementary Education programme (or *Sarva Shiksha Abhiyan*), was aimed at strengthening the base of the education system, the primary levels of schooling. The DPEP strategy was to restructure the primary education system in selected districts, and had as its particular focus the securing of education opportunities for underprivileged social groups. The programme had 'hard' targets, in terms of improvements in enrolments, retention and achievement within a time-frame, and had resources allocated for infrastructure development, such as building more schools and improving water and sanitation provision in existing schools. However, within the resource and target framework, DPEP emphasised the use of mobilisation campaigns, and built links between government agencies and community bodies empowered to make recommendations to government about aspects of the programme. DPEP also focused on retraining teachers in terms of both curriculum changes as well as the more process-based aspects of the programme.

Despite the differences in focus, Mahila Samakhya and DPEP (as well as the *Sarva Shiksha Abhiyan*, which now incorporates both Mahila Samakhya as a distinct programme as well as the lessons of DPEP, as discussed earlier) share several features which provide concrete attempts to put the key policy shifts in the NPE into practice.

- They both specifically targeted underprivileged and traditionally excluded social groups, in terms of mobilising their participation in education and also committing government resources to investment in infrastructure.
- Both programmes restructured management to make it responsive and flexible. This is particularly so in the case of Mahila Samakhya, though DPEP also stated that 'capacity-building' and establishing appropriate management structures are important components of programme strategy.
- Both programmes built their strategies on a network of community organisations and community decision-making as an integral part of their programme functioning.

Each of these aspects reflects the framework of the NPE, and provides a crystallised and tangible context within which policy shifts in education can be investigated, monitored and evaluated.

1.3.2 Four levels of policy investigation

The case study in Section 1.2 revealed how shifts in transport policy in Britain have necessitated shifts in the type of information required to support policy structures. Clearly, investigations are relevant to different points and levels in the policy process, and can use existing information systems in different ways and to greater or lesser extent. Investigations can be designed to identify the need for change and the content and direction of change; or they can be designed in the aftermath of policy change to provide an evaluative perspective. If policy is conceptualised as an iterative and dynamic process, rather than a linear progression from design to implementation and then outcomes, it will help to locate information systems within the constant process of policy change. Policies are rarely written on 'clean sheets', but are, variously, responses to 'problems' that are perceived to exist based on evaluation and feedback, or prompted by a sense of 'crisis', or brought about through changing social and political environments.

Whereas the UK transport policy case was written to reflect the change in the type of investigation needed to inform policy-makers, in this Indian case we are looking at how the whole policy process may be investigated from a more independent viewpoint. From this perspective, we suggest a framework for independent policy investigation based on four parameters, each of which leads to research at a different level. They are:

1 the *concept* underpinning policy change;
2 the *contexts* of policy change, in terms of the environment within which the concerned policy is designed, as well as the complex of 'reality' in which it seeks to intervene;
3 the *capacities* for change, particularly with regard to the institutions involved in implementing the policy change; and
4 the *experiences of change* of those who are the intended beneficiaries of policy.

In terms of the distinctions used in the discussion of research questions in Section 1.1, the first three levels are about the policy itself (mostly top right box of Table 1.1), while the last is about the field of policy (bottom right box in Table 1.1).

Researching concepts

Locating policy goals and targets within debates about the kind of change that is desirable is an important first step in evaluating the viability of policy goals. If policy goals are situated within an ideological perspective that does not correspond to the perspectives and needs of a majority of targeted users, will it impede the realisation of those goals, and if so, to what extent? In the case of education planning, there are interesting ideological conflicts. Formal education has largely been a twentieth-century concern, and discussions of its value and importance continue to be debated. As Jones notes, 'The history of education in the twentieth century has been very much concerned with the need to choose between the moral and the material purposes of education. Were education's principal effects the unlocking of individual potential or rather the enhancement of social administration? Did education foster liberty or stifle it? Did it promote creativity and entrepreneurship or rather passivity and subservience? Was it a vehicle for the renewal of society or its mere reproduction?' (Jones, 1992, p. xiii). Conflicting perceptions of the importance of education are central to the relationship between the system and its users in India, where attendance at schools is not compulsory. This makes the policy arena in education a particularly contested one, where different actors are likely to define the value of education in different terms, and possibly expect different outcomes from the system on offer.

Researching political context

Beliefs about the importance or direction of policy goals are not the only influence on policy design. The chosen boundaries of policies and programmes also reflect *political* decisions on what is viable and what is desirable. Hence, investigating the political factors that contribute to policy shifts as well as the selection of design and strategy is often a critical aspect of research on policy change. At the level of decision-making and political authority, questions could include:

- What were the influences on the policy shift (both individual and institutional)?
- What are the roots of the policy shift? (in political ideology? in crisis? in responses to evaluation?)
- Is the timing of the introduction of the policy shift politically significant? (election? crisis?)
- What is the extent of the change desired? How different is the policy from previous efforts?
- What is the history of the ideas involved in the change?

The political context of decision-making is relevant at all levels of the policy process, and so investigation involves looking into the contexts of power and authority that determine policy design.

Education policy has the power to shape and transform the lives of those who benefit from it in a variety of ways. A commitment to equality would necessarily involve transforming existing social relations to remove the barriers that exclude disadvantaged sections from schools. Management of the education system in a local context would require information about local social relations so that the achievement of policy goals of equality and empowerment can be monitored. Thus, policy research should include identifying the organisations and actors participating in the policy process and locating them in a network of relationships, both social and organisational. Within this framework of structures and agents, it will then be easier to identify which relationships are likely to have which impacts on the realisation of policy goals, and the direction of change. A suggestive 'map' of policy actors in the context of an education programme aimed at rural areas could look like that in Figure 1.4.

The 'map' in Figure 1.4 is merely a subjective draft, but could be as detailed as required within a given context. What it does help to do is to identify the key actors involved at the different stages of the policy process. A map of this kind is useful in the process of updating the researcher's knowledge of the context and can serve as a reminder of the complexity of the policy process.

Researching institutional capacity

A third level of analysis involves the stage at which policy goals are made operational. The implementation stage of the policy process is an integral link between policy design and the realisation of outcomes. In the two education programmes discussed, the administrative and management structures form a critical component of the process of change. Research would need to focus on the capacity of implementing agencies to adapt to the changes in policy, and locate the analysis within an understanding of these agencies as organisations with specific histories and internal relations. To what extent are implementing organisations flexible in their structure to adapt to changes in practice that policy shifts may necessitate? How responsive are they, and do they need to be, to users' interests around the resources that they have the power to disburse? This analysis may be critical to understanding the dynamics of policy change at the interface between organisations representing the state and wider constituencies representing civil society. A representation of this is shown in Figure 1.5.

Researching the field of policy

A final, important level of analysis would need to focus at the level of the people whom policy change is expected to benefit. Researching change at the level of users is necessary not just to evaluate 'impact' in a linear sense, but to evaluate the likelihood of policy changes meeting the expectations, needs and interests of users. Here it may be important, as in the UK transport policy example, not only to find out what underlies or causes change in expectations or needs, but also to ask 'What if?' questions. If policy aims to develop or manage demand, existing expectations may be a poor guide. It is also useful to distinguish needs from interests. This kind of investigation is particularly vital in a context where policies claim to be concerned about the interests of disadvantaged

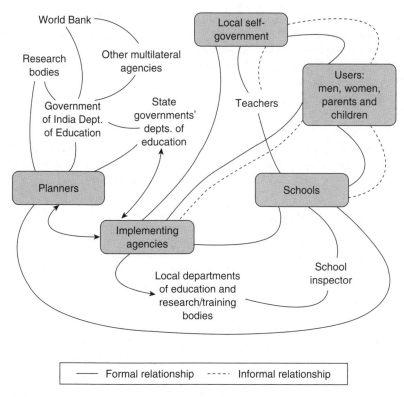

FIGURE 1.4   Mapping policy actors in the socio-political context of education policy in India

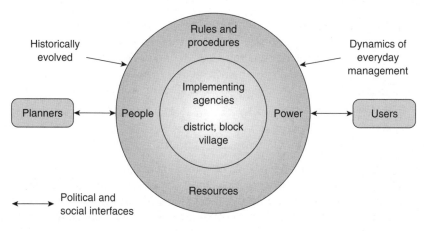

FIGURE 1.5   Organisational context of implementing agencies

sections of the population, whose voices may not be heard by planners situated in offices removed from the field. However, one should not confuse interventionism with the imposition of external values. The experience of users can provide a perspective on policy change that can point to gaps in analysis or information, and help to explain why outcomes may not match expectations.

Research and investigations on policy change at all these four levels are integral to the completion of the loop between the implementation of policy, user responses and the design of policy change. If designed and carried out by individuals or institutions working outside government, research can play an important part in promoting public action and advocacy for change. The ideas and evidence that research offers can provide the basic backdrop against which policy is put into operation.

1.4 Policy change and information needs • • •

A number of general points about policy investigation can be made from the areas of contrast as well as the common themes emerging from these two case studies.

Implications of change from reactive to developmental policy

A stable and purely reactive policy regime requires only answers to 'What?' questions about the field of policy. However, once there is a policy change towards demand management or developmental policies there will also be a change in the type of question which needs answering. This could be a change towards needing to understand causes and the likely impact of new policies, i.e. a change from 'What?' through 'How?' to 'Why?' and 'What if?'. It could also be a change towards investigating not just the field of policy but also the policy itself and the context of policy change, including the multiplicity of stakeholders and policy agencies involved as well as the capacities of various agencies for change and the competing concepts behind changing policy goals.

Stakeholder involvement
A shift towards a policy-as-process approach involves a change in the role of stakeholders – planners, researchers, activists/advocates and users/beneficiaries/clients, etc. There is a need to involve and empower stakeholders in policy change to achieve acceptance and success. In both case studies, existing institutional structures have proved a barrier to this happening.

Role of research

As noted in the Introduction to the book, investigation also becomes a tool or means for policy change through the entire process. This is the case whether it is undertaken or commissioned by policy-makers with the direct aim of informing policies, or whether it is undertaken from a more independent perspective, when its results might be used for lobbying or advocacy.

In the UK transport policy case study, research tended to show that the traditional policy approach was not working rather than to inform a new process that did work. This gap remains at the time of writing. In the Indian education study, investigation of new programmes such as DPEP may aid the improved design and development of such programmes within the new approach.

The need for research results to be available throughout the intervention

A policy change could involve the outline of a broader parameter of change, while the information gathered can help to develop the direction of change in greater detail. Often the research can be the only contact that planners at higher levels have with reality; it thus provides not only a symbol of the 'public' for planners, but also their means of defence, justification and legitimacy. Having research results available throughout an intervention also helps them to be open to incorporate feedback, lessons of evaluation and so on, to complement the dynamic of the policy process.

How identification of information needs depends on the nature of the policy change

Policies can be changed in different ways:

- the change could represent a shift in ideology underpinning policy;
- the change could be an improvement on previous efforts based on feedback or complaints, i.e. lessons from evaluations;
- the change could be about the recipients of benefits rather than about content;
- the change could be about implementing agencies or management structures.

In both examples here, the change was from a reactive to a developmental orientation. In the transport case study, the policy change centred on the abandonment of a failed 'road-building' approach, and the adoption of the idea of managing demand in order to achieve goals such as accessibility. This included the realisation that traffic growth had to be controlled, but with only a vague idea of what was needed to achieve this. In consequence, information needs have not been adequately identified. In the Indian education study the change is from administration of schools and other educational services towards recognising the developmental role of education and an interventionist stance, targeting certain socio-economic groups and reforming management structures.

The need to identify the sources and contexts of policy change

This relates to the above point. Policy changes are principally, or ultimately, an issue of political will. However, the key catalysts of policy change do vary, depending on the sector, the particular policy, the country, political structure and so on.

In the transport case study, lobbyists that had for many years been on an uninfluential fringe rapidly became part of the core political process. These included the public transport or environmental lobby, such as Transport 2000 and Greenpeace. They joined the traditionally powerful industry lobbies, such as the British Road Federation and the Confederation of British Industries, both of which have changed their stance in response to the failure of traditional road-building policies. The extension of political recognition to wider stakeholder interests was perhaps epitomised by the awarding in 1996 of an OBE to the Director of Transport 2000, something unthinkable a few years before.

In the Indian education study, political context was recognised explicitly as one of the levels of investigation required, and Figure 1.4 showed the kind of result to be expected, in terms of a 'map' of policy actors.

Contexts could include both crisis situations and those where changes are more gradual. They also include the nature of the political system which can determine the boundaries of policy change; the time-frame planned for the policy; the capacity of implementing agencies; and so on.

The framework for designing the investigation will need to be based on assessments of the key actors involved in policy change as well as the political context which shapes the direction of the change. This will provide more 'realistic' parameters within which the policy change can be investigated or information to feed into it can be collected.

The scope of policy change

This is suggested in the earlier points above, but needs to be reiterated.

The 'scope' of change is not just about the influence of political variables or institutional agendas on policy change, but also could be more simply about the extent to which new institutions are likely to be created, or new actors embraced. If the policy change is a shift in the criteria developed for building new schools (a simple example), it could range in scope – on the one hand, it could be the simple commission of research to identify new criteria, retraining for old implementors etc., or on the other, it could be a complete change in the institutions that formerly were involved in planning, building, etc., and the creation of new community institutions in order to identify criteria in a participatory way. Identifying the scope of change will help to focus the direction of the investigation, and help to ensure that information is relevant, presented in a way that is directly useful, and not overly ambitious. The 'scope' is essentially a combination of assessing the nature and content of the direction of policy change and the sources and contexts of change.

The key point here is that investigations are not designed in a vacuum; they only exist around a bounded rational entity called 'policy', but are rooted in several traditions or histories, intellectual, cultural, political and developmental. What they offer to planners will depend on the 'field of vision' of those who carry out the research, what is perceived, understood or interpreted by those who use it, and then what is realistically 'do-able'.

Boundaries for thinking and action

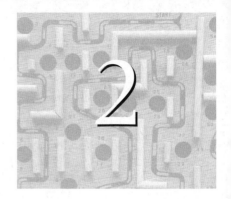

Chris Blackmore and Ray Ison

T he focus of this chapter is on using boundaries for thinking and action. It is not confined to the process of investigation but stands back from it to look at the overall conceptual framework within which investigation takes place. It challenges the thinking from which investigative processes start, which in turn shapes the design and conduct of an investigation.

Investigation is an iterative process but once it becomes channelled in a particular direction it can be difficult to change course without tools and concepts to help. This chapter, in the main, uses the term boundary as a 'systems' concept. Systems thinking and practice has a well established intellectual and practical history (Ison, 2008; Chapman, 2004). A system is a set of components that are interconnected for a purpose. The boundary is the conceptual line, distinguished by someone, that demarcates what is inside the system from what is outside the system, in its environment. In other words, it separates what is directly relevant for a particular purpose from what is not of direct relevance or interest. Should the purpose change the system boundary needs to be redrawn. Translating this to the context of investigation, the suggestion that you use boundaries for thinking and action is intended to challenge you always to be clear about the purpose of your activity. If your purpose changes you need to reconsider where the boundary needs to be redrawn and what and who should and should not be included in your investigation. We return to this point later.

We have interpreted 'investigation' quite widely in this chapter as we consider much thinking and action for policy and development management to be part of a 'finding out' or a 'learning' process. Your own interpretation of investigation may be narrower than ours. Don't use the chapter uncritically but do at least try to use it to widen your thinking so that you recognize what is relevant in an investigative situation.

2.1 Why boundaries? • • •

Drawing boundaries is relevant to the development manager or policy investigator in many different contexts. They help to separate, simplify and focus on what is important in a particular situation and what is less important and can be ignored.

For example:

1 identifying the geographical location of boundaries within which new development activity might take place under a policy, project or programme;
2 identifying people who are involved in an activity who might need to participate in investigation and action;
3 separating your own professional responsibilities from those of a colleague – identifying the boundaries of your role;
4 becoming sensitive to how others are using boundaries whether explicitly or implicitly;
5 working out the expected effects of interventions; and
6 defining where responsibility and accountability might reside.

In some situations it might be difficult to place boundaries (not all situations are easily bounded or they may be fiercely contested) but thinking through where the limits lie can help in planning, challenging, negotiating and evaluating many different activities.

Whilst some boundaries are physical and can be easily seen, others are more abstract. They are constructs used to develop and communicate understanding and to define and negotiate limits. In this chapter we will define boundaries in abstract terms and in relation to the concept of a 'system'. Thus a boundary is determined by stakeholders (which may or may not. include you as development manager or investigator) and relevant actors when they differentiate a 'system' from its 'environment' or a 'sub-system' from the 'system'. Depending on their perspectives and purposes, different people in the same situation will recognize different systems, and constituent sub-systems. That is, they will put the boundary in different places.

We shall differentiate between 'open' and 'closed' systems, which may be distinguished by the nature of their conceptual boundaries. Thus a project for which there are fixed, perhaps highly specified, outcomes from which little or no deviation is anticipated or tolerated, can be seen as a *closed system* with a fixed boundary. In such systems we can say that the boundary is closed to new inputs to the system, such as the experiences and learning of the actors in the process of implementation, or data about changed or changing factors in the environment of the system. Projects developed within a blueprint approach to development, as described by Korten (1980, 1990), typify closed systems.

In contrast *open systems* have flexible and 'permeable' boundaries which allow the system to adapt – to respond to inputs and to generate new forms of output. This process of change occurs through iteration and learning. We would argue that one of the needs in development management is to move away from the notion of projects as closed systems towards more open systems. Likewise, policies which are prescriptive, and are unable to be adapted to diverse, local contexts can also be conceptualized as having closed boundaries. However, they can be viewed as either open or closed systems depending on how they are formulated, articulated and implemented. This is not an either/or situation but one in which 'open systems' are the context in which certain 'closed systems' might be found. This is why development managers need to be able to negotiate, help resolve conflict and evaluate processes and outcomes in order to manage boundary formulation and reformulation as an open process.

An example of this might be a particular investigation as part of the process of policy formulation. An investigation into, say, infant mortality in a particular region, as a precursor to the development of post-natal health care services policies, may have a fixed time frame and be recognizably discrete or bounded. In systems terms we would say that it might be helpful to consider this investigation as a sub-system of a 'system to develop regional post-natal health care services'. Conceptualizing it in this way means that the investigation can be seen as part of a greater whole. In turn this may help shape the design and conduct of the investigation because thinking of it in these terms creates a constant reminder that the investigation is *related* to this greater whole – the policy. Of course the policy would be unsustainable if it did not contain within it provision for the regular collection, analysis and interpretation of infant mortality data. In this way it is possible to see what is described as a *recursive relationship* between an initial investigation, policy and the ongoing implementation of policy, or one in which feedback from data collection and analysis is constantly informing action.

2.2 Using boundaries in development management • • •

The concept of a 'boundary' is fundamental to the study of systems, which employs systemic or holistic thinking to guide action in complex situations (Checkland, 1981, 1999). A point which is frequently made in the teaching of systems is that our actions in a given context are very much shaped by our ways of thinking. Hence it makes sense to think about how we think – what particular theories, metaphors, experiences shape how we react, plan, manage, etc.?

Thus, one way of using the concept of 'boundaries' is as a tool to guide your thinking (examples are given below). A development manager might be more interested in linking theory to action for some purpose in a given context rather than thinking about theory itself. But this can mask a whole set of complex questions: What theories? Who are or should be the actors? Who specifies the purpose? What is the context and how is it understood and by whom? These are all boundary setting questions that need to be considered at the beginning of any investigation and are developed in Box 2.1. The answers to these questions result in sets of premises for the design of a system of interest.

The checklist of questions in Box 2.1 can be divided into four groups of three (Ulrich, 1987). They are:

- the *sources of motivation* of those involved – what is the value basis of the design? (questions 1 to 3)
- the *sources of control* – who has power or authority and on what basis? (questions 4 to 6)
- what are the *sources of expertise* or *know-how* and is it adequate? (questions 7 to 9)
- what are the *sources of legitimation and its basis*? (questions 10 to 12)

Box 2.1   A checklist of boundary setting questions

1   Who ought to be the *client* (beneficiary) of the system being designed or improved?
2   What ought to be the *purpose* of the system; i.e. what goal states ought the system be able to achieve so as to serve the client?
3   What ought to be the system's *measure of success* (or improvement)?
4   Who ought to be the *decision taker,* that is, have the power to change the system's measure of improvement?
5   What *components* (resources and constraints) of the system ought to be controlled by its decision taker?
6   What resources and conditions ought to be part of the system's *environment,* i.e. should not be controlled by the system's decision taker?
7   Who ought to be involved as *designer* of the system?
8   What kind of *expertise* ought to flow into the design of the system; i.e. who ought to be considered an expert and what should be their role?
9   Who ought to be the *guarantor* of the system; i.e. where ought the designer seek the guarantee that their design will be implemented and will prove successful, judged by the system's measure of success (or improvement)?
10   Who ought to belong to the *witnesses* representing the concerns of the citizens that will or might be affected by the design of the system? That is to say, who among the affected ought to get involved?
11   To what degree and in what way ought the affected be given the chance of *emancipation* from the premises and promises of the involved?
12   Upon what *world-views* of either the involved or the affected ought the system's design be based?

(From Ulrich, 1987)

Of course there are no simple answers to these questions and they are often contested and the basis of conflict. Under such circumstances it is necessary to have some appreciation of power relations (see Chapter 8) and how they might be understood.

For example, John Heron (1989) identifies three levels of power to be consciously recognized in the process of project or activity design:

1   hierarchical, with 'power over' leading to 'deciding for';
2   co-operative, or 'power with' leading to 'deciding with'; and
3   autonomous, or 'power to' leading to 'delegating deciding to'.

Choice of any one of these frameworks will lead to very different outcomes in a given context because the systems that result will be very different. There is no right answer as to which conception of power might be used in a given context but these distinctions do exemplify:

(a) how the boundaries around a given system of interest might vary depending on the perspectives which different participants bring;
(b) how this might be consciously incorporated into process design; and
(c) how open to conflict and negotiation the whole process might be understood to be.

2.2.1 Acknowledging individual perceptions and perspectives

The point has been made that individuals confronted by the same situation are likely to recognize different 'systems' because they have different perspectives. It is worth considering this notion of *perspectives* further. When we stop to think about it we know that each of us has a unique experiential history – even within families, groups or cultures no human beings share exactly the same experiences. From this unique cognitive history it follows that all we have at our disposal is the ability to communicate about our experiences. We never have exactly the same experience as another. Thus, we each bring to any situation, and into any conversation, sets of unique perspectives. There is a tendency to forget this, although when reminded it seems like common sense.

Unfortunately many factors act against us remembering that human communication lies in a complex process. One of the most powerful constraints is the common metaphors associated with human communication – e.g. 'information transfer', 'information sharing', 'getting the message across'. Hidden in these metaphors is the notion that human communication is just like two computers linked to each other, i.e. that the message sent will be exactly the same as the message received. Clearly, however, human communication is not the same as two computers 'talking'. We can never be sure that the meaning attributed to what we said is the same as we intended. In fact the meaning attributed will be an *interpretation* of the message from the unique perspective of the other person.

Recognizing that human communication is often misunderstood and that some pervasive metaphors seem to conspire to perpetuate this misunderstanding enables us to understand the importance of designing and developing effective communication processes. As discussed further by Chataway and Mordaunt in Chapter 4, we cannot think in terms of investigation as leading to results which are then simply transmitted to policy-makers who act on them. It is better to think of an investigation as including writing up and feeding back results to particular audiences, and this whole process as a negotiation – including the changed meanings constructed by the members of the audience as they interpret the investigation and its results from their own unique perspectives.

2.2.2 Moving boundaries to get out of traps in thinking and behaviour

Many boundaries are those of our own making and they affect the way we think and behave. For example, at some time in your life you have probably experienced a situation where you constructed a boundary between what you could and could not do, but later managed to overcome fears, develop skills or see different opportunities that enabled you to change the boundary. There might be no physical reason why you can't speak up in a public meeting, jump across a ditch or travel to another country, but if you tell yourself you can't do it, you often won't be able to. If, however, you can begin to think of a task differently you might find ways you can do it. This process is one of moving the boundary between what you perceive you can and cannot do.

In the context of development management, perceptions of resource limitations provide an example. Resources are elements which are available within the boundary of a system. Before working out where the boundaries lie, it is important first to identify what system or sub-system you are considering. Take the case of a team of three busy people with a small fixed budget, tasked with running a major series of training events as well as maintaining an existing activity. If the boundary of project resources were drawn around these elements the task would seem unachievable. However, if other resources can be identified – involving other people, sharing the task with another team, obtaining additional funds from those with a complementary agenda – then it might indeed be achievable. In this case it is only the system for organizing training events we need to consider, not the system for running the project as a whole. Working out where the particular activity boundary might lie (in this case training) rather than the project boundary enables us to consider the situation quite differently.

One common trap in using systems thinking is the belief held by many scientists or development managers that it is possible to stand outside any 'system' in a so-called objective position. This is often manifest in behaviour in which one person or group claims to have access to the 'truth' rather than recognizing that in a given situation there may be many 'truths'. The relationship between individual and collective experiences with respect to investigation for action is another area in which it may be useful to think in terms of how people construct and draw boundaries around knowledge.

For example, knowledge can be seen as a commodity or a body of understandings (based on data, analysis and interpretation) which can be passed on in verbal or written form to others. Knowledge can also be seen as a process of 'knowing' which is very personal and involves experiential learning. Moreover, different people will place different emphasis on scientific and traditional perspectives. Redclift (1992) points out that when we observe local resource management strategies we must acknowledge that we are dealing with multiple epistemologies (knowledge systems) possessed by different groups of people. There are many different ways of interpreting a statement such as 'we do not have that knowledge'. It could range in meaning from 'we do not have that data' to 'we have not had that experience'. Finding out what individuals understand by knowledge – where they draw the conceptual boundary – can help to communicate different perceptions and build a more coherent understanding. It is in turn a way of finding out what action might be taken.

These different ideas about knowledge and ways of drawing boundaries around knowledge suggest that any attempt to 'find out' should be open to the many possible stories or interpretations of a scenario or situation. For example, in many parts of

Africa and other countries with semi-arid rangelands where pastoralism is the most common land use, there has been acrimony between scientists and pastoralists for many years focused around the so-called 'land degradation debate'. This is a contest between different epistemologies but one in which the players are often unaware of their own epistemological positions. In Botswana, Louise Fortmann's case study of rangeland use over a 50-year period showed how official policy consistently defined the major problem of the pastoral regions as overstocking leading to certain ecological disaster (Fortmann, 1989). For the officials the problem was clear, as was the technical solution (destocking). Local experience on the other hand defined the problem as too little land. The local solution was also very different: renting, or using land previously let to a European mining company. The local experience was that the local range could and did carry an increased cattle population and that, besides localized problems, the dire official predictions of ecological disaster did not happen. While there is general agreement that the quality of the environment (as indicated by the quality of the grazing, the number of trees and the extent of erosion) is deteriorating, there is clearly no agreement on causes or solutions. It is significant that the story has been told consistently from both perspectives for 50 years; this shows how different and how unconnected traditions of knowledge or understanding can be (Russell and Ison, 1993; Ison and Russell, 2000).

Stephany Kersten, in an Australian study (Kersten, 1995), found a similar contest between researchers and pastoralists over the nature and causes of the so-called 'rangeland degradation problem'. In her research she used particular techniques to design participatory workshops with the aim of enabling researchers, pastoralists and advisors to break out of this historical trap. One approach she adopted was to invite the participants to draw pictures, using mind-maps or spray diagrams, of who they were as people. One of the diagrams drawn by the participating Landcare co-ordinator (an employee of a local community Landcare Group, funded by the government) is shown in Figure 2.1.

By doing this Kersten was inviting the participants to move their conceptual boundaries; from belonging to, or representing groups of researchers, pastoralists or advisers, to a large single group of individuals coming together as individual people with a common concern about the future of the rangelands. Her research showed that this was one necessary precursor to the generation of dialogue (as opposed to debate).

Some differences between debate (the original meaning of which can be interpreted as 'to put down') and dialogue ('has meaning running through') are given in Table 2.1. Dialogue in this sense is an ideal which cannot always be realized, and it is often necessary to think in terms of negotiation between interests as another alternative to 'debate' (see also Section 2.2.4 below). Factors that enhanced or restricted dialogue, arising from meetings between pastoralists, researchers and advisors, are summarized from Kersten's research in Table 2.2. The research by Kersten is a good example of the design of a communication process which recognizes the multiple perspectives that we bring to our conversations.

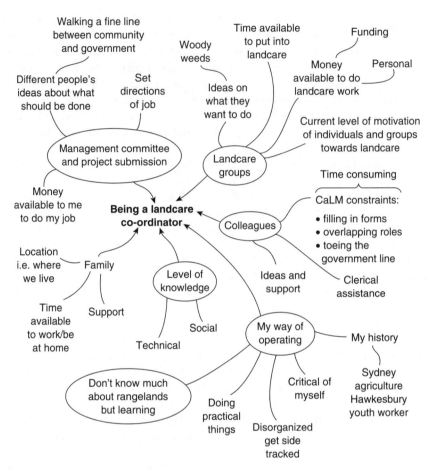

FIGURE 2.1   Spray diagram drawn by the Landcare Facilitator; CaLM is Conservation and Land Management (source: Kersten, 1995)

Another factor which affects the way people view the world and set boundaries is their profession. One of the more common traps is narrow disciplinary thinking. Many professionals see the world in the light of their disciplinary perspective and all too often have a tendency only to recognize problems and opportunities accordingly. For example, Figure 2.2 shows a situation and how different experts view their system of interest, depending on their area of expertise. Such thinking has caused many difficulties in project formulation and is a strong argument for the use of interdisciplinary perspectives and systemic (or holistic) as opposed to systematic (step-by-step) methodologies in the project formulation process. Note that in Figure 2.2 the perspective of the

TABLE 2.1   *Some of the key distinctions between 'debate' and 'dialogue'*

Debate	Dialogue
Participants tend to be leaders of groups with a specific opinion, to speak as representatives of a group, or be committed to a particular view	Participants are not necessarily leaders, they speak as individuals about their own unique experience, expressing uncertainty, as well as deeply held beliefs
The atmosphere is threatening, attacks and interruptions are expected	The atmosphere is one of safety, ground rules exist and promote respectful exchange
Differences within the group are set aside or denied	Differences between individual participants are revealed
Participants listen in order to refute other ideas, questions are often rhetorical challenges or disguised statements	Participants listen to understand and gain insight into the beliefs and concerns of others; questions are asked from a position of curiosity
Statements are predictable and offer little new information	New information surfaces
Success requires simple impassioned statements	Success requires exploration of the complexities of the issue being discussed
Participants operate within the constraints of the dominant public discourse, which defines the problem and the options for resolution; this assumes that fundamental needs and values are already clearly understood	Participants are encouraged to question the dominant public discourse, to express fundamental needs that may or may not be reflected in the discourse, and to explore various options for problem definition and resolution

(Kersten, 1995; after Roth *et al.*, 1992, p. 44)

interdisciplinary team reflects far more fully the situation as a whole and, of course, involving local people adds further to the capacity to understand a complex situation.

Another example is that in completing the logical framework plans used by certain development agencies, many disciplinary 'natural' scientists consistently name organizational, institutional and other socio-economic factors as likely or possible constraints to 'natural science' research success. In other words many of the complex people- and policy-related issues are seen as outside the system boundary by those who proposed the projects. The use of multi-disciplinary teams in rapid rural appraisal (RRA) and participatory rural appraisal (PRA) constitute attempts to break out of such disciplinary traps, though the quality of these approaches varies depending on the practice skills of those responsible (Armson *et al.*, 2001). (See Chapters 7 and 8).

Historically much agricultural and rural development has been managed by scientists and technologists, including agricultural economists who have focused on the concept of the 'farm'. This has been exemplified in 'farm management' and 'farming systems research' (FSR) where the tendency has been to define the boundary in terms

TABLE 2.2 *Factors that enhanced or restricted dialogue*

Enhancing dialogue	Restricting dialogue
Participants come to a meeting as individuals	Participants come as representatives of a group
Participants articulate their personal understanding at the meeting	Participants are at the meeting as groups and participants act as part of their own group
Time has been spent on building relationships before the meeting and during the meeting	Little time has been spent on building relationships
Participants are prepared to relax preconceived ideas about other participants at the meeting	Participants have fixed general or stereotyped ideas about other participants
Participants do not know each other beforehand	Participants know each other beforehand and are not prepared to relax preconceived ideas about each other
Listening actively to other participants with an open mind that is not blocked by preconceived ideas	Participants listen to re-establish preconceived ideas
Participants are open to ideas and asking for suggestions of other participants	Participants are defending or attacking statements made
Participants respect other meanings and understandings. Multiple realities are acknowledged	Participants do not respect meanings and understandings other than their own. They believe in one reality
Participants feel they can benefit from a good discussion with people who see the same issue from different perspectives	People have the feeling they are 'being participated'

(Kersten, 1995)

of a 'farming system' whilst neglecting the wider rural context. For example, seeing the desired system as a 'rural livelihood system' would also allow artisanal, craft and wage labour to be considered within the system boundaries. In recent years FSR's remit has expanded tremendously to include this wider perspective. Figure 2.3 illustrates how farming systems are now seen as sub-systems that contribute in one way to 'rural livelihood' or in another to 'food' systems (Bebbington *et al.*, 1993; Bebbington, 1994).

Development managers can make important contributions to the investigation and design of interventions which enable clients or stakeholders to break out of traps or self-imposed boundaries to their thinking that they themselves may not appreciate. We believe that this is most effective when the participants are enabled to take responsibility for their own learning and insights (McClintock and Ison, 1994; McClintock *et al.*, 2003). Such enabling processes require a high level of self-awareness among development managers themselves (see Chapter 8).

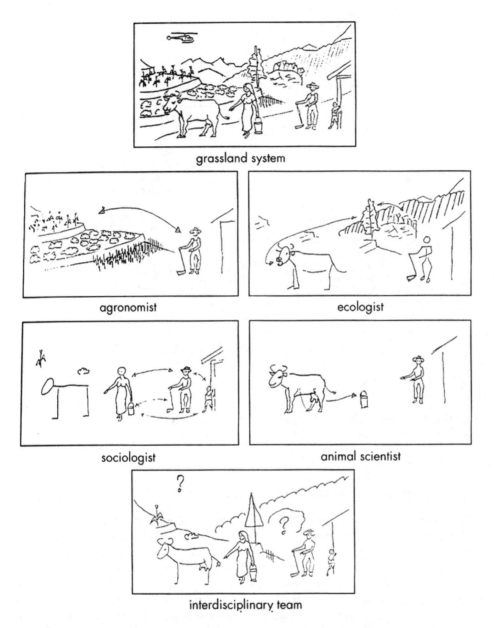

FIGURE 2.2 Perspectives of a farming system taken by disciplinary experts differ from that taken by an effective interdisciplinary team (Adapted from U. Scheuermeier, unpublished)

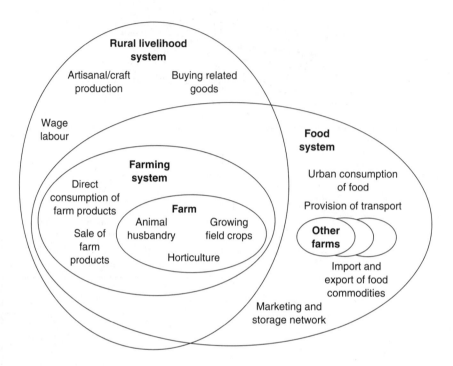

FIGURE 2.3   A systems diagram of a farming system as a sub-system both of a rural livelihood system and of a food system

2.2.3 Boundaries to simplify and communicate

Many situations under investigation by development managers are complex, messy and apparently unbounded. Drawing boundaries and diagramming can help to *simplify* a situation and act as a powerful means to *communicate* different perspectives among participants as we saw in the study by Kersten. There are many forms of diagramming which could be part of any development manager's 'tool-kit'. One of the simplest is the systems diagram (similar to a Venn or 'chapati' diagram), of which Figure 2.3 is an example, which shows what is considered to be inside and outside particular system boundaries and how systems and sub-systems overlap. Some other useful diagramming techniques are given in Figure 2.4; the figure is itself an example of a tree diagram. These and other forms of diagramming approaches are used extensively within RRA and PRA, while Chapter 8 includes other examples.

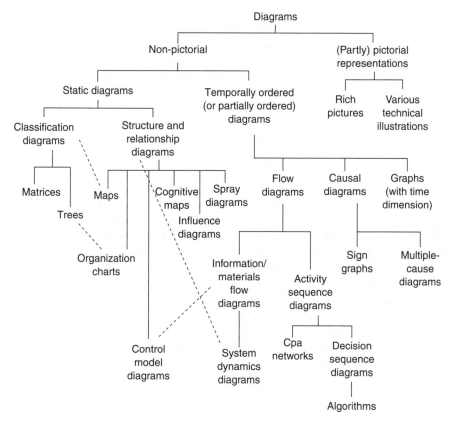

FIGURE 2.4 Different diagramming techniques available to the development manager for use during investigations (Open University, 1996)

Diagrams can be a very powerful means of cross-cultural communication although their effectiveness in communication differs depending on whether:

(a) the diagramming is done as part of a process in which there is joint learning and appreciation of why things were done in a particular way; or
(b) the completed diagram is simply presented to an audience, which is a qualitatively different experience.

An important point to remember in developing systems diagrams is that they should not be restricted to what already exists. In fact they lose much of their utility if they do not picture 'what might be' as well as 'what is' and thus may also include components and linkages which do not actually exist in the situation under consideration. When used in the early stages of any investigation, systems diagrams, as well as other diagramming and creativity techniques, are an important means of finding out fast.

Development managers undertaking an investigation may produce their own completed systems diagram as a way of simplifying a complex situation and providing a basis for discussion. For example, a diagram may be used as a stimulus for discussion, and with reactions providing new information for the investigator. Alternatively, diagramming may be done collaboratively, as a tool for negotiation (see, for example, Figure 12.2 in Chapter 12).

Development managers have a responsibility to try to be transparent in the boundary judgements they make and to trace their possible consequences. Ulrich (1987) argues that planners and managers cannot take upon themselves the 'political' act of approving the consequences of their boundary making. We would like to agree with Ulrich and say that only the affected can do this (see, for example, Figure 8.3 in Chapter 8). However, this would seem to negate the realities of power in many situations.

The development of conceptual models through the process of diagramming is also a valid means to start the policy formulation process. Some approaches to systems modelling stress the importance of using verbs – 'doing' words – as the modelling language (e.g. *gather* data, *analyze* data, *identify* stakeholders; see Checkland and Scholes, 1999). Particular functions are then incorporated within the system of interest through the choice of appropriate boundaries. For example, Figure 2.5 was used as part of the process of formulating a livestock sector development programme in Nepal. The figure also makes the system a lot easier to conceptualize than a description of the same model in words:

> a system to influence the living standards of people in Nepal's rural communities by concurrently developing the productivity of the livestock sector in an environmentally sustainable and equitable manner, while enhancing the capacity of the people to manage an on-going process of development. The system is dependent on long-term policy support from government and donor agencies and requires the development of institutional arrangements and capacities to facilitate people-centred development.

Systems practitioners, such as Macadam *et al.* (1995), rely on a simple but powerful tool to generate descriptions of possible systems of interest. This is the 'PQR' formulation of root definitions proposed by Checkland and Scholes (1999). It is simply a definition of an ideal system in the form:

A system to do <what, P> by means of <how, Q> in order to <why, R>.

This definition identifies:

(i) a system of interest in terms of what it does – its core transformation (e.g. 'living standards not influenced ® living standards influenced' is one of the transformations in the Macadam *et al.* system of interest), together with

(ii) its subsystems in terms of its constituent activities and the wider system of which it is a part and to which it contributes.

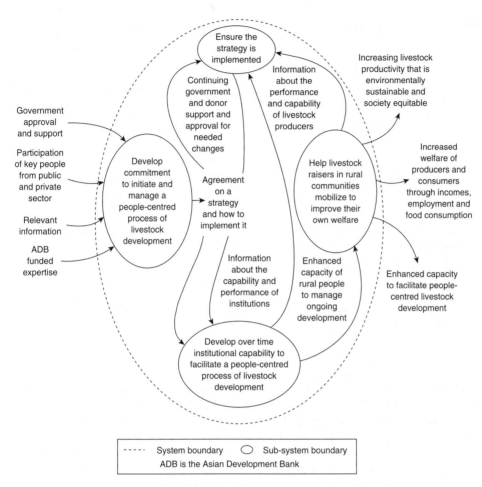

FIGURE 2.5 A form of conceptual modelling, using verbs as the modelling language, which is based on soft-systems methodology. (Macadam *et al.*, 1995)

Like many systems ideas, the PQR definition is a simple concept that is both demanding to formulate and revealing when finally identified.

2.2.4 Boundary setting as a process for negotiation

Getting people to explain – either verbally or visually – what they consider to be inside or outside a boundary is a starting point either for 'dialogue' or for 'negotiation by

TABLE 2.3 *Some contrasts between verbal and visual modes of working collaboratively*

	Verbal (interview, conversation)	Visual (diagram)
Outsider's roles	Investigator	Initiator and catalyst
Outsider's mode	Probing	Facilitating
Outsider's interventions	Continuous and maintained	Initial and then reduced
Insider's roles	Respondent	Presenter and analyst
Insider's mode	Reactive	Creative
Insider's awareness of outsider	High	Low
Eye contact	High	Low
The medium and material are those of	Outsider	Insider
The poorer, weaker, and women can be	Marginalized	Empowered
Detail influenced by	Etic categories (imposed from outside)	Emic perceptions (constructed from inside)
Information flow	Sequential	Cumulative
Accessibility of information to others	Low and transient	High and semi-permanent
Initiative for checking lies with	Outsider	Insider
Utility for spatial, temporal and causal information, relations, analysis, planning and monitoring	Low	High
Ownership of information	Appropriated by outsider	Owned and shared by insider

(After Chambers, 1992)

interests' as discussed in Section 2.2.2. *How* this is done needs careful thought. Slim and Thompson (1993) stress the importance of *listening* to the voice and experience of people, particularly in cultures with a strong tradition of oral testimony. Table 2.3 shows how Chambers (1992) highlights some differences between verbal and visual modes in the context of participatory rural appraisal. The right-hand column shows the potential of participative group-based techniques using visual representations, particularly when, in Chambers' terms, the outside investigator 'hands over the stick', but this potential is not always realized (see Chapter 8). Chambers points out that the verbal will always remain important and suggests that a combination of the verbal and the visual can express more than either on their own.

People who are in actual or potential conflict can often reach a better understanding of each other's point of view by working together and modifying the boundaries of their views. In some cases people may find they have closer or more complementary views than they think. An example where this has been done is in the UK where the 'Planning for Real' approach has been used in housing areas in Glasgow, Leicester, Nottingham, Tyneside and Sheffield (Gibson, 1994). Three-dimensional models with movable parts were used as part of the methodology so that participants could experiment with different scenarios and design their future amenity areas together. The process started with residents' suggestions. Officials and politicians were then drawn in to add their advice and experience, for example of legal and technical constraints, costs of proposed developments and sources of money and materials. Several stages of working out priorities and resources followed the modelling. No limits were put on the number of initial suggestions but part of the process involved removing duplications and having second thoughts about proposals that on reflection didn't look so good after all. In some cases this approach provided a way for residents to work with officials and politicians with whom they had previously been in conflict. Overall, residents used the technique to explore their own ideas and to negotiate with each other and the officials to find the limits of what is acceptable and desirable to all those involved.

2.2.5 The need for iteration in boundary setting

Views, understandings, values and beliefs are not static. The experience of engaging in discussion and dialogue, listening to others and deepening understanding and negotiation is dynamic and the boundaries constructed will change. For development managers this raises two important issues:

(a) the need to consider boundary setting as a continuous or *iterative* process; and
(b) who are relevant *stakeholders* in the construction of any system and how might they be involved in the boundary setting process?

There are various tried and tested ways of working out what system you need to consider and where its boundaries lie so that you can think about it in different ways, build understanding and work out appropriate forms of investigation and action. Facilitating a meeting where different perspectives and ideas can be heard, brought together and built on, is one such way. Such an approach places value on diversity of perspectives and data, in contrast to many standardized modes of investigation which seek to homogenize and normalize. Using more formal methodologies such as *soft systems methodology* (Checkland and Scholes, 1999) and *participatory and rapid appraisal* (Chapters 7 and 8) are other possibilities.

It is not possible here to expand on soft systems methodology (SSM) in detail. It is among the many formal methodologies which are potentially useful to the development manager or policy investigator. It was developed (Checkland, 1981, 1999) as an approach to resolving complex, human-centred problems where there was no agreement about either the problem or the possible improvements (SSM avoids the language of solutions, recognizing that most 'solutions' in complex situations bring with them unintended consequences). Elements of SSM have been used creatively by ActionAid in Somaliland to negotiate and renegotiate the boundaries to systems of concern to them. Example 2.1 shows the use of a statement about a 'system of interest' (called a root definition) which is generated in a group process going through several iterations. During the process the mnemonic CATWOE has been used as a tool to check that the description of concern has all the elements necessary for the subsequent conceptual modelling of this system of interest (Figure 2.5 is an example of a conceptual model developed using SSM). Research has shown that the best statements refer to:

- Clients (C);
- relevant Actors (A);
- the Transformation (T) carried out by the system (in this case non-availability is transformed into availability of drugs by the system);
- the World-view or views (W) held by those developing the system;
- Owners (O) of the system; and
- the Environment (E) in which the system will exist.

The process of refining the root definition and checking it using CATWOE statements is an iterative process. In this example it has enabled ActionAid to develop boundaries around five specific activities that need to be carried out to meet one of its strategic objectives. ActionAid has also used SSM to evaluate its activities from three perspectives: its own; the funders Overseas Development Administration (ODA – now Department for International Development, DfID); and local pastoralists.

Such participatory multi-perspective evaluations are likely to increase in the future. They are another example of an open system – the process reveals the many trade-offs and contrasting judgements of what is, or is not, a success. It also sees evaluation as starting at the beginning of any policy or project development activity and continuing through the life of the activity.

One of the important features of SSM is its focus on iteration – of 'learning your way' to new appreciations of complex situations.

Example 2.1 Use of soft-systems methodology by Action Aid Somaliland

ActionAid Somaliland (AAS) used a modified soft-systems methodology (SSM) to generate their strategic objectives. This is a description of one strategic objective, written as a system of interest or root definition, and which contains reference to the elements of the mnemonic CATWOE. The activities which AAS will carry out to implement this system are also listed.

Strategic objective

An AAS-owned system, managed by traders and herders, to make at least five essential veterinary drugs available to the traders, PVAs (primary veterinary assistants) and herders, so that livestock remains healthy and food security of the region is maintained.

(Continued)

(Continued)

Elements

C   client: traders, PVAs, herders.

A   actors: AAS, ODA, herders' fora, traders and NGO committee.

T   transformation: non-availability of the essential veterinary drugs to availability of five essential drugs.

W world-view: food security in the area depends on livestock, so that it is necessary to keep the livestock healthy.

O   owner: AAS.

E   environment: lack of enough experience of veterinary-drugs trading business by the Sanaag community, poor communication facilities with the outside world and security.

Activities

1   AAS provides communication facilities to allow the traders to be linked to outside drug companies.

2   AAS shares experience of the progress and constraints of the programme with the other international organizations involved in this sector.

3   AAS stores a stock of essential drugs for emergency purposes.

4   AAS provides information on the veterinary drugs available in the region to the herders and PVAs.

5   AAS provides information on the diseases existing in any given period of the year to the traders.

2.3 Who participates in boundary setting? • • •

As we have already seen, where boundaries are drawn depends a lot on who is involved in drawing them. Concepts are frequently understood differently by different people; for example, the notion of family or household. As Feldstein and Jiggins (1994) point out, one of the most important starting points is deciding who to ask to draw a particular boundary. Thus, for example, explicitly asking women at the start makes it easier to incorporate gender concerns into any boundary construction. Asking men and women to draw boundaries around the same concept may also reveal different perceptions (see Chapter 8). This relates back to stakeholder analysis and the processes by which stakeholders are identified and perhaps invited to participate (see Chapter 12).

Boundaries can help us to work out who is or should be involved in a given process, such as decision-making. An example is provided by Uphoff (1986, 1992) when

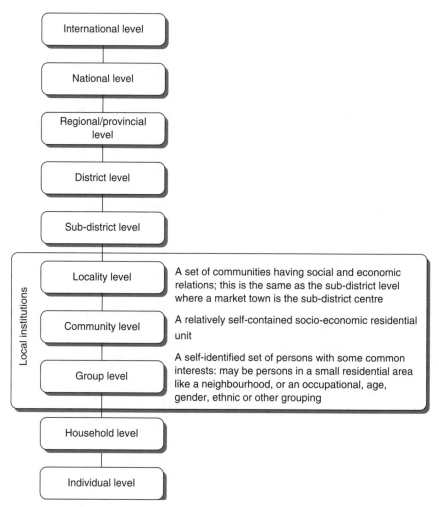

International level

National level

Regional/provincial level

District level

Sub-district level

Locality level — A set of communities having social and economic relations; this is the same as the sub-district level where a market town is the sub-district centre

Community level — A relatively self-contained socio-economic residential unit

Group level — A self-identified set of persons with some common interests: may be persons in a small residential area like a neighbourhood, or an occupational, age, gender, ethnic or other grouping

Local institutions

Household level

Individual level

FIGURE 2.6 Ten levels of decision-making and activity (After Uphoff, 1986, p. 11)

considering the types of local institutions involved in development activity (see Figure 2.6; each level represents a boundary identified as being of relevance).

Uphoff uses boundaries in two ways to analyze and explain what he means by *local* institutions. Firstly, he distinguishes between *levels* of decision making and activity – ranging from individual to international. He constructs boundaries around different groups of decision-makers and activities in order to define these levels and by naming and describing the levels he is able to communicate his understanding to others. Secondly, he challenges the way many people use the word *local* by constructing a further boundary around three of the levels – the locality, community and group levels. The distinction is important because, for example, the involvement of local level institutions is recognized (by Uphoff and others) as essential for mobilizing resources and helping to resolve resource management conflicts in an adaptive way. Picking out just one of the three local levels for decision-making may well mean that opportunities are missed.

Such an approach to boundary setting can be helpful for investigation. It is often extremely important to know what the potential levels of any investigation are and how boundaries might be drawn around them to:

- challenge accepted views where appropriate;
- act as a means of communication to those who are participating in the investigation; and
- decide at which level or levels it is appropriate to carry the investigation out.

2.3.1 Keeping boundaries open

The rapidly changing nature of the challenges of development management means that there is a conscious need to keep boundaries open. Many factors relating to projects and policies will change over time. Different people, who offer new perspectives, will be involved. And there will be a need to respond – both proactively and reactively – to events that occur and resources that become available (or unavailable). There is a need for iteration – for the 'system of interest' to be constantly constructed and reconstructed. Otherwise, there is a tendency to work with closed systems or blueprints without reference to the wider dynamics (or open systems) of which they are a part. In development, this can lead development managers to think of targets (human and physical) rather than processes.

NGO involvement in the United Nations Commission on Sustainable Development (CSD) process of follow up from the Rio Earth Summit provides an example of action based around policy. The CSD was initially set up by the UN General Assembly in December 1992 to review progress on the resourcing and implementation of the Summit's major plan of action, Agenda 21, and the Rio Declaration on Environment and Development, and to make recommendations on them through the Economic and Social Council (EcoSoc) to the UN General Assembly. From 2002 the CSD also became responsible for providing policy guidance to follow up the Johannesburg Plan of Implementation (JPOI). The JPOI re-affirmed the CSD as the high-level forum for sustainable development within the United Nations. Although this CSD system of interest might appear closed in that there are many rules and regulations (originally set down after the Rio conference) about who can participate, both the governments and the NGOs associated with the CSD have set out to facilitate involvement of stakeholders and enable it to be an open system. For instance, the CSD initially broke down Agenda 21 so that it could be reviewed and NGO involvement in the review process was continually negotiated, with the result that, following the Earth Summit, the role and access of

NGOs and 'major groups' (see below) in the CSD process increased greatly. Following the Johannesburg-based World Summit on Sustainable Development in 2002 the CSD further opened up its sessions, through other initiatives, such as a 'Partnerships Fair', which became part of the official CSD programme. This Fair aimed to encourage further participation from both governmental and non-governmental actors through networking, identifying partners, creating synergies between partnerships and learning from each other's experiences. The facilitation role played by individuals within the UN, governments and some NGOs to ensure that individuals who can bring relevant new perspectives are able to participate effectively, might be thought of as 'demystifying' the process or interpreting the rules. It can also, however, be thought of in terms of recognition of the need for iteration, acknowledgement that the systems of interest are changing in the review and partnership process as different areas come up for review, and thus as a process of questioning and repositioning the boundaries.

Some individuals within the international NGO community have been particularly active in this process and this example highlights the way in which skilful facilitation can change a potentially closed system into a more open one. Another point illustrated by this example is that it is not enough to rely on self-selection for participation in formulating policies and projects. It is often necessary for an intervention to be made to encourage and facilitate participation of groups that frequently do not get heard in a process. Some of these are included in the 'major groups' involved in the CSD: women, children and youth, indigenous people, NGOs, local authorities, workers and trade unions, business and industry, the scientific and technological community, and farmers. It is interesting to trace the reasons why these groups were selected above others. It was due at least in part to them organizing themselves, or being helped by others, so that they had a voice in the process. Boundaries for participation can also be changed by ensuring that different forms of communication are taken into account. The CSD focuses on formal dialogue sessions among Government Ministers and Major Groups, and other dialogue through panels, roundtables and side events. The importance of oral testimony and listening must not be forgotten in policy and project formulation processes such as the CSD, especially where there is heavy reliance on written material. However, it is unlikely to be accounted for unless facilitated, for example as in Section 2.2.4.

Stakeholder analysis (see Chapter 12) is one technique that can be used to work out who *should* and who *does* participate in formulating policies and projects – it is a boundary setting process (SLIM, 2004). To date it has not been well developed for policy formulation but has had increasing use in project formulation (e.g. Grimble *et al.*, 1995; Montgomery, 1995a and b; Grimble and Wellard, 1996). A challenge for the future is how to create the political and institutional space that might enable stakeholder analysis to be used more in the policy formulation process. Such a move would challenge existing conceptions of time (e.g. the common three-year project), value (e.g. an overnding concern with outputs at the expense of concerns with the design stages) and of course vested interests, including the nature of relationships between donors and recipients.

Keeping boundaries open is also important for conceptualizing and reconceptualizing investigative processes. One area in which this has been attempted is that of investigation or data collection for impact assessment. 'Impact assessment' is a term applied to a whole range of techniques that have evolved from environmental impact assessment (EIA) which was first introduced in the USA in 1969. This evolution was itself due to changes in perceived boundaries of development activities. Different dimensions have been incorporated to meet a growing range of needs around predicting the effects of development activities.

Roe, Dalal Clayton and Hughes (1995) identify details of

- environmental impact assessment;
- cumulative effects assessment;
- (environmental) health impact assessment (E)HIA;
- risk assessment;
- social impact assessment;
- strategic environmental assessment;
- technology assessment.

These techniques are useful for a range of different purposes but all involve elements of boundary setting and resetting. In general they all include a preliminary stage of *scoping* – a process of defining the scope of the full study in terms of which geographical area, which types of impact and which affected groups should be included in the study, as well as the minimum impact to be regarded as significant. This implies deciding what is outside the boundary of the study, in other words not worth looking at further. Thus, the process of scoping in EIA should involve exploring and identifying key issues under investigation with interested parties. There are different ways in which this process is interpreted, particularly around who is involved. One drawback is that it can provide opportunity for vested interests to surface (though one could also argue that, if vested interests are there, an investigator needs to be aware of them). However, scoping can also provide opportunities for information, ideas and proposals to emerge and for building an understanding of the impact of given processes based on a wide range of experience. Development managers involved in this process can play an important role in facilitating local community involvement and helping to ensure that boundaries are kept open and that there is scope for iteration.

2.3.2 Managing personal and ethical boundaries

It is desirable that development managers and policy investigators are able to identify and articulate their own personal and ethical boundaries. Robert Chambers (1993) has pointed out how many professionals may be part of the problem rather than part of the process of generating improvements. Development is replete with examples of those who have come to help but who have made things worse. From a systems perspective it is necessary to acknowledge that in collaborating with others there is a mutual dance of responsibility. The blurring of the relationships and thus boundaries in this process has too often led to development practitioners taking responsibility for others such as local people, clients, staff, etc. The contrasting position is to attempt to design contexts in which each is 'response-able' – able to respond for themselves (McClintock and Ison, 1994).

Personal and ethical boundaries have a particularly important role to play in investigative processes, especially when they are linked to policy development. One aspect is the relationship between the development manager and/or investigative team and those communities, organizations and individuals who are helping to provide information or are participating in some way in the investigation. The boundaries may be ones of 'expertise', education, social position, etc., issues discussed earlier in this chapter. Decisions to blur these boundaries may result in expectations about action or outcomes that are impossible to meet, while the 'reversals' discussed by Chambers and others in using participative approaches (see Chapter 8) can also be difficult to achieve.

Another aspect is the relationship between the development manager or investigator and the individuals and institutions involved in policy formulation. Do boundaries that might exist or be constructed allow development managers or investigators either to challenge or to collaborate with a given policy direction? Such challenges or collaboration may be within their own institution or take place in a wider institutional arena, and may raise complex personal and ethical issues.

TABLE 2.4 *Four types of boundary where feelings need to be managed*

Key questions	Boundary	Necessary tensions	Characteristic feelings (positive)	(negative)
Who is in charge of what?	Authority	How to lead but remain open to criticism How to follow but still to challenge superiors	trustful open	rigid rebellious passive
Who does what?	Task	How to depend on others you don't control How to specialize yet understand other people's jobs	confident competent proud	anxious incompetent ashamed
What is in it for us?	Political	How to defend one's interests without undermining the organization How to differentiate between win–win and win–lose situations	empowered treated fairly	powerless exploited
Who is (and isn't) with us?	Identity	How to feel pride without devaluing others How to remain loyal without undermining outsiders	proud loyal tolerant	distrusting contemptuous

(After Hirschorn and Gilmore, 1992)

One approach to managing such situations has been suggested by Hirschorn and Gilmore (1992). They argue that managers should use their own feelings as the primary tool for managing boundaries. Table 2.4 outlines some of the key questions, boundaries, tensions and feelings that may well apply to situations that development managers find themselves in. We have all had experiences of working effectively in groups and of the satisfaction that comes from this – these are the positive experiences that are possible. If a group is not working effectively and negative or 'bad' feelings predominate then we need the skills to encourage a process whereby these feelings can be discussed openly and strategies developed to make changes. This means being in touch with our own feelings and being able to decipher frustrating and difficult personal relationships and diagnose why they have gone wrong.

2.4 Conclusion • • •

The ideas about 'system' and 'boundary' that we have used encourage a systemic approach to investigation and action which helps make sense of complex and messy situations in which exactly what to do is uncertain and possibly contested. More importantly, people who use these ideas have found them to help with their own practice. That said, some of the ideas and examples outlined in this chapter could be articulated in other terms besides using the concepts of 'system' and 'boundary'. Such is the nature of constructs.

When conceptualizing at the start of a policy investigation it is useful to think in terms of different possibilities for placing boundaries as well as in terms of different possible research questions (Chapter 1). Reconceptualizing can mean a new choice of boundaries and new questions, but this is often necessary if an investigation is to be effective (Chapter 3).

Systems practitioners have developed a range of tools, methods and heuristics to help with the practice of making boundary judgements (e.g. Checkland and Poulter, 2006). Becoming familiar with these can assist your investigative or research practice. 'Systems thinking' involves considering a number of partial and simplified views of a situation to better understand the whole situation. Focusing on boundaries is a particularly useful way forward in many of the examples given because it enables those involved to both think and act differently and to recognize that investigation and policy formulation are iterative processes. It particularly helps us to avoid the either/or trap associated with the distinctions between process or learning approaches (what we call systemic), and goal or objective driven approaches (what we call systematic). Within an open-systems framework, in which learning and feedback takes place, it is also possible to have well defined guidelines or specifications which could be described as goals or possibly even blueprints, recognizing at the same time the constraints and possibilities they offer.

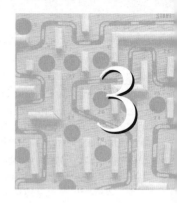

Grabbing attention

Joseph Hanlon

The article on the front page of today's newspaper or the first item on the radio news were probably written by journalists in less than a day. Even the longer 'feature' articles in newspapers and magazines are often written in less than a week. Journalists have developed techniques to 'find out fast' and present the results in a way that attracts attention.

The problem of a policy investigator is often remarkably similar to that of the journalist. With limited background knowledge and little time, the investigator must find an answer and present it convincingly. As a development journalist who is also a consultant and author I am using this chapter to share some of my tips or 'tricks of a different trade'.

The methods I suggest may not always be appropriate. They involve a lot of quick 'thinking with documents' (mainly grey materials – compare O'Laughlin's Chapter 6) and 'thinking with people' (mainly contacts – people who know about the issue already, 'experts' or those already involved in the policy debate). They are useful in cases where someone commissions me to answer a policy question directly: what's the best way to provide funds for a project? How can we put pressure on government? (see Examples 3.1 and 3.2 and Section 3.6). You may need to answer a more specific field-based question: how do people make their living in a region? What is the impact of a new policy on poverty? My methods will probably be useful if you are investigating a policy question. If you are carrying out a more fundamental study, you may need some of the more formal methods of 'thinking with people' (survey or PRA/RRA) discussed in Chapters 7 and 8 or of 'thinking with data' (Chapter 10). Still, if your study is to be useful it has to link to a policy question, and the methods discussed here are probably useful as well.

3.1 Four steps • • •

Because flexibility is central to journalistic investigations, there are no firm rules. But my investigative process commonly involves four steps. I summarise them here, with the remainder of the chapter fleshing them out:

1   Throw the net out wider or 'Find the woman who knows'.
    Journalists lack the time to reinvent the wheel, and our primary skill is making good use of people who have already thought about the issue. This means gathering existing reports and studies, using the internet, and talking, usually informally, to anyone who has investigated a related topic. In this phase, informal, unofficial, and 'off-the-record' contacts are key. It is essential in this phase to look more broadly than the narrow initial brief, throwing out a net to try to catch people and reports that look at the subject from different perspectives. This is essential because the journalist then must:
2   Redefine the question and select the key issue.
    Most investigators will admit, at least privately, that their first formulation of the question is normally wrong – often wildly so. Using the initial broader trawl of material and ideas, I decide on a priority issue as early as possible (certainly no later than the half-way point in an investigation). At this point I make a first attempt to define the outcome – the broad outlines of the story or recommendations. This is the most problematic point.
        The question needs to be redefined so that it is likely to provide both a useful answer and one that can be presented well. 'Usefulness' takes into account the assumptions, goals, and agendas of the people who commissioned the report or will read it. Both as a journalist and as a consultant, I already begin to think about presentation at this point. The best reports and articles make only one point, or at most very few. This is the time for discarding peripheral issues and selecting the one which will be the focus of the report or article.
3   Discard and deepen.
    Having thrown the net out wider to draw in new ideas and material, it is vital not to be smothered in too much information. At this point, I ruthlessly put aside all irrelevant material. A good journalist will discard at least two-thirds of the material initially collected. This is the opposite side of throwing out the net wider; it is selecting the relevant and discarding the irrelevant. What proves relevant is often surprising and different than what I expected at the start – the whole point of throwing the net wider.
        This phase involves actually answering the newly defined question; numerous points must be clarified. This is the time to reread good reports and talk again to the best contacts, officially and 'on the record' if possible.
4   Having the desired result.
    Investigators need to be clear what action they want – is the report just for the file, or does the investigator want something done? The report needs to be written with that outcome in mind. Most people only read the summary or introduction, which becomes more important than the main report, and can be angled to push the desired result. Also, if you really want action, you need not stop with this report. You can write briefings for ministers or officials with your results, or media articles. You may want to give copies of your report to campaigners or the local press.

Deadlines are the biggest difference between an academic investigation and a journalistic one. An academic doing a study for a PhD or a journal paper must cover a narrow area completely, often taking many years to complete the investigation. A journalist always has one eye on the deadline, and investigates a broader area only to the depth that time allows; nevertheless, the result must be credible and accurate. Decision-makers, administrators and consultants are much closer to journalists than to academics, which is why the journalist's tools are useful.

3.2 Step 1: Find the woman who knows • • •

Other people have already thought about the problem – whatever it is. The first rule of any journalist is to find the people who know. In a sharp change from my practice a decade ago, I often start with the internet, to try to find what has been written on my problem and related issues. If I find anything really interesting, I look for other articles and papers by the same person or organisation. But the internet cannot automatically be trusted; it has a lot of false and silly material (see Box 3.1).

Next I hit the telephone, chatting to people informally. I start with friends and contacts and then quickly move on to people met at meetings. I often make 'cold' calls, telephoning an agency and asking 'Do you have someone who deals with X?'. The telephone directory remains the journalist's most important reference book, but I now often use websites to find telephone numbers.

In talking to people, I find that admitting ignorance is always a good start, even when it isn't true, because people are more willing to help when they feel superior and more knowledgeable. As well as asking people to talk broadly around the subject, I always ask two things:

- if they know of any related reports, studies, articles, etc. – both published and confidential – and
- who else has written about the subject and would it be useful to talk with them (and I make sure to get a telephone number or e-mail address, at least).

And I always take notes, even of an informal conversation.

This sets up a telephone tree, with each person suggesting two or three others. In a few hours, it is possible to talk with a wide range of people about the issue.

In parallel, I use e-mail, sending notes to friends and contacts asking if they know any people or articles linked to my problem. For busy people who are hard to contact on the telephone, it is sometimes easier to use e-mail to set up a time to talk on the phone. If someone has written an interesting article which I find on the web or by recommendation, and I cannot find anything else on the subject by the person, I will often e-mail them to ask if they have other unpublished reports on the subject or can suggest others who have written.

And I go back to the internet. First, I look up people and organisations that have come up in e-mails and telephone chats. One problem with the internet is finding the right keywords and search terms, so when I am talking to people I am always on the lookout for words or phrases that might be useful for internet searches, and I try these in later searches.

Often, there already exists a whole string of reports on the same subject or related ones, frequently commissioned from consultants and academics. In Chapter 6, Bridget

O'Laughlin talks of 'grey material'; these are reports that are not published but which are often not secret either – or if they are officially confidential, they are still widely circulated. People are often pleased to share them – it is just that no-one asks and there is no central archive. Remember how few people will ever see your report, and how easy it would be for someone else to do the same thing again, without knowing what you did. For example, for a book I was writing, I found 15 different studies of poverty in Mozambique.

Journalists are never 'experts' in anything; rather, our skill is in searching out the experts and in drawing on that expertise. At this stage, I give equal time and weight to people and paper. Hiding in an office and simply searching the web and reading reports will never give an adequate picture. I want at least to skim as much as possible that has been written on the subject, but I also want to talk to as many people as possible who have already thought about the issue.

There is the danger that particular views get repeated and gain credence that way with no-one ever checking to see if they are correct. However, reinventing the wheel is hard work and time consuming. The journalist's key to 'finding out fast' is finding people who have already done the hard work.

Box 3.1 Internet – gold mine and junk shop

The internet transformed research by making available a wealth of information. The relative lack of censorship and ease of posting information is both the boon and bane of the internet.

On one hand, reports and grey literature are increasingly posted on the web, both because it costs nothing to do so, and because of pressure for increased transparency and openness. Also, many people are posting eye-witness accounts, reports and opinions which might otherwise have been censored or simply never been written.

But, on the other hand, conventional publication imposes at least a slight filter – someone must read the item and agree to publish it. The internet has no such restriction. An item on the web can be complete lies or total fantasy. Total nonsense can be dressed up in scientific jargon. Conspiracy theories abound – for example, that the moon landings were faked and that no human has ever been to the moon. Bizarre religious sects and weird political groups have highly professional websites. Equally dangerous has been the growth of false websites, for example those which pretend to be pressure groups but are really funded by cigarette or pharmaceutical companies.

This is not the world of the library, where librarians have chosen the books and journals. This is the world of the junk shop, of buyer beware. There may be treasures there, but there is also a lot of dross. And yet, the good and useful material makes the internet much too useful to avoid.

So that means the internet must be used with much more care than many other sources of information. One key test is to assess the source or writer. There is no such

(Continued)

(Continued)

thing as absolute truth and no guarantee of perfect accuracy. But we are instinctively more likely to trust the science correspondent of a major newspaper than we are to trust the flat earth association. Similarly, we are more cautious about listening to someone outside their area of expertise – a Nobel Peace Prize winner deserves to be listened to on war and peace, but speaks with less credibility on science.

Here are my three levels of credibility:

1 Known source. A person or institution which I already know and might already be part of my telephone tree, or which is directly referred to by a known source. This also applies to websites I already use regularly and consider credible and trustworthy. I have a list of bookmarked sites, like the BBC, which I use and trust.
2 Official or semi-official source. A website from a government, a government agency, a well known international NGO, a journal or newspaper known to be reputable, a person widely cited in the literature, a known university, etc. In other words, a website from a person or organisation you feel is trustworthy.
3 Verifiable source. You may never have heard of me (Joseph Hanlon), but if you do a web search you will find a range of articles I have written, and you can make a judgement on my credibility. Look for articles that touch on something where you already have some slight knowledge and ask if the article seems credible. And don't just look at my articles – look at what people have had to say about me, in other articles, book reviews, etc. But, also, I automatically have some credibility because I am writing for the Open University. At this point, if I cannot easily establish a writer's credibility, I tend not to use the article – I don't have time to waste. But, once in a while, someone I have never heard of says something new, interesting, or intriguing. Then I do more searches to see if I can find any references to the writer, and send e-mails to friends, saying 'Have you ever heard of X?' Often I get a reply from someone I trust with a thumbs up or down.

Once you know the source, you can move on to consider biases. No one is unbiased. Governments and pressure groups all have positions they wish to promote. All will be selective in their use of evidence. Elsewhere in this chapter we talk about agendas and biased sources. In this, websites are no different from other sources of information. A useable source will be both known and biased.

There are other kinds of trade-offs. A person who you do not know but who has actually been on the ground, interviewing peasants, may have written a more accurate report than a senior government official who has not stepped outside her office. More reports and grey literature are now posted on the web. And an important use of the web is to find a range of articles covering your subject area, which you can then compare and contrast.

But remember that the web is a basically dishonest place – people can lie and cheat, invent names and credentials, and dress up the most bizarre claims in scientific or literary jargon. In the internet era, photos can be faked, so seeing is no longer believing. Knowing your source is the first step.

Keep it unofficial

In talking to people, there are three reasons to avoid official channels – it takes too long to get clearance, you are often forced to speak to the wrong person who does not actually know anything about the subject, and people are more cautious when they are speaking officially. If I want to use the material, I go back later officially. Informal chats on the telephone, or over lunch or a coffee, are always more productive in the initial stages of an investigation, because they show how people are thinking on the subject. Like you, they will not commit to paper or official statements material about which they are unsure, or which goes against official policy, but they will be interested to discuss it informally.

Confidentiality is essential. If I promise not to say you talked with me, I keep that promise at all cost. A record of keeping confidences helps in the future, because I can return to useful and talkative sources time and again. Recently, a government official referred an inquirer to one of my books, saying it was an accurate reflection of his views – even though he was never named in the book!

Be sure of the rules. Journalists use the phrase 'off the record' to mean that what you are told can be printed, but you cannot say who told you. By contrast, 'background' means that you cannot use the material or identify the source – unless you can find someone else to tell you (which I can often do – once I know the basic story). Again, there are dangers here. Compare my suggestions with Bridget O'Laughlin's more considered academic approach in Chapter 6. In my opinion, although you should give references wherever possible in your final report, there is nothing to stop you using journalists' pet phrases like 'ministry sources say' or 'it is reported that' if you need to protect a source.

Sometimes possibly useful grey material is confidential or secret, often because reports are critical or came up with the 'wrong' answer. More commonly, a person is afraid to release a report because they are not sure of its status. At this early stage, an investigator is more interested in the information and analysis, rather than quoting from the report or saying you have it. I use three techniques:

- Ask for a copy in confidence, and respect that confidence.
- Find out who else might have copies; someone more sympathetic may let me see it.
- Ask to read the report. Often an official will let me sit in their office and read a report, even if they won't release a copy.

Finally, reciprocity is essential. If I ask people to talk with me unofficially, I must do the same with them when they need it.

Using biased sources

Openly biased people and groups can often be useful sources of background information. Pressure groups, trade unions, and others with an interest in the outcome may have done extensive research to bolster their case, and that material can prove useful for background and for further sources. Groups with a strong agenda are also useful in obtaining questions to challenge their opponents.

In the study on land in Mozambique (Section 3.6 below), a key issue was whether land should be leasehold or freehold. Talking to strong proponents of both sides made clearer the implications of the differences in tenure, particularly with respect to loans and mortgages. Advocates of freehold argued that the only way peasants could obtain credit was through a mortgage, and this had forced the leasehold advocates to do research on alternative credit systems – saving me substantial work.

Clearly, care must be taken when using biased sources. But as I note later, and as Bridget O'Laughlin notes in Chapter 6, all sources have some bias and the researcher must take this into account. The danger in 'finding out fast' is that the researcher will be fooled; every journalist has examples of apparently bona fide reports being false, with numbers changed or conclusions distorted. I often cite the case of the World Bank claiming in several widely distributed reports that a study of vegetable marketing showed that price deregulation had improved vegetable supply in Maputo – when the study itself said no such thing.

Equally serious is the problem set out both by Chris Blackmore and Ray Ison in Chapter 2 and by Linda Mayoux and Hazel Johnson in Chapter 8, as well as by O'Laughlin – power relations bias investigations. Outside investigators often misinterpret what relatively powerless people say – because they do not hear, or because people are telling them what they want to hear. This is linked to the issue set out by Sue Mayer in Chapter 11 – that 'expert knowledge' often excludes key elements of 'local knowledge' because of the way the outside 'experts' codify and interpret. Participatory research techniques have been developed (see Chapters 7 and 8), but journalists do not have time to use them – we are dependent on studies already done by others.

In assessing the validity of other's people's work, I am guided by two things – my own sense of what seems reasonable, and the hope that I talk to enough people and see enough reports that some will challenge other dishonest or distorted reports. In the end, though, we all make mistakes and misjudgements; the best I can ever do is keep them to a minimum. Step 3 includes further attempts to reduce errors.

Widening the net

Telephone and e-mail trees, the internet and collecting existing reports are all ways of throwing the net out further. In the terms of Blackmore and Ison's Chapter 2, this can be seen as extending the 'boundaries' which define thinking on the subject. Often people have approached the same question from a different angle, and this will come up in informal discussions. For example, to draw together evaluations of hand pumps, it is not sufficient to look just to the rural water sector of government, but also to other development agencies that may have done project evaluations which, in passing, touched on problems or successes with hand pumps. Informal chats on the telephone direct you to relevant reports.

Widening the net is also about related questions. Starting out with a question of which hand pump is easiest to maintain leads to issues of spare parts supply and maintenance arrangements – is someone hired? is it done by an agency? is it done by a volunteer water committee? etc. Successful maintenance may prove to have more to do with organisation and less to do with the pump itself.

In a 1987 investigation of tightening sanctions against the then apartheid-ruled South Africa, a Commonwealth study team I headed obtained a study of United States sanctions against Cuba. This presented a different perspective on the issue – the United States was trying to make sanctions work against Cuba when most countries were looking for mere token sanctions against South Africa. Thus it introduced alternative ways of thinking about what was possible and what was effective.

In the internet era, widening the net also shows new search terms – jargon and catch phrases I had not seen before, alternative technical terms, more experts' names, or simply different ways of looking at the issue. At this point I often do another web search, using the new key words. This almost always produces new articles and often new ways of thinking about issues.

The final point about throwing the net wider is time and speed. If someone is away on holiday or won't talk to me, I stop and try someone else. If, with a bit of effort, you can't get to see a report, forget it. You do need to be aware if there appears to be a whole area where people don't want you to find out. Still, widening the net means drawing in more people and reports, which makes it easier to ignore those which are difficult to get access to.

3.3 Step 2: Redefine the question • • •

Having thrown the net wider, the investigator then returns to rethink the question – and to look at those asking the question. It is essential to consider three issues: assumptions, agendas, and goals. As Examples 3.1 and 3.2 show, these may only become clear during the investigation.

The initial question is usually formulated on the basis of an implicit set of assumptions. Some are encapsulated in slogans such as 'small is beautiful'. Others relate to the assumption that your employer – be it a government department, a bilateral donor, an NGO or a private company – is necessarily the best for the job. Some relate to skills and capacity – that foreigners or consultants are needed, or that peasants are too stupid. Key ones relate to the root of the problem, and whether it is technical, financial or organisational. It is worth listing as many of these assumptions as possible; by making them explicit, they can be tested against the information drawn in through the earlier trawl. Note should be made of any assumptions which do not obviously hold up. Example 3.1 shows a case of how this was done in a study of co-operatives in Zimbabwe.

Example 3.1 Zimbabwe co-ops: changing the question

Several hundred producer co-operatives were formed in Zimbabwe in the first years after independence in 1980. Demobilised guerrillas and released political prisoners played an active role, and the government gave the movement political backing. Many co-operatives received technical and financial support from government and international NGOs. But by 1986 it was clear that many of the new co-ops were in trouble, and I was commissioned by a European NGO to do a study. I was to look at:

(a) tensions between the government and the co-op movement; and
(b) ways in which NGOs might provide further funding to co-ops 'without increasing the tensions with the government institutions'.

The underlying and stated assumption of the study was that the co-ops were in trouble because the government bureaucracy had turned hostile to them, despite political rhetoric, and that the solution was further funding by foreign NGOs, in some way bypassing the government.

In Zimbabwe, I talked informally to a wide range of people in the co-operative movement, in government, in the university, and in agencies supporting co-ops. I visited a number of co-ops – some successful, some struggling, and some failing.

Informal chats and personal contacts confirmed two key assumptions:

• most producer co-ops were, in fact, facing serious problems; and
• there were sharp divisions within government and the civil service with respect to co-ops, and, indeed, key people who were supposed to be helping were in fact hostile to producer co-operatives.

But I also found that government hostility was not the heart of the problem, and that in some cases the assumed solution – foreign NGO help – had actually been harmful to co-ops by creating dependency. Throwing the net wider made it clear that the question had to be redefined if my answer was to be useful to the co-ops. Further thinking showed that the core problem was attitudinal – foreign NGOs, government officials, and many members of the less successful co-ops all treated co-ops as political, charitable and social organisations. On the other hand, the successful co-ops saw themselves as small businesses which eventually had to be commercially viable. I decided that this had to be the key point of my report.

Throwing the net wider also produced two surprises, even to me:

• I discovered that, in the six years of independence, some sectors of the largely white business community had significantly shifted their attitudes toward the largely black co-operative movement. At least some commercial finance was now available, which my commissioning agency – and, indeed, many co-ops – did not realise.

(Continued)

(Continued)

- I also found that the white colonial government had provided substantial agricultural extension and other support to inexperienced new white farmers in the 1950s and 1960s, and that the new majority rule government was expecting farming co-ops with a similar lack of experience to thrive with much less support.

My problem was that spreading the net wider challenged the core assumptions of many co-op members and – most importantly – of many international NGOs working in Zimbabwe. It became clear that two further unstated underlying assumptions were that co-ops were passive recipients of charity, and government and business were hostile. These, in turn, masked an agenda of many NGOs to continue to provide direct support to particular partner co-operatives, and not to encourage self-sufficiency or to build the co-op movement in general. Others wanted to build the co-op movement, but make it dependent on foreign funding rather than local business or government.

Keeping in mind the sensibilities of all concerned, I reformulated the question to be:

How can foreign NGOs help co-ops to become more politically and commercially independent and make the best use of government and private resources?

Thus, my proposals were to call for foreign NGOs to:

- use their funds not to finance co-ops directly, as in the past, but to guarantee and support private commercial loans – thus setting up a sustainable system and routeing more money to the co-ops;
- support co-ops in political lobbying and pressure on the government to provide more agricultural extension and other technical support, and help co-ops create their own technical support units.

For some co-ops and NGOs who enjoyed the cosy direct relationship involved in cash handouts, these proposals were unacceptable; NGO workers would lose the power that comes from direct funding, while co-ops would have to be productive and profitable.

But others found it useful. The report was one of many inputs that led to the establishment of a co-operative loan fund which had both commercial and NGO money.

Next is the question of agendas. Everyone involved in any project has personal goals and agendas. When you do a study, you want to keep your job, or earn a promotion, or gain future contracts. I originally wrote this chapter not only to help you learn, but also to earn money and in the hope of winning more contracts from the Open University. Agendas are sometimes seen as shameful and illegitimate and thus to be kept hidden, because development agencies and charities are supposed to be altruistic and concerned only with the poor. But decision-making is easier when agendas are recognised and made explicit.

In particular, this means making clear those agendas which may work against the long term development goals. Agendas of this type can be loosely grouped into four categories:

1 Something to show. Development agencies need quick results to show to their paymasters – parliaments, national or international development agencies, or the general public making donations. This often involves photos of white women helping black children.
2 Corporate stability. Many development agencies are large businesses with headquarters' staffs and overheads to support; this is as true of non-government organisations as of ministries of health or agriculture. The agenda may be how to win a contract over another agency, in order to protect jobs or to expand.
3 Power and importance. Everyone needs to feel that their role is important; every agency wants to believe that recipients of aid are better off for it. Individuals, departments and agencies often simply want to increase their power base.
4 Other benefits. For example, at one time, the highest priority for the Irish aid programme was 'to increase the number of Irish people working in developing countries' (Irish Department of Foreign Affairs, 1993).

Finally, questions are often muddled because of lack of quantifiable objectives. Too often, goals are vague, such as 'empowerment' or 'helping the poorest'. In their study *Non-Governmental Organizations and Rural Poverty Alleviation* Riddell and Robinson (1995) noted that in the projects they studied objectives were 'imprecise' and frequently altered. This was both because NGOs wished to remain flexible, and because they didn't want quantifiable goals because 'northern NGOs tend to exaggerate the potential impact they can make'.

But for rapid decision-making, it becomes essential to define a clear goal, even if one does not exist for the overall programme. Example 3.2 looks at the issue of goal definition. Goals must take into account both assumptions and agendas.

Example 3.2   Matching a new question to the agenda

Peasants in Namialo in northern Mozambique are poor and malnourished, so you are asked to propose an improved extension service. Throwing the net wider means looking not only at extension models, but also at peasant poverty. That immediately points to an assumption: that extension is the answer to peasant poverty. Namialo is a cotton producing area, and poverty and malnutrition are common in cotton out-grower schemes. This leads to three very different choices:

(Continued)

(Continued)

1 increase food production (perhaps at the expense of cotton), for which extension is probably most appropriate; or

2 raise the price paid to peasants for cotton, which may be an issue of state setting of minimum prices or negotiating different contracts with officially recognised cotton buyers, or it could be an issue of campaigning against cotton subsidies in the United States which are depressing world prices; or

3 improve the marketing structure to ensure that peasants can buy food at the lowest possible price, which may require state support for the private trading sector including loans and road building.

Other more radical options range from promoting marketing co-operatives to providing better water supplies so that women spend less time collecting water and more time growing food.

But assume your analysis of the agenda of the commissioning agency (an NGO, the Ministry of Agriculture, or a UN agency) is that it needs a rural extension scheme even if that is not the most productive, so your immediate goal is to work out the best extension scheme. But 'best' for what? There are a range of possible goals:

- reduce chronic malnutrition levels;
- reduce acute malnutrition levels;
- increase cash incomes of the poorest 20% of families;
- increase women's income;
- increase total marketed production;
- raise food production of the poorest in the village;
- raise total food production in the village;
- richer farmers providing more jobs to the poorest;
- total production up;
- productivity up.

And so on. Which extension system is chosen depends strongly on which goal is chosen. Throwing the net wider also raises questions about the immediate objectives of extension itself. Is it to introduce better food crop varieties, to encourage best practice relating to existing crops and techniques, to introduce new forms of pest control, or to introduce entirely new forms of cash crops (in Namialo this might include oil seeds or tobacco)?

This last point raises another agenda issue – is cotton production to be defended or can cotton production be allowed to fall? Assume that because of the need to support private cotton companies and to encourage exports, peasants must continue to grow cotton.

With all of this in mind, the question might be redefined as follows: what would be the best form of agricultural extension to bring chronic malnutrition below 5% of children and to increase the food production of the poorest peasants without reducing cotton production?

When goals do exist, they are too often short-term, such as number of wells dug rather than number still in use in three years, or number of health centres built rather than number of people using health facilities. A standard measure for the success of cancer treatments is five year survival rates – what percentage of those treated are still alive five years later. Similar longer term goals are needed for development projects, but are rarely used.

The new question

New information almost always convinces me that the original question is not the best one. Initial research also makes clear the assumptions, goals and agendas that underlie the initial question. With these in mind, the question is redefined in a way to provide a useful answer and which can be presented well.

Often it is worth making explicit more than one goal – a corporate goal and a development goal. Thus a simple question about the best hand pump might be turned into a new one: what is the best combination of pump and maintenance system which will give the donor short term publicity pictures and have the best chance of surviving for five years? Agendas are important too, so a question which started out being about rural health care might end up being one about making the best use of foreign volunteers in rural health posts.

It is not too early to think about presentation. If I expect people to take notice (not always the case, see step 4), I make sure that my article or report makes only one central point, and perhaps a small number of subsidiary ones. Thus it becomes essential to define one key issue, and one or two points to be made about that issue. All the examples in this chapter show how this can be done.

Having key points is not the same as having answers. For me, key points are usually clearly defined questions to answer. It is important to note that the new question may not be harder to answer than the original one – but the answer surely will be more useful and easier to present.

Trying not to get it wrong

This phase is the most problematic and riskiest, because it requires choices. There is no single right choice, no single key issue or single right question. But there are wrong choices. In part, decision-making is intuitive and comes from experience. Usually a key issue will jump out at me during the initial investigation; the problem comes when there is more than one issue competing for attention, and I know I must choose one.

A chat with a friend or colleague is useful at this point; even with a very tight magazine deadline that may only leave me a couple of hours, I find it useful to take two minutes to discuss the topic with someone. Indeed, being forced to spell out the issue quickly often makes the decision for me – if I cannot explain it in a few words, then I probably cannot find out fast either.

Expected outcome (step 4) is an important criterion. There is no point in a report which so contradicts agendas and assumptions that it is ignored. My Zimbabwe redefinition (Example 3.1) came very close to being wrong because the new question was unacceptable to many donor NGOs. On the other hand my Mozambique redefinition, in the example in Section 3.6 below, actually fitted better with the needs of all parties than the original question.

A good journalist must be prepared to take risks. If I do not improve on the initial question, my articles will be too boring to be published. Any failures or mistakes will be outweighed by the successes. For a government official, the rewards for success may be lower and the penalties for failure higher. Each investigator must make their own choice. But I remain convinced that good investigation always involves some risk of failure – if you can be sure in advance, then there is no need for research.

3.4 Step 3: Discard and deepen • • •

Having redefined the question, you are now faced with a pile of reports and notes which are no longer relevant. Get rid of them. Now.

It is hard to force yourself to think more broadly as you cast the net, but even harder to narrow down again and throw away what you do not need. At this point an unusual degree of ruthlessness is required – to exclude all issues not relevant to the main story. Since redefining the question is an iterative process, and you may redefine again, it's as well to keep notes and reports you think you don't need somewhere where you can retrieve them, at least until this particular job is finished. Some will then be filed away for future use; others will be forgotten. But no matter how interesting, 'finding out fast' means keeping an eye on the deadline and only following the most important issues.

I find this one of the most difficult steps. It hurts to discard reports or interviews that took hours of hard work or a long trip to obtain. I have to admit that I cheat. Sometimes discarded reports sit in piles on my office floor for months, because I cannot bear to throw them away. And on a longer project, if my initial investigations generate something that I find interesting but which is not directly relevant to the key issue, I sometimes put it into the report as an appendix; I know no one will read it, but I gain pleasure writing it up.

But, as I have already noted, a journalist always keeps one eye on the deadline, whether it is minutes or days away. When half of the available time is used, if I have not passed through steps one and two and moved on to defining the key issue and revised question, and being reasonably sure of the story, I am in trouble because I won't meet my deadline.

In part, this step revolves around answering a personal question: Why am I writing this report or article? It is essential to select the key point to be made, and structure the report – and the remainder of the investigation – around that. If you listen to a good radio news item or read a good news article, you will see they rarely make more than one key point and the rest of the article is to support that point. The best reports make only one point; never make more than a handful. Even if the report has dozens of conclusions, some must be more important than others, and need to be prioritised.

Deepening understanding

The task is now to answer the revised and much narrowed question. I never find the material already gathered and interviews already done to be sufficient.

By this step, the deadline is in sight; time is precious and cannot be wasted following up all issues. Articles are written and decisions taken based on limited information; not even historians have all the facts. The goal is to collect as much as possible of the most relevant information. I make a list of remaining issues in order of importance to the final report, and start with the most important. Another journalist's trick is simply to leave out unanswered questions or doubtful material that cannot be verified. Reports and articles are never 'complete' and my personal rule is: when in doubt, leave it out.

This is where I go back to the most interesting reports and most useful contacts, to ask this very limited set of new questions. Having put the issue in context, clarified agendas and goals, and revised the question, I usually have new things to ask my most productive contacts. There is no harm in going back two or three times to the same person, when new research throws up new topics. Indeed, I find that when I go back a second or third time to people who have previously looked at these issues, they find my new information interesting and there is a useful exchange of ideas.

Having started out broadly and then chosen a narrow focus, this is the phase of deepening understanding. Unresolved issues need to be followed up. Conflicting opinions which were simply recorded in step 1 now need to be clarified and either resolved or spelled out clearly. Quick internet searches on new key issues and to clarify details and disputed points are useful here. This is also the time to go back to pressure groups and others with overt biases, and put to them the arguments of the other side.

This is also the final chance to prevent mistakes. If my conclusion rests on one or two key items, I try to verify their accuracy further – by looking in more detail at research methods, by talking to others who were there, or by talking again to people who disagree with the conclusions. Many of the other chapters in this book outline warning signals to watch for – is it possible, for example, that 'experts' have missed a key point or that the received wisdom is wrong? Do the spokespeople of the intended beneficiaries of a project really speak for them? Even at this late stage, it is better to have second thoughts and delay than to go ahead with something if you have strong doubts. For a journalist, there is an intangible sense of 'feel' that comes from experience (and from having got things wrong before) – if the story 'feels right' I go ahead, but if nagging doubts make it 'feel wrong', it's back to step 2.

This is also the time to confirm sources and check facts. I was recently writing an article on economic development in Manica province, Mozambique, and I had a handout from a PowerPoint presentation claiming that 2000 jobs had been lost in two years.

But the governor said no jobs had been lost. The presentation had no source, so I telephoned the person who gave it to me, and she sheepishly admitted she did not know the source either. So we both hit the e-mail, to ask people we knew. The next day a message came from someone I did not even know, but who had been sent a copy of my e-mail query, giving me the source (a Manica business association) and the date and place of the lecture. Without e-mail, I never would have found the source and would not have been able to use or trust the information.

Finally, in this deepening process, I think much more about the final report. That means I try, where possible, to move 'on the record' so that I can quote people. It may now be useful to go through the proper channels and request formal permission to speak to people with whom I previously had an informal chat. Sometimes this is not possible and another informal chat is the only way forward. If confidence is promised, I always keep that promise.

3.5 Step 4: Having the desired result • • •

Presentation is one-quarter of the job. Proper presentation improves the chances that the report will have the desired effect. Goals and agendas are important here, too, and we consider three cases.

For the file

Many reports are only written for the file 'just in case' – they are to prove that something was done or that warnings were properly considered. Many are done by consultants, but civil servants trying to protect their own jobs often do such reports.

There is no harm in reports for the file, and presentation should be designed to discourage reading:

- no summary or introduction;
- use lots of jargon; and
- bury the key points.

As to be read but not acted on

Many reports are written to demonstrate good intentions, for example on gender equality, or to justify a decision already made. These reports are to be read by donors, funders, auditors, etc. in the hope that they accept the report and do not demand further action. You will have seen many such reports in your internet searches, since these are often posted on websites.

Most people only read the summary or introduction, and this should be encouraged by making the main report as dense and impenetrable as possible. The introduction should take the form of an executive summary, which precisely follows the report section by section and simply summarises what has been written. Be careful not to highlight key points; only suggest actions that have already been agreed.

Take action

If action is desired in response to an investigation, then the entire report should be tailored to that end. The writer of the report must decide on the desired outcome before writing the report. Such outcomes need to be clearly and simply stated – a new kind of water committee, changing the form of agricultural extensions, support for the peasant union in rewriting the land law (see example in Section 3.6 below), a campaign against the World Bank, etc. It should be possible to state the desired outcome in one short sentence.

Of course the investigation may lead to a whole series of subsidiary recommendations, but it is essential to keep the main one to the fore. In writing the report, recommendations need to be justified and key ones highlighted. Debated issues must be discussed, but irrelevant issues should be dropped – even when you worked hard to find the information. To make the report easy to read by non-experts who may need to take decisions, jargon should be excised and replaced by plain English; acronyms should be shunned.

Keep the report interesting. Journalists' tricks, like telling stories and quoting the more colourful speech of some sources, can be used in reports just as well as in articles. Concrete examples and real names and places make reports and articles feel more real. (Note how I mentioned Manica province by name and gave the actual number of job losses in my example in Section 3.4.)

If the investigator has a clear recommendation but there is a strong opposing view, then the summary should only make the case for the investigator's view, while the main report should also clearly explain the opposing line.

The introduction or summary is critical, because few will read the entire report. It should take the form of highlights and not a précis or exact summary. Instead of a formal 'executive summary', I usually write what is actually an article pinpointing the key points and the action proposed. It must be short (only one or two pages) and, like any good article, it can only make one point – the action I want taken. I may call it a 'summary', although I often try to use a different kind of heading such as 'key points', but in reality I am writing an article.

There are two good ways to begin an introduction:

1   Start with a strong quote or brief story that either sets the scene or backs up the course of action proposed. A few words from a government minister, a bishop, or a real peasant (with a name and village) proposing the course of action I want immediately makes the recommendation seem reasonable and broadly acceptable. The alternative is to set the scene; a report on pumps might start: 'Anna Mpofu had to

walk 10 km each day to the river for water after the Chifunde village hand pump broke and no one could fix it'; or

2 Start with the key conclusion or single most important recommendation, stated briefly and without caveats – I always leave the 'ifs' and 'buts' for the main report. If I start with a quote or story, I give the key conclusion immediately afterwards.

I would never start a report the way Open University books often start their chapters, with the phrase 'this chapter' – only dedicated students read on. If you want people to read what you write, make it interesting from the very first words.

The introduction/summary/highlights should never cover all points – that is the purpose of the main report. Instead, the introduction should make the case for the most important desired action. In any case, a good and provocative introduction is more likely to push people into reading the whole report.

An important point here is that, until now, we have made an implicit assumption that the outcome of your investigation is to be a report, study, article or briefing note – a single written document. But if you really want action taken, you will need to do more. First, you need to ensure that your report (or an unofficial version of it) is widely circulated – to the people you interviewed, to other interested parties, perhaps posted on a website, distributed to the press and campaign groups, and so on. If you want action, then you need to make a special effort to ensure that you get information to the people who can use it. This may mean presenting information in more than one way – a formal report to the commissioning agency can be backed up with articles in the media or the web, interviews with press and TV, seminars, public meetings, and so on. If you feel strongly that your research points to important action, then you cannot stop when you have written your first report.

No answers

The fear of all investigators and journalists is of failing to find a clear answer. Journalists have two responses to this.

- Change the question again. Step 2 of the process is to redefine the question, and it needs to be defined in a way that has an answer. Go back and define it again.
- Admit you don't know. Journalists often use phrases like 'opinion remains divided on ...' or 'the debate continues about ...'.

The whole process of throwing the net wider encourages a reconsideration of the initial question and redefinition of the issues. If the investigator genuinely remains unsure even at the end of the study, then a recommendation for more fundamental consideration is justified. Usually, however, simply proposing more study is a way of avoiding choices and delaying decisions. If that is not the goal (see step 2) then it is better to make a choice.

3.6 Step-by-step: Land in Mozambique • • •

'Peasants are being pushed off their land in Mozambique and people are afraid to talk about it; tell us how to put public pressure on the government to stop this'.

That was the original request on the telephone from a British NGO one day in 1996. Finding out fast started even before accepting the job; a few telephone calls showed that some peasants were indeed being pushed off land, but others were defending their rights, and there was actually a massive public debate. With the brief rewritten to a broader one of helping to protect peasant land rights, I set off to Mozambique.

Step 1, throwing out the net, involved two days of intensive telephoning. As the telephone tree expanded, I found myself pursuing four different but overlapping lines:

1 Identifying people already working on land rights – finding the people who know. I discovered that the government had already established a National Land Commission which was working on just this issue, trying to draft revisions to the existing land law. (My commissioning NGO had not known of the existence of this commission.) Several Mozambican lawyers were also working on aspects of the problem and anxious to talk; women's land rights had been raised in the Mozambican submission to the Beijing Women's Conference in 1995. Two different groups at the local university were studying land issues. The issue had been raised by the parliamentary agriculture committee, and there had been substantial press coverage.
2 Locating other studies. Land turned out to be fashionable with donors, in part because of a debate about whether privatisation of land would lead to landlessness, as it had in Brazil. Thus there was a whole bookshelf of studies.
3 The first few telephone calls produced three Mozambican organisations already working with peasants on land issues; during the next few days, four more Mozambican groups – including the Catholic Church and the national women's organisation – and three donor agencies all working on land rights were identified. Remarkably, no single organisation knew about all the others in the field.
4 Looking for first hand evidence of peasant land struggles, and their success or failure. What was striking was how successful peasants had been in defending their land. I found instances where someone came and claimed (often falsely) that the land belonged to them or a 'minister' and peasants left without protest (respect for authority remains strong). But I found no case where peasants with some right to land had been pushed off if they defended those rights. Indeed, I discovered a variety of groups successfully gaining land titles for peasants.

Step 2, redefining the question. The original brief was based on three false assumptions – that peasants were unable to defend their land, that the government was uninterested in the problem, and that there was little public debate. I concluded that the government was sincere about getting a revised land law on the books by the end of 1996, that the National Land Commission was open to discussion and lobbying from outside agencies (and even had peasant representatives on it), and that in most instances peasants could defend their land (although the procedures were often cumbersome and they needed assistance). The Commission had already approved a national land policy under which peasants would confirm land rights through a mix of customary law and collective titles. My commissioning NGO had two relatively open agendas – supporting its partner agency in Mozambique and gaining publicity at home – and one hidden one – keeping control in London and not yielding too much power to its Mozambican partner (which was one of those agencies already working with peasants, and which already had links with the Commission). The original vague goal had been simply defending peasant land.

Based on initial research and the constraints defined by the agendas and vague goals, I defined a new question: How should the ongoing process of revising the land law be influenced so as to defend peasant rights, and how should the partner agency play a role in the process? My personal agenda was to shift power to Mozambique, and to counter the hidden agenda of the commissioning NGO to keep control. I kept at the back of my mind the need for publicity for the commissioning NGO.

Step 3. First came discarding and error avoidance. Many of the studies on land tenure systems and arcane debates about Mozambican law could now be put aside. A check against an important possible error was to return to lawyers and others to confirm my view that many peasants had successfully defended their land rights.

Next my focus was on deepening my understanding of the ongoing political and legislative process and how to influence it. Further discussions with the Land Commission and its technical advisors, with peasant pressure groups already identified, and with the most interesting lawyers and researchers, highlighted two sides of the 'how' question – what mechanisms should be used, and which areas should be targeted.

It was clear that peasants needed a louder and clearer voice in the ongoing process, and to do this I concluded that some form of lobbying was needed. This would work directly with the Land Commission and feed into the ongoing press debate.

The other part was more complex. It seemed that the mix of customary and collective titles could be made to work, and further research highlighted key issues that needed to be dealt with in the land law. These related to how decisions were taken, transparency, rights of women, and dispute settlements.

Step 4, having the desired result. My agenda was that action should be taken, so my report was aimed in that way. Having two recommendations and accepting my own rule of only making one point, I concluded that the key point for my paymasters in London was that they should support peasant lobbying, and my introduction highlighted this. It also stressed ways in which original assumptions were false and how the Land Commission was doing a good job. The debates over customary law and key issues in the land law were relegated to the main report.

The second point, about key issues that the land law needed to consider, was more for Mozambican consumption, so I wrote an article for a local newspaper setting out those recommendations. To satisfy publicity demands, I also wrote two general articles for the British press, which named the commissioning NGO.

In summary, we see that the initial question, despite its false assumptions, hid a real question which could be usefully answered to the benefit of all parties.

3.7 Risks and benefits • • •

For a journalist, the point about 'finding out fast' is to meet the deadline and publish an article. For the investigator, the point is to make a recommendation of some sort.

Journalists are notorious for making mistakes. Pressure of time means we do get things wrong. I have written stories where I believed people who lied to me and where I quoted dishonest or inaccurate reports. Conclusions based on limited information have been wrong. I have made a bad choice, missing the main issue and following up a less important point.

But if you check press reports against your own experience, you will find the press is far more often right than wrong. These techniques do work. Perhaps most important, taking no decision at all is usually worse than making a wrong choice. Quick decision-making moves development forward.

Go ahead. Take the risk.

Communicating results

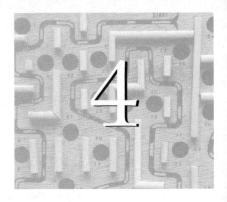

Joanna Chataway, Avril Joffe and Jill Mordaunt

The world of policy change is complex, contested and therefore highly political. Many of us working in development often identify serious problems which, if they are to be overcome, require substantial and difficult changes to occur. Research can be one of the motors for initiating change but communicating research findings to initiate a process of policy change can be very difficult. There are some messages that powerful stakeholders simply do not want to hear. In these cases, no amount of skill in communication will facilitate the adoption of that policy change. However, it *is* the case that poor communication can prevent the adoption of research findings and inhibit the implementation of otherwise acceptable and politically appropriate policy recommendations. Communication therefore is an important aspect of policy-oriented research. Policy issues can be politically sensitive, and successful communication of results involves complex judgements and a sense of timing. Good communication is particularly important where the research seeks to advocate on behalf of a particular group or cause. Here we consider a set of related issues together with some challenges involved in how to communicate results.

Policy investigation often involves finding out about people, organizations and people in organizations (see Chapters 6 and 12). However, securing the implementation of research-based policy that requires significant change implies much preparation and forethought about who are the key stakeholders and who needs to be persuaded to allow policy change to occur. Although results are prepared for those charged with formulating and implementing policy or those who commissioned the research, there are always other interested parties affected by any proposals. This means that your research has many audiences, some of whom you will have taken into account, while others may emerge at later stages, and these will also need acknowledging and you may also have to seek their approval. Communicating results to those directly affected by policy changes may be a particularly delicate and important task, particularly if the changes appear to threaten their interests.

Moreover, the deeply political nature of the relationship between policy research and policy change needs to be revealed and acknowledged. Nearly 30 years ago Weiss

(1979) presented a cogent argument about the 'loose coupling' of social research and social policy. She argues that social research does not follow simplistic linear models of implementation. The first myth, she argues, is of the 'decision-driven model', where the research is done, missing knowledge is provided and interpreted to lead to policy choice. The second myth is of the 'knowledge-driven model', in which basic research leads to applied research and then to development and application. She says that social research is rarely actually used in these ways despite a mythology perpetuated by government departments about a mutually advantageous relationship. Thomas (1982) argues that this means policy research is often used:

> 'as political ammunition;
> to delay action;
> to avoid taking responsibility for a decision;
> to win kudos for a successful programme;
> to gain recognition and support;
> to discredit an opponent for a disliked policy;
> to maintain the prestige of a government agency through supporting prestigious researchers;
> to keep universities and their social science departments solvent...' (Thomas, 1982)

Although today we are in an era where evidence-based policy is much discussed and a great deal of thought has gone into the relationship between research, evidence and policy (Crewe and Young, 2002; Young and Court, 2004), we suggest that many aspects of Thomas' argument still hold good. For example, Pawson (2002) notes that evidence rarely speaks for itself and Nutley *et al.* (2000) suggest that, even in highly scientific and technical policy areas, technical arguments do not appear to have a great impact on policy decisions. The best that policy researchers can hope for is to illuminate and influence the process of policy change. There is no simple direct relationship between research findings and policy change. Moreover, as Mayer points in Chapter 11, the relationship between research findings and acceptance of particular policy positions is complex. This means that the communicator of research findings needs to be both politically sensitive and adept.

In this chapter we argue for the importance of thinking through how to communicate results and that this often involves investigation and planning. Ideally, communication between researchers and other stakeholders in the project is a two-way process: flexibility and some degree of sensitivity to a range of different interests and concerns may be necessary.

Ideally, communicating results is integral to the design of projects from the outset rather than something that is only considered when the research is completed. In Section 4.1 we discuss the benefits of planning a politically sensitive communication strategy for a piece of policy research.

In Section 4.2 we discuss some of the constraints and political considerations which in reality often impact on the sequencing and substance of communication. While ideally communicating results is integrated fully into the research process from early on, thus maximizing participation, in some instances it may be necessary to think about the impact of research from other angles. Some stakeholders may demand that communication is much more circumspect or that some results are not publicly reported. This may, or may not, be legitimate but in any case decisions about the when, what, who and how of communicating results often raises questions about power, ethics, accountability and responsibility.

4.1 Communication and the research process ● ● ●

4.1.1 An iterative process

Communicating results is an activity which is often thought of as coming at the end of a project – you define the project, do the research and present the results. If the conclusions include clear policy recommendations, these will then be implemented. This is a rather linear and naive way of thinking about the research process. Good communication of policy related research requires layers of iteration (Hovland, 2005). When research is commissioned, the initial questions often uncover more complex issues. Or, through preliminary investigation, it may become apparent that the initial design of the project is lacking or that a key stakeholder has been overlooked. Alternative research designs will need to be thought through. Sometimes the researcher will realize the need to change and will, in discussion with other stakeholders, be able to make the appropriate alterations. This process may also lend insight into the explicit and implicit motives behind the commissioning of the research.

Joseph Hanlon provides a good example of this in Chapter 3 (Section 3.6) when writing about his work on land issues in Mozambique. Here the initial enquiries made it clear that the original brief should be revised. In the course of discussions with the commissioning NGO about this, the NGO's agenda became clearer. Hanlon was able to suggest a set of revised research questions, based both on his new understanding of events and situations in Mozambique and on the NGO's aims and objectives in commissioning the research.

In this case, the researcher realized there were problems in the way the brief had been defined. But most often communicating preliminary results to others will uncover problems which the researcher may have missed and which can then be discussed. Thus, one reason for integrating communication and presentation into the process of research at an early stage is that design faults can be dealt with. This process also builds support for any recommendations arising from the research results, as key stakeholders will feel that they have played a part in their development.

Sometimes, however, the brief itself is highly political and cannot be changed. Policy research is often commissioned to meet political objectives. For example, one of the authors was part of a consultancy team commissioned to provide evidence to develop strategies as part of the UK government's new thinking about the role of the voluntary sector. Although we had opportunities throughout the whole process to communicate with a reference group and the civil servants commissioning the research (and they agreed with our conclusions), we did not have the same access to the politicians. It transpired that they wanted a much simpler and less complex message. The problem for the researcher/consultant then is how to second guess how the final arbiter will view and react to the findings, particularly when they are not party to the iterative process.

4.1.2 Thinking about communicating conclusions

Thinking about communicating conclusions and presenting tentative conclusions can shape the research in productive ways. The process of reaching a set of conclusions involves trying to pull out essential elements from the work carried out and weaving a coherent 'story'. Conclusion making and testing is a part of the conceptualizing and reconceptualizing of the issue under investigation, which Alan Thomas refers to in the Introduction. It often encourages the 'two-way relationship between ideas and evidence'. In Chapter 5 Stephanie Barrientos points out that sometimes it is not until writing up that you know if your argument will work and you can provide a conclusion. In this respect it is the same when you have been thinking about people and organizations as when doing a literature study.

Communication of initial results can also highlight any misunderstandings about the appropriateness and consistency of the methodology being used and how the research is understood both by those carrying it out and by those who are interested parties in some way. The former is particularly important when several people, or teams of people, are engaged in the research. A recent project looked at risk regulation of biotechnology in several European countries. Although early discussions had defined a common methodology, nationally based teams carried out research independently of each other. At an interim meeting, about a third of the way through the project, the research teams discussed the progress of the work and how the final report should be written. This brought to light several discrepancies in the methodology in each country. For example, the way in which interviews were carried out in different places meant that there was a difference in the amount of 'formal' statistical data that could be used from each survey. While it had been assumed that the same type of information was being collected in each place, detailed discussions about presentation of results revealed substantial differences in the *nature* of the data.

Communicating ideas generated early in a study helps to provoke feedback on the way you are thinking about the topic. If you have an interesting or new approach (or even if not), communicating your ideas early (for example, in a workshop to a variety of interested parties) may prepare the ground. People you are presenting to are likely to respond better to new ideas if they are not surprised with a radical approach at the end of a project, but have a chance to think through the implications before final recommendations or conclusions are made. Additionally, you may find yourself being more open to critical feedback before you have become too wedded to an approach.

Philip Woodhouse (Chapter 7) notes the importance of establishing rapport with research subjects. Feeding back tentative conclusions and ideas formulated on a work-in-progress basis can be a good way of building rapport among different stakeholders, including interviewees. The process of presenting or discussing tentative conclusions may well generate new information and perspectives.

However, this approach sometimes assumes a degree of separation between researchers and other stakeholders that is not always reflected in reality. Those commissioning policy research are often less concerned with academic rigour, important as that is, and more concerned with 'getting things done'. Indeed much policy research is of the 'action research' model where the researcher is a co-creator with the other stakeholders of devising new ways of resolving social problems. This can make the whole issue of communicating findings much more problematic. The situation in which the researcher is working may be crosscut with organizational politics that at the outset may be opaque to someone coming in from the outside. Often government departments commissioning research happily assume a unity of purpose in organizations working with the same client group that does not exist in reality. Before deciding what to communicate to whom, it is worth undertaking a mapping of the stakeholder environment to find out what is the agenda of each of the participants in the research. This means trying to talk to all the interested parties separately rather than relying on group meetings. Also, being commissioned by a state body can render the researcher automatically 'suspect' in the eyes of particularly disadvantaged or stigmatized groups.

For example, one of the authors was commissioned by a local council to work with groups supporting people affected by HIV/AIDS to design a resource centre for all the groups. There was some political pressure as a very influential local businessman had offered a building at a peppercorn rent. The council simply wanted a quick and tidy solution. However, the groups were suspicious of each other, concerned that the Resource Centre would obtain resources that might otherwise go to their group and highly distrustful of the motives of the local businessman. The researcher needed to understand the situation and be very careful about her communication strategy. One wrong word to the wrong person could bring the whole fragile structure of collaboration crashing down. By careful talking to those involved on an individual as well as a group basis (people often do not say what they really think in a group, particularly one that is riven with conflict), she was able to identify a core group that would help the project to progress.

4.1.3 Research as advocacy and involvement

A critical question when communicating results to advocate a position is: Who owns the research? In the case of the HIV/AIDS resource centre, the work was commissioned by a local authority but the centre was to be an independent voluntary organization. All the local politicians wanted was a recommendation for a course of action about how to respond to the offer of a building. However, the other stakeholders needed a detailed and carefully argued case which was perceived as both fair and convincing about how those recommendations had been reached. To have simply communicated what was required by the (rather short-sighted) commissioner of the research would have led to the project falling at the first hurdle.

Much policy research seeks to consult and establish user opinions and views on the operation of public services. Here two issues arise. Firstly, users do not always have the kind of language about their situation with which policy makers are comfortable. In a UK study of the views of peoples' experiences of poverty in a local area, a number of council tenants expressed very forthrightly their opinions on the offer by the council to allow them to buy a new front door for their rented house. Not to take up the offer was a public declaration of poverty but most could not afford to buy one and expressed their views colourfully. When these views were fed back to an informal meeting of stakeholders prior to the public launch of the report it was clear that the council had not considered this aspect and were stunned that what they thought had been a generous offer had these implications. They demanded that this mention be withdrawn from the report. What to do? The commissioner of the research, a local regeneration project, was dependent on the council for funding, and so this feedback was removed from the published report – however there is no doubt that the message got through to the council.

The second issue is that these concerns get heard because of your own status as a researcher. The problem for many disadvantaged groups is not that they are incapable of identifying their problems and articulating their concerns but that nobody takes their individual views seriously and listens. They have often been trying to be heard for a very long time. Collating these views into a piece of work with the status of research seems to change how things are heard. As researchers we need to be very conscious of this phenomenon and therefore aware of the potential power that this can give us.

4.1.4 Presenting results

It is helpful to present research findings throughout the research process to participants, funders and other stakeholders in order to clarify analysis, try out ideas and deepen understanding and knowledge. There are a variety of ways this can be done and decisions about which format to use for meetings and which tools to use need to take into account political dynamics and aims of the research (Court and Cotterrell, 2006). Iterative processes can often enrich research and provide an opportunity to check approaches and results. There now exist some excellent resources and toolkits to help with planning research communication (Hovland, 2005; Start and Hovland, 2004). However, it is important that you think through exactly what you need to communicate rather than simply relying on templates created by someone else. Culture and context can radically change what works. For example, sometimes the language used can lead to misunderstandings, particularly if the research findings are of a technical nature that normally uses a lot of jargon. It is always important to make your audience feel comfortable and enable them to ask what they may consider 'silly' questions.

There are various ways to communicate results, including the following:

- formal and informal presentations to stakeholders;
- breakfast/lunch/dinner talks;
- newspaper/popular journal articles;
- public workshops with selected invitees from the policy world, experts, academics and participants in the research.

Decisions about how to organize communication will depend on a range of factors, including the scale of the project, the relationship between researchers, funders and other stakeholders, the extent to which the research is 'public' and the extent to which participation and feedback from the 'subjects' of research is required. How you choose to structure presentation of results will clearly depend on what stage you are at and what you hope to get out of the presentation.

The wide range of different fora and circumstances which might be associated with communicating results makes it vital that some thought is given to how to construct communication. One way of thinking about this is to ask some simple questions. Box 4.1 outlines some 'Who? What? Why? When? How?' questions which may be helpful in thinking this through.

**Box 4.1   Start by asking the five questions:
Who? What? Why? When? How?**

Who are you communicating with?

- What are their levels of knowledge?
- What are their roles?
- Who holds the power?
- How many are there?
- Are they the right people to communicate with?
- How are they likely to react?

What do different stakeholders want?

- What are their needs, their concerns, their expectations?
- What matters to them?
- Consider this before you decide on your own objective and strategy for handling the presentation.

(Continued)

(Continued)

Why are you making the presentation?

- What is the purpose of the presentation for you?
- What is your message?
- What is your objective?
- What ideas, products, services are you presenting?
- What kind of feedback are you interested in?

When will you make the presentation?

- At what stage of the project or process are you making the presentation?
- Do you have the information you need to make your points?
- Is the physical space (or document format) appropriate?

How will you do it?

- What tools will you use to help put your message across – notes, visual aids, documentation, amplification, props, etc.?

(Adapted from Stanton, 1986 and JSB, 1996)

4.1.5 Integration into the research process

The main point of this section has been that communication of results is not something that only happens at the end of your research or consultancy – rather it needs to be built in at various stages of the process. It needs to be viewed as a two-way process and you need to be able to respond to input from stakeholders if you wish to make your research relevant and useful. The communication process itself should also be thought through and constructed so as to make the most of the work you have done.

This view of research and communicating results as a non-linear process has implications for researchers and those using the research and funders. Among other things, the way in which research is structured and the way in which it is evaluated needs to reflect the non-linearity of the process (Crewe and Young, 2002). If research is being done in the context of ongoing policy reform, policy initiatives may change during the course of the research. Researchers and funders will want to build in plenty of space for ongoing discussions about the design and progression of the research. A degree of flexibility is desirable, so that time, benchmarks and perhaps even the people working on the research project can be changed. If you are doing 'action research', making changes and examining their impact as part of the research, you will obviously need to build in frequent review sessions. In this case, policy and implementation will be directly part of the remit. This increases the extent to which you need to network with stakeholders and will mean that your communication strategy will be an even more integral part of your work.

Building a pilot phase into the research or consultancy framework can be extremely useful. Pilot periods allow funders and clients to assess the relevance and usefulness of the research question and to amend the design, methodology and tools to be utilized in the research. If the research time is too tightly scheduled or if the clients and funders are not kept informed about the importance of their input at this early stage, the flexibility of the project will be diminished and it may not yield the results required. Researchers and consultants need to be open and honest about what is working and what is not and be prepared to go back to the drawing board if necessary.

However, policy-making is often messy! If communication is not possible throughout the life of a project, a whole range of issues may have to be addressed. We end this section with an example of a difficult project where timing and communication decisions contributed to complications (Example 4.1)

Example 4.1   The need for continous communication

In research done for the South African Department of Labour, a lack of communication compounded an already difficult and complex piece of research. The consultants' brief was confined to governance and financing issues. However, this brief formed part of a broader project of the department to write a new policy framework for human resource development. Other researchers, including officials of the Department of Labour, were investigating a new national, integrated system of human resource development and its governance and financing. However, this work only consolidated into a clear framework towards the end of the consultants' contract. At that stage the consultants were testing tentative policy conclusions with all relevant stakeholders. Not surprisingly, there were then major contradictions and cross-purposes between the consultants' recommendations and the overall framework. It was clear the consultants needed to go back to the drawing board to align, amend or totally reconsider their recommendations in the light of this new knowledge.

Or was it? Realistically, it is to some extent the clients' (or funders') prerogative to put new information on the table as they see fit, and it is the consultants' (or policy researchers') job to respond flexibly. Yet, sometimes consultants or researchers will be put in a position where they have to set limits. Here, an alternative response would be to say 'This was not the brief; these are the recommendations, the client should

(Continued)

(Continued)

have given us this information earlier; and the consultants have fulfilled their brief'. If the client commissioning the work is unreasonable, this will sometimes be an appropriate response. In the case above, the consultants felt that, while decisions about timing could have been better, all relevant information had been passed on as soon as was possible. They decided that they should try to cope with the misunderstanding and spend the extra time to reconsider their recommendations in the light of the new framework from the client. This proved a valuable lesson for the future both for the consultants and those commissioning the research.

4.2 Communication and policy formulation • • •

Research connected to policy formulation and implementation raises a host of issues about accountability, responsibility, power and ethics, as we have noted already in Section 4.1.3. A very simple example immediately brings to light a number of questions about the role of different actors:

> If a researcher or consultant is hired by an NGO to formulate policy relating to small-scale farmers, to whom is the researcher accountable? Is it the NGO? Is it the small farmers? Is it the director of the research unit or consultancy firm? Who makes decisions about controlling the flow of information? Who should be responsible, particularly if things go wrong?

In practice, the picture is almost always too complicated to give a single answer and indeed the aim in most cases should not be to arrive at a single answer. These questions point to the importance of understanding the key actors, structures and power relations that may affect who appropriates (or ignores!) research (Keeley and Scoones, 2003; Crewe and Harrison, 1998; Crewe and Young, 2002). It is important to understand the complexity in general terms and also the implications, in terms of power and ethics, of different answers. This section explores aspects of the intricacies of policy-oriented research.

4.2.1   Is research an intervention?

Policy-oriented research itself constitutes an intervention. It can often be unsettling to those involved by asking questions. Or by approaching one group on behalf of another a new dynamic can be set in motion. For example, a research project to assess the needs of medium-sized enterprises in Poland entailed extensive interviewing with the diverse community of support agencies operating in the country. The project created awareness amongst some providers of development assistance and services that more co-ordination and communication was necessary. A new set of discussions began as an indirect result of the research, independent of the formal progress of the commissioned work. In another example, asking board members of an organization questions about their understanding of their role led some to remark that the questions made them aware that they could be fulfilling their role a great deal more effectively. In both cases the research itself acted as intervention and stimulated a new dynamic among those interviewed.

In the first example this aspect of the research was not anticipated but was welcomed. The research began to stimulate activity in the process of interviewing people. In a sense, communication of results began there; approaches to people signalled that policy was being thought about. In this case some people were receptive to the work and began to act accordingly. In the second example, the chief executive of the organization was not happy that her board members became more questioning as she had felt more in control with an 'approving' and less questioning board.

Research 'subjects' will clearly respond in very different ways depending on their position and context. They may welcome the research, or feel threatened by it. They may feel that the right questions are being asked or that the research is not addressing the right issues. Whatever the response, it is often the case that an approach by a researcher doing policy-oriented work (especially if the research is commissioned by a policy-implementing body) will generate concern and interest on the part of those being asked to participate in the research. The way researchers choose to handle this can have far-reaching implications for the final outcomes, as shown in Example 4.2.

Example 4.2   How research can provoke unexpected inputs

As outlined in Example 4.1, the South African Department of Labour commissioned a new human resource development strategy. For the section on the implications of this strategy for training providers, the consultants decided to bring together different groups of providers half-way through the brief to present their tentative proposals. Each group of providers had not only an opportunity to hear the proposals long before they came out in an official government paper, but were able to comment, criticize and amend the proposals from their point of view – which was often in competition with another group of providers. The training providers were unanimous in their appreciation of this unique opportunity (never afforded them by the previous South African government) and used it to carry out a substantial assessment of what would be in the best interest of human resource development rather than simply how to secure more protection for themselves by privileged access to government funds! The feedback it gave to the consultants led them to revise some of their initial ideas and proposals. For instance, instead of an initial proposal to protect a small group of state-aided training providers through an extension of long-term capital funding, they chose to provide for differential contracts to any training providers, thus allowing any particular training provider to access longer term funding.

One of the most important implications of this analysis of policy-oriented research as an intervention is that researchers require an awareness of the nature of power in their work. Much has now been written on this subject (Court and Cotterrell, 2006). One important area that has received relatively less attention in the literature is the need for researchers and consultants to be reflective about their own actions and political dynamics that they themselves set in motion.

Often researchers have strong feelings about what they regard as the right course of action that flows out of their findings. This poses dilemmas about how they should present these. Should they be honest about their preferences whilst trying to present the evidence for all the options even-handedly? Or should they present the findings as if they feel neutral about the options?

In Chapter 3, Hanlon argues for the first option. He says 'If the investigator has a clear recommendation but there is a strong opposing view, then the summary should only make the case for the investigator's view, while the main report should also clearly explain the opposing line'. This opens a debate – does this approach lack transparency or is it rather being honest and saying that some options are better than others – whilst recognizing that the commissioners of the research may agree to differ? The danger lies in the differentials of power. Where the commissioner is well-informed and powerful, they may feel empowered to disagree with the researcher.

However, where the commissioners lack experience in dealing with researchers, they may not feel able to disagree. In this case, there is an argument for presenting a range of options and leaving the commissioners to make the decision. However, here there is a temptation to skew arguments to the researchers' preferences without being honest and open about this. As we observed earlier, the problem is that the facts do not speak for themselves. It is therefore important to be sensitive to the needs of your audience and reflect on how your biases and preferences might shape their decisions.

4.2.2 What are the dangers of research becoming public relations?

Although there are always exceptions, most researchers and consultants do pursue their work with a sense of the importance of accuracy and honesty. The researcher is often likely to be the person most intimately connected to the details of the project and will want long fieldwork hours reflected in the outcome of the project. It can therefore be discouraging, to say the least, if other stakeholders are uninterested in the process of research.

In some cases research is commissioned and formulated with a very clear idea of the outcomes. Research is often carried out with political objectives being of primary importance. The researcher will have to negotiate these politics and as long as the research adheres to an ethical code, this approach is not a problem. Research that has more or less predictable outcomes but is useful at a particular time, or in a particular place, can be valuable in arguing a point or gaining support for certain policies. Research into the state of the manufacturing sector conducted through the South African Industry Strategy Project aimed to show the extent of the problem in order to identify a set of policies in the areas of trade, competition, human resource development and technology. The fact that South African manufacturing was performing poorly was well known, but the nature of that performance, the depth of the problems and the implications for the general economy were not agreed upon. In carrying out tightly defined studies for each subsector of manufacturing, the Industry Strategy Project (ISP) was able to gain support for supply-side measures to be undertaken by government. The former South African Minister for Trade and Industry, Alec Irwin, was asked 'What impact did the ISP have on government?' He responded 'It's the decisive position that's been taken. That's what makes South Africa a little unusual in the world economy at the moment. It was the decisive basis for forging a trade and industry policy that is compatible with the broader RDP [Reconstruction and Development Programme]' (Irwin, 1996). The research in this case was clearly carried out with a potential agenda in mind. Nevertheless, it was also undertaken with rigour and the findings and analysis were based on detailed investigation.

The dangers are that research is not undertaken in an ethical manner and 'results' are concocted with reference mainly to desired ends and outcomes. There is a difference between commissioning a piece of research for purely political purposes without regard for the validity of results and commissioning serious research at a particularly advantageous time. In practice, the issues are often not this clear cut. Sometimes, although the end 'public' outcome of a piece of work may appear to be a gloss on reality and a piece of PR, commissioners of the research may have taken on board the more serious research findings. For example, if a report is very critical of a project, the promoters of the project may be reluctant to have a negative report made public, but may in private be willing to rethink their approval. It is often the practice, particularly in evaluations, to produce two reports – one for public consumption and another with a limited internal circulation to enable organizational learning. Researchers and consultants draw their own 'ethical codes' around their practices. Researchers and consultants are interested in accuracy, not only to satisfy their ethics, but also because ultimately it is not good for individual reputations if results are seen to be concocted for political purposes. People who do not retain a sense of integrity in their work are not seen to be credible. Few funders want to hire people whose work is not considered as legitimate. The greater danger, however, is lack of courage on the part of researchers. It is always easier to deliver 'good news' rather than bad and there can be a tendency to avoid including critical findings. Part of the integrity of the researcher is to tell the whole story of their findings rather than a partial one. There are many grey areas, however, and pressures related to donor demands that projects demonstrate policy impact further complicate the environment in which researchers work (Mosse, 2005).

4.2.3 Is it ever too early to release results?

Sometimes the timing of when to release results also presents difficult choices and raises questions about accountability. An example from South Africa demonstrates some of the difficulties that sometimes confront policy-makers when they think about how to strike a balance between openness, on the one hand, and effectively completing the brief on the other. The Labour Market Commission (LMC) in South Africa (a presidential commission and therefore publicly accountable) decided at a certain stage of its deliberations to stop communicating with the public via the press. Its logic was twofold: first, that the expectations of the public were growing and that releasing information piecemeal exacerbated this; second, the differing positions of the commissioners would be made public by such comments 'along the way' rather than the commission utilizing its time to develop consensus positions. Being open with the press would create an opportunity for different ideological views to be fought out in public, allowing different stakeholders (particularly business and labour) to 'score points off one another'.

This example clearly raises important issues of public accountability. Although the LMC was a publicly accountable body, the decision was made that it could best serve the public by handling its communication in a more circumspect manner than it had done previously. There are, of course, potential pitfalls to this strategy. The LMC could well have been accused of being secretive, of concealing results and conclusions from the public eye. However, it is certainly a political reality that stakeholder views (as reflected by the various commissioners) on labour market policy are diverse and at times contradictory. The final outcome of the LMC's work was a consensus report which may not have been possible otherwise. In some cases the issue can legitimately be identified as one of controlling communication of results in order not to obscure the process of research and policy formulation. In other cases, however, lack of communication on the part of the commissioning body can mean a more worrying attempt to 'package' research.

There are, of course, no set rules for dealing with situations such as these. Decisions will depend on political judgement and the stance taken by the different individuals and stakeholders involved. This is clearly a very delicate and sensitive issue. Experienced researchers would usually negotiate protocols and agreements about the ownership of the research at the outset that clarify who owns the intellectual property, what expectations the commissioners have about communications and when, what needs to remain confidential and what the researchers can and cannot communicate about the findings to the wider stakeholder group. However, sometimes this remains unclear and a decision not to communicate should not be taken out of any individual motive but rather based on what will be best for the outcome. There needs to be clear and agreed support from the team for the strategy adopted. Individuals on the team will need to be clear about why this is done and have the opportunity to voice their dissent if necessary. There are always dangers in a more democratic approach. A decision not to communicate could be undermined if one of the researchers on the team decided not to abide by the decision. This would exacerbate whatever conflict situation existed and allow the public/media to focus on this dissension rather than on the content of the reports. This media focus could then bring into question the legitimacy of the research. Nevertheless, the underlying principle of discussion among the main groups and individuals involved is a very important one and may well, in the longer run, be the least 'dangerous' of all. In general, if people feel they have had a stake in decision-making, they are less inclined to undermine decisions.

4.2.4 Is not communicating results ever justified?

In some situations researchers or funders of research may feel that it is not appropriate to communicate certain findings or some sources may be sensitive about being named as holding a particular view. This can lead to difficult ethical considerations. One such scenario is when interviewing happens 'off the record'. As noted in a number of other chapters in this book, often the most valuable information is given by informal sources who do not wish to be formally quoted. There are often good reasons for this. For example, when one of the authors of this chapter was researching the dynamics of workplace change in a small appliance factory in Kwazulu, Natal, many hours of interviews were conducted with the shop steward committee. They were keen to give the researchers a side of the story that they believed management would omit but were also adamant that management should not be told of their views for fear of reprisal. Management were convinced that their productivity improvements were due to worker motivation and willingness to co-operate, whereas the shop steward committee believed this was due to workers' sense of insecurity and desire not to lose their jobs – they did not trust management.

The researchers were trying to understand the conditions under which South Africa's manufacturing industry would become more productive so as to withstand competition from the international environment. The request from the union produced a dilemma. If the researchers did not communicate these results back to management, the productivity increases may have been unsustainable in the medium-term and an opportunity to put in place the conditions necessary for these initiatives to be sustained may have been missed at enormous cost. On the other hand, if these results were communicated back to the management, the researchers would be betraying the trust of respondents and opening themselves up to being blacklisted by the union community from this kind of research.

Eventually, a decision was made to communicate the general lack of security of the workforce back to management without being explicit about the fears and concerns raised, in so far as they pertained to the union. Like Hanlon in Chapter 3, we would stress that confidentiality is essential. In the end, the situation remedied itself by the union re-establishing itself in the factory once the new facility was opened.

This example highlights a number of issues, including the importance of acknowledging power relations between informants and researcher or investigator, or between different sets of informants and the expectations of one set of respondents about the influence of the researcher/investigator on another set of respondents. It also highlights the importance of recognizing that respondents may be viewing an investigation from a very different angle from the investigator.

There may well be other circumstances where you or other stakeholders may view the best public communication strategy as silence – temporarily, at least. It has long been a principle of those advocating responsible journalism that news reports which increase the vulnerability of already vulnerable groups should not be released. The same principles need to be adopted in policy research which is taking place in violent or emergency contexts.

Woodhouse (Chapter 7) and Mayoux and Johnson (Chapter 8) point to several of the pitfalls which can be associated with participatory methods of research. Some of these points relate more generally to issues of communication. For example, even good research may be used by more powerful groups to sanction their own demands. It may also expose but not deal with conflict. These circumstances do not necessitate a strategy of silence or legitimate not communicating research, but they do highlight the importance of carefully constructing results and being aware of the impact they may have.

4.3 Conclusion • • •

One of the points from this chapter is that the term 'results' can be a misleading way of describing the output from investigation. 'Results' tends to imply an end point, but it is often more productive to think about communicating findings on an ongoing basis. There are many ways in which research and investigation can be understood differently by the different actors involved, or can miss the point without those being involved realizing that their work is not focusing on the appropriate target. This view of communicating results as an iterative process has implications for the way in which research is structured. Time must be built into the research process for reflection and communication about findings. This can be built in as 'pilot projects' or interim reviews, or an ongoing process of meeting with different stakeholders in the investigation.

We have put forward the view that policy-oriented research is itself an intervention. In development management, interventions often involve many actors who can have very different levels of access to resources. Researchers and consultants enter into relationships with multiple stakeholders, and issues to do with power, ethics, accountability and responsibility need to be examined, particularly where the stakeholders include vulnerable groups who may have a lot to lose or gain from policy changes. There are many questions which involve consideration of the researcher or consultant's 'place' in the research process and who is accountable and responsible to whom.

We have not presented definitive answers to these questions. Contexts are too diverse and complex for formulaic answers. Nevertheless we have raised and discussed some of the questions which researchers and consultants may have to confront and suggested some ways to think about responses. Communication is an essential part of the research process and learning how to communicate more effectively and thinking about some of the ramifications around issues of communication will, we think, improve your research and consultancy efforts overall.

PART II

Thinking with documents

Interrogating information through a literature study

Stephanie Barrientos

Any kind of research or investigation in policy is going to involve, at some level, a study of the relevant literature. If you are the investigator yourself, this study may be the main focus of your work, or it may simply serve as background for other forms of research. Either way, you should be able to analyze and use literature in order to support your own research project. It is likely this is going to involve you in a search for information using literature from a diverse range of sources, be they academic, non-governmental organizations (NGOs), governmental or community groups. You may well need to combine your use of literature with other sources of information such as interviews, surveys or data, and all may form part of any final report you present. However, a literature study can also constitute a policy investigation in its own right, if enough evidence can be obtained from analyzing what others have written.

It is useful to distinguish the idea of a literature study from that of a literature survey. A literature survey involves you primarily in summarizing the material as accurately as possible. A literature study involves a process of critically assessing and evaluating the same material in order to develop your own analytical approach and/or relate it to new aspects of inquiry. While a literature study is more focused, a literature survey is generally a necessary preliminary phase in any such study.

In this chapter we will examine the aims of a literature study, the methods by which a literature study can be carried out, the interface between literature and other sources of information, and, finally, how you can use literature to formulate your own argument and present your own analysis. It is important that you learn to evaluate the literature you read in a critical way, and develop your own arguments and structure so that your final written work stands up as a coherent piece of analysis. Even if you are in a position of commissioning and using the results of others' research, rather than doing the investigation yourself, the same skills will be useful. On the one hand you need to understand what the researchers have to do and the difficulties involved; on the other you have to evaluate their reports critically yourself – and those reports are themselves contributions to the literature!

It is important to stress that literature-based research is a constantly iterated process of:

(a)   gathering and assimilating;
(b)   evaluating and analyzing;
(c)   formulating your own arguments on the basis of your analysis of what you have gathered;
(d)   structuring and writing up your arguments.

Although you will be focusing more on gathering/assimilating information at the beginning and evaluating/analyzing later, they are not completely separate or discrete stages. Throughout we will consider the problems of time constraint. You will need to structure and plan your research in order to progress and achieve results within a realistic time-frame, and in this respect it is important to divide your research into different, if overlapping, stages.

The chapter has four main sections, related to the different stages you will need to go through in order to complete your own literature study. At the same time the sections are interconnected, discussing the process you are likely to go through in your research. You may find some sections more relevant than others, depending on your own purposes in using the literature. The main focus of this chapter is on literature-based research. But even if you are only using literature as a background to other types of research – participatory rural appraisal (PRA) or data analysis, for example – you still might find it useful to think about all aspects of literature-based research, as in your final outcome you will probably be integrating results from your primary and secondary data sources with information gathered from the literature.

This chapter mainly deals with published or accessible literature, and should be read in conjunction with Chapter 6 by Bridget O'Laughlin, which considers many of the same issues using 'grey material' and institutional literature.

Section 5.1 considers aspects of the literature search, possible sources that can be used, internet search engines and problems of timing and information availability. It highlights the advantage of using systems for logging and referencing data and generating bibliographies. It considers the related issues of surveying the literature you acquire, and using this to trace further sources and to help focus your own study so that it is manageable and leads to productive results. This focusing involves posing a central question, which will guide your study throughout.

Section 5.2 examines how you can approach studying the literature you read. Having already posed the main question of your study, you can analyze the available literature in that light. This is broken into three parts: (a) how to evaluate an argument or approach; (b) how to locate an argument or approach; and (c) how to compare different arguments or approaches. There are no hard and fast rules for these, but this section attempts to give you guidelines, and indicates problems you might encounter.

Section 5.3 discusses the next stage, which is the process of formulating your own argument. The step from summarizing other people's ideas to articulating your own can be a very difficult one. Again there are no hard and fast rules, but once again posing the right question is central to this process. Your analysis of the literature was related to the central question you posed. Now you draw your own conclusions from this analysis which forms the basis of your own argument. It is this process which is essential to completing a coherent, well-argued study based on the literature.

Section 5.4 examines the final stage of structuring your study, linking all the material you include to the central argument, and writing it up in a way which is readily accessible to the reader. If you have been successful in formulating your own argument, this stage of your study should fall into place fairly easily.

In this chapter, I will develop and use a single example of a literature-based study throughout. The example I use is part of a study examining 'The rise of female employment in global export production?'. This example study is based on similar research that has been carried out in a number of countries engaged in export production – Barrientos (1997), Kabeer (2000), Lim (1990), Elson and Pearson (1981), Pearson (1998), Collins (2003). Of course, your own study could be completely different from this example, but it provides concrete indications of the types of problems you might encounter.

While this chapter can give you insights into the process of literature-based research, ultimately there is *no* single formula or set of hard and fast rules. You will need to use your own initiative, logic and intuition to achieve the results you are aiming for. The main thing is that, whatever your topic, you consider it from the different aspects this chapter explores, even if you arrive at the conclusion that certain angles are more relevant to your specific research design than others. Research can be a bumpy road, but hopefully this chapter will help you to think objectively about the process you are involved in, and help you avoid some of the potholes – thereby making the journey all the more worthwhile.

5.1 Literature search and survey • • •

This initial phase of a literature study is intended to be wide ranging to help you acquire a broad understanding of the topic, and then progressively narrows down to focus on a more manageable area to survey. The aim is to define the central question for the literature study that will guide the later analytical phases.

5.1.1 Literature search

It is likely that once you initiate your investigation of a topic, you will be operating under tight constraints, both in terms of the time you have available and your physical access to sources of information. If you have little knowledge of the topic, this is going to be more problematic than if it relates to a similar area you have already researched. When starting from scratch, your first aim should be to try to find literature which gives an overview of the topic: any articles, books or pamphlets which survey or summarize the field. This is a quick way of familiarizing yourself with the area of the project; getting to know what work has *already* been done (there is no point in reinventing the wheel) and giving you key sources or references. You might find these through an internet search, by contacting key institutions or organizations, visiting relevant bookshops or libraries, or by talking to someone who has already done related research.

Where publications are available through the internet, they can increasingly be accessed from most parts of the world. The internet has become a powerful source of information. Using search engines such as Google Scholar allows you to trace published data, often on quite obscure topics (see http://scholar.google.com/scholar/about.html). You are now able to download documents directly, including papers put up by different institutions and articles from an increasing number of e-journals. Some universities and other research organizations have electronic subscriptions that give you access to journals and other published material whose circulation is more restricted by copyright. Even where you are unable to download material directly, the internet gives you greater access to information about published information, either through references or abstracts. You can then chase up the original material through other means.

A greater challenge is where published material is only available in hard copy but is not accessible in local libraries or bookshops. If it is a book that is still in print, it can normally be ordered by mail through internet based companies such as Amazon. If it is out of print, access to the material may be restricted to locations that are at some distance or in other countries. If you are researching in a developing country, you may find that publications you need are located in one or more developed countries (which have the main publishers and libraries and many institutional headquarters). However, if you are in a developed country, you may find that important primary sources are only easily available within developing countries to which the information relates. Ideally you will be able to visit both, but if not, try and find contacts who might lend you information, and write to people or organizations abroad to try and obtain information you are lacking (do this early on as it will take time). Ultimately your research will be constrained by the information you have access to, and you should remember this in determining the focus of your study.

Wherever you are based while doing the work, you may be able to visit specialist libraries. Many libraries now have computerized cataloguing and search facilities. You will hopefully be able to gain access to search facilities, such as CD-ROMs, to search for sources in your specific area of interest. Ask librarians for help. If they become interested in your quest, they can give important leads. Most large international organizations have regional libraries, and many government and non-government organizations have sources of information in both published and unpublished form. O'Laughlin in this volume deals with the latter type of material in depth, and from the beginning you should gather as much relevant information as possible from all sources (the most frustrating thing in a literature search is not picking up something you had access to which you later find you need). You may also need to contact the original source of the information, such as authors, NGOs, banks, international institutions, government departments, or other bodies that have produced publications relevant to your field. You will need to allow time for this. You can do this most easily through email, building up a contact list for information in the process.

When you use formal or computerized search facilities you are going to have to start defining the focus of your study by the key words you use to initiate your computerized literature search. Equally, you must try different key words and combinations to be sure you are accessing all the relevant literature available. This is shown using my example study in Example 5.1. Not only should you put in obvious key words and as many related combinations of key words as possible, but also try and think of alternative words for the topic you are searching, and don't forget to search for material related to particular institutions as well.

Example 5.1   Finding key words

Example study title: 'The rise of female employment in global export production?'. Obvious key words: 'employment', 'female', 'global exports'.

Other key words and phrases which you might try in different combinations include: 'global production', 'export processing', 'trade', 'gender', 'women', 'work'.

Related institutional searches might include: UNIFEM, ILO, Oxfam, Global Union Federations.

One word of caution is that modern computerized searches can generate large quantities of references. You may find you have acquired access to so much material it is difficult to know where to start in terms of unpacking it. A first tip is to carefully log all the references you acquire, and where possible keep a short summary or abstract of its content. This can most easily be done using reference software systems such as Endnote that allow you to enter all references you encounter and/or read. When you come to write, these also generate automatic bibliographies, saving a lot of time in the final stages. Even without such programmes, you can keep a reference record yourself in Word or Excel.

The next issue is deciding what to read, given you do not have time to go through every piece of published material you acquire. Initially, it is useful to look for fairly general books, journal articles, or reports in your area. This gives you an overview of your field before you narrow your topic down. Where you see certain works being referred to repeatedly by different authors, you are getting an indication of the main works and debates in the field of your study.

But you will need to focus your topic as soon as you can so that you use your time productively. How you narrow your topic may be largely influenced by your brief and your organization's policy requirements, but your own particular interests will play a part, as well as the availability of material, resources, and the time you have available. It should also be driven by the central question you decide upon. It is very easy, through your interest and enthusiasm in a subject, to be overambitious in your aims. However, any research project has to be of manageable size and have clearly stated objectives if it is to be successful in fulfilling those objectives.

Having defined the scope of your topic, you must now start pursuing references and leads in the literature in a more specific direction. Only pursue references or read literature that directly relate to your question. You will probably continue your literature search, although less avidly, quite far on into the research for your study, as you continue to encounter and chase references you had not seen before, or decide to explore new angles you had not initially considered. But gradually its importance will decline as you move further into your study, and your own work becomes more focused.

5.1.2 Literature survey

As you accumulate and read material, so you embark on your literature survey. When you first start surveying the literature, you do so fairly 'blind', taking in much of what you read as it is presented. You might have noted different ideas and approaches in the literature, and certainly papers, articles and books will have examined the topic from different angles.

Initially this will be a fairly broad survey, but as you narrow and define your topic, so you will begin to concentrate your survey on the literature of most relevant interest to you. As soon as you have defined your topic, you need to write a brief plan of your study, which acts as a guide for your further search, survey and analysis of the literature. It is very easy when you are doing a literature project to read *ad infinitum*, but you could well be wasting time which you do not have. A plan helps you to focus and also to allocate your time appropriately. This early plan is not definitive, can easily be amended, and can be integrated into your terms of reference if it is part of a broader research project involving, for example, field study.

5.1.3 Focus: initial plan and central question

The initial plan should give you a central focus and framework for your study. You achieve this by identifying the specific aim of your project – which is the central question you want to address. Each section of your project should then relate to this central aim, which acts as a backbone to your project. We are going to explore this in some detail later on, as this is an essential part of carrying out a literature project. But the earlier you identify this central aim, the more you are able to focus your research productively. As a general guide this initial plan should be as brief as possible (one side of A4 paper is enough). It should contain the following information:

- Title
- Aim (problem and central question you are going to address)
- Key issues (with short summary of each)
- Other research methods to be used (summary of methodology)
- Time schedule

This outline acts as a 'photograph' of your project which you can keep in mind at all times. It helps you to organize your material, discard literature which is not relevant to your specific needs, concentrate on the sections of any book or article of greatest importance, and search for new relevant material. At the same time you should write a time schedule for your work, detailing your time allocation for:

- literature research;
- other research methods (interviews, participatory methods, data analysis, etc.);
- writing, allowing time for redrafting and polishing at the end.

This helps you to organize and divide your research time proportionately between the parts of your project, within a manageable deadline.

5.1.4 Literature study

As you progress with your literature survey, so you will need to begin to study the literature analytically. In Chapter 6, O'Laughlin writes of moving from a survey to a study of the literature. Here I prefer the idea of search/survey as the first phase in a literature study, followed by analysis. However, there is no single point of transition from a survey to the later phases of a literature study. As you begin to analyze, you will continue to search and survey new work, guided in part by the ideas you are beginning to form. But, increasingly, you should be able to read from a more critical standpoint and be able to relate it to any additional research (field work, survey material or data analysis) you are going to use.

When you critically assess material, you do not do so in a vacuum. An essential ingredient in this is that, as early as possible, you will have posed a question which you want to address, and from then on you approach the literature in the light of analyzing its relevance to your question. Having a central question is important both in giving focus to your reading and in framing any further research design. It will play a central role through to the final conclusion of your investigation. In Example 5.2 I consider how this might affect my example study.

Example 5.2   Posing a question

In my example study, I started with a fairly broad title 'The rise of female employment in global export production?' But this is still fairly general, and could involve uncritically summarizing a range of case studies, without any yardstick for comparing or assessing them.

   Posing a central question helps to resolve this, and the question I will pose is: 'How can employment in global export production help to empower women?' This is not directly a policy question, but such research could help to underpin a gender sensitive approach to policy formulation. The question can help to inform the literature search.

- 'Empowerment' needs to be entered as a keyword in the computer search. In general the search should explore literature on the empowerment of women.
- It helps to focus analytical reading of the literature. In any book, article or document, I am interested in the information given, but now I particularly want to ask how this affects the empowerment of the women themselves.
- It helps to evaluate *critically* the literature used. Even if an article doesn't mention empowerment, what are its implications?
- It helps to interpret and unpack any given policy and data.
- It poses a framework for carrying out further in-depth research such as semi-structured or focus group interviews with temporary women workers, and helps the design of that research.
- Ultimately, it will provide the basis for writing up the research.

5.2 Analyzing the literature • • •

We now need to consider how to analyze the literature we are surveying. One problem you are likely to face in development or policy studies is that the literature may be from a range of different sources: academic, government, non-government or other organizations. They are going to be written from different perspectives, in different styles, using different 'in-house' language. O'Laughlin examines the use of grey and institutional material in Chapter 6, but let's consider the general issues. First, we'll look at how to assess articles or reports individually, before going on to comparing them.

5.2.1   Evaluating an argument

The process of critically assessing a piece of literature starts with evaluating its position or argument and logical construction. Evaluating a position or argument can be broken down into two important parts. Firstly, you have to identify the argument accurately. If you misunderstand or misrepresent an argument, your own final analysis of it will be flawed. Secondly, you have to consider whether the argument you are examining is logically consistent internally and meets its own objectives. In other words, do the conclusions follow from the premises? We will consider each of these separately.

Identifying an argument

The extent to which identifying an argument is easy or problematic will depend largely on the author you are reading. Some authors present their ideas very clearly and systematically in an articulate form. They will start at the beginning with a summary of their views, the questions they wish to address, the material they are going to examine, the methods they are going to employ and the conclusions they aim to draw. So long as they fulfil their objectives clearly, then your main role is to take accurate notes.

Often, though, written work appears very complex, and cannot be easily summarized in a few paragraphs. In this case you have to be very patient in working through the argument, accurately recording all the essential points, in order to get an overall view of the main features and their interconnections. Sometimes, a piece of writing *looks* highly complex, but once you have isolated and identified its essential points, it is actually quite simple. Do not be intimidated by the fact that some writers have perfected the art of dressing up mundane ideas in sophisticated language. Therefore, you need to question everything you read, but at the same time be accurate in distinguishing and recording the main features of its argument. Remember, too, the points Joseph Hanlon made in Chapter 3 about writing to impress. He was thinking about how you might improve your writing style and write with different aims in mind, but of course similar considerations also applied to others writing up the reports which are now part of the literature to you.

Alternatively, you might encounter an empirical piece of work containing a large amount of factual information and data, but no clear argument. The way data are selected, organized and presented often reflects a particular perspective, whether or not that perspective is explicitly stated. In this situation you need to stand back from the piece of work, and consider what type of data have been considered relevant and how these data have been selected and are organized. You might also need to consider what data or evidence have *not* been included. Often you can evaluate a piece of literature just as much by what has *not* been considered, as by what has (see Mayer, Chapter 11).

The other problem you might encounter is when, however hard you try, you are unable to identify exactly what the author is trying to say. It is not easy to give advice on this, except to suggest that (a) you try to get as close an approximation to the argument as possible, and (b) if you decide to use the argument in your own final report, you indicate that this was the argument as you understood it.

The logical consistency of an argument

Examining a piece of work for logical consistency will depend partly on its structure. In turn, the structure might vary, in accordance with the methodology employed by that author, with the particular approach or institutional perspective of that author, and with the nature of the work under examination. The main thing to look for in determining logical consistency is whether the conclusion logically follows from the premise, given the assumptions made, and is supported by the evidence given.

In determining the internal consistency of a piece of work, you must be aware of the criteria that piece of work sets itself. Does it pose a central question or issue that it is going to address? Does each stage in the argument or procedure adopted follow logically from the previous one? Do the data and empirical evidence support the argument, or are there contradictions? Are there dislocations in the argument? Does it arrive at a conclusion consistent with its original aim and supported by the evidence given? I am trying to provoke you, when reading, to ask yourself whether you think a piece is consistent, or whether it contains contradictions in terms of its own argument or approach which undermine its validity as a piece of analysis. Example 5.3 considers the type of literature encountered in my example study.

What we have been considering so far is the evaluation of a piece of work in its own terms. When making notes on a particular piece of writing, you may want to add comments of your own. This can be useful for the comparison stage and for formulating your own arguments (see below). However, be sure to make a clear distinction between your own comments and your evaluation of a piece of work *in its own terms*. The next stage is to locate each argument in relation to others, before going on to a comparison between one argument and another, and weighing them up in relation to available evidence (data, surveys, etc.) which has not necessarily been included. Finally you will need to consider the importance of an argument for your own study.

Example 5.3 Evaluating the literature on female employment in global export production

Let us consider this process of identification and evaluation using my example study. Assume that the literature I have encountered through my search and survey can be broadly divided into three categories:

1 *Global exports.* Much of the literature is easy to identify and categorize. Some more economic literature extols the success of global exports, and argues that trade liberalization, improved efficiency and high productivity (no mention of gender) have been key to expanding global exports and creating new job opportunities. Other literature is directly critical of global export production, arguing it generates wasteful consumerism, drives out local producers, and provides low paid and exploitative jobs.

2 *Female employment in export production.* There are a number of case studies on female employment in export production. Many are quite descriptive, but often

(Continued)

(Continued)

they reflect different standpoints. Some take a negative perspective, highlighting poor labour conditions, the multiple burdens that women workers carry. Others take a more positive view, emphasizing the opportunities this has created for income generation by women, and overcoming barriers to female employment. Some weigh up the benefits and costs to women of working in global export production.

3   *Women and empowerment.* Again, we will find different perspectives in the literature. Some authors emphasize the repressive nature of women's employment in export production and its disempowering effects. Others emphasize that this employment has facilitated greater empowerment of women through economic independence, control over their income, bargaining power within the household, and voice in the wider community. However, some take a more ambiguous position, weighing up both the pros and cons of working in export production.

So far I am assessing the direct literature relating to the particular question I have posed. I have been taking notes of the different positions in each article or book. But, on its own, it might not provide sufficient analytical tools to answer the question posed in depth. To interrogate the literature further I may need a set of sub questions, which in my example of women's employment in export production could look like this:

(i)   Why has global export production drawn in a large female workforce?
(ii) What are the employment relations experienced by women in this type of work?
(iii) What are the wider gender relations that condition women working in export production and how do these affect women's empowerment?

To explore the sub questions further, I am likely to need to draw on a wider literature that informs, but does not necessarily directly deal, with the central question. In my example, sub question (i) can be further examined through the literature on global value chains and production systems and a more technical literature on product innovation and specialization in the global economy. Sub-question (2) may involve exploring the literature on flexible employment, and work risks more broadly in a global economy. Sub question (iii) can be further examined through feminist literature on a gender bias in the economy, and debates on women's empowerment in other contexts.

At this stage you are not necessarily taking a position on whether you agree or disagree with an author. Even if you have your own position, it is important you examine all perspectives in the literature thoroughly to ensure you are fully informed. Your main activity is to have a good record of the different positions held by different authors. You are also looking for consistency in their arguments. Do they substantiate their arguments with facts, do they use well documented evidence, do their conclusions follow from the logic of their argument and evidence presented?

Drawing on a wider literature gives you more substantive information for assessing your own questions in more depth. It provides a basis for coming back to your central question, and weighing up the different perspectives you have encountered in the literature dealing directly with women's employment in global export production.

5.2.2 Locating an argument

In order to weigh up the different arguments you have encountered in this diverse literature, you need to be able to place it in the context from which it arose and also to identify where it fits in terms of different analytical approaches and paradigms.

1 *Examining the context*
It is likely that the literature you are going to compare comes from a number of different time periods, institutional sources, theoretical approaches, and ideological perspectives, each reflected in different paradigms or policy agendas. None of it was written in a vacuum, and examining the context can provide important insights into a better understanding of it. The greater your understanding of the problems different authors have sought to address, and how those problems arose, the greater your understanding of their analytical perspective and any conflicts between the different approaches you encounter.

The extent to which you need to look at the context will partly be dictated by the type of topic you are researching. In most policy-based research, you may need to identify the development process and the specific problems which arose in order to contextualize the different policy proposals, and also consider the position of the different actors within any given situation. This is particularly important in comparing work from different agencies, in which you need to consider the institutional context, whose interests are being represented, and what is the underlying policy agenda (see Chapter 6).

Exploring the context of a topic can involve consulting a wide range of literature on economic history, social and political and policy related issues, both in relation to the country or countries and to the topic you are examining. This can be very time consuming. If you decide upon this course, you will only be able to consult a sample of sources; try to look in the literature for any overviews, literature surveys, and summaries already carried out by other authors. You might also find it helpful, for example, to see if similar work to your own has been carried out for another country, from which you might gain contextual insights. You will need to use your own initiative on this, but you must be very careful to limit the time you spend, and stick rigorously to your original time schedule.

2 *Different analytical approaches*
Development and any other field of policy studies are also composed of a number of quite different approaches, which you must also be aware of in evaluating the literature, contextualizing your project, and developing your own analysis. You will not have time to go back and familiarize yourself with each different approach (unless you are specifically examining one of these in your study), and will have to fall back on previous knowledge and overviews. It is often possible to find a comprehensive review article which also sets out the main schools of thought on an issue – though,

of course, it will be that author's view on what the main schools of thought are! (for example, Kabeer, 1994 on gender and development; Gereffi and Kaplinsky, 2001 on global value chains, and Collins, 2003 on women working in global apparel).

Whenever you read an article, book or piece of analysis, it is important to try to locate it in terms of which approach it reflects. When an author indicates clearly the viewpoint he or she is starting from, this is quite easy, but many authors will not render you this service, or might be combining ideas from different schools. There are four aspects you need to concentrate on when attempting to identify the approach of a particular author, although the relative importance of each will vary according to the type of literature you are reading.

- What are the key theoretical assumptions?
- What empirical evidence or data are used?
- What are the policy prescriptions?
- What references are cited?

Let us assume that you are looking at two pieces of work on structural adjustment and poverty written from different perspectives, for example. If the author assumes free markets and free trade are the most efficient method of development, cites key macro-economic indicators, argues that greater economic liberalization is the most beneficial policy prescription, and cites authors such as Krueger (1974), the work is of neo-liberal origin. If, conversely, the author starts with an analysis of entitlements and capabilities, appeals to social, poverty and equity indicators, and advocates community-based social policy as an essential element in resolving problems of economic development, citing authors such as Chambers (1997) and Sen (1999), the work is drawing on a capabilities or participatory perspective.

These, however, are two fairly clear-cut examples. The problem of locating a piece of writing in terms of a particular approach can be difficult. A piece of writing may contain a number of competing influences in explaining a particular phenomenon. This is more likely in recent development literature, where increasing credence is given to a multi-dimensional perspective on poverty and development. Once you focus on policy analysis, which by necessity involves a degree of pragmatism, pinning a proposal to a specific analytical approach can be even more difficult. Also, some authors may not want to be pigeon-holed. They may try to present themselves as having taken everything into account and then put forward a balanced view. This may ultimately be unhelpful in that it tries to gloss over differences between approaches, and it can be difficult to pin down the particular author's argument. However, it is up to you to gauge the main influences and general perspective of any work, and weigh up the relative importance of its theoretical perspective to the given literature you are studying.

How you do this again will depend very much on the type of topic you are researching, but, for example, you could develop a chart to group the literature you are using, and if necessary break it into component parts according to its leaning. Let us assume, for example, your study involves using material from two approaches (neo-liberal and capabilities), and you want to examine the background, analytical, empirical and policy angles of the topic. Much of the literature you are dealing with might not neatly fit into one approach

TABLE 5.1 *A simple breakdown of the literature*

	Neo-liberal	Capabilities	Multi-dimensional
Background material cited			
Theoretical assumptions			
Data and empirical evidence used			
Policy prescriptions			

or another, so a chart of the key aspects you are examining could help you break down an individual article, and help as a method of comparison of the literature.

A possible example of such a chart is given in Table 5.1. Using this you could note (or tick) the leaning of each component part of an article, use this to weigh up its overall approach and compare it with other articles similarly deconstructed. This is a fairly mechanical method. You would need to evolve your own version of such a method with which you feel comfortable, and which would help you to think logically through the process of evaluation and comparison.

5.2.3 Comparing arguments

The next stage in a literature project is when you begin to compare and weigh up arguments, which may be from different theoretical perspectives. There are no hard and fast rules for comparing different arguments. Hopefully, you will begin to do this intuitively as you are reading, but it is important that you are aware of this as an essential transition to developing your own arguments and conclusions.

The *problem* of comparison really lies with the literature which is not easy to group by approach. For example, two articles might appear to agree in the main about analysis of a problem, but come to quite different or opposing conclusions in terms of policy. Here you will need to question each article. What context were they written in? What are their unstated theoretical assumptions? What are their institutional agendas? What evidence do they appeal to? What authors do they cite? What are the unstated implications of their policy prescriptions? All of these types of questions will help you to unpack and weigh up the literature. But, ultimately, you will have to use your own initiative in comparing this type of literature.

However, one additional test, which is vital, and leads on to the next stage, is: How do any two pieces of literature relate to the central question *you* are asking? At this stage you are not simply comparing the literature 'blind' or in a general way. You are weighing it up and comparing it in preparation for your own use, i.e. in order to formulate your own argument or to integrate it with other forms of research which your question is leading to. Therefore, analyzing and probing it in terms of your own central question is a way of comparing literature, not in and of itself, but in terms of its relative importance to the project you yourself are carrying out. To what extent do two articles relate to your question? To what extent do they throw new light on your question (whether or not you agree with them)? To what extent do they refute or support the available evidence and data?

What further research do they necessitate? How do they relate to the arguments you are developing, and conclusion you are now beginning to arrive at? You are now involving yourself, and your own research project, in the process of comparison, and, at the same time, using the literature as part of the process of formulating your own arguments and further analysis. However, it is important to re-emphasise that when making notes on any piece of writing, make sure you (a) summarize and evaluate it in its own terms; (b) make your own comments as part of a comparison with other writing and formulating your own arguments; and (c) distinguish clearly between (a) and (b). It is this process which ultimately constitutes the advancement of research.

Example 5.4 uses my example study to consider the problem of evaluating the literature in more detail, and the type of chart which might help us to break down the literature into its component parts for the purpose of comparison.

Example 5.4   Comparing the literature

My example study deals with issues relating to women's employment in global export production. I have also formulated my question regarding the empowerment of women workers, which I want to use in analyzing the literature for my own purposes. I have drawn up a set of sub questions that help to interrogate the issues further. I thus need to elaborate a chart as a means of breaking down and evaluating the literature I am studying. Table 5.2 gives a simple example of a chart I could use. Here it is very simple, but could be expanded to help sieve all the issues touched on by any piece of literature, and the perspective taken in relation to each issue.

Any literature which clearly supports a free-market, free-trade approach to global exports, argues that it generates positive employment opportunities for women workers, and that this employment is empowering would clearly be grouped in the first of each pair of sub columns: 'Pro' in the global export column, 'Positive' in the women's employment column and 'Empowers' in the women's empowerment column.

Conversely, any literature which is critical of the effect of global export production, and which emphasizes the problems faced by women workers and the importance of improved pay/working conditions, transport, health provision, social provision and reproductive rights for women workers, will clearly be grouped in the second of the subcolumns: 'Critical' of global export production; 'Negative' on women's employment; and 'Disempowers' on the outcomes for women workers.

The problem is going to be in locating literature – for example research or policy documents coming from government organizations – which advocate a combination of the above. For example, such documents might be critical of global export production but ignore the problems faced by women workers altogether. Conversely, they might support global export production but also argue that women workers are adversely affected and need more support. The sub questions provide an important mechanism for sieving and comparing different pieces of this type.

TABLE 5.2 *Simple chart to evaluate literature on temporary women workers in agribusiness*

	Leaning of literature					
	Global Export Production		Women's Employment		Women's Empowerment	
Issues covered: Economic/ industrial Employment Gender analysis Empowerment	Pro	Critical	Positive	Negative	Empowers	Disempowers

5.2.4 Moving the literature boundary

So far we have concentrated on examining literature in a published form (quite likely including pamphlets and institutional literature). But we must remember that all published literature has a 'vintage', be it new or old. The information contained in a recently published book, for example, could be at least one to two years old, allowing for the process of writing and printing, etc. (although some non-academic publishers can speed up the process). The information contained in an article or pamphlet might be more recent, but, once published, it has entered the public domain and there is little point in simply reiterating it.

An examination of the existing literature is always an essential part of research, but it is likely you will need to move beyond this boundary if you are to produce material of additional value. Within the context of a literature project itself, this could involve trying to find unpublished material (see Chapter 6), or material which is still in the process of being developed, by attending relevant talks or conferences. Through this you become familiar with similar work which is in progress (again no point in simply reiterating it), or gain access to new sources of information such as discussion or policy documents.

The main way of gaining access to this type of supplementary material is to contact other people, be they key informants, professional experts, or other researchers (see Hanlon, Chapter 3). It is usually beneficial before talking to such people to have done your own groundwork first, so that you can hope to have an informed discussion with them, and understand the context and background to any new information. But you can also see some of the problems and issues other researchers in the field are grappling with, which can help inform the process you are going through. Research is often an isolated process, and simply talking to someone who is knowledgeable in the field can help you to formulate your own ideas. If you are working in a developing country, with little library access, this could also be a means of access to published literature you cannot easily obtain.

Moving the literature boundary is also the point of interaction with non-literature forms of research. Other chapters explore these in detail, but you should always remember that a literature project can contextualize, inform and help to direct. Literature is ultimately a means of communicating the results of other research mediums. So, for example, you may want to supplement your literature project with semi-structured interviews, or a survey in the field. In both, the literature will have helped you to examine the general issues, and to identify weak areas which have not been addressed. This will help you in the formulation of your questions, and the design of any questionnaire (Mikkelsen, 1995). You might choose to pursue the data you have encountered in the literature. At the simplest level you may go back and analyze the original data source, or you may have obtained new secondary or primary data you wish to analyze in order to supplement, advance or question the existing literature in the field (Mukherjee and Wuyts, Chapter 10, and Mayer, Chapter 11, discuss these issues in more detail).

Alternatively, your primary aim may not be a literature project, but rapid or participatory rural appraisal (see Mayoux and Johnson, Chapter 8) or an econometric project, which the literature simply helps to inform. Again, the literature can be a means of contextualizing the research agenda, or getting a handle on the data or evidence you are analyzing (Section 5.3 examines this), and help you to confirm or interpret the results you obtain. The research process often involves constant interaction between quantitative and qualitative analysis at different levels (micro, meso and macro), especially in innovative policy analysis. Finally, your main aim may be to undertake case study analysis (see Thomas, Chapter 13), where literature provides one of several forms of evidence.

5.3 Formulating your own arguments ● ● ●

Once your research is well under way, you will need to start formulating your own argument or analysis of the topic. This can be a very difficult part of a literature project. Summarizing other people's ideas can be fairly simple, but formulating your own involves a lot of energy and critical thought. Don't worry if you find it difficult; the best ideas will not necessarily come easily. There are three aspects to formulating your own argument:

1 the central and sub questions you want to ask;
2 the approach you want to take;
3 the conclusion you want to draw.

I will examine each of these in turn so that you can consider the role each plays in formulating your own logical argument.

Central question

We have already seen the importance of posing a central question for your analysis of the literature, and this now becomes a key element in formulating your own argument. However, it is worth standing back for a moment and thinking through whether your question as originally posed is quite the right question. You may want to modify it a little or even reconceptualize around a rather different question that makes it easier to formulate your own argument.

The central question can act as the 'pivot' on which you hang your own argument, and provides the backbone for articulating your own written work. Having a central question provides the linkage between your sub questions, which should all be connected to the central question. It is this which will provide the backbone of the project, allowing it to stand as an integrated whole (see Section 5.4 below).

Argument

It is possible that when you started the project, you knew the argument you wanted to develop. If you are working for a particular institution or organization, this might have been given to you as part of your original brief. If not, identifying a question can also help you to decide your argument.

In literature-based policy analysis, you will often be dealing with debates. You will need to develop and articulate your own argument through exploration and critical examination of the existing approaches you consider. In doing this, you might decide to align yourself with one particular approach on the issue, although you should always consider alternatives and possible criticisms of the stance you take. Alternatively, you might decide different approaches have valid contributions to make to understanding the problem you have chosen to project. Whichever line of argument you decide upon, it is important that the analysis of it is clear and consistent and leads ultimately to your final conclusion. Remember that others will be analyzing what you write, using the kind of critical approach put forward in the previous section!

Conclusion

For your own argument to be logical and coherent, you also have to arrive at an endpoint in this process. Your argument is the logical series of steps you have gone through – in your analysis of the existing literature and supporting evidence or research – which link the original question to the final answer. The argument you develop must be rigorous and the conclusion you draw should be logically consistent with your original question and supported by the evidence you present. Your argument has also got to be able to stand up to criticism. The argument you develop should be tenable, either in terms of logical reasoning or appeal to empirical data, and should consider potential refutations or criticisms. And each stage of your argument should be connected (however indirectly) and lead towards your final conclusion. Once all these elements are in place, you are in a position to write a well-structured and coherent report, which we will consider in more detail in the next section.

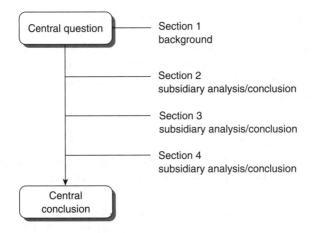

FIGURE 5.1   Literature study framework

5.4 Structuring your argument and writing up your report ● ● ●

Early on in your study you should have written a short outline of its structure. As your research progresses, this outline must be expanded into a fuller structure through which you can develop your argument. The outline should encompass the central question and sub questions. The more coherent the argument you have elaborated, the more easily this structure should fall into place. The difference between the outline and this more elaborate structure is that you are now developing the complexities of the argument, and integrating into it the more peripheral points, while still ensuring that they are connected to the central question. Some points may not be relevant to the final argument, so, as Hanlon suggests in Chapter 3, you should be prepared to leave them out, even if they represent a lot of reading on your part.

The final written report must stand as an interconnected whole. Each section should clearly be linked to the central question of your study, and those connections should be logical, as shown in the integrated literature study framework in Figure 5.1. Further, the progression from one section to another should be determined by and encompass the overall progression of the central argument of your project from its initial question to its final conclusion. Hence each section is connected to the whole like a skeleton to the backbone, which in our case is the central question. This skeletal form is summarized in Figure 5.1. The key here is that you are now structuring your own argument, drawing on but not simply reviewing the existing literature. It is through your own independent evaluation and argument that you advance understanding of the issue.

If you already have a well-formulated argument, the structure of your overall study will probably fall into place fairly easily. But, conversely, it is often through developing the structure and beginning to write your report that you 'test' the coherence of your argument, and you might find you need to refine it. The aim of the final structure, therefore, is to achieve the overall balance between sustaining the central argument of the study, while simultaneously exploring its various facets through analysis of the relevant literature and supporting evidence. Example 5.5 gives a concrete example of this, using my example study.

Example 5.5   Literature study outline – formulating an argument and structuring the report

Returning again to the example study, we have already decided the central question: 'Is employment in global export production empowering for women?'. This central question has been supplemented by a number of sub questions. These have helped in the process of focusing on exploring and comparing the literature. The question is then used as the basis for formulating a substantiated argument, which frames the structure of the final report itself, drawing on the sub questions as a guide.

Female employment and empowerment in export production

1   *Introduction*
    Brief outline of project and statement of aims: to examine the growth of female employment in global export production, the nature of their employment, and whether or not it is empowering for women workers. May provide a brief summary of key literature on this topic. Can also set up the central question 'How can employment in global export production help to empower women?' It may outline the different perspectives within the literature, but at this point does not answer the question.

2   *Global export production and female employment*
    Considers the background and expansion of global export production, and the growth of female employment within it. Draws on literature on global value chains, production systems and product innovation. Links this with empirical information on global export production and rise of female employment. Assesses why demand for female labour has grown, and what role this employment plays in producing 'just in time' high quality products. Thus addresses sub question (i) Why has global export production drawn in a large female workforce?

3   *Gender and employment relations*
    Assesses the type of employment relations and conditions of employment experienced by women workers. Draws on literature on flexible employment and work risks. Assesses why this type of employment relations have been generated in 'just in time' high quality export production and why women workers preferred.

(Continued)

(Continued)

Assesses changes in employment conditions through buyer codes of labour practice, and whether these have in any way affected employment relations. Thus addresses sub question (ii) What are the employment relations experienced by women in this type of work?

4   *Women's empowerment through global export production*

Probes the gender basis of women's employment. Draws on wider literature on gender bias in the economy, and different dimensions of women's empowerment. Links this with empirical information on the realities of women's lives, issues they face in juggling insecure work and childcare/domestic responsibilities in global export production. Weighs up other factors constraining the empowerment of women of working in export production, such as lack of adequate skills training or enforcement of good working conditions for temporary workers that are mainly women. Addresses sub question (iii) What are the wider gender relations that condition women working in export production and how do these affect women's empowerment?

5   *Conclusion*

The conclusion, based on the analysis undertaken, can then examine how policy can help to enhance the empowerment of women working in export production. This may be through more state provision of childcare, better occupational training for women, or stronger enforcement of labour regulation for temporary workers. This section draws together all the analysis and empirical information to answer the original question. Whatever conclusion is drawn, it must be substantiated by: (i) a critical review of the literature covered; (ii) weighing up the analytical perspectives and relevant empirical information provided. This must have been logically demonstrated through the previous sections.

In this example, the formulation of the central question regarding empowerment helps to link the analysis in each section, and thus the articulation of the argument which leads to the conclusion. The above structure provides the basis for writing the final report. It is only when you come to write that you will finally be sure whether you can sustain your central argument throughout, and you are able to tie all the separate parts of your analysis into an integrated whole. Always allow time for preliminary drafting, as it is bound to be fairly rough and disjointed at the beginning, and will need polishing to produce the final integrated whole.

5.5 Concluding remarks • • •

In this chapter, I have attempted to guide you through the various stages a literature study is likely to involve, and the types of problems you will need to address at these different stages. The aspect of this I have concentrated on is how to transform a broad summary of the literature into an analytical study through which you can develop your own argument and policy analysis.

A problem with this is that literature studies can vary widely in both the types of issue they are addressing, and how they address them. I have attempted solely to give you some guiding principles. It will be your final decision to choose what is relevant to you, given the topic you have been assigned or have chosen, and the approach you want to take. The main thing is that you approach your study with your eyes open, and an analytical mind, that you question what you read, and question what you do, and that you use your own experience and initiative to achieve your objectives. The result will be a report that is consistent and clearly argued, and with which you can be satisfied as a piece of your own work and a useful contribution to policy.

Interpreting institutional discourses

Bridget O'Laughlin

In policy-oriented research, we rarely choose our own topic; we are assigned it. In the course of our research, however, we often come to challenge the terms or boundaries of the topic we were given. We construct our own account, and then decide how to present it to the policy makers or activists who commissioned the research, or how to reach a wider audience. The production of policy documents, our reading of them and the construction of our own accounts are shaped by the politics of the policy-making process. What policy-oriented research tells us is not self-evident; it has to be interpreted politically to be understood.

In this chapter we will be looking at how, in the process of constructing and presenting our own account, we can get the most out of *grey materials* – unpublished or semi-published documents that are often short-lived, have not been through academic review and are not commercially available. It was once difficult to find such documents, but since the advent of the internet and powerful search engines the problem is sorting through them to identify those that are useful. We will be looking particularly at policy-oriented reports on development issues written by trained researchers working either as employees or consultants for governmental or non-governmental organizations (NGOs). The examples used here derive mainly from my own experience as a researcher on development issues in two different contexts: first in a research and teaching centre within the national university in Mozambique, then in a development institute in the Netherlands, looking at research on poverty, gender and health in Africa. The issues raised here apply, however, to using grey material from other regions and on other topics as well.

This chapter should be read as a complement to Chapter 5 on literature study. Whereas Stephanie Barrientos stressed the importance of locating an author within a particular school, here I am emphasizing the importance of locating research reports within particular institutional discourses. Research reports are often written anonymously so that their author becomes the agency that commissioned them. But, even when signed, such reports must be located institutionally. They are the product of an explicitly political process – though often couched in technical language. The final report is the outcome of a process of negotiation between researchers and the commissioning institution. To use this material well, we must locate the choice of questions and conclusions within this political process. We must recognize key words and interpret both messages and silences as part of socially constructed institutional discourses.

6.1 Problems in using grey materials as sources of information • • •

The politics of producing grey materials is an explicitly political process, which can compromise their usefulness as sources of information in some persistent ways. The first is censorship – either explicit or implicit. Agencies that request reports can simply refuse to accept conclusions they do not like, assigning drafts to the dustbin or negotiating bland and uncontroversial conclusions. The World Bank, for example, disagreeing with an outside evaluation of its own assessments of poverty programmes in Africa, simply withheld it. In a study of the poverty impact of an increase in the fuel tax in Mozambique, the IMF wanted the final report to point out that, ultimately, the impact would depend on how increased government revenues were used, a point that is obviously true but which minimizes the immediate impact of an increase in transport costs on the livelihoods of urban workers.

   To avoid censorship, researchers often exercise self-censorship, since they wish both to have their research reported, and to be commissioned to do further research. In practice it is very difficult to write a definitively negative report on any on-going project supported by those who commissioned the research. Motives may be political as well as financial. In researching agrarian issues during Mozambique's socialist period, for example, we deliberately put little emphasis on class differentiation of the peasantry; we were concerned that evidence of differentiation would be used by certain voices in the ruling party as a justification for forced collectivization. There is thus a drift toward consensus in grey material, often at the cost of coherence. The conclusions drawn and executive summaries do not always reflect the findings and information presented in the body of the report.

   Not only conclusions, but even the general premises of research, may be subject to implicit assumptions about suitable solutions. Ferguson (1990) has noted that development institutions have preconceptions about acceptable policy options for rural Africa. There is a standard package of projects – usually emphasizing greater integration of traditional peasants into the market – that they are prepared to implement across a wide range of situations. He also argues that these packages tend to be technical – removed from the different political situations in which they must operate. In the case of Lesotho, an independent country located in the heart of South Africa and long a source of migrant workers, this package included technical measures such as rural road construction and improved livestock production. This was intended to improve commercial smallholder production. Ferguson argues that for this package to look like a solution to Lesotho's problems, World Bank research on Lesotho had to rewrite its history and political economy to present it as 'a nation of farmers, not wage labourers, a country with a geography, but not history, with people, but no classes; values, but no structures; administrators, but no rulers; bureaucracy, but not politics' (Ferguson, 1990, p. 66). The migrant workers moving constantly back and forth to South Africa thus became traditional peasant farmers, isolated from the market.

Preconceptions about solutions may also explicitly figure in negotiation of research questions between researchers and those who commissioned the research. During my time with the research centre in Mozambique we were asked to investigate worker absenteeism in the harbour of Maputo, considered by management to be the principal cause for the long turn-around time in ship-handling. Preliminary research convinced us that low productivity in the port was rooted in the organization of the work rather than in the recruitment of the workers. It took hard bargaining to extend the terms of our research to the operational zones of the harbour.

The focus of much grey material is on 'problems' and this in itself leads to some predictable silences, even without political censorship. Neither space nor time is sufficient to locate the problems within their relevant historical and social context. These contexts are often assumed to be understood by both researchers and readers, sometimes, as Ferguson (1990) points out, most inappropriately so. The immediate political context that made certain points fundamental may no longer exist, and thus make the concerns of a particular report unintelligible or even trivial to the reader. For example, in reports produced by the research centre on co-operatization in Mozambique, we included what may now seem to be disproportionate detail on the ownership and cultivation of cashew trees. This was because forced resettlement in communal villages was still an option preferred by some within the ruling party. We wanted to make it clear why disputes around ownership of cashew trees had become a symptomatic focus of opposition to resettlement.

The politics of the policy process leads to a dichotomy in the types of grey material it produces: (a) reports with a national focus, of the sort that ministries and large international agencies tend to commission; and (b) project reports, commissioned by NGOs wanting to know how their money was spent, often focused on a particular community or region and concerned with issues such as the competence of individual project staff. The critical analytical space in between these two types of reports – the links between macro or sectoral policies conceived at a national level and their disparate effects at local and regional levels – is rarely covered in grey material.

Finally, the unequal power relations that dominate the policy process in turn dominate the production of grey materials. The voices of the poor, the oppressed, and the exploited are under-represented in grey material, and the voices of the powerful echo loudly. In their review of studies of malnutrition in India, for example, Kumar and Stewart (1992, p. 278) observed that the discussion on targeting has tended to focus exclusively on leakage of benefits beyond the target group, ignoring failure to reach all in the targeted group. They note that narrowly targeted interventions often show apparently favourable cost–benefit ratios, of great importance to officials, but this does not tell us the costs incurred by leaving out groups in need of nutritional supplementation. The voices of the latter group are not so easily heard as those of officials concerned with showing the efficiency of their work.

To respond to this problem, many policy studies on poverty now include material drawn from participatory poverty assessments, as mentioned in Chapter 8. The research agenda, decisions about what material should be included in the report, the interpretation of the voices and the drawing of policy conclusions still depend, however, on the authors and sponsors of these studies. Take, for example, Narayan-Parker's (1997) study in Tanzania. The report chooses some of the many things village focus groups said:

> In Arusha and Kilimanjaro regions the poor said: 'We have land but nothing to work it with. All I have is a small hoe. You have to bend your back to work with a small hoe and after two hours you are tired.' 'The land is exhausted from overcultivation. Ten years ago, I got eight bags per acre; today I get two bags.' 'I cannot afford fertilizer or hybrid seeds, and I do not qualify for credit. Without fertilizer, the land does not produce even enough to feed the family' (Narayan-Parker, 1997, p. 10).

In drawing out the policy implications of such statements, the report concludes that 'The poor do not advocate a return to government subsidies. However, they cannot afford to buy farming inputs at current prices without access to credit and other non-farm income-earning opportunities' (Narayan-Parker, 1997, pp. 16–17). Actually there is nothing in the report that shows that the poor would rather have credit than subsidized inputs. Only two percent of village groups mentioned lack of credit as a cause of poverty though 17 percent mentioned lack of farm inputs and implements (Narayan-Parker, 1997, p. 16). Under the neo-liberal regimes of the 1990s credit was an acceptable policy option whereas subsidies were not.

The dominance of the discourse of international consultancy in grey materials on development issues reflects unequal power relations between countries that are the focus of development studies and the countries that commission such studies. Problems of reliability that arise in the politics of the policy-making process are exacerbated by the prevalence of short-term consultants who must couch their reports in funders' fancies. In discussing possible research on the consequences of sharp cutbacks in the recruitment of Mozambican miners in South Africa with a staff member of the United Nations Development Programme (UNDP), researchers from the Centre for African Studies tried to explain that the principal problem was not unemployed miners, but rather the young rural unemployed men in Mozambique who needed wage-income but had never been employed in the mines. The staff member from UNDP understood the point, but explained that unemployed miners were a 'sexy' issue, whereas rural unemployment was not.

Short-term international consultants are prone to characteristic defects in research practice; the quick and dirty methods described by Chambers (1980), which this book is designed to counter. They rely for background information on previous consultancy reports, often furnished by the commissioning agency, so that the same stereotypes are passed on from one report to another, acquiring the appearance of truth, the well-known fact, with each telling. They tend to concentrate their attention on centres of power, speaking with those who can rapidly mobilize facts and information: ministry officials, embassy desk officers, technical staff of international agencies. While we can learn from the best of such consultants (see Chapter 3), they all too often play the role of the 19th century sociologist Georg Simmel's stranger – the outsider brought in to hear contradictory and conflicting accounts, order them, and present back to the people in power what they themselves said in a more orderly and acceptable way. Such consultants may also try to find sources of hard quantitative data which will give an appearance of substance to their reports, although the methodologies used to collect these data are often illusively presented. The methodological basis of qualitative information is typically even less rigorous. Short-term consultants tend to rely on gossip and anecdotes acquired in the corridors of the capitol and in semi-social encounters with other international personnel.

6.2 Why use this material at all? • • •

If there are so many problems of interpretation in institutional discourses, why would we want to use grey material for finding out fast? Why not just put it aside and look exclusively at measured and critical academic research on our topic?

The most important reason for finding and interpreting grey material is that it is itself an important part of the world that we are studying. It tells us the ways in which important institutions in the politics of development, such as the World Bank, UNICEF, COSATU (the South African trade union federation), and national governments view problems and solutions in the domain we are studying. When Ferguson (Ferguson, 1990, p. 66) noted that World Bank research on Lesotho erroneously presented it as a nation of farmers not wage-workers, he showed both why the Bank policy favoured smallholder agricultural development to alleviate rural poverty in southern Africa and why the policy wasn't working. Similarly, a 1989 poverty study on Mozambique argued that 'the prospects for off-farm employment in Mozambique as in much of Africa have never been very bright' (World Bank, 1989, p. 102). This was in line with the policy consensus of the moment that saw promoting the development of smallholder marketing as the key to poverty alleviation in Africa. As long as we remember that what we learn from such studies is not the truth but the representation of particular points of view, they can be ideal key informants in the sense used by Chambers (1980): knowledgeable, interested, anxious to inform – and open to interpretation.

Analyzing such reports as part of a political process clarifies the context of policy formulation. This in turn helps us to think about how we want to write up or present in our own study. We can sound out the audience and determine what is likely to be assumed, what is likely to be contested and what is politically acceptable to different institutional actors in the policy context within which we are working. When South Africa was debating restructuring the mining industry in the 1990s, for example, all policy actors agreed that raising productivity was important. But, whereas reports done for the mine workers union, the NUM, emphasized greater stability and equality of employment as ways of improving labour productivity, research published by the Chamber of Mines, the owners' cartel, saw high labour costs as the principal problem of the industry. Knowing both positions would help us to read the African National Congress (ANC) government's Green Paper on restructuring and to locate its strengths and silences.

Grey materials can also be a source of information about the topic we are studying that academic literature may not yet be able to provide. Consultants often have access to recent statistical information, registered either by governments or by the agencies for which they work, which is not in the public domain. Their interventions must be timely, thus reports are finished much more rapidly than are academic studies. Consultants may also work in situations where conventional academic research is difficult or unauthorized. For many years, for example, information on Mozambican refugees came mainly through people working with agencies involved in refugee work.

Finally, there is a high moral and political cost to be paid for repeated research on the same topic and in the same areas, particularly when this involves surveys, even though we may be able to detect many methodological and conceptual problems in previous studies. Research is always an approximation, never a reproduction of reality. Critically reading, cross-checking, and recasting a series of fragmented, incomplete or even biased reports on our topic can contribute to giving us a reasonable understanding of the policy area we are studying.

6.3 Where to begin? Not with grey material • • •

How then do we undertake this critical reading? As Barrientos (Chapter 5) observes, the way we read and take notes depends on the phase of our research. Initially, to find the topic, or to develop alternative approaches to the topic we have been assigned, we survey the literature. The literature survey makes it possible both to define the topic more clearly and to identify material which is worth reading closely and analytically in the literature study. In both survey and study phases, grey material is not the place to begin. Just as we would never try to conduct a key interview without first having thought carefully about the topic and identified the social and political position of the person we are going to interview, we must also prepare ourselves before reading grey material. General historical information about the place we are studying and similar studies from other areas sharpen our awareness of alternative theoretical and political approaches to the topic under investigation.

It is easier to spot assumptions and incomplete arguments if we already know something about the history, geography, and political economy of the region under study. It was easy for Ferguson (1990) to recognize the absurdity in the Lesotho *Country Economic Report* (World Bank, 1975) of characterizing the peasantry as traditional subsistence cultivators, because he had read work such as Murray (1981) that traced the consequences of a long history of labour migration and the decline of marketed peasant production.

Reading key sources on the issues and areas under study also makes it possible to recognize and evaluate the original sources of hand-me-down data. In Mozambique, Wuyts (1981) used data from colonial agricultural censuses to estimate regional differences in the proportion of peasant production that was marketed, thus making it possible to estimate total peasant production. Ten years later, these estimated proportions had become facts, and were used to estimate the impact of structural adjustment on peasant production. Total peasant production was inferred from registered marketed surpluses, producing a remarkable increase in estimated GDP. If one has read the original work by Wuyts and is also broadly familiar with the history and political economy of Mozambique, one doubts that estimates based on conditions of production and marketing in the 1960s could be carried over to the late 1980s in the midst of a destructive war and after prolonged scarcity of consumer goods in rural markets.

6.4 Identifying grey material for interpretive analysis • • •

Chapter 5 shows you how to approach the literature in different ways in different phases of your research. In the literature survey you are still defining your topic and locating the directions of future study. In the literature study you are developing your own argument. Since grey material is just a sub-set of the literature in policy-oriented research (though a particularly important and distinctive kind), you should approach it in the same way. However, I will distinguish between two ways of reading – the structured skim, and a more thorough analytical and interpretive reading. The former is particularly useful in the literature survey whereas literature study demands the latter. The deeper interpretive reading always depends, however, on the structured skim having first identified what is useful for study.

6.4.1 Finding possibly useful grey material

The first problem to be solved in identifying grey material for finding out fast is obtaining access to it. The second is separating the wheat from the chaff. The advent of the internet has simplified the first task but made the latter much more taxing. Many development actors, from the World Bank, to SIDA to national AIDS councils or local NGOs post 'publications' (usually grey material) on their websites. None the less, it is still very difficult to obtain many current research reports, particularly if findings or topics are controversial. Some consultancy firms do not distribute their reports widely, as these are the only product they have to sell. Government officials continue to be suspicious of researchers and reluctant to share previous reports, particularly those that are critical of government.

Finding out that an important report exists is usually the first step to obtaining access. Locally based researchers often know about useful grey material. Some grey materials are covered by bibliographic data bases. ELDIS (http://www.eldis.org) and the British Library for Development Studies (http://blds.ids.ac.uk/blds/) cover grey material related to development issues, much of it directly downloadable. The local World Bank offices and NGOs keep copies of reports they have commissioned and often have access to government reports that are not in the public domain. Copies of consultancy reports can sometimes be obtained from their clients, particularly the development-oriented NGOs. The United Nations Development Programme (UNDP), United States Agency for International Development (USAID) and central planning ministries generally have documentation centres for the use of their employees and consultants. Specialized government agencies are sometimes willing to allow researchers access to material in retired archives, though reluctant to release current studies for research they do not control.

6.4.2 Sorting the wheat from the chaff: the structured skim reading

After obtaining access to grey material, the second major problem is deciding what is really useful and well worth reading in our literature study and putting aside the rest, much of which is weighty but useless. The abstracting services provide good help for deciding whether a report is worth looking for, but they are not usually a sufficiently reliable guide to their content. A structured skim reading helps us sort out the material we have accumulated. It is particularly important for grey material, because sometimes it turns out to be our only reading – we may not have another opportunity to look at a report. Government or agency officials may allow you to look at reports but not to take them out of the office or perhaps not even to photocopy them. On a return visit a report may no longer be available to you, or even its existence recognized. Thus the steps summarized in Box 6.1 and expanded below are useful in carrying out an effective structured skim reading.

> ## Box 6.1   The structured skim reading: 7 steps
>
> Step 1   *Register the complete reference.* You may not gain access to the material again.
> Step 2   *Note and identify the source.*
> Step 3   *Study the title page.* Note down the title, date of publication, institutions, etc. All this information helps to locate the political, social and institutional context of the report.
> Step 4   *The executive summary.* This is good for reconstructing policy discourses and debates on the issues, but may not reflect the body of the report.
> Step 5   *Skimming the substance.* Differences between the body of the report and executive summary indicate areas of controversy and negotiation.
> Step 6   *Survey the quantitative data.* For all useful data note the source, years, types of data and method of data aggregation. Copy any useful primary data – it may be your only chance to do so.
> Step 7   *Review the bibliography.* This may provide useful references or give an indication of the depth of the research.
> Step 8   *Note taking.* Make notes about the report itself, about any useful information, and of any points you think are important to verify or deepen in further reading.

Step 1 Register the complete reference

The first look at possibly useful material should be done with pen (or pencil or computer) at hand. For anything that is even remotely relevant to your study, note the complete reference. Much grey material is not catalogued by library systems and has limited or restricted circulation.

If you don't record the complete reference now, including the URL if they are web-based, there may never be another chance. Reports that seem useless in one phase of your research may become important later on, and you have to know the titles and authors to find them again. Further, grey material often circulates in different drafts, with wording and even conclusions under debate. Documents that were downloadable from a website suddenly disappear. Note carefully the date of the particular draft in hand. Even if you discard a report, it is useful to note the complete reference and to add a note as to why it is not useful, particularly if, like mine, your memory sometimes fails. When a title sounds particularly relevant to my study, I am more likely to forget that I have already chased down a reference and found it unhelpful. This can be time-consuming and embarrassing, especially if you must formally request authorization or have hounded a ministry official to see a particular report.

Step 2 Note and identify the source

Include a short note on where you found the report. This may be a person – someone working in a ministry or NGO – but increasingly it is a website. If the material proves to be useful, you may want to go back to check on the reliability of the source or to see if you can get other good documents there.

Step 3 Study the title page

The next step is a close look at the title page. Consultancy reports are not sold commercially, and so they don't depend on catchy titles. The title is often a long and accurate guide to their content, as for example: *State Farm Divestiture in Mozambique: property disputes and issues affecting new land access policy – the case of Chokwe, Gaza Province.* Key words in titles sometimes indicate the institutional discourse in which they are rooted. Following the study by Cornia *et al.* (1987) *Adjustment with a Human Face* (which criticized some of the dimensions of structural adjustment programmes) for example, a rash of reports with 'human face' in the title appeared, generally concerned with alleviating poverty and minimizing the decline of social services under structural adjustment programmes.

The title page often bears the names of the agencies who commissioned the research, and sometimes an indication of their relative importance to those who wrote the report. The report on state farm divestiture mentioned above, for example, was carried out by researchers from the University of Mozambique, Land Tenure Centre for USAID, and the Government of the Republic of Mozambique, Ministry of Agriculture, listed in that order on the title page. If, on further reading, the report proves interesting, you might want to investigate whether there were points of dissension between the two agencies, whether these were suppressed in the final report, and whether the viewpoint of the prime financing agency dominates the report. Reports are often parts of a series, so noted on the title page.

The date of publication can be an important indicator of whether or not the report will be useful for a particular study. Mozambique's structural adjustment programme was introduced at the beginning of 1987. A national household income and expenditure study, based on surveys carried out in 1981, was published in 1984. Although this study may help us to understand change (since subsequent household surveys, using similar methodology, were carried out in 1994 and 2004), we cannot use the 1981 data to establish rural/urban income and expenditure gaps for a study of the immediate consequences of structural adjustment for urban poverty.

Step 4 The executive summary

After inspecting the title page, move on to the body of the report. One of the particularities of grey material is that most consultancy reports prepared for international agencies have an executive summary on the main findings and arguments of the report. The prevalence of the executive summary is based on the realistic assumption that many of the policy makers for agencies that commission consultancy studies will not have the time, interest or technical background necessary for reading the entire report. The executive summary is thus a particularly good source for reconstructing policy discourses and current debates on the issues we are researching.

The executive summary may not be, however, a very good guide to the actual content of the report or a summary of its findings (see Chapter 3 for some reasons why this may have been done deliberately). Assumptions easily become conclusions when the evidence and argument to support them is compressed in a summary. An executive summary may conclude, for example, that in the country under study poverty is principally a rural phenomenon. We cannot understand the meaning of this statement without reading the body of the report. It could mean only that most of the population live in rural areas and hence that most of the poor also live there, i.e. not a very interesting finding. Or it could mean that a higher proportion of people in rural areas fall below the poverty line than do those in urban areas. In this case we need to know how poverty lines were defined in rural and urban areas. Or, if we are dealing with a migrant labour system, the body of the report may show that rural incomes are dependent on remittances from urban areas and hence that the conclusion that poverty is principally a rural phenomenon is deceptive. Thus, we use our background reading to note questions and issues raised by the executive summary that should be carefully examined in the body of the report.

Step 5 Skimming the substance

Given that the executive summary can be a polemical document with a message different from that of the body of the report, your skim reading should not stop with it. A quick look at the table of contents (or skimming through chapter sub-headings in the body of the report if there is no table of contents) may reveal that there is information not covered at all in the executive summary. Introductions and conclusions to chapters sometimes phrase policy issues and summarize findings in language different from that of the executive summary. Differences may give us indications of areas of controversy and negotiation.

Step 6 Survey the quantitative data

In your first structured skim of a report, check the list of tables, figures, and appendices, to see whether the report is likely to have quantitative data which will be useful in your study. If you see that there are data that are definitely useful, it is worthwhile to note the source, years, types of data and the way the data are aggregated. If the source is primary, you may not be able to find the data elsewhere. If the data come from a secondary published source, it is more reliable to obtain them from that source. If you have access to a photocopier, you can copy relevant tables, but often you must transcribe the data yourself, an arduous procedure.

Some reports include lots of graphs, but not the source data. Note whether quantitative data are included in tables and appendices within the report. If there are only graphs, we can reproduce or interpret them in our own report, but we cannot verify the data nor analyze them in different ways. Authors of grey material use graphs because their readers can understand images quickly, but do not have the time or capacity to see patterns in quantitative data. Sometimes, however, motives are not didactic. The data may come from restricted sources and cannot be reproduced, or authors may know that in quality terms the data are not very reliable and should not be reproduced. And sometimes consultants withhold quantitative data because they consider them their intellectual property, to be used in future publications.

Step 7 Review the bibliography

Even in a quick skim of a report, it is useful to look at its bibliography. In our initial phases of research, it may provide references that we can follow up. Later on, when we ourselves know more about the topic, it may help us to determine whether the report was itself based on a good mastery of existing studies. If, for example, in reports on Benin or Mozambique, most references are in English, we can infer that the researchers did not speak French or Portuguese, the respective official languages, and thus that their understanding of local issues may be superficial.

Step 8 Note taking

After this first structured skim reading, you should know whether a report is useful and should be put aside (or photocopied) to be read again more carefully. At this point, stop to take three different kinds of notes.

1   Notes about the report itself. Thus, the fact that a poverty study on Mozambique sponsored by the World Bank observed that prospects for off-farm employment have never been very bright is important information in itself, whether or not we think that observation is correct. To determine whether the evidence of the report supports the conclusion, we have to dig into the report.
2   Scraps of relevant useful information that we have noted in passing, quite often quantitative data, in a report that will not merit further close study. A detailed study of a women's micro-credit group, carried out for an NGO that sponsored the scheme, may, for example, contain data on overall credit coverage in the region. For both these first two types of notes exact citation and complete references to page numbers are important.
3   Perhaps most important in interpreting institutional discourses, are the preliminary notes to ourselves about points we think are important to verify or deepen in further reading. These notes reflect what we bring with us to our reading – our theoretical baggage and what we have already learned about our topic and the area under study.

6.5   Locating the report institutionally • • •

To interpret institutional discourses, we have to locate a report institutionally. This means placing it in its political and historical context, establishing the institutional identities of its source, authors and audience, and attending to the objectives and scope of the study as defined by its terms of reference and the ways in which research was carried out.

Before beginning the substantive reading of the report, try to recreate the context in which the research was carried out and the report written. The date should serve as an indicator if we have already constructed a rough chronology of the recent history of the place we are studying in our minds, and reviewed recent policy debates around the topic under research. In development discourse around the position of women in African agriculture, for example, it was commonly assumed until the 1980s, following Boserup's (1970) work, that women were subsistence producers. In the late 1980s, following work by Mackintosh (1989) and others, the importance of women's work in cash-cropping, even though men often controlled the cash, began to be recognized. If we are looking at a report on rural poverty in Africa, we can check to see whether the researchers simply assumed the subsistence role of women or actually looked at intra-household organization of both labour and income.

Similarly, political issues can shape the language of the report, its silences as well as its focus. In Mozambique, for example, a gradual collectivization of agricultural production was official policy for many years. At the research centre where I worked at that time we argued that voluntary co-operatization would depend on the improvement in marketing position provided for the broad mass of peasants. Research reports written later under structural adjustment take the need to improve the marketing position of family farmers as a given fact and devote little attention to co-operatization. Today the focus is on 'smallholder associations' – but many of their activities are the same as those organized through co-operatives.

Gaps between the dates of publication of different versions of reports and policy documents are often good indicators of political controversy and hence contested drafts. Identifying differences between the Interim Poverty Reduction Strategy Paper and the full version accepted by the World Bank and IMF as the basis for Highly Indebted Poor Countries (HIPC) funding may point to areas of disagreement between national governments, the Bank and the Fund. Locally based researchers often know about the existence of such controversies and are thus able to reconstruct the political context of a final report by locating omissions from it.

If we have learned (from the title page or terms of reference) that the report is part of a particular series, we then think about where it fits and how that may affect its language and concerns. In the first round of poverty studies emerging from the critique of structural adjustment in Africa, for example, almost all reports took care to propose how well-defined and restricted groups should be targeted for special assistance. Hence, there was a great deal of attention to the issue of whether or not it would be possible to identify and subsidize a staple (generally one in glut on world food markets), which the poor and only the poor eat – such as sorghum or yellow maize. A later World Bank report on structural adjustment in Africa concluded that poverty was so widespread that tightly targeted measures probably would not satisfactorily reach the poor (World Bank, 1994). Today food markets in most African countries have been liberalized and privatized. The World Bank's PRSP Sourcebook (World Bank, 2002) now recommends that 'They [governments] can mitigate the effects of low income on health outcomes by reducing the price poor people pay for health and other key goods and services, through, for example, health insurance, fee-waivers, and targeted food subsidies' (p. 203). Interpreting what particular country studies say about targeting means locating them within the shifting terms of this debate.

The questions and conclusions of a particular report reflect the political context within which they were written. Some of the most extensive work on poverty in Southern Africa was done in the series of Carnegie studies on poverty in South Africa co-ordinated by SALDRU, a research centre located at the University of Cape Town. In the early 1980s, these reports were written by researchers opposed to the apartheid regime, but their language reflects the context of political repression in which they were written and their recommendations show that few thought that by the end of the decade the regime would be politically ruined. Similarly, research on agrarian issues at the Centre for African Studies in the first decade of Mozambican independence was focused on the importance of understanding peasant production within an overall strategy of socializing production. In both cases the information contained in the reports continues to have relevance today, but some of their immediate concerns now seem anachronistic and limited.

6.5.1 The institutional identity of the source

Organizations differ in the kinds of studies they consider worth circulating, and that applies to the information they post for download on their websites as well. Both the World Bank and Oxfam, for example, post research reports on land policies in Africa on their websites. Though there is some overlap between them, Oxfam focuses on land rights for the poor. We would not expect to find comparative studies of agricultural productivity under different forms of tenure there as we would on the World Bank site. Though the World Bank has become much more interdisciplinary in some of its research, economists still predominate in the papers posted on its site.

What about organizations that are not so familiar to us as the World Bank or Oxfam? How can they be placed institutionally? Let's take, for example, The Corner House (www.thecornerhouse.ac.uk). We can see from its URL that it qualifies as an academic site, but what areas does it cover? Like many sites, it provides an 'About us' section:

> Since its founding in 1997, The Corner House has aimed to support democratic and community movements for environmental and social justice. It is motivated by the concerns of such movements, whether they be locally-based struggles for land or water rights or better health care; campaigns against destructive mining, dam or forestry projects; or struggles against racial discrimination. We aim to pay constant attention to issues of social, economic and political power and practical strategy. We try to take a 'bottom-up' approach, filled with examples, to issues of global significance which are often handled in a more abstract way. As part of our solidarity

work, The Corner House carries out analyses, research and advocacy with the aim of linking issues, of stimulating informed discussion and strategic thought on critical environmental and social concerns, and of encouraging broad alliances to tackle them.

Here terms such as 'social justice', 'locally-based struggles', and 'solidarity' indicate that this is probably a left-wing site. We would expect its postings to overlap with some of those on the Oxfam site, but very little with the World Bank. Many websites provide the names of staff or of a board of directors. Searching on their names can give us further information about the orientation of the site. In the case of the Corner House, for example, staff publications indicate that they have particular competence on environmental issues, a fact confirmed by a rapid review of the titles of publications. The list of funders also gives some idea of what kinds of positions are likely to be advocated by a particular source. It is always risky of course to rely only on what people say about themselves, so it is also useful to return to the net to see what other sources are saying about the organization, its staff and its funders.

6.5.2 The institutional identity of the researchers

To interpret the report, we have to think about the institutional identity of the authors. Are they employees of the agency that commissioned the research or are they specialized researchers or academics contracted especially for this research? Are they locally based researchers or were they part of an internationally recruited short-term consultancy team? If the authors are named, what do we know about their disciplinary background and their previous research experience?

The name of Harold Alderman, for example, appears on several studies done on poverty and food-security related issues under structural adjustment in Mozambique. A quick internet search can tell us a lot about his probable research orientation. He has done previous work for the World Bank and for the International Food Policy Research Institute (IFPRI) and was affiliated with Cornell University when he did the studies in Mozambique. He did research on food issues in Pakistan and now works in various African countries. He is a neo-classical economist whose work is generally concerned with making markets work better. The solutions he recommends, such as the introduction of food stamps, are marked by the institutional world of the United States; they would not be envisioned by Mozambican academics (unless trained in the United States), nor even perhaps by consultants from the Institute of Development Studies (IDS) in Sussex. His work tends to differ in its language from that of consultants from the Wisconsin Land Tenure Centre (LTC), another university-based applied research centre in the United States, which also worked in Mozambique. LTC researchers were of course more specifically concerned with agriculture, they had varied disciplinary backgrounds in the social sciences, and they tended to be more critical of strategies of market liberalization than do those from Cornell.

A close study of the bibliography can help us locate the institutional identity of the authors – telling us something about both what sources were consulted and which sources were thought important to record. Work undertaken in the framework of Social Dimensions of Adjustment (SDA) more often referred to the work of anthropologists and sociologists than did previous World Bank studies – although arguments need not have changed. The critique by Ferguson (1990) of the 1975 World Bank *Country Economic Report* on Lesotho appears in the bibliography of a much later World Bank poverty assessment of Lesotho, even though its conclusions bear a much stronger resemblance to those of the 1975 report than to Ferguson. Since we approach grey literature already armed with a good control of the field, we can also note significant gaps or silences in sources. Reports done by the Centre for African Studies on agrarian structure in Mozambique are rarely cited in consultancy studies done under the aegis of the World Bank, in part because this work is associated with Frelimo's discredited socialist period.

6.5.2 Identity of those who paid for the study and their interests

Attending to how a study was funded helps to identify the audience the report was intended to reach and thus to interpret its findings and its silences. At one extreme are confidential reports commissioned by a specific agency that controls the choice of researcher and terms of reference of the study and has right of veto over acceptance of its results. In the research centre in Mozambique, by contrast, our salaries were paid by the university, and our research funded mainly by long-term grants from the Nordic countries. Although we responded to research requests from government agencies and always required authorization from both national and provincial authorities to carry out research, we did not have to submit drafts to government agencies before publication. This did not mean however that there was no self-censorship. We were careful to weigh what was said against probable reactions; we did not want to be excluded from key national debates on agrarian strategy. We saw our audience, however, as much larger than a particular government agency; we tried (not always successfully) to write in a style that would be accessible to most educated Mozambicans and to produce reports that would introduce information about Mozambique into university teaching.

6.5.3 Institutional constraints in carrying out research

We can often tell a lot about the limitations of a study by analyzing the terms of reference and what is said about when and how the research was carried out. There are usually references to the locations that the research team visited and a list of people who were interviewed. Even expressions of thanks may give us information about the scope and limits of the research.

Sometimes the terms of reference of a study will show us that there is a link between a study and an ongoing project. This tends to affect the conclusions of a report and sometimes even the questions it asks, particularly if those who have commissioned or execute the research are also responsible for the execution of the project itself. Schubert's (1993) evaluation of a cash-transfer scheme for the alleviation of urban poverty in Mozambique, for example, has to be read with care since he was involved with the conceptualization and earlier evaluations of the scheme.

Some actors have much more institutional presence than others in grey material, a fact which may already be clear from the terms of reference and sources of a study. Reports on international migration policy in Southern Africa, for example, tend to deal with the situation of documented workers, such as miners, whose movement back and forth from South Africa is registered. Solid quantitative data on formal migration can be obtained from the Chamber of Mines and from the governments of labour-supplying countries. Undocumented migration, which for countries in the region exceeds legal migration, is notoriously difficult to research and hence its extent is not reliably estimated in most reports. Looking at the terms of reference and sources consulted in research will tell us quickly whether or not the report has attempted to grapple seriously with the issue of undocumented migrants. The institutional presence of research projects varies with the consistency of their funding. The Canadian-based Southern Africa Migration Project (SAMP), for example, continues to make reports and briefings on undocumented migration available on its website, but most of its research was done when migration reform was a more openly debated topic in South Africa.

Locating where the research was carried out helps us to determine whether its findings are generalizable at a regional or national level. Reading a study on peasant marketing in a war-torn country like Mozambique with a good map in front of us, for example, we try to reconstruct the experiences of those rural communities studied during the war. Areas visited by consultants tended to be close to urban areas or to complexes with military protection; they did not visit regions where they could not be protected from attack by Renamo, the armed opposition movement.

6.6 Interpreting institutional discourses in construction of argument ● ● ●

Grey material can be a privileged direct source of information about the ways in which policy issues are posed in our area of study – a good informant – persuasive, sometimes deceptive, with fixed ideas not always revealed. Hence, when we have identified grey material useful for our literature study and located it institutionally, we approach it in the same critically constructive way outlined by Barrientos in Chapter 5. Here, then, we will look at some specific issues in the interpretation of grey material in the construction of our own arguments. Box 6.2 summarizes problems in the interpretation of grey material that we have discussed in this chapter and what we do about each in the process of our literature study (steps 1 to 6).

Box 6.2 Overview of interpretive tasks

Since grey material is predictably limited because of:	Use of this material requires:
• questionable but unstated underlying assumptions	• identifying and rethinking assumptions (step 1)
• the questions it asks	• formulating alternative questions and extending the range of possible answers (step 2)
• a tendency to simplify opposing arguments or alternative answers	• reading both sides of key debates (step 3)
• illusive methodology	• confronting the data: how well they answer old and new questions (step 4)
• the conclusions it finds acceptable	• rethinking conclusions (step 5)
• the audience it intends to reach	• rethinking the audience (step 6)

In the following sections, we will move through each of these steps in interpretation one by one, with examples of each. In reality, however, this process is never a linear set of sequential steps – it is an iterative process. Rethinking the answers helps us to locate and criticize implicit assumptions; alternative interpretations of the data help us to locate methodological weaknesses in the analysis of the data, and so on. As your own argument takes shape, what you find, and reject, in the report will change.

Step 1 Identifying and rethinking assumptions

Background reading in the history and political economy of the place we are studying helps us to uncover and rethink assumptions. We have discussed how Ferguson's (1990) previous reading on Lesotho, for example, led him to challenge the assumption of the World Bank (1975) study that peasants in Lesotho were subsistence peasants weakly integrated in the market.

Background reading on different theoretical approaches to our problem can help us uncover and recast assumptions. Some reports on rural poverty, for example, make general statements about what peasant households or smallholders do. There is an implicit assumption that the interests, attitudes and behaviour of all within the household are reducible to those of the male head of household. Feminist criticism of this assumption has led us to recognize that men and women often have different and contradictory interests within households. Recent studies of households in Africa in particular emphasize that, despite co-operation and male dominance within households, there are domains controlled by women.

Step 2 Formulating alternative questions and extending the range of possible answers

Once we have recast underlying assumptions, we will also find alternative questions. Studies like that of Ferguson have led us to question the presumption in studies of rural poverty in Southern Africa that rural problems have agricultural solutions. In other words, we no longer accept that if poor people live in rural areas the way to improve their incomes is necessarily by improving their farming. Thus we may recast the questions in our study to focus on how to improve off-farm employment and non-agricultural activities in rural areas. Or, if we refuse to assume that the household is a basic unit of analysis, we may choose to ask specifically how gender differences shape or express the experience of poverty. Posing new questions means extending the range of possible answers or working hypotheses that we bring to interpretation of data.

Step 3 Reading both sides of key debates

When the question we are considering is highly contested, it is important to find the strongest arguments for the main positions, even those with which we do not sympathize. In developing an argument it is easy to simplify or even stereotype the arguments with which we do not agree. Most websites provide us with grey material written from a particular point of view. On the Corner House site (www.thecornerhouse.org.uk), for example, you can download a briefing paper, 'Too Many Grannies? Private Pensions, Corporate Welfare and Growing Insecurity', by Richard Minns with Sarah Sexton. According to the introductory blurb on the website, this paper 'summarizes and critiques the main justifications given for expanding private pension schemes, and analyzes the motivations of the groups that perpetuate this model'. The paper is well-argued and informative, but it is clear that the authors are opposed to private pension schemes and we know we can rely on the Corner House to provide briefings that make a robust critique of corporate interests. We should, however, also look directly at the arguments made by advocates of private pensions, not just at critical summaries of their positions.

Step 4 Confronting the data: how well they answer old and new questions

Once we have recast our questions, we can confront the data to see if they provide information on a new set of questions. Quite often, however, when we confront the data to see whether they allow us to answer the questions posed by the report and support its findings, we will also think further about assumptions and questions. This process is discussed by Mukherjee and Wuyts (Chapter 10). Here I will only signal some of the specific things to look for in confronting data presented in grey materials.

First, attend carefully to the original source of the data and return to it if possible.

Most World Bank studies (and many others) depend on the economic data collected and assessed by the country study team. In the country study you will usually find an explanation of how the data were collected, what the limitations were, which figures are based on estimates, etc. – information that tends to disappear in successive reproductions of data.

If you can locate the original source of data, you can check not only whether data have been correctly reproduced, but also if they have been selectively lifted. In interpretation of time series data, for example, the choice of a base year often establishes a direction of interpretation. A report critical of structural adjustment may find, for example, a sharp rise in infant mortality in urban areas in the year after the introduction of a structural adjustment programme. But if we include the ten years prior to introduction of the structural adjustment programme, the data may show a long-term tendency toward rising infant mortality, associated, perhaps, with the breakdown of public health services.

Second, see whether the categories in which data are grouped correspond to the questions that are asked in the report and the answers found. Much grey material is not based on new surveys or independent research – data are found and made to speak. There is nothing wrong with this in itself (indeed, doing it is one of the prerequisites to finding out fast), but it means that we must be particularly careful about verifying interpretations. As the result of feminist criticism of research methods in the social sciences (cf. Eichler, 1988), for example, we are now much more careful about over-generalization and lack of gender and age sensitivity. Take, for example, a study on the consequences of a cash-crop farming scheme for rural incomes based only on interviews with household heads, most of them male. The study may tell us many things, but it cannot tell us about intra-household distribution of income and thus it cannot generalize about the effects of the project on rural poverty.

Third, integrate the qualitative studies you have read into the interpretation of quantitative data, and micro-level studies into the interpretation of macro-level studies. For example, where migration is clandestine, registers of migrants are unreliable sources of data on the extent of migration. Male/female ratios can be an indirect indicator of emigration by men, as long as there is little emigration by women. To relate changes in male/female ratios to contemporary shifts in migration patterns in Southern Africa, we therefore need qualitative information on the legal changes in the 1960s and 1970s that restricted access to women from Lesotho, Botswana and Swaziland to the South African labour market. Case studies and the collection of individual labour histories cannot be aggregated to provide a quantitatively secure picture of the extent or shape of migration, but they can alert us to patterns to probe at a macro-level and provide direct evidence on underlying mechanisms (see Chapter 13).

Conversely, we can integrate quantitative data into the interpretation of qualitative data and macro-level information into the interpretation of micro-level studies. In part because of its policy orientation, there is, often, a tendency towards over-generalization in grey material. Conclusions based on the phrases 'most of' or 'the majority of' cover a range from 50.1% to 99.9%, and are not necessarily based on exclusive categories. Without quantitative data, it is impossible to determine the meaning of such phrases. A report suggesting that the majority of rural households obtain most of their income from agriculture may lead us to under-emphasize the importance of off-farm income for rural households that depend both on farming and non-agricultural work. Processes that may appear general and inevitable at a micro-level may become specific and transient when we locate them within a macro perspective. Sharply falling rural incomes in the 1970s in Mozambique did not neccessarily apply to communities in southern Mozambique relying heavily on remittances from migrant miners in South Africa, whose real wages were rising.

Step 5 Rethinking conclusions

Having located assumptions, recast questions and possible answers, and confronted the data, you should compare the conclusions of a report with those you would draw yourself. There may be conclusions that are simply wrong or misleading, or there may be significant silences. The observation on off-farm employment in the report on poverty in Mozambique discussed above, for example, is not precisely false, if we think that the 'brightness' of employment prospects has to do with the levels and conditions of that employment. It is, however, deeply misleading if it is read to imply that off-farm employment is not central to the economy of many rural households.

In interpreting policy-oriented documents your conclusions about the findings of the document become not only a basis for developing your own arguments, but information about the world you are studying. In the case above, for example, the fact that an important World Bank report on Mozambique generalized about all of sub-Saharan Africa and emphasized the marginality of off-farm employment is itself a finding about an important institutional actor.

Step 6 Rethinking the audience

Sometimes it is easy to identify the audience for which a report was written and to recast its information for a different group. An evaluation report on a particular development project, for example, will attend to the competence of particular project staff. If we are writing a more general assessment on the co-ordination of NGO activity in rural poverty alleviation for the Ministry of Planning, we are not interested in the details of individual competence, but in the recruitment process that underlies general problems in staff competence in NGO projects. We may draw important economic information from a highly technical report on public sector management written for economists at the World Bank and present it in simpler and more accessible ways for public sector trade unions.

Sometimes, however, rethinking the audience means not only identifying the objectives and experience of different actors in the policy process, but also recognizing that institutional discourse itself may have changed. A Mozambican researcher assigned to work with an early World Bank mission on agriculture told me, for example, 'They think that all Mozambican peasants are subsistence cultivators, so I'm going to take them to Manica to see specialized commercial growers'. Later, when the stereotype of the entrepreneurial smallholder had replaced that of the traditional tribesman in the minds of international consultants, it became important to take them to see women-headed households dependent on wages and remittances. Reports that seem anachronistic or limited in their concerns can become relevant when we locate their findings within a different set of issues for an audience with different expectations and experience.

6.7 Conclusion • • •

This chapter has emphasized that grey materials – policy-oriented reports prepared for and by governmental and non-governmental agencies – can be important sources of information. We must treat them as we would other key informants – locating them institutionally, reconstructing the context in which they spoke, analyzing and interpreting both their statements and their silences. This is only possible if we are both informed and reflexive about our own assumptions and concerns in the developing dialogue that we pursue with all our sources – and our own projected audience – in the construction of policy-oriented arguments.

PART III

Thinking with people

People as informants

Philip Woodhouse

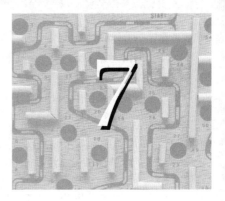

This chapter is concerned with investigative approaches which development managers and policy investigators need when 'finding out' from other people. In it I shall consider two basic issues:

- Why should development managers and policy investigators be particularly interested in using people as a source of information?
- What methods can be used to improve the accuracy and reliability of ideas and information people provide?

I wish to emphasize at the outset that I consider these issues from the standpoint of the investigative development manager; that is, from the perspective of the *initiator* of the investigation – the one who wants to find out. Thus, my concern with accuracy is: does the information people provide tell me what I want to find out? Similarly, my concern with reliability is: can I have confidence that what I have found out will not be contradicted or easily undermined by other, similar investigations? My prime concern is, therefore, with the rigour of investigation where people are the source of information.

It is important to note that this leaves largely for the next chapter a key issue in using people as information sources, that of power. Power relationships are incorporated in all forms of knowledge, even those in documentary form, as discussed in the previous chapter by Bridget O'Laughlin. However, working with people brings out power relations in a very immediate way. Investigators determine what information is being sought and what it will be used for. Informants decide how much information to disclose. Seeking information from people is always, therefore, an interactive process, and the investigator stands to find out more from it if it is also a collaborative process. If informants are to collaborate, should their participation in the investigation extend to shaping the purpose of the investigation, and to deciding what information is considered valid? Some have argued (Chambers, 1994a) that when working with disadvantaged groups (for example, with the rural poor in Africa or India) investigation should always seek to 'empower' those providing the information. That is, development managers' investigation should encourage informants also to 'find out' by prompting them to reflect and analyze their own experience. From this 'participatory' perspective, development managers should be 'convenors, catalysts, and facilitators' (Chambers, 1992, p. 12)

I shall return later to the issues of *rigour* raised by participative enquiry and other techniques used in finding out from people. I wish to emphasize at this point that, for the purposes of this chapter, I shall step back from any such assumptions about the *objectives* of development managers' investigative activity, and simply recognize that these will be determined by the investigator or by those to whom she or he is accountable. There are clearly a number of factors which will operate in shaping these objectives, including the legislative and policy framework, and contractual obligations, within which the development manager works, and the political values which she or he holds – for example, in relation to environmental conservation or the living standards of disadvantaged social groups. One consequence of stepping back from making assumptions about the purpose of investigation is recognition that the investigator's purpose is not necessarily shared by all those from whom information is to be sought. Thus, while not excluding the possibility that a development manager's goal is to empower people who act as informants, my discussion in this chapter does not assume that this is always the case.

The chapter is organized in the following way. Section 7.1 examines why development managers should particularly want to turn to people as sources of information. Section 7.2 looks at ways of dealing with difference and diversity in the information people provide, contrasting the two major approaches of structured survey and semi-structured interview. Section 7.3 discusses rigour with respect to these two contrasting approaches. Section 7.4 explores ways of improving communication between investigators and informants. Section 7.5 considers issues of accuracy and reliability raised by participatory enquiry, with particular attention to methodologies now referred to as 'Participatory Learning and Action' (PLA), and their application in 'Participatory Poverty Assessments'.

7.1 Why find out from people? • • •

It may seem obvious that development managers need to consult people whom their decisions affect, but it is worth reflecting briefly that people know things that development managers would be unable to find out from any other source. Two types of information of this kind can be identified.

Firstly, development managers may wish to seek *knowledge* not available elsewhere. Examples of this might be oral histories of rural communities, details of the rules governing customary land tenure, or indigenous technical knowledge relating to the use of plant and animal species.

Secondly, development managers may need to know the *perceptions* of individuals or social groups in their capacity as 'stakeholders', such as users of services or resources, or participants in particular events or processes, and how these perceptions or experiences are manifest in particular patterns of decision-making.

Some issues that development managers may need to investigate may be a mixture of both. For example, farmers' views on agricultural topics may be sought, both because farmers have technical insights into the behaviour of plants, animals and soils, and also because farmers' perceptions of their priorities may dominate the way these resources are used. Or the staff of a development agency may know the inside story of how the agency works and also have preferences with respect to its various stated development aims.

It is worth noting here how this emphasis differs slightly from that of Joseph Hanlon's account in Chapter 3 of a journalist's approach to 'finding out'. Both use people as sources of information but, whereas Hanlon's journalist seeks 'those who know', my concern is also with the knowledge and perceptions of all those who have some interest in, or are affected by, the issue being investigated. In many cases this means finding out about the people concerned themselves, as a group. In other words, I am concerned with ways of finding out not only with those who fund, plan, design and implement an irrigation scheme, say, but also with all whose livelihoods are affected by the scheme. I identify 'who is important' to the enquiry not *only* by 'what they know' but also by 'who and where they are' – that is, their position in a particular social situation. Having made this distinction, I must hasten to add that I am only distinguishing between the emphases in the two chapters. I am *not* making a distinction between journalists and other types of investigators: each will seek informants according to the purpose of the investigation. The approach taken in this chapter should reinforce the point that, for development managers, understanding the perceptions of 'non-experts' may be as important as understanding those of 'experts'.

Setting out in these terms the need to find out through talking to people reminds us of the 'subjectivity' of information which people provide. It can be argued that all knowledge is subjective. That is, what we know is shaped by how we know it, as illustrated by Blackmore and Ison's images of a 'grassland system' through the eyes of agronomist, ecologist, sociologist and animal scientist in Chapter 2. This subjectivity is even more strongly apparent when knowledge is generated from an encounter between 'investigator' and 'respondent'. An agronomist asking a farmer about farming problems, for example, will obtain an understanding which is the product not only of two (possibly quite different) perceptions of farming activity, but also of the efficiency of communication between them. Here, again as noted by Blackmore and Ison, 'message sent' is not the same as 'message received'. Section 7.4 explores techniques for improving the efficiency of communication between investigators and their informants.

For those investigating development issues by using 'people as informants', an important consequence of the subjective nature of information is that informants' views will tend to be diverse and possibly contradictory, reflecting differences in what individuals know and also how that knowledge affects their interests. During the course of an enquiry, development managers are likely to accumulate a large amount of information, much of it from quite divergent standpoints. A key question in investigative approaches which involve seeking information from people is, therefore, that of how to manage the diversity of views which will be generated: how to reduce the data to an amount that can be understood.

7.2 Dealing with diversity: structured survey and semi-structured interview ● ● ●

This section will look at strategies for dealing with the diversity of response that inevitably confronts an enquiry seeking people's views. It is organized under four main headings:

- defining the population;
- deciding who to speak to;
- formulating questions to ask;
- analyzing the response.

7.2.1 Defining the population

By 'defining the population' I mean identifying the boundary from within which the investigators will select people to take part in their enquiry. Where this boundary is drawn will depend primarily on the purpose of the enquiry. As I observed above, this may involve decisions about the relative importance of 'expert' and 'lay' views. Is the investigation concerned, for example, with the whole range of interests and opinions in a given geographical area, or is its purpose to investigate the views of a particular social group (e.g. women, landless households, charcoal-makers), perhaps one whose interests are felt to have been underrepresented in decision-making? Is it sufficient, like Hanlon's journalist, to find out second-hand from 'those who know', or is it necessary to find out directly about a particular group or population?

Drawing this boundary may require some preliminary investigation in order to find out who should be involved in the enquiry. In a study in Mali (Woodhouse *et al.*,

2000), for example, the objective was to interview a sample of rice cultivators in order to understand the impact of rice-growing – a new activity in the area – on their live-lihoods and on land tenure. Initially, it was assumed that all the cultivators would be living locally. However, preliminary enquiry revealed that some cultivators were seasonal migrants from distant villages. The boundary of the enquiry therefore needed to be extended from the immediate vicinity of the rice fields to include these distant villages.

7.2.2 Deciding who to speak to

Investigators select their informants according to the type of information they are seeking, which, once again, is determined by the purpose of the enquiry. There are two principal, quite distinct, approaches which may be followed. The first of these is that of a *sample survey*, the second is that of *focused interviews*. The decision as to which approach to use depends on what kind of information is sought. It is quite pos-sible that both approaches could be useful in a single enquiry, but it is important to be aware of the strengths, weaknesses, and very different criteria for establishing rigour, in each approach. The main characteristics of the two approaches are set out later in Table 7.2.

The point of a *sample survey* is to generate a description of a wider population with-out actually talking to every individual in the population. It is important to note that the objective here is mainly *descriptive*, providing answers to 'What?' questions (e.g. number of households owning livestock or cultivating more than one hectare of land, number of households with off-farm income, percentage of a workforce satisfied with their jobs, etc.), and that the emphasis is generally on *quantitative* aspects, although some qualitative data can also be obtained. Sample surveys can be useful in contexts where information is needed on populations with large numbers of people, or where comparative data are needed.

In order to describe the wider population, the sample of informants for a structured survey is selected, on *probability* criteria, to be representative of the population (see Box 7.1). Probability sampling requires a 'sampling frame': that is, a means of identi-fying all the elements of the population so that they can be included in the sampling procedure. In the simplest version, they all have an equal probability of being included in the sample. While a sampling frame may be obtainable from existing documentary sources, such as census data or an organization's employment records, these need to be checked for inaccuracies and omissions. It is quite possible that in remote and rural areas a sampling frame can only be obtained by undertaking from scratch a form of census of the population to be sampled. This was, in fact, the case in the Mali study of rice cultivators.

Box 7.1   Probability sampling

At its simplest, probability sampling means the sample of informants is selected at random in the population. In practice, populations usually are known to contain subgroups which are significant to the purpose of the survey, and these subgroups are used to 'stratify' the sample: that is, the informants are selected from subgroups, either following the proportions which each subgroup represents in the population as a whole or deliberately favouring certain subgroups known to be more important to the study than their numbers would indicate.

For example, in the Mali study mentioned above, the sample of rice cultivators in a single village was stratified among five subgroups. The sample aimed to include 20% of cultivators in each category (Table 7.1).

TABLE 7.1   *Example of stratified sampling for rice cultivators in a single Malian village*

	Cultivator subgroup	Number in village	Number in sample (% of subgroup total)
1	Heads of extended households (managing fields for household consumption)	88	19 (22%)
2	Individual men (married and unmarried) cultivating on their own (or immediate family's) account	65	13 (20%)
3	Individual (married) women	119	24 (20%)
4	Locally resident immigrants	55	10 (18%)
5	Seasonal immigrants	80	17 (21%)

(Data from Woodhouse *et al.*, 2000).

In the other main approach – *focused interviews* – selection of informants is governed by the need to identify as wide a range of different viewpoints as possible, or by Hanlon's criterion of talking to 'those who know', but the selection is not necessarily linked to the wider population in any quantitative sense. The numbers of informants from minority social groups, whether powerful élites or socially marginalized, may be disproportionate to their presence in society as a whole. Thus, in a rural community the same number of informants may be sought among the 80% of households owning land as among the 20% without land. As a result, the number of informants can be much lower than for a sample survey.

There are two main variants to the approach. One is referred to as *purposive* or *theoretical* sampling, where different subgroups are sampled more or less heavily, depending on their importance to the purpose of the research or to certain theoretical distinctions which the investigator is testing (e.g. in the above example, how strategies for coping with drought differ between the landless and those with land). The other is the use of *key informants* ('those who know') who are not necessarily representative of a population in any sense, but are chosen simply for their knowledge or distinctive viewpoint. In both variants, selection of informants is driven by the investigators' need to test or clarify elements of their evolving hypotheses about the issues they are investigating.

This idea of evolving hypotheses highlights a further distinction between sample survey and focused interview approaches. Whereas in a sample survey the sample of informants and the questions they will be asked must be defined before starting the survey, the focused interview approach allows investigators to decide who to talk to, and what to ask them, as their understanding is shaped by earlier interviews.

7.2.3 Formulating questions to ask

As with deciding who to speak to, there are two main approaches to formulating what to ask: the structured questionnaire and the semi-structured interview schedule.

Structured questionnaires are generally used in sample surveys, primarily to answer 'What?' questions. The questions are standardized. Mostly of the 'tick the box' variety, they may be phrased 'Which of the following ...?', 'How much ...?', 'To what extent ...?', and so on, where the boxes to be ticked give a choice of options or a number of points on a scale. Questionnaire design is a detailed technique in its own right, requiring various types of expertise. Individual questions may need testing, and the overall design and mode of 'administration' (face-to-face, self-administered, postal, telephone) has to be adjusted to the circumstances so as to obtain a high percentage and reliable response.

Can structured questionnaires also be used to answer 'Why?' or 'How?' questions? One possibility is to analyze the relations between the answers to different 'What?' questions (see 'Analyzing the response' below), although as we will see it is difficult to be sure about causal relationships by this means alone. Another possibility is for the questionnaire to include such questions directly: e.g. How did you negotiate to borrow land? Why do you lend land to people from outside your village? How do present farming practices represent a change in relation to the past? Questions such as these can be answered by means of predefined options or in the respondents' own words, in 'open ended' format questions. Quantification is less straightforward, however, if the latter is chosen. In practice, answers to such questions tend to be complex, requiring further questions for clarification, and, unless investigators already know their informants fairly well, it can be difficult to frame such questions in a manner that is both appropriate and standardized.

For these reasons, structured questionnaires are often an ineffective way of answering 'Why?' or 'How?' questions, which are better addressed using a *semi-structured interview schedule*. This allows investigators to explore issues with informants in a much more flexible way, using supplementary questions to clarify complex responses, and developing new lines of enquiry – perhaps unforeseen but relevant to the investigator's purpose – as these arise during interviews. The semi-structured interview approach is also useful for answering 'What?' questions, where investigators are unfamiliar with the social situation in which they are working. By providing answers to 'Why?' and 'How?' questions, semi-structured interviews allow investigators to go beyond describing 'what is' to *develop theories* or hypotheses about the nature of relationships and decision-making which explain why people think or act they way they do. Addressing 'Why?' and 'How?' questions leads to an emphasis on *qualitative* information in semi-structured interview approaches, although not necessarily excluding quantitative data (as exemplified in Section 7.5).

A semi-structured interview schedule generally has a number of headings or standard but open-ended questions, but each interview will vary in the way the investigator follows up interesting lines of enquiry that could not have been foreseen, using supplementary questions. It is possible to use semi-structured questioning within a sample survey, perhaps as an adjunct to a structured questionnaire. However, it is more usual for this form of questioning to be part of the technique of focused interviewing, where, as described above, those interviewed are either a purposive sample or else key informants, who may be chosen to throw light on new issues brought up by previous informants.

Thus, the most usual approaches to finding out from people are, on the one hand, sample surveys done by administering structured questionnaires ('structured survey' for short), and, on the other, focused interviews using semi-structured interview schedules ('semi-structured interview'). In the latter case, the 'design' of the approach, in terms both of adding new interviewees and of asking new questions, continues while the enquiry is in progress. This 'iterative, learning-process' design provides great flexibility, and makes the semi-structured approach particularly suited to situations where development managers are trying to understand unfamiliar social situations. It has seen wide application in various forms of PLA, known earlier as 'rapid rural appraisal' and 'participatory rural appraisal'. More recently it has provided the methodological basis for large-scale investigations known as 'Participatory Poverty Assessments' in many developing countries.

7.2.4 Analyzing the response

In any investigation a major task is to gather together the ideas and the evidence that the enquiry has generated in order to summarize its findings. In the case of structured surveys, each informant is asked an identical set of questions, and the responses are recorded on specially prepared questionnaire forms. The questionnaire responses are collated and subjected to statistical analysis, usually using a computer. The response to any given question can then be expressed as a statistic (mean and standard error) for the sample or subsets of it, taken to be representative of the population. Characteristics of the population are 'inferred' from statistical analysis of the sample. Statistical analysis will also show the extent to which certain characteristics of the population are associated, or correlated, with other characteristics. For example, in the study of rice cultivators in Mali, statistics showed that mean rice production per hectare was lower on hoe-cultivated plots than on those tilled by ox-drawn plough. Statistical analysis also provides clear indications as to how significant such differences are: that is, how much confidence we can have that they are not the result of some chance pattern occurring in the response data.

Note that above I stated that statistical analysis shows *correlations*. It does not prove *causality*. However, this is where attempts may be made to throw light on certain 'Why?' (or 'How?') questions through relating the answers to different 'What?' questions to each other, as signalled above. Although statistical correlations may be useful in exploring such questions, this type of analysis will not give definite answers by itself. Thus, though higher rice yields were correlated with cultivation by ox-drawn plough, this does not prove that ploughing with oxen was the cause of higher yields (even though this may be a reasonable supposition). It is equally possible that those cultivators wealthy enough to plough with oxen had other advantages, such as better quality seed, more labour for weeding, or plots with better access to water, which were a more direct cause of higher rice yields. At a further extreme of interpretation, cultivators may have become wealthy enough to plough with oxen because they fortuitously occupied more productive plots of land. This indicates that great care should be exercised when using responses to 'What?' questions to answer 'Why?' questions.

This brings us back to weaknesses in structured surveys. While they can provide rigorously defined descriptions, they are notoriously open to misinterpretation, giving rise to the phrase 'lies, damn lies, and statistics'. A crucial point to bear in mind is that the interpretation of statistics from structured surveys is only as good as the qualitative information available to guide interpretation. An example from the Mali study (Example 7.1) demonstrates that the influence of households' wealth and status on the productivity of their rice-growing only became apparent when statistical comparison was guided by information from semi-structured interviews, in this case villagers' own criteria of who was wealthy and who was poor.

Example 7.1 Interpreting survey data using information from semi-structured interviews

At the outset of the structured survey of rice cultivators, it was believed that inherited access to land suitable for rice cultivation was a key indicator of wealth and status. However, a comparison of productivity (in terms of mean weight of rice produced per hectare) on inherited and borrowed plots showed hardly any difference (1.2 t/ha on

(Continued)

(Continued)

inherited fields, against 1.4 t/ha on borrowed fields), suggesting that the wealthy were no more productive than their poorer neighbours. However, in the course of semi-structured interviews, village elders had been asked to rank all households according to wealth. They had identified three categories of wealth in the village:

1   Wealthiest: self-sufficient in food, and owning more than five head of cattle.
2   Middle: self-sufficient in food with one or two head of cattle.
3   Poorest: food-deficit households.

Considering each household in turn, they had allocated 51% to the first category, 32% to the second, and 17% to the third. Since it covered all households in the village, the wealth ranking of each household included in the structured survey sample could be used in statistical analysis. When this was used to compare rice productivity, the mean figure for the category of wealthiest households was more than double that of the category of poorest households, with that for the middle category lying in between (1.2 t/ha, 1.0 t/ha and 0.5 t/ha).

Example 7.1 illustrates the important point that in many cases the descriptive data from structured surveys can only be accurately interpreted – and hence give *valid* findings – for populations with which investigators are already fairly familiar. Where this is not the case, a structured survey can be preceded by semi-structured interviews in order to establish an adequate 'theory' with which to design the structured survey and interpret the statistics it generates.

7.3 Rigour in structured survey and semi–structured interview • • •

Structured surveys are often criticized for giving invalid results, as with certain well-known examples of opinion polls of voting intentions giving incorrect predictions of election results. This is similar to the mistake of assuming correlation implies causality. There are two aspects to establishing the reliability of results supposedly obtained from structured surveys: how the survey results are used to obtain a description of the population, and an interpretation of that description.

Thus, in the example of electoral opinion polling, a properly conducted sample survey can tell us reliably what proportion of the population say they will vote for a certain party. Whether that can be interpreted to mean they will in fact vote that way depends on whether some of them were misinterpreting the questions (e.g. answering 'Which party do you prefer?' rather than 'Which party will you vote for?', which might be different), giving misleading answers, or answering in a way they thought would please the interviewer ('interviewer bias').

Similar criticisms were raised when data from national questionnaire surveys of expenditure by Ugandan households were used to interpret rising expenditure levels as indicating increasing living standards and household well-being. Critics pointed out that aggregate household expenditure included certain items (particularly alcohol consumption, school fees, medicine purchases) for which increased expenditure was not consistent with improved well-being (McGee, 2003).

Rigour in *interpretation* therefore requires a structured survey to be backed up with other, perhaps more qualitative, information, that might be obtained as just suggested by combining the survey with semi-structured interviewing. However, rigour in *description* is much more straightforward, particularly if interviewer bias is minimized through careful wording and paying attention to how the interviewer is perceived by the interviewee (see Section 7.4 below). One of the undoubted attractions of the structured survey approach is that, however potentially misleading – or invalid – the interpretations, the procedures for undertaking and presenting the investigation are subject to definite rules. This means that, so long as rules of probability sampling are followed, the statistics produced by the survey can be taken as a reliable description of those aspects in the population as a whole. Thus, in the rice cultivator study, it could be said with confidence that hoe-cultivated plots had less rice productivity, even though one could not say why.

Conversely, one of the consequences of the flexibility of semi-structured interview approaches is that procedures for establishing rigour are less simple. In the ethnography literature from which semi-structured approaches were first developed, considerable attention has been devoted to discussing ways of improving rigour (Robson, 1993). Essentially, the investigator needs to ask a number of questions:

- Are my findings compatible with all the evidence?
- To what extent could other investigators reproduce and corroborate my findings?
- How far can my findings be applied to other situations?

For investigative development managers to be able to answer these questions, two main principles need to be borne in mind: *triangulation* and *documentation*.

Triangulation refers to the use of multiple sources of information to test and modify one's understanding (or 'theory') of a given problem or situation. In practice this involves using different methods of enquiry, different informants, and different investigators to see whether the ideas and information they generate can be accounted for by the developing theory of the issue under investigation. In semi-structured interview approaches, this forms part of an iterative cycle of interview, analysis, evaluation, and design of the next interview. Each interview is thus used to test the 'working hypotheses' that have originated from earlier interviews. In principle, this process should be pursued until the working hypotheses can credibly account for all the available ideas and information, and further interviews confirm, rather than modify, these hypotheses. In practice, the time and other resources available for this process may impose constraints on how completely this can be achieved, and such constraints are likely to be tighter in large-scale investigations, where an investigative team may be allocated only a few days in a study site (see Section 7.5). The rich repertoire of interviewing and other techniques that has developed within PLA methodology, reviewed below, provides additional scope for triangulation by providing alternative ways of visualizing and interrogating social activity. Although some of these techniques involve group rather than individual responses, they can be considered within the broad framework of the semi-structured interview approach. However, the principle of triangulation should also remind investigators pursuing their enquiry by talking to people that they need to cross-check their interview findings against other relevant sources, such as earlier research findings, documentary material, and so on.

Documentation refers to the need to record not only the substance of what informants say, but also key features of the investigation 'process', such as interpretation of what informants say which incorporates investigators' observations on the context of interviews, and reflections on investigators' (changing) rationale and understanding of the enquiry. The basic concept here is that ideas and information can only be understood with reference to the circumstances in which they were generated. This is the same as the notion that 'what we know is shaped by how we know it' mentioned earlier in Section 7.1. It means that if you wish to assess how far your findings may be applicable elsewhere, or reproducible by other investigations, you need to be able to examine the possibility of differences not only of subject matter and methodology, but also in the enquiry process itself. In order to do this effectively, investigators need to reflect upon their own role and influence on the interview, and the nature of the communication between themselves and those whom they are interviewing. I return to this need for 'reflexivity' in the next section.

In this section and the previous one I have considered investigation which relies on people as informants in terms of two principal approaches: structured survey and semi-structured interview. Table 7.2 summarizes the differences between the two approaches. I have organized the discussion this way because the two approaches differ fundamentally in the way rigour is established. Structured survey uses theories of probability to select a sample of informants whose circumstances and perceptions are taken to be representative of a wider population. Valid structured surveys require considerable prior knowledge of the population involved in the enquiry, however, both to select a sample and to interpret the survey findings. Semi-structured interview approaches select informants in order to obtain a wide range of viewpoints. Validity is sought not through statistical analysis but by generating explanations (hypotheses) to account for what informants have said and pursuing further information until investigators feel able satisfactorily to explain all the evidence the enquiry has yielded. The reliability of the findings of semi-structured interview approaches is further established through documentation: careful recording of the context and process of the enquiry.

TABLE 7.2 *Structured survey and semi-structured interviews compared*

Structured survey	Semi-structured interviews
Design completed before interviewing starts	Design continues in interviewing phase
All informants selected before interviewing begins	Informants identified progressively, making use of findings from earlier interviews
All questions defined before interviewing begins	Questions are identified and modified in response to understanding or information gained in earlier interviews. New questions or aspects of enquiry may emerge during the course of an interview
Identical question set (questionnaire) addressed to all informants	Questions or topics of interviews tailored to different informants, and different stages of the enquiry (e.g. to elaborate or check on earlier findings)
Informants chosen as representative sample of the wider population following *probability* criteria	Informants chosen to explore a range of different types of knowledge or perspectives, not linked to a quantitative representation of the wider population
Data 'reduced' to understandable patterns using statistical analysis	Data 'reduced' to understandable patterns by comparing what different informants say about specific themes or questions
Findings validated by probability criteria: the calculation of the likelihood that patterns observed in the data have arisen by chance	Findings validated by triangulation: does information from different sources lead to the same conclusions?
Most suited to answering 'What?' questions, less effective in answering 'Why?' questions	Well suited to answering 'Why?' questions. Can answer 'What?' questions but findings cannot be used to calculate (infer) the distribution of characteristics in the wider population

It needs to be recognized that discussion of the reasons for choosing one or the other approach is frequently polarized. The view advanced here is that one approach is not better than the other, but that they produce different kinds of information and thus are suited to different types of investigations. To undertake either method rigorously needs an awareness of the method's strengths and weaknesses. In practice the two approaches are often used to support one another. A common procedure has been illustrated already in the Mali study where semi-structured interviews with villagers identified what kind of people were rice cultivators, the extent of the village's rice cultivation lands and the forms of land tenure. This constituted the basis for designing a structured survey of the way rice was grown on those lands. Equally, however, semi-structured interviews can be used to follow up and explore questions suggested by gaps or contradictions in the findings of a structured survey. In the Mali study the structured survey suggested that the practice of charging rent to those borrowing rice land was one such question that needed further exploration through semi-structured interviews.

In these instances semi-structured and survey approaches are used sequentially. However, as mentioned above, elements of semi-structured interviewing may also be undertaken concurrently with structured surveys, by including 'open-ended questions', in which the form of response is largely determined by the informant, as part of a questionnaire schedule. Alternatively, separate semi-structured interviews may be conducted with some of the informants who are taking part in a structured survey. In practice, therefore, the clear separation between structured survey and semi-structured interviews may become blurred. Even where combined in a single enquiry, however, it is essential that investigators retain a clear distinction between which information is being generated by which approach, for this will determine the process through which findings need to be validated.

Awareness of the differences and scope for complementarity between approaches is particularly important when evaluating claims that semi-structured interview approaches are more rapid or more cost-effective than structured survey. Firstly, the methods produce different kinds of information and one should not be seen as substituting for the other. Secondly, semi-structured interviews require a much higher level of decision-making during the course of each interview than does the questionnaire in the structured survey. Consequently, the level of training, experience, and maturity required of field interviewers is much higher in semi-structured interviews than in structured surveys. If this is not recognized, and there is evidence that in many cases it is not (Cornwall and Fleming, 1995; and see Section 7.5), the invalid structured surveys widely criticized in the past will merely be replaced by unreliable semi-structured interviews in the future.

7.4 Improving communications • • •

I suggested at the start of this chapter that all investigations which use people as sources of information are necessarily interactive, and that they are more likely to be successful if they are collaborative. Investigators therefore need to pay attention to establishing a collaborative context for the interview. A key aspect of this is informants' perceptions of an investigator's identity and the purpose of the enquiry. This may not be as straightforward as it might first appear. Hanlon's remarks about personal goals and agendas are relevant here, and, as he observes, decision-making is easier when agendas are made explicit. However, I noted at the beginning of this chapter the possibility that a development manager may need to 'find out' from people who may be unsympathetic to that manager's agenda. In such cases the investigative manager may prefer to identify herself or himself with a different agenda, more likely to be viewed positively by potential informants. This raises ethical questions to which I shall return, but a more immediate concern is that whatever identity an investigator adopts she or he needs to be clear about the purpose of the enquiry. I am not asserting that the goal of the enquiry should be regarded as immutable. In real research, investigators' perceptions of the question they wish to answer alter as they learn more about it. My point here is that investigative managers need to *reflect* on the enquiry process and maintain a clear sense of their own purpose, how this is presented to, and perceived by, their informants, and the consequences in terms of the kinds of relationships established, and the type of information generated, in the enquiry.

One of the most important elements establishing an investigator's identity is the way in which she or he is introduced to informants. Most commonly this is through a 'gate-keeper' – someone in authority whose approval is needed before investigators can proceed to contact individual informants. The gatekeeper's approval acts to legitimate and sponsor the enquiry. Typically, gatekeepers are community leaders in rural areas, but could be company managers or union officials in more industrial contexts. It may be that a gatekeeper is not hierarchically related to other informants, but merely agrees to introduce the investigator to potential informants in a social group of which the gate-keeper is a member (e.g. traders' associations).

Depending on the degree of hierarchy between the gatekeeper and the other informants, introduction and sponsorship by the gatekeeper may be a more or less important element in establishing a climate of collaboration for the investigation. In general, however, investigators are advised to be prepared to adjust the time and place of interviews to the convenience of informants, and to explain the purpose of their enquiry. The collaborative climate between interviewer and interviewee is often referred to as 'rapport', and it is recognized that certain investigators have better possibilities for establishing rapport with particular groups of informants than others, such as female investigators working with women's groups. Differences of language, ethnicity, age, and class are also recognized as barriers to rapport between investigator and informants. However, it should not be assumed that greater similarity between social background of investigator and informants is always conducive to better rapport. Classic ethnographic methodology seeks rapport by casting the researcher as the ignorant outsider seeking instruction in local history and custom. Similarly, informants may feel discussing sensitive issues with strangers from another culture poses less risk of what they say coming to the ears of neighbours and relatives.

I think it is essential to be clear that establishing rapport is important both for structured questionnaires and for semi-structured interviews, although particularly critical for the latter. Rapport should therefore be seen as a necessary part of effective interviewing. Further, this is so irrespective of the purpose of the research. Thus, although rapport may be an essential ingredient in participatory research which seeks to empower its informants, it may be equally critical for investigators who seek information from powerful groups in the hope that the findings can be used to restrict or reduce their power. My point here is that establishing rapport can be manipulative. Indeed, some researchers have suggested – and deplored– that rapport is regarded as a form of social lubricant to elicit disclosure (Oakley, 1981). Establishing rapport is therefore not the same as empowering informants.

For this reason, investigators using 'participatory' forms of enquiry such as PLA, discussed in Section 7.5, have a particular need for careful reflection on the enquiry process and a clear sense of their own purpose in undertaking it. I believe that this 'reflexive' practice is important in maintaining investigators' awareness of the power relations, to which I referred at the start of this chapter, inherent in any enquiry, and which can be masked where rapport creates the sense of an egalitarian relationship between investigator and informant. Some formulations of participatory research that envisage outsiders taking part in enquiries only in a neutral, facilitating, role, for example, can be interpreted as implicitly denying the underlying power of the investigator in the enquiry process. This raises difficulties, firstly in the sense that denial of power suggests a denial of investigators' responsibility in the enquiry. Secondly, as argued in the next section, it denies the 'outside' perspective that may be essential to investigators' ability to draw valid conclusions from the enquiry.

I noted above that rapport is important in all interviewing, but it is especially critical in semi-structured interviews which have the format of an informal conversation guided by the interviewer to cover the issues of interest to the enquiry, but free to pursue other unforeseen, but relevant and important, issues that arise during interview. General interviewing skills include the use of open-ended questions, probing (e.g. Who, what, when, where, why ...?) to encourage more detail on points of interest, and exploring reactions to hypothetical (What if ...?) scenarios. In addition, the approach known as participatory learning and action (PLA; see also Chapter 8) brings together a variety of diagramming techniques which allow information to be set out visually. This has many advantages over purely verbal description in improving clarity (see Table 2.2 in Chapter 2 for a comparison of verbal and visual). It also generates a new focus of discussion, in which questions can be addressed to the diagram rather than direct to the interviewee. The principal types of diagramming are set out briefly in Box 7.2.

Box 7.2   Improving communication through visual techniques

Time line. A drawn line is used to locate different events in chronological sequence.

Activity/seasonal calendar. Variation in rainfall, work (agricultural work, migration), health (disease incidence, food scarcity), and other factors showing regular seasonal variations are recorded on calendar diagrams. The technique offers considerable scope for informants to create diagrams using their own calendars and systems of measurement, and identifying their own priority concerns.

Transect. An interview conducted while walking a traverse of an area of interest to the enquiry. Allows the identification of different zones resulting from variations of topography, ecology, resource use, or ownership. The mobile interview prompts further exploration of the patterns of variation along the transect, and diagramming can be used to summarize the zoning pattern for further discussion.

Venn/Institutional diagram. Circles are drawn or cut out of paper to represent different organizations or groups. Organizational relationships can be represented by the overlap between different circles.

(Continued)

(Continued)

Mapping. May be used to map natural resources and resource use, ownership (e.g. of village land), residence, social differences, incidence of disease (e.g. within settlements). Mapping may be undertaken by different individuals or groups to visualize different perceptions, or may be a public activity to encourage discussion and the visualization of a 'consensus' perception.

Ranking exercise. These often use diagrammatic techniques to record the outcomes of comparing two alternatives (e.g. which tree species is best for firewood) through pairwise ranking, or a number of alternatives through matrix ranking. Wealth ranking is undertaken through informants identifying wealth categories, recording each household on a card and then allocating the cards to the wealth categories.

The use of diagramming techniques has been developed for interviews with individuals and with groups. In participatory investigations, diagramming by groups has been developed into public activity in which informants are encouraged to identify their own questions and lines of enquiry (see examples in Chapter 8).

7.5 Participatory methods of enquiry • • •

Widespread advocacy of participatory forms of development has been associated with the development of participatory methods of enquiry, of which participatory learning and action (PLA) is the best known. Originally developed for work in rural communities, the approach has also been widely applied in urban contexts. Biggs (1995) has observed that such methods are fast taking on the form of a new generalized orthodoxy for solving development problems. However, critics of participatory approaches have suggested that they may 'override existing legitimate decision-making processes ..., involve group dynamics that reinforce the interests of the already powerful ..., and drive out other (methods) that have advantages participation cannot provide' (Cooke and Kothari, 2001, p. 7). Much of the critical literature on participation (e.g. Hickey and Mohan, 2004) has focused on the first two of these concerns that relate particularly to issues of power relations and claims that participatory approaches achieve empowerment for disadvantaged people in processes of governance. These issues are addressed in Chapter 8. My concern here is to examine the possibility that participatory approaches are being used in ways that do not improve the validity or reliability of information, and, in particular, what issues participatory methods raise for development managers in relation to the rigour of enquiry – 'Does it tell me what I want to know?' and 'Can I have confidence that what I have found out will not be contradicted or easily undermined by other, similar investigations?'.

As a method of enquiry, PLA has the following characteristics:

- It is firmly rooted in ethnographic traditions of semi-structured interviewing, and thus depends on the criteria for validity appropriate to semi-structured interview approaches.
- Interviews commonly make use of diagramming techniques to construct visual forms of information, and this can be a powerful way of answering 'What?' questions, as well as providing a focus for addressing 'Why?' and 'How?' questions.
- PLA techniques are often used with groups in a public forum, with the aim of assisting all members of the group to contribute to a consensus response to the questions raised, whether in verbal or visual form.
- A central concern of many proponents of PLA is that the enquiry process should encourage a process of empowerment: of informants in relation to investigators, and of socially disadvantaged groups in relation to the prevailing power structure. This process of empowerment requires that investigators become 'convenors, catalysts and facilitators', encouraging informants to take the initiative and set priorities for the enquiry, and that the enquiry 'gives a voice' to those whose opinions are not generally given prominence in the public arena.
- The current designation 'Participatory Learning and Action – PLA', with which a leading network concerned with the methodology replaced the earlier 'Participatory Rural Appraisal' (PRA), reflects the idea that those participating should be able to use the enquiry as the basis for planning and implementing action to bring about change.
- Some proponents of PLA (notably Chambers, 1992) have counterposed 'participatory' modes of enquiry, committed to empowering informants, to 'extractive' modes of enquiry which are guided by investigators' agenda of 'finding out'.

Development managers who wish to use PLA activities as a means of understanding the situation in which they have to take decisions need to consider the following points, which have emerged from the experience of those using such approaches in participatory poverty assessments (PPA). The Ugandan PPA (UPPAP) is of particular interest because it is well documented (UPPAP, 2000, 2002) and has been the subject of reflexive analysis by those involved (Yates and Okello, 2002). The aim of the first cycle of the UPPAP was 'to bring the voices and perspectives of the poor into central and local governments' policy formulation, planning and implementation, as well as strengthen and complement quantitative monitoring of the planning and implementation processes'. (UPPAP, 2000: vii). Field researchers were contracted from nine different Ugandan organizations, including NGOs, research organizations, and a government department. These participated in a planning workshop and then joined field staff seconded by 9 districts in a three-week residential training programme 'to create a shared vision for the project' and to gain 'theoretical and practical knowledge in participatory methodologies' (UPPAP, 2000, 6). The 36 researchers then undertook participatory research in a total of 24 rural and 12 urban sites over a period of eight months, with a team of six researchers covering four sites over a 35-day period and each site being researched by a 'sub-team' of three.

At the end of Section 7.3, I observed that the semi-structured interview approach demands a high level of skill and experience of interviewers. PLA in particular requires highly practiced facilitators if it is to avoid a routine (but 'participatory') production of village maps, calendar diagrams and other artefacts. It is important to recognize that such artefacts have no interpretive value unless accompanied by documentation that enables an understanding of the context and process by which they were produced. (When, where, why, and by whom were they made? Who has seen them? What has been said about them since? And by whom?)

It seems that the preparatory workshops for UPPAP field researchers did not fully overcome this hazard. A primary source of difficulty was field researchers' confusion over the purpose of the PPA: whether the workshops and meetings were simply to obtain information, or whether they were also to act as catalysts for development projects. In the event a number of PPA researchers encouraged the villagers they worked with to formulate 'Community Action Plans' in the expectation that financial support would be provided to implement them, although there was no planned budget for this support (Yates and Okello, 2002). A second problem was noted by mid-term reviewers of the second cycle of UPPAP: 'The site reports offer varying levels of analysis, with differing implications for "understanding poverty and poverty trends". There is a clear difference ... for example, between those reports that merely record the respondents' "voices" and those that include the researchers' observations ... [I]nsights on subjects such as "gender dimensions of poverty" or "locally specific poverty dimensions" can be greatly enhanced through independent researcher assessments' (Yates and Moncrieffe, 2002: 63).

A second, and fundamental concern in the interpretation of participatory research has been identified by Mosse (1994, p. 510):

> ... as public and collective events, PRAs tend to emphasize the general over the particular (individual, event, situation, etc.), tend towards the normative ('what ought to be' rather than 'what is'), and towards a unitary view of interests which underplays difference. In other words, it is the community's 'official view' of itself which is projected ... (O)ften the very structure of the PRA sessions – group activities leading to plenary presentations – assumes and encourages the expression of consensus.

An example of this from the Mali study referred to earlier concerns the lending of land to cultivators from outside the village. A census undertaken in landholders' own homes revealed a much greater extent of land lending to outsiders than a public mapping exercise which conveyed a 'consensus' that this was a relatively uncommon and unimportant practice. The difference suggested that lending land to people from outside the village was a controversial practice that landholders feared would expose them to criticism from others within the village. Further enquiry showed that this was indeed the case.

Mosse argues that the public and consensus-building nature of many participatory approaches to investigation, exemplified by PPAs, offers opportunities for dominant groups or people in authority to influence public opinion so that their private interests become 'officialized' by incorporation in the 'community consensus'. Conversely, the public arena sets considerable barriers for the expression of the views of groups – women in the case of Mosse's work in India – who would normally simply not be expected to be present in formal public encounters, and who are unaccustomed to expressing themselves in terms suitable for a public audience.

These observations raise the paradox that the more 'participatory' the enquiry, in the sense that it is undertaken in the public arena – following an agenda set by 'the community' – the more the outcome of the enquiry will mask the power structure of the community. Mosse (1995, p. 29) observes: '... public participatory research methods are unlikely to prove good instruments for the analysis of local power relations since they are shaped by the very relations which are being investigated'. As a consequence, actions developed to meet 'community goals' identified in PLA risk reinforcing, not changing, those power relations. From the point of view of development managers who wish to use participatory methods to understand social relationships as a basis for decision-making, this is a serious limitation of PLA. In terms of validity criteria, the consensus-building nature of PLA restricts the expression of difference and hence the scope for triangulation. Two important points flow from this.

Firstly, investigative development managers using PLA must ensure adequate triangulation by talking to different types of informant, in different, less public social contexts. They need to reflect on and document the context and process of these encounters, including their own influence on the information generated. Seeking out, interpretation, and use of information is guided by the *investigators'* purpose in the enquiry. As Mosse (1995, p. 32) says:

> The often-used polarity between 'extractive' and 'participatory' research modes thus overlooks the fact that certain types of knowledge employed in participatory projects is [sic] *necessarily* external and analytical. Indeed, knowledge of social relationships which helps project workers identify the conditions for participation itself, to bargain with villagers on issues of equity, gender, or cost recovery ... is of this kind. [original emphasis]

This need for investigators to establish their own understanding of social relationships in order to pursue their own purpose leads to a second point: the need to acknowledge that the investigator is an active agent and, no matter how participatory the enquiry, will affect its findings. This reinforces the argument, made earlier, that investigative managers need to be explicitly aware of their agendas. If their purpose is to identify opportunities to alter power relationships in favour of disadvantaged groups then investigators must keep this clearly in mind as they pursue the enquiry, irrespective of how they ultimately 'negotiate' this agenda with the local power structure. I noted earlier that the investigator as a purposeful change agent conflicts with the rather neutral-sounding role of 'convenor, catalyst and facilitator' allocated to outsiders in PLA. However, acknowledging this role and making explicit the investigator's purpose is necessary to the rigour of the enquiry by allowing adequate documentation of the investigator's own influence on the context and process of the enquiry.

The widespread use of participatory research methods to undertake PPAs raises further sets of hazards to rigour, in addition to those already discussed above (Woodhouse, 2004). The Ugandan PPA illustrates a desire to present the findings of PPAs in some aggregate form 'representative' of the national poverty situation. This is perhaps a response to what Mohan (2001, p. 161) has termed 'the "economism" of development agencies' that requires that '"soft" information has to be made acceptable through its pseudo-scientism to hardened decision-makers'. The UPPAP reports provide case studies that provide sharp insights into the causes and consequences of poverty, but it is also apparent that the national reports of UPPAP findings (UPPAP, 2000, 2002) emphasize aggregate 'top ten' rankings of particular 'causes' and 'effects' of poverty based on the relative frequency (number of sites) with which particular aspects of poverty were mentioned. This raises problems of validity of representation. Not only does this aggregation effectively isolate information, such as 'causes of poverty', from the contextual detail we need in order to interpret it, but the impression is also given that the rankings somehow describe the relative extent of these 'causes' of poverty nationally. In fact, in neither cycle of UPPAP were study sites chosen to be representative of the country as a whole, but rather to enable a focus on particular problems (e.g. extreme poverty, HIV/AIDS, insecurity). Since the selection cannot strictly be considered nationally representative, it cannot be used to 'represent' a national picture in a quantified, aggregate sense.

7.6 Conclusion • • •

This chapter has set out issues which development managers will need to consider when finding out by talking to people. I have contrasted structured surveys with semi-structured interviews, and emphasized the underlying ground rules by which investigators try to improve the accuracy and reliability of information generated whichever approach is taken. I have argued that establishing a collaborative content is important whether or not the methods used are specifically labelled 'participatory'. Those which are so labelled, such as PLA and PPA, require similar criteria before they can be considered rigorous and reliable as semi-structured interview approaches generally. The widespread adoption of participatory methods at a large scale raises additional problems of validity of the information obtained, and demands particular attention to the distinct criteria of validity applicable to different research methodologies. In this discussion I have begun to consider the power relations inherent in encounters between investigators and informants and how these affect the confidence which development managers can allow themselves in the findings from such studies – questions dealt with more fully in the next chapter.

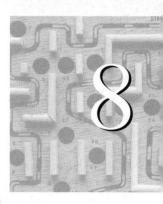

Investigation as empowerment: using participatory methods

Linda Mayoux and Hazel Johnson

Many investigators concerned with policy development may want or be asked to use participatory approaches at some time. Participatory methods of investigation and policy development are increasingly promoted by development agencies of varying perspectives and influence, including the World Bank and non-governmental organizations (NGOs). In many northern aid agencies, participatory approaches have long been a required component for funding development programmes (Chambers, 1995; Richards, 1995), and participatory *research* is an important part of a participatory approach. The most comprehensive and fully documented initiative was the World Bank's own Participatory Poverty Assessments (Narayan *et al.*, 2000; Narayan and Petesch, 2002) culminating in the 2000/2001 World Development Report *Attacking Poverty* (World Bank, 2000).

Empowerment is also a stated part of the policy of many development organizations. Given the explicit link often made between participatory investigation, participatory development and empowerment (e.g. Narayan and Srinivasan, 1994) but also evidence of limitations and pitfalls (e.g. Mosse, 1994; Guijt and Shah, 1998; Cooke and Kothari, 2001), it is important to decide whether, with whom and how participatory methods are likely to promote empowerment and when they are less likely to be effective.

In Chapter 7 Philip Woodhouse questions whether participatory investigation (specifically, participatory learning and action or PLA, which he takes to be the most recent terminology incorporating the older 'RRA' and 'PRA') can overcome inequalities in power relations between investigators and their 'informants', or reveal the power structures within communities. The chapter concludes with advice to investigators to triangulate their findings, be aware of their own influence in the process of gathering information, and keep in front of them their own agendas in carrying out an investigation.

In this chapter, we suggest some areas of investigation in which participatory methods of investigation for policy development can be potentially empowering for subjects, and discuss some of the limitations of trying to use participatory approaches as an empowering process. The chapter is concerned with the following questions:

- Can a participatory approach to investigation act as an empowering mechanism, particularly for the poorest and most disadvantaged?
- How do power relations affect the use of participatory approaches to investigation?
- What are some of the key considerations for investigators and development agencies wanting to use participatory investigation as a means of empowerment?

Section 8.1 examines the concept of empowerment and its presumed relationship to participatory approaches to investigation and action. Section 8.2 reviews some of the empowering experiences of using participatory methods while Section 8.3 looks at the ways in which power relations affect, create and even magnify inherent challenges in the research process. Section 8.4 summarizes some of the critical issues which need to be addressed in using participatory approaches.

8.1 Participatory investigation and empowerment • • •

Labelling a research process 'participatory' does not mean that it will automatically lead to 'empowerment'. The language of participation and empowerment is used differently by different people and has been appropriated by organizations with different ideologies and intentions. Unpacking the term 'empowerment' and reflecting on its relationship to participatory investigation are thus important tasks for any investigator concerned with the effects of research on participants or 'informants'. The following reflections can act as a starting point.

8.1.1 What is empowerment?

Many researchers involved in policy development hope that their research will benefit those they are studying by enabling the views of marginal groups to be heard, and by stimulating debate within communities and development agencies. This is often true of those using other qualitative methods and surveys as well as participatory methods. However, empowerment is a contested concept used in different ways by individuals and organizations of differing world-views and political persuasions. There are disagreements about what is meant by power and hence the aims of empowerment, who is to be empowered, and the role of intervening agencies in empowerment processes. This has implications for the ways in which participatory methods have been used, why they have been used and whether or not they have been considered 'empowering'. Before using participatory methods for empowerment, therefore, it is necessary to be clear about what one means by empowerment and hence the implications for design of the research process. Some dimensions of empowerment debates are summarized in Box 8.1.

Empowerment is by definition concerned with power relations. However, power has different dimensions and operates in different, interrelated and often mutually reinforcing ways (see Box 8.1). In what follows we build on a commonly used distinction between 'power within', 'power to', 'power with' and 'power over'.[1] 'Power within' refers to awareness of life choices, possibilities of change and confidence in one's own abilities to bring about change. This is also related to the idea of 'voice' and confidence to express one's views in public. 'Power to' refers to people's abilities to act on these aspirations and choices – having the necessary capacities, resources and knowledge to realize choices and exert increased control over and/or to change their conditions of existence. 'Power with' signifies a less individualistic form of 'power within' and 'power to', stressing mutual support, alliances and joint action. 'Power over' signifies means of control over other people. These distinctions are important, because the notions of 'power within', 'power to' and 'power with' imply that increasing the power of some people does not necessarily diminish that of others and therefore have attractive and positive connotations for development agencies (Rowlands, 1995, p. 102). This is in contrast to the idea of 'power over' which suggests that the power of particular individuals, groups or institutions only exists in relation to the greater or lesser power of others, and that an increase in the power of one implies a decrease in that of another. In practice, however, the types of power are inevitably interlinked, with changes in 'power over' often being necessary for increases in 'power within', 'to' and 'with' and vice versa.

---

[1] There are many different frameworks for empowerment and a full discussion is outside the scope of this chapter. Compare for example the framework by John Heron mentioned in Section 2.2 of Chapter 2. The treatment here derives from Rowlands, 1995 (building on Kabeer, 1994) and also attempts to incorporate discussion of choices, voice and agency from other recent frameworks, e.g. Kabeer, 2002 and Malhotra, Schuler and Boender, 2002, while retaining an emphasis on the importance of addressing structural context and constraints, as in Thomas, 1992.

Box 8.1   What is empowerment?

Types of Power Relations

'power within': awareness of choices and the possibility of change, and confidence in one's own abilities to bring about change
'power to': having the knowledge, capacities and resources to change the condition of one's existence
'power with': ability to achieve control through joint action with others
'power over': control over other people

Dimensions and Levels

Different dimensions: economic, social, political, psychological, etc
Different levels: individual, household, community, market, institutional, national, international, etc

Potential Contribution of Development Agencies

'power within': increasing confidence and giving voice
'power to': increasing skills, knowledge and resources
'power with': building networks and capacity for collective action
'power over': changing attitudes and behaviours of the powerful and changing discriminatory and unequal institutional structures and policies

It is clear also that power operates on many different and interlinked dimensions of people's lives, and at many different levels. Power generally has easily identifiable material dimensions, determining access to resources, levels of poverty and the range of choices and constraints affecting people's ability to achieve their aspirations. Power also has more subtle manifestations in ideologies, values and discourses which might be shared unquestioningly by those who are disadvantaged by them (Lukes, 1994). Conformity to unequal social relations can be sustained in this way, and can have the effect that both the subordinate and the relatively powerful are protected from potentially threatening processes of change. Moreover, these inequalities in access to resources and underlying or dominant values may reinforce each other at many levels of social interaction: between individuals, within households and families, in communities, and in national policy agendas as well as among international organizations.

For example, gender, age and ethnic discrimination are complex mixes of material deprivation and ideological subordination operating through many levels of social organization. Such interlocking relationships mean that it can be difficult and often impossible to identify any one single strategy for empowerment. For example, is it possible to address material inequalities without also changing underlying values which may be shared by those who are subordinated? Is it possible to challenge power relations among individuals, households and communities without also making changes in national and international structures and processes?

These complexities of power relations make investigatory processes for policy development which aim to empower inevitably subject to potential differences of opinion or even conflict over the aims of investigation, how it is to be carried out, and what use is made of the outcomes. These relate also to differences in views of the role of development agencies in the empowerment process. Is the role of the development agency mainly to increase confidence and voice, capacities and/or collective action ('power within', 'power to' and/or 'power with')? Or is it also to directly address issues of 'power over'? If investigation is intended to assist policy development, it almost inevitably has to confront ways that power relations maintain the *status quo*, which they do by acting to resist change or influence the direction of change in particular ways.

Finally, investigators are themselves embedded in power relations by their membership of institutions and their social position – and/or their subordinate position in relation to employers in development agencies. This also affects how the investigation is carried out and how far and in what ways it can be linked to action. In some cases investigators may have considerable control over the research process and the outcomes. The main concern then is constantly to reflect on power relations between themselves and the people they are investigating. In other cases, even when asked to use participatory methods, the scope for changing power relations either during the investigation or through any subsequent action may be extremely limited – with consequences for the types of methods used and degree to which expectations can be raised.

The complexities of power at all levels means that any empowerment brought about through using participatory methods is also inevitably limited. At the same time, these different dimensions of power relations indicate a range of potential contributions of the research process itself to empowerment and some key questions for investigators to reflect on at the outset of the investigative process:

1 *What are the aims and boundaries of the investigation?*
   How and by whom should aims and boundaries be decided? Is the investigation concerned with 'power within', 'power to', 'power over' or 'power with'? How far and in what ways do power relations themselves need to be a subject for investigation?
2 *Who is to participate in the investigative process?*
   Among whom and at what level is the investigation taking place (individuals, households, communities, etc.)? Is the main aim to try and involve the participation of the

relatively powerless or most disadvantaged? Or is the main aim to examine the behaviours and structures of the powerful? Or is the aim to involve a full range of interests to see how attitudes and actions can change? Is this possible?

3 *What are the implications of power inequalities for design of the investigation?*
How will the relatively powerless or most disadvantaged participate and how can their participation be ensured? How will the powerful participate? What are the different factors to be borne in mind in each case? What are the factors to be borne in mind in bringing the different interests together?

4 *How is the investigation to be linked to action?*
How can benefits to participants, including the relatively powerless, be ensured? Is action trying to enhance 'power within', 'power to' or 'power with', or to challenge 'power over'? Can action be limited to particular levels (individuals, households, communities, etc.) or dimensions (economic, social, political, etc.) or must it address different interlinked levels and/or dimensions? Must the research also investigate the processes of implementation?

5 *What role is to be played by any intervening agency or agencies in both the research process and related action?*
What is the role of outside investigators and development agencies in influencing the design and aims of the research, the research process and outcomes? What are the decision-making procedures preceding, during and following the research? How does the agency expect to use the findings? To what extent is it able to learn from and change its policies as a result of the investigative process?

6 *What contribution to empowerment can be made by the research process*
Contribution to increasing confidence and voice ('power within')? contribution to understanding and knowledge or 'power to'? contribution to building networks and linkages between people ('power with')? contribution to behaviour and attitude change or 'power over'?

8.1.2 Participatory investigation and empowerment

Participatory methods have been described by Robert Chambers, one of their key promoters and developers, as 'a growing family of approaches and methods to enable local "rural or urban" people to express, enhance, share and analyze their knowledge of life and conditions, to plan and to act' (1994c, p. 1253). There are currently many different participatory methods – different acronyms, differences in details of processes and differences in diagrams used and the ways they are used. Some of these distinctions signal substantive differences in aims and approach, and others a progressive engagement and synthesis with other participatory methods.[2] Some, but by no means all, of the many methods are summarized in Table 8.1.

---

[2]Overviews of early developments in participatory methods can be found in Chambers, 1994a,b,c. More recent and personal accounts of developments of the different strands of participatory methodology can be found in Cornwall and Pratt, 2003; Brock and Pettit, 2007.

TABLE 8.1 *Participatory investigation: selected approaches*

Approach	Date	Description	Key sources
Activist Participatory Research (APR), also known as Participatory Action Research (PAR)	1970s	The basic ideology of PAR is that 'self-conscious people, those who are extremely poor and oppressed, will progressively transform their environment by their own praxis. In this process others may play a catalytic and supportive role but will not dominate' (Fals Borda, 1991) The main aim is not so much knowledge per se, but social change and empowerment of the marginalized and oppressed.	Paolo Freire, 1972; Fals Borda, 1991; Mohammad Anisur Rahman, 1995
Democratic evaluation (DE)	1970s	Evaluators should ensure their work contributes to dialogue and preservation of democratic principles and particularly inclusion of the underprivileged. 'Deliberative Democratic Evaluation' combines democratic evaluation with DIP principles (below).	Barry MacDonald, 1976; House, ER and Howe, KR, 2000; Segone, M, 2000; Floc'hlay, B and Plottu, E, 1998; Critique: Lizanne DeStefano and Katherine Ryan, 2004
Rapid Rural Appraisal (RRA)	1970s	Diagramming and visual techniques originating in a number of scientific disciplines for analysis of complex systems: biological science, ecology, agricultural economics and geography. From the 1980s applied anthropology added oral and other methods to gain a more sophisticated understanding. By the end of the 1980s these techniques had been combined into a flexible methodology for working with rural people to explain their responses to development programmes.	Chambers, 1980, 1992, 1994a
Participation Rural Appraisal (RRA)	1980s	Initially the term PRA (Participatory Rural Appraisal) was used to describe the bringing together of RRA and activist research. It was emphasized that the most important aspect was not the diagramming tools but their flexible application based on a number of underlying principles: • embracing complexity and seeking to understand it rather than oversimplifying reality in accordance with predetermined categories and theories, recognition of multiple realities to be taken into account in analysis or action. • prioritizing the realities of the poor and most disadvantaged as equal partners in knowledge creation and problem analysis.	Chambers, 1992, 1994 a,b,c; PLA Notes

(Continued)

TABLE 8.1   (Continued)

Approach	Date	Description	Key sources
		• grassroots empowerment: aiming not only to gather information about impact, but to make the assessment process itself a contribution to empowerment through linking grassroots learning and networking into policy-making.	
Appreciative Inquiry (AI)	1980s	Appreciative Inquiry is a methodology for organizational change. It was first formulated by Cooperrider and Srivastava (1987) as a critique of what they termed a 'problem-centred approach' to inquiry where the focus is on problems to be solved by a change agent. Appreciative Inquiry in contrast adopts an appreciative stance towards organizational change to lead to more innovative and long-lasting transformation. It consists of four main steps: • Discovery: where bottom-up open interviews bring out stories of the 'peak moments of achievement' which the community or organization values most. • Dream: where the interview stories are combined to create a new dream for the future. • Dialogue: where all those involved openly share exciting discoveries and possibilities. Through this sharing of ideals social bonding and shared vision occurs. • Destiny: construction of the future through innovation and action. Because the ideals are grounded in past realities, there is confidence to make things happen.	Cooperrider, DL and Whitney, D, 1999 Fry, R *et al.*, 2002
Fourth Generation Evaluation	1989	Identified as a new and emerging innovative form of evaluation by Guba and Lincoln (1989). It emphasizes evaluation as a process of negotiation, incorporating various stakeholders more centrally into the process. It is a development from, and reaction to, earlier forms of evaluation which focused on measurement and description. In developing these judgements fourth-generation evaluation takes into account stakeholders' consensual and competing claims, concerns and issues. Through negotiation, fourth-generation evaluation helps identify courses of action for stakeholders. The evaluator plays a role primarily as facilitator in negotiation processes with stakeholders, who participate in the design, implementation and interpretation of the evaluation as full partners.	Guba and Lincoln, 1989

(Continued)

TABLE 8.1 (Continued)

Approach	Date	Description	Key sources
Participatory Learning and Action (PLA)	1990s	The successor to PRA, Participatory Learning and Action (PLA) is seen as more effectively incorporating the underlying human rights tradition through emphasizing the importance of: • changing from appraisal to learning and hence moving away from the use of participatory methods as an extractive process by outsiders to a sustainable learning process involving different stakeholders as equal partners. • the importance of relating learning to action incorporating programme and policy improvement as an integral part of the learning process.	Chambers, 1994 a,b,c; PLA Notes
Beneficiary Assessment (BA)	1990s	Beneficiary Assessment is a qualitative research tool used in the World Bank to improve the impact of development operations by gaining the views of intended beneficiaries regarding a planned or ongoing reform, particularly the very poor. The approach relies primarily on conversational interviews, focus group discussions, and direct and participant observation. Furthermore, Beneficiary Assessment increases the participation of stakeholder groups, which leads to their ownership of the development operations and increased likelihood of its support and success.	Salmen, L, 1992; World Bank, 2002
Deliberative and Inclusionary Processes (DIPs)	1990s	These approaches were developed in a number of countries in the 1990s, in order to extend the notion of democracy to allow greater deliberation of policies and their practical implementation through the inclusion of a variety of social actors in consultation, planning and decision-making. Key features are: 1 Focus on deliberation defined as careful consideration of the discussion of reasons for and against particular forms of action. 2 Inclusionary decision-making processes based on the active involvement of multiple social actors and usually emphasizing the participation of previously excluded citizens. 3 Use of a range of procedures, techniques and methods, including citizens' juries, committees, consensus conferences, scenario workshops, rapid and participatory rural appraisal, and visioning exercises.	PLA Notes, 40, February 2001; PLA Notes, 44, June 2002

(Continued)

TABLE 8.1 (Continued)

Approach	Date	Description	Key sources
		4 Although the goal is usually to reach decisions, an unhurried, reflective, informed and reasonably open-ended discussion is required.	
Empowerment Evaluation (EE)	1990s	Use of evaluation concepts, techniques, and findings to foster improvement and self-determination. Focusing on training people in evaluation techniques to conduct their own evaluation, it employs both qualitative and quantitative methodologies. Although it can be applied to individuals, organizations, communities and societies or cultures, the focus is usually on programmes.	Fetterman, Kaftarian and Wandersman, 1996; Fetterman, 2005
REFLECT	1990s	Methodology for literacy generation piloted by Action Aid and currently implemented by over 350 organisations in sixty countries. Based on pedagogy and political philosophy of Paolo Freire and merged with techniques from PLA, it proceeds by engaging participants in discussions about their socioeconomic problems. 'Keywords' emerge from these and form the basis for literacy learning. Alongside this, individuals and communities conduct research and keep diaries related to these problems which then form the basis for lobbying and advocacy.	Archer and Cottingham, 1996; Archer, 1998
Participatory Action Learning System (PALS)	2002	Methodology currently being developed by Linda Mayoux with Kabarole Research and Resource Centre and partners in Uganda, ANANDI in India and LEAP in Sudan. Here people as individuals and as groups use diagram tools to collect information they need in order to improve their lives in ways they identify and record this in individual diaries and group minutes. This information is then supplemented by programmes through participatory and conventional quantitative and qualitative methods for programme evaluation and policy advocacy.	Mayoux and ANANDI, 2005

Underlying these methodologies is a concern with power inequalities in society and in the investigative process, and an attempt (realized or not) to somehow challenge and change these unequal power relations. For example, Chambers (1994c) identifies some important reversals in how investigative work is carried out in participatory methods:

(a) reversals of *frames*: a shift from the categories and values of outsiders to those of local people, enabling them to help define the frame of investigation;

(b) reversals of *modes*: the greater use of group work rather than individual informants; the use of visual rather than verbal techniques; and using comparison as a means of finding out quantitative data rather than direct measurement;

(c) reversals of *relations*: establishing rapport and involvement with local people rather than reserve and distance from them;

(d) reversals of *power*: enabling local people to enhance their own capacities for finding out and using and improving their own knowledge, rather than investigators extracting information for use elsewhere.

In this way participatory methods are seen as contributing to different dimensions of empowerment:

1 Those 'under investigation' will be able to make their voices heard and increase their own awareness and understanding through participatory discussion. A focus on local categories and issues helps systematize local knowledge, increase awareness and enable groups which are not generally heard to have more say in defining development needs and action. Added to this the use of diagrams enables inclusion of hitherto excluded groups and helps to systematize the information being obtained. In addition to empowerment this is also seen as increasing the accuracy and relevance of information obtained.

2 There is generally a strong emphasis on linking participatory investigation and action. The collective nature of the discussions in itself may lead to local solutions being identified and taken forward by participants themselves. Through making people's voices heard they are more likely to have a determining role in policy development which is directed towards – or is likely to affect – them (Nelson and Wright, 1995).

3 There is an emphasis on reversing power relations between investigators and those being investigated. Such processes in turn call into question the role (and power) of the investigator (or investigating team) as well as of agencies which might be involved in designing and implementing policies and interventions. In some cases there are attempts to help people take control of their own research so that their capacities and skills are built for the future (Schrijvers, 1995; Mayoux, 2003).

Development agencies' use of participatory methods adds other perceived benefits centred upon contributing to the empowerment process in a number of ways:

• Relevance: Participation of the main stakeholders is said to increase the relevance of the questions being asked to the realities of people's lives and policy processes and hence their voice in decision-making.

- Accuracy: Use of participatory methods may overcome the limitations of fragmentary individual views to increase the reliability of the information collected and likelihood of identifying realistic recommendations.
- Effectiveness: Involvement of the main stakeholders in collecting information increases awareness of the issues and ownership of the learning process and hence likelihood of implementation of recommendations – the main stated aim of much development research.
- Process: The participatory research process, through building skills, capacities and networks, can be a contribution in itself to pro-poor development, civil society and empowerment.
- Rights: Participation, and particularly and explicitly participation of the poorest and most vulnerable participants, is a human right and thus arguably an inherent and indivisible component of pro-poor development strategies and empowerment.

8.2 Positive experiences of participatory investigation and empowerment • • •

The degree to which participatory methods have lived up to the above claims of empowerment has been a subject of much debate. As will be discussed in Section 8.3 there are some inherent tensions and challenges which need to be taken into account when using participatory approaches. Nevertheless, as discussed in this section, there have been very important contributions of participatory investigation to empowerment which would be impossible, or at least more difficult, to achieve through other methods.

8.2.1 Giving voice and investigating difference

One of the main aims in using participatory methods is to help those 'under investigation' to make their voices heard, increase their own awareness and understanding through participatory and public discussion rather than being the object of individual private questioning in surveys or qualitative interviews. The design of the participatory research process aims to help people systematize local knowledge, including understanding differences and conflicts, and enables them to have more say in defining development needs and action to be taken. A key feature is that participatory methods are not intended to impose external categories of analysis, but try to reach understanding of local categories used by otherwise often 'invisible' groups such as elderly people, poor women or children.

For example, The World Bank Participatory Poverty Assessments brought together and compared subjective experiences from 60 countries into an overall analysis of poverty (Narayan and Petesch, 2002).

Local wealth rankings can take into account a wide range of considerations such as types of ownership of land and livestock, types and amounts of debts and repayment capacity, types of job, whether permanent or temporary, capacities to educate children, and so on (Chambers, 1994c).

Mapping exercises have been a well-established method for investigating differences by gender and age in representations of physical space and access to local institutions – and hence in priorities for development. Figure 8.1 shows an early example given by Welbourn (1991) of two mental maps from a village in Sierra Leone, one drawn by men and the other by women. The men's map includes all the roads which lead out of the village whereas the women's map concentrates more on the village centre. The men have identified boundaries and objects of status, such as the cotton trees, the (broken) chairman's tractor, the village drum, while women did not show any of these. When asked to mark changes they would like to see, men marked a series of important buildings lining the route of the main road leading to the village, including an administration hall near to the centre. However, when the women were asked to mark changes, they first explained that this was not their role: 'women do not have any power to decide where any of these things should be. The men have the last say' (Welbourn, 1991, p. 17). When they were encouraged to imagine changes, they drew a huge hospital, close to the centre, followed by a school and wells to serve them. In another, poorer village, when women were asked to draw changes on their maps, they replied 'we can't draw changes on this map, because the kind of changes we need can't be drawn' (ibid). The unmappable issues they were concerned about were overwork, breakdown in co-wife support and beatings from their husbands.

More recently diamond exercises have been used in India, Pakistan and Sudan to investigate local definitions of empowerment and poverty. Diamonds are used to investigate the extent and criteria of social differentiation within communities and/or groups. They start by identifying where the majority of a population are as the middle of a diamond. Then the numbers of people or examples at the extremes of the diagram are identified together with the reasons and criteria. Diamonds are good for rapidly gaining an idea of the extent of differentiation within a group or community and particularly for identifying criteria for differentiation and extreme cases. Their reliability as quantification of differentiation, however, needs to be crosschecked, either by extensive probing or voting or by other means like social mapping and surveys.

In Kashf, a Pakistani micro-finance programme, diamond diagram exercises conducted with women and men found that for women definitions of poverty included serious problems of domestic violence, drug addiction and female suicide, whereas these aspects were absent from men's definitions (Sardar, Mumtaz and Hussein, 2004). In ANANDI, an Indian NGO working with women in marginalized communities, empowerment diamonds were used to investigate tribal women's concepts of empowerment. This revealed that top of women's criteria were women's ability to defend their interests against forest officials and lobbying with the local panchayat – countering a widespread misconception in many NGOs that women's empowerment is an external imposition (Mayoux and ANANDI, 2005). In the Taraqee Foundation in Baluchistan, diamond diagrams were used to compare women and men's concepts of gender roles in 'happy families'. Women's concepts focused on issues like mutual respect and joint decision-making and wanting more knowledge of the outside world and education. The exercises with men served to counter NGO preconceptions about men's lack of support for at least some changes in gender relations – focusing on the importance of women's education and the challenges of changing the 'culture' of women's seclusion (Mayoux and Taraqee Foundation, 2006). In all these cases the analysis led to greater understanding by participants of their own aims and also to changes in the programmes.

8.2.2 Investigating sensitive issues and raising awareness: reproductive health and domestic violence

Participatory methods can also be used to research sensitive areas which are very difficult to investigate using conventional methods. One example is in relation to women's knowledge of reproduction, often a taboo or mysterious area but vital to increasing women's control over their lives as well as their health and general wellbeing. An early study used interviews and body mapping techniques in Zimbabwe to examine women's knowledge about reproduction and non-indigenous contraceptive methods (Cornwall, 1992). Interviews were used to find out what women had been told about contraception and what they thought about oral contraception. Maps of reproductive organs were drawn by women (individually or in groups) on paper or on the ground (see examples reproduced in Figure 8.2). After an initial discussion of their body maps, women were asked to draw where conception took place and describe the processes from fertilization to birth, referring back to their maps. Using these maps, researchers were able to work together with the women towards explanations of contraception and ways of preventing conception which were locally appropriate. For several women in Cornwall's study this was the first time that they had drawn anything, and for most of them, it was the first time they had thought about their internal anatomy in such a way. Use of visual methods was useful to help clarify ambiguities (for example, in understanding the term 'womb'), and provided a shared reference point for participants and researchers. The maps increased women's confidence in their own knowledge and also served to highlight some of the researchers' own biases by contrasting the biomedical frame of reference of the researchers with the ideas about human biology held by the women.

Another issue where participatory methods have proved effective has been in investigating definitions and incidence of domestic violence. Sometimes, as in the examples from Sierra Leone and Pakistan above, domestic violence comes up out of participatory discussions about poverty. Gender violence takes many different forms, some of which are so common as to be seen as 'natural'. Other forms are very extreme, leading to serious injury or death, but are hidden behind closed doors, and even disguised as 'suicide' or attempted suicide. In many cases women are reluctant to talk about such violence for fear of reprisals, and also often fear of being blamed by other women as well as men for 'bringing it upon themselves'.

Gender violence in the household and community were key issues which had come up again and again in ANANDI's work in India. However, explicitly initiating discussions of gender violence was difficult. There was an obvious gap between what ANANDI knew about violence and what emerged 'naturally' from participatory discussions. The issue of domestic violence had never once been mentioned in ANANDI's broad-based participatory needs assessment in the women's groups. But when ANANDI made a decision to explicitly include a question on violence at one of its networking fairs, 80% of group

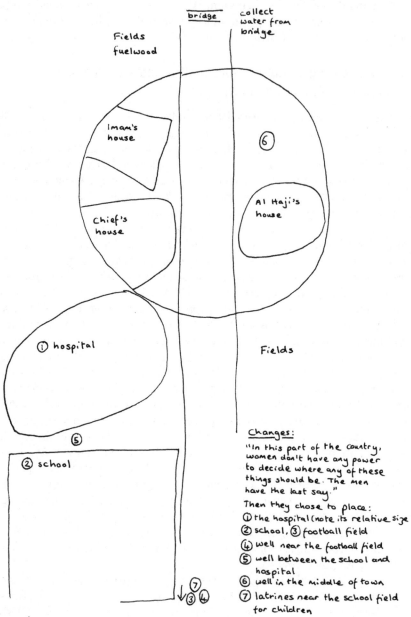

bridge

collect water from bridge

Fields fuelwood

Imam's house

⑥

Chief's house

Al Haji's house

① hospital

Fields

⑤

② school

Changes:
"In this part of the country, women don't have any power to decide where any of these things should be. The men have the last say."
Then they chose to place:
① the hospital (note its relative size
② school, ③ football field
④ well near the football field
⑤ well between the school and hospital
⑥ well in the middle of town
⑦ latrines near the school field for children

↓ ⑦
③ ④

Women's

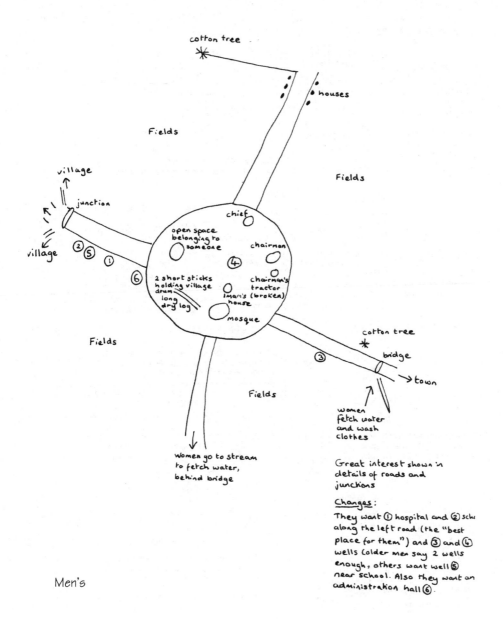

cotton tree

* houses

Fields

Fields

village

junction

village

chief

open space
belonging to
someone

② ⑤

①

chairman

④

⑥

2 short sticks
holding village
drum

chairman's
tractor
(broken)

long
dry log

Imam's
house

mosque

cotton tree

③

bridge

→ town

women
fetch water
and wash
clothes

Fields

Fields

women go to stream
to fetch water,
behind bridge

Great interest shown in
details of roads and
junctions

Changes:

They want ① hospital and ② sch
along the left road (the "best
place for them") and ③ and ④
wells (older men say 2 wells
enough, others want well ⑤
near school. Also they want an
administration hall ⑥.

Men's

FIGURE 8.1   Men's and women's village maps in Sierra Leone

1. INDIVIDUAL MAPS

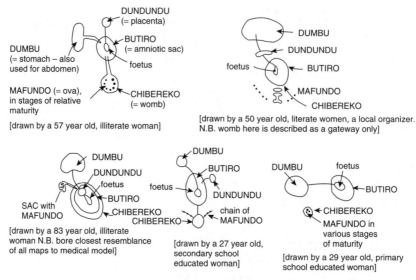

[drawn by a 57 year old, illiterate woman]

[drawn by a 50 year old, literate women, a local organizer. N.B. womb here is described as a gateway only]

[drawn by a 83 year old, illiterate woman N.B. bore closest resemblance of all maps to medical model]

[drawn by a 27 year old, secondary school educated woman]

[drawn by a 29 year old, primary school educated woman]

2. GROUP MAPS – drawn first to explore processes of conception and pregnancy, then used to discuss oral conraception

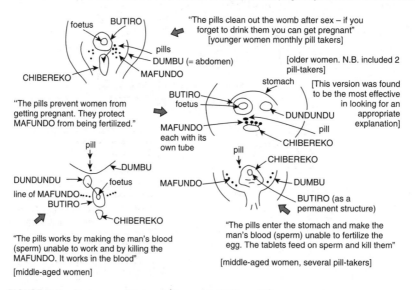

"The pills clean out the womb after sex – if you forget to drink them you can get pregnant" [younger women monthly pill takers]

[older women. N.B. included 2 pill-takers]

[This version was found to be the most effective in looking for an appropriate explanation]

"The pills prevent women from getting pregnant. They protect MAFUNDO from being fertilized."

"The pills works by making the man's blood (sperm) unable to work and by killing the MAFUNDO. It works in the blood" [middle-aged women]

"The pills enter the stomach and make the man's blood (sperm) unable to fertilize the egg. The tablets feed on sperm and kill them" [middle-aged women, several pill-takers]

FIGURE 8.2   Body map diagrams (Cornwall, 1992, p. 71)

representatives reported domestic violence as a serious issue in their groups. ANANDI was therefore looking for a method which would help to understand the different forms which violence takes, the incidence of such violence and whether or not ANANDI's work was leading to increase or decrease in conflict. During a participatory review staff used the

Violence Diamond, ANANDI, India

Looks at different levels of violence: from 'acceptable levels of violence'
to extreme, numbers of people and strategies

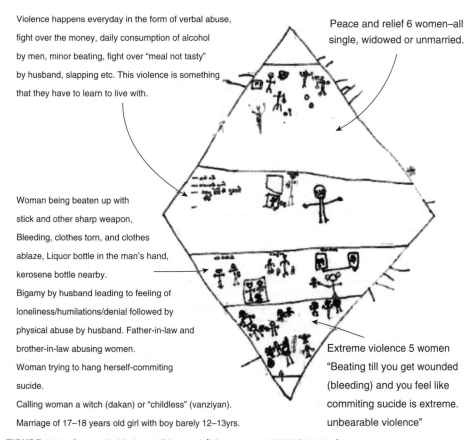

Violence happens everyday in the form of verbal abuse, fight over the money, daily consumption of alcohol by men, minor beating, fight over "meal not tasty" by husband, slapping etc. This violence is something that they have to learn to live with.

Peace and relief 6 women–all single, widowed or unmarried.

Woman being beaten up with stick and other sharp weapon, Bleeding, clothes torn, and clothes ablaze, Liquor bottle in the man's hand, kerosene bottle nearby.
Bigamy by husband leading to feeling of loneliness/humilations/denial followed by physical abuse by husband. Father-in-law and brother-in-law abusing women.
Woman trying to hang herself-commiting suicide.
Calling woman a witch (dakan) or "childless" (vanziyan).
Marriage of 17–18 years old girl with boy barely 12–13yrs.

Extreme violence 5 women "Beating till you get wounded (bleeding) and you feel like commiting sucide is extreme. unbearable violence"

FIGURE 8.3 Domestic Violence Diamond (Mayoux and ANANDI, 2005)

diamond tool (see Figure 8.3) with 20 women from one village to examine the different types of violence and how women ranked their relative seriousness. In two hours, use of the diamond helped women to move from denial of any existence of domestic violence to discussing their distressing experiences for the first time, including five cases of attempted murder which the women had never before discussed, even between themselves. As in the body mapping, women themselves did all the drawing and this focus on the pictures helped women to be more open and spontaneous. They then used a Road Journey diagram where women drew how they saw themselves coming out of this situation and the role of ANANDI in facilitating this process (Mayoux and ANANDI, 2005).

In both the Zimbabwe and India cases it was the combination of diagrams and drawing with participatory discussion which gave women the confidence to open up and discuss difficult and sometimes painful issues. In ANANDI a further key factor was the women's trust in ANANDI as an organization with the will and capacity to take the issue forward in ways which would not make them even more vulnerable.

8.2.3 From voice to action: investigating institutional and policy contexts

Most development research aims to be in some way action-oriented. However, the link between research and action is much more explicit and often immediate in participatory methods because the analysis is often done by participants. REFLECT and PALS methodologies in particular enable people to carry out their own analyses, even after the research process has ended (Table 8.1).

In many cases participatory investigation has been useful in informing or challenging the agendas set by outsiders. In some of the examples above women's and men's priorities were shown to be very different. Some were previously invisible or deemed less important by development agencies. In another example from Bangladesh (from Welbourn, 1992, p. 6), the main concern of the researchers was health. However, a problem priority matrix ranking carried out with landless women showed that the women's overriding concerns were for means of livelihood, the future reduction of access to natural resources (the river bank on which they lived), and lack of business opportunities. Although a survey could have shown the same results, the participatory ranking method was quicker, did not rely on literacy and also revealed interesting insights into the reasons for differences in the women's priorities which energed during the discussions. Such insights would not have been evident from simply combining individual rankings.

Participatory methods can be used to raise the awareness of the more powerful. For example, participatory methods are widely used to raise men's awareness of gender subordination, as in the Baluchistan example above. In another example in Gujarat (Bilgi, 1992), men had resisted the introduction of labour-saving devices such as biogas, pressure cookers and flour mills because they found the food produced by these methods tasteless and they were not particularly concerned to reduce women's workloads. PLA methods were used to raise men's awareness of women's work and enable them to reflect on their initial perceptions. The men then went on to look at the nature of the women's tasks and to evaluate how 'hard' they were compared with their own. These participatory discussions are very useful in investigating attitudes and preconceptions and to explore this new awareness can provide the basis for change.

Participatory methods are increasingly used for investigating institutions. Institutional mapping has been widely used to look at the different types of institutions affecting people's lives and how they can be changed and influenced (MYRADA, 1992; Mayoux and ANANDI, 2005). Participatory value chains analysis is being used to look at ways to improve the incomes and working conditions of textile workers and workers in multinational companies (McCormick and Schmitz, 2001; Auret and Barrientos, 2004). Participatory methodologies have also been used to do institutional analysis for grassroots-based advocacy and lobbying strategies (Veneklasen and Miller, 2002).

8.3 Some limitations and pitfalls of participatory methods • • •

It is nevertheless important not to idealize the empowering capacities of participatory methods. In designing a participatory investigation it is important to bear in mind the following:

(a) increasing participation cannot substitute for a proper understanding of power relations within the boundaries of research;
(b) participatory methods do not automatically ensure empowering outcomes;
(c) using participatory methods requires constant awareness of inherent power inequalities in the research process itself

We look briefly at each of these three issues in turn. Some ways of addressing these challenges are then outlined in Section 8.4.

8.3.1 Power relations within research boundaries

There has been a tendency in many discussions of participatory methods to present an idealized picture of 'local knowledge' and 'communities'. These have tended to treat local knowledge as somehow infallible and ignore the many ways in which power relations within communities structure the generation and control of knowledge both by individuals and by social groups. However, reliance on spontaneous expressions of 'local knowledge' may lead to very erroneous conclusions – as illustrated by the example of ANANDI above where initial participatory group discussions failed to identify the problems of domestic violence. It is important (as highlighted also in Chapter 2) to treat critically the outcomes of participatory discussions and be aware of: what is and is not seen as 'up for discussion'; who can (or does) communicate with whom, about what, and for what reason; what types of knowledge are generated, who has access to which types of knowledge and how different types of knowledge are used.

Participatory methods may not necessarily either produce reliable information or enable different voices to be heard. In a recent discussion of the implications of findings in social psychology for participatory processes, Bill Cooke argues that participatory discussions may distort rather than reflect people's views and consequently decisions based upon them – even without significant inequalities between participants. He outlines four main ways in which this can happen: discussions may produce decisions which are more risky than might be the case if made by individuals; discussions may persuade people to support decisions with which no one agrees because they are carried along by what they think is a group consensus; 'group think' may stifle dissent and critical thought; and intentional design of the discussion process may lead to 'coercive persuasion' to agree certain outcomes (Cooke, 2001). Power inequalities are likely to significantly increase these distortions.

The outcomes of participatory investigation need to be treated with some caution. Local knowledge needs to be treated as critically as any other type of knowledge, even that which has been subjected to 'community' discussion and scrutiny. For example, Mosse concluded from a PRA exercise in India (1995, p. 32):

The essential material for our social analysis is not found so much in the agreed output (on map, chart or diagram), but in the absences, the gaps and corrections, the after-thoughts, the errors and false-starts, the disagreements or conflicts, even the complete failure of a PRA exercise. Through these we get glimpses of how power operates in the community ...

Participatory approaches can still exclude people from investigation. 'Key informants' are often used and the definition of who is 'key' is inevitably based on rather subjective value judgements. Even where key informants are not purposively selected participation is rarely 'equal'. In an early study using wealth rankings in Malawi, Welbourn found that the people who spoke in meetings and showed researchers around were generally those who had more respect and self-confidence and were from relatively high status social groups. They presented their own problems, outlooks and needs. By contrast, the richest people did not attend meetings or show researchers around because they had little to gain and had their own means of access to resources, while the poorest people did not attend meetings because they did not think that the processes would be relevant to them (Welbourn, 1991). Minorities or groups in danger of violence are particularly unlikely to participate. Research by Mosse has shown that women often do not participate unless they are specifically targeted and encouraged (Mosse, 1995). It can be difficult to get children to participate and sustain their interest (Guijt *et al.*, 1994; Baker, 1996). Even in targeted exercises, it cannot be assumed that the poorest are being reached. For example, a mapping exercise in a low caste area in Tamil Nadu missed out some households. On talking to the large number of local women and men involved, they stated that the missing households were 'only huts, we didn't count those, they are the downtrodden who depend on daily labour' (Pretty *et al.*, 1992, p. 42).

Use of participatory methods is not therefore a substitute for in-depth investigation of power relations in the community. Rather an understanding of these power relations is necessary to both design and interpret participation in discussions. Such an understanding can be built up through a series of participatory investigations which build one on the other, or it may require complementary use of other qualitative or quantitative methods. Equally importantly, it requires careful documentation of the participatory process rather than only relying on any one single diagram output.

8.3.2 Difficulties in achieving empowering outcomes

The potential fallibility of local knowledge has particularly important implications where the investigation is linked to action and where the outcomes of research may have negative as well as positive outcomes for participants. It cannot be assumed that local participatory discussions will necessarily lead to wise strategies for action, even in relatively egalitarian settings and without 'distorting' influence from outsiders. The nature of poverty means that, although poor people have certain types of knowledge which are of critical importance for development decisions, they are also excluded from other types of knowledge and are as likely as anyone else to be just plain wrong. For example, one very active REFLECT group in Uganda had done a thorough community mapping. They had also done body mapping as part of their identification of health problems. Linking the two processes of investigation they had identified two major community problems: firstly, AIDS/HIV and male sexuality in particular; and, secondly, population pressure within the village, leading to families, including young people, living very closely together. This led them to conclude that close proximity of young people was somehow related to spread of AIDS/HIV. The solution they identified was to persuade young men to build their houses outside the village or to move to urban areas. Questions of women's control over their own bodies and gender inequality were not raised. This may have been partly because of participation of some older men in the group, some of whom were related to some of the young women (Mayoux, 2003).

The passage from discussion to action needs to be treated with even more caution where power relations are very unequal and certain parties have a vested interest in the outcomes. Where they are not carefully targeted, participatory approaches may be used to legitimize the demands of the more powerful. This was a problem encountered by the Mosse study cited above. Another example is given by Richards (1995) of a study of the Mende in Sierra Leone. It describes how village elders created space for people to express differences of opinion in public meetings. However, the elders' management of this space ensured that the decisions made generally favoured the village elite.

Even when decisions are not made in the interest of powerful vested interests, it is likely that they will be oriented towards the interests of those who have been most active in the research process. While this may not be a 'pitfall' as such, it is important to be aware of the implications. For example, Ison (1996) describes using an action participation research approach to investigate why graziers in New South Wales, Australia, were not adopting new practices to limit rangeland degradation. The project attempted to construct and constantly negotiate shared meanings and understandings of what it meant to be a pastoralist, and of the practices and problems of rangeland farming. Using a six-person team over nine months, graziers were given semi-structured and in-depth interviews and then were invited to attend joint discussions, become co-researchers, and present and discuss particular 'enthusiasms' for action. At this point, the main difficulty for the researchers was to stand back and allow the graziers to identify points of action. In addition, although the graziers came with a diversity of 'enthusiasms', the process of arriving at consensus for action resulted in a relatively small number of graziers carrying it forward. Those who did continue to be active were the graziers whose ideas had become the consensus.

Participatory approaches may expose and reinforce rather than address conflicts of power relations. Such tensions can be a particularly difficult area for development managers and development agencies to handle. For example, Shah and Shah describe the consequences of a participatory appraisal of natural resources in a village in Gujarat. The investigation showed that a low caste group, the Gadvis, had little access to surface water resources. A high caste group, the Rajputs, owned the large fields and controlled most of the common property resources, including water. Both groups wanted wells dug on their land and NGO engineers identified suitable sites. The Gadvis raised the capital required and the group started constructing its community well. They developed a land use plan and started preparations for cultivating in the winter season. However, in the process, the Rajputs had lost their source of cheap wage labour in the Gadvis, because the Gadvis had previously needed to do wage work to supplement their low incomes from their unirrigated fields. Several meetings were organized between the groups during this period for negotiations and bargaining. But while the Gadvis were still working on their wells, they were ambushed and beaten up by a group of Rajputs. Two of the Gadvis died and others were injured. The NGO facilitators had not been able to contain the effects of the participatory process of investigation on this power struggle. Rather than initiating further programmes, the NGO then spent more time facilitating negotiations between the two groups (Shah and Shah, 1995, p. 50).

8.3.3 Tyranny of the research process?

Using participatory methods does not automatically remove power inequalities between researchers and those being researched. It is just as important when using participatory methods as using any other research methods, that researchers should be aware of their own biases and preconceptions and work consciously to counter them. Otherwise the benefits claimed for using participatory methods are undermined.

At the same time, in view of the unequal power relations in many group discussions, it is important to balance participation with facilitation. It may be necessary for investigators to raise and suggest issues if they have good reason to feel that they are important, but are somehow being hidden in the participatory process. This is particularly the case with sensitive issues like domestic violence and/or where local analyses are ill-informed.

When to intervene and when not to intervene will inevitably always be a difficult decision. There are inherent requirements in any research process which are likely to pose certain limits on empowerment. Firstly, most policy-based research has to reach some conclusions which can then lead to action. This may be within the limits of one participatory consultation or over a longer period. Nevertheless, decisions have to be made about when to allow 'free flow', when to ask certain voices to be quieter in order to let other voices come through and when to direct investigation to be able to come up with conclusions and action.

Secondly, development research very often requires large amounts of data in order to convince policy-makers. Eliciting certain types of quantitative information by using participatory methods can be relatively quick (and cheap) compared with other methods of research. Chambers (1994c) relates how in Kabripathar village in Gujarat an illiterate woman from a neighbouring village facilitated census mapping by women on to cards, leading to a full village census of 87 families, giving numbers of women, men, girls, boys, bullocks, cows, buffaloes, goats, donkeys and other information. This process was completed and checked in about four hours. Seasonal calendars and flow diagrams have also been rapidly elicited from groups of poor and illiterate children, women and men showing important information which would otherwise take a long period of field research to gather using conventional methods. Numerous other examples where participatory methods have led to more rapid collection of more reliable information are cited in Mayoux and Chambers (2005).

Nevertheless there are questions as to how empowering these exercises are for participants unless linked explicitly to action outcomes. In particular the use of locally-produced categories and classifications must often be weighted and reduced to figures similar to those in surveys in order to be aggregated for macro-analysis. The difference is that, when using participatory methods, this weighting can at least take some account of local priorities.

8.4 Investigation as empowerment: critical considerations • • •

Although participatory methods of investigation can act as empowering mechanisms under certain circumstances, some of the challenges are also clear. The contributions and pitfalls we have mentioned are summarized in Box 8.2, but more can be found in the now extensive literature (see Box 8.3). What is evident is that using participatory methods of investigation as a means of empowerment requires a high level of awareness on the part of investigators and their institutions as to what the investigative process is for. It also means being highly aware of researcher preconceptions and bias, of the link between investigation and action, and of ethical considerations. We now look briefly at these aspects.

Box 8.2   Investigation and empowerment: potential contributions and challenges of participatory methods

Potential contributions

power within: may enable those 'under investigation' to increase confidence and increase their own awareness and understanding to make their voices heard.

power to: a focus on local categories and issues may help groups which are not generally heard to have more say in defining development needs and action to gain access to knowledge, resources and power itself. Methodologies used may also develop people's analytical and learning skills to do their own research on issues of importance to them.

power with: the collective nature of the discussions in itself may lead to local solutions being identified and taken forward by participants themselves. The research process may also develop skills and networks for collective discussion and action.

power over: making people's voices heard may give them a more determining role in policy development which is directed towards – or is likely to affect – them. Can help to break down barriers beween the powerless and those with more power and between investigators and investigated.

(Continued)

(Continued)

Use of diagrams and/or explicit targeting enables inclusion of hitherto excluded groups and expression of their points of view.

Potential challenges

-   Local knowledge is not infallible
-   May be exclusive rather than inclusive unless carefully designed
-   May expose, but may not deal with, conflicts and may be used by the more powerful to legitimate their own demands unless power relations are understood.
-   May raise confidence, aspirations and expectations without fulfilling them and hence make people feel and/or be more disadvantaged and vulnerable
-   May give illusion of 'empowerment' which may be token and not integrated into decision-making or lead to action.

Box 8.3   Further sources on participatory investigation

A number of recent publications contain papers on the pros and cons of participatory approaches to development in general, notably Cooke and Kothari (2001) 'Participation: The New Tyranny?' which contains critiques of the unthinking application of participatory development. This was followed by a 'counter-volume' by Hickey and Mohan (2004) 'Participation: from Tyranny to Transformation?' which sought to move away from the timely critiques of participatory tools in Cooke and Kothari's collection towards situating participation within political processes of citizenship building. Personal stories of those using participatory methods and current innovations can be found in Cornwall and Pratt (2003) and Brock and Pettit (2007).

Continually updated bibliographies on participatory investigation and action can be obtained from the participation website of the Institute of Development Studies, Sussex University, UK (www.ids.ac.uk). The International Institute for Environment and Development (IIED) in London, UK, publishes the journal PLA Notes which has detailed discussion of innovative methodologies (www.iied.org). Further information can be found by doing a web search on 'participation', 'participatory methods,' 'participatory investigation' and so on, each of which comes up with different useful sources. You can also search on the different types of participatory methods outlined in Table 8.1 above.

8.4.1 Focusing on processes as well as outputs

One area of awareness involves being clear about the purpose of the research (see also the discussion at the start of Chapter 6). Although never an easy task, this is probably more straightforward using conventional research methods than when the research process is intended to include other people in the definition and design of it. However, participatory approaches can have advantages over other research processes, which might meet obstacles at a later stage if local social dynamics and relations have not been taken into account earlier on.

In participatory investigation, there is also a difficult balancing act between research process and obtaining research outputs. Investigators might have a set of concerns or an agenda which requires specific outputs – for example, finding out about local healthcare needs to develop a healthcare policy for their organization. However, the concerns of researchers and participants may be different (as in the priority ranking exercise from Bangladesh mentioned in 8.2.3). Thus, if investigators want people to have a say in how the research is carried out and to be able to influence policy and action outcomes, decisions will have to be made about whose agendas should have priority or how different agendas can be combined.

The tension between process and output in participatory investigation can also affect the time required to carry out such research. Although particular methods can produce rapid results (as in Chambers' example of doing a village census in a few hours), the time between the beginning of the investigative process and outcomes can also be quite extended (as with Ison's nine month study of graziers). This means that there is a temptation to concentrate on the output by using a semblance of participatory approaches rather than actually allowing the investigative process to have the time and depth it may require to enable participants to gain investigative or organizational skills ('power to') and have more control over outcomes ('power over' or 'power with').

Steering an investigation which is intended to have an empowering effect on participants in a multiple-actor situation suggests that there are likely to be conflicts – or, at least, differences – of values over the purpose, process and desired products. To be an effective investigator in these circumstances requires a number of skills, such as: the ability to sustain a dialogue across different social groupings about their needs and interests; the ability to negotiate; and the ability to build consensus about process and outcomes in order to get something done. An equally important task could also be enabling other participants to gain such skills. However, the investigator must also try to steer a research process through the concerns of other stakeholders or interested parties, such as other organizations working in the area, government ministries, and international organizations. Knowledge and understanding of the institutional arena and its dynamics is necessary to inform reflection on the research goals, processes and outputs (Chapters 4, 6, and 12 address this point in different ways). As a final point investigators also need to be highly aware of and to manage their own 'power relations' – both with respect to other participants and stakeholders in the research process, and to their own position in their organization.

8.4.2 Preconceptions and exclusions

The construction of boundaries – which is a necessary part of the investigative process – must be carried out with a great deal of care in participatory research. (The concept of boundaries is explored in detail by Blackmore and Ison in Chapter 2.) Care is needed not only in deciding what is and is not within the investigative boundary but also in the focus or course of inquiry within it. Questioning assumptions about boundaries is therefore an essential part of the investigative process, especially if particular categories of people are not to be excluded. An obvious example is the now commonly debated concept of household. Households may be seen as single units of analysis by both participants and facilitators; for example, in investigating poverty and livelihoods. However, the composition of households, what differences exist between members' access to and control over resources and over decision-making, how perceptions of the roles of the old, the young, men and women are constructed, might all be important dimensions in investigating and understanding a given set of livelihood issues.

People can be excluded from participation because of the greater influence of powerful groups within communities, or because of the interests, agendas and world-views of other organizational stakeholders. How can investigators try and ensure that the people relevant to a particular investigation take part? Part of the answer might lie in greater awareness of one's own and others' preconceptions of social relations and dynamics – and encouraging dialogue and debate about firmly-held ideas. However, it may also involve setting up checklists directed to the needs of a specific investigation and for specific groups of participants, including the following, adapted from Dent (1996):

- *Timing*: are people able to join in the activities?
- *Location*: where are people allowed to meet? Where will they feel comfortable and able to speak?
- *Representation*: are disadvantaged groups, e.g. women or ethnic minorities, represented in the participatory team?
- *Relevance:* are issues covered which are relevant to the different participants? Are there issues relevant to some participants which are excluded?
- *Equal roles*: are all people able to have an equal voice in mixed meetings, perhaps with the facilitator's help? Or will separate meetings for different participants be more effective?
- *Marginalized groups*: are minority or marginalized groups within generally disadvantaged communities, e.g. widows, divorcees, disabled, and the elderly in women's meetings, seen and heard?
- *Capacity building:* do the methods and processes used build the capacities and confidence of disadvantaged groups to enable them to participate effectively in future?

8.4.3 Investigation and action

The reality of much policy development is that, at least in the initial stages, information is required quickly and is often incomplete, even if information gathering over the longer-term can be set up through monitoring procedures. Given the often finite periods of time which any investigator or worker for government or other organization is likely to spend in a particular site of investigation, follow-up processes can only be seriously pursued if there is local control over and desire for continuous knowledge-building – that is, the empowerment process.

Ideally researchers need to seek out a suitable local institutional base for linking investigation to action. An isolated piece of participatory investigation may raise expectations among participants about future action which cannot be realized by investigators or their organizations. At the same time, participatory research may raise institutional awareness of necessity to set up structures for ongoing dialogue. For example, a DFID review of Participatory Poverty Assessments concluded that: 'Cumulative evidence from this review shows that the poor can provide analyses of the complex states of poverty and furthermore analyze policy solutions ... In all the PPAs reviewed the poor showed an impressive ability to identify differences and suggest specific and realistic reforms tailored to their situation. These types of specificities highlight the need for policymakers and sector planners to listen carefully to the voices of the poor. The complexities and multifaceted nature of their lives are difficult to understand without engaging in continuous dialogue. If policymakers wish their services to be accessible and relevant it is clear the demands of messages of the poor are paramount' (Brocklesby and Holland, 1998, pp. 25–26). This in turn may require changes in the institutions themselves, as Narayan and Srinivasan (1994, p. vii) state: 'in order to have significant impact, participatory approaches must be accompanied by institutional reform supportive of local initiative'. However, assuming an institutional context which is favourable to local action, participatory investigation can in principle provide a basis for ongoing dialogue about the nature and direction of policy development.

Even given a favourable institutional environment, who takes action and on what basis is also open to question. For example, there may be a choice for an external investigator between standing back and allowing other participants in the investigative process to determine what action should be taken (for example, in Ison's New South Wales graziers case above), or ensuring that an external agency takes responsibility and intervenes. Instances when it is extremely important to do the latter include conditions of extreme social conflict.

8.4.4 Ethical considerations

Finally, as we have illustrated, it would be naive to assume that participatory investigation will necessarily be empowering for participants. Rather than empowering people, participation can make them extremely vulnerable, if sensitive information enters the public arena, or if knowledge and understanding which enables marginalized people to cope with difficult social situations is appropriated by others already more powerful than themselves. Such possible effects place a high level of social and ethical responsibility on those initiating and supporting the investigation.

How rights and responsibilities are to be established in the investigative process is a crucial consideration for those carrying out participatory research. This is particularly important in the ownership, and thus acknowledgement and use, of research output, as well as in issues of openness and confidentiality. Although ethical concerns apply to all forms of research, they are brought even more sharply into focus by the anticipated reversals that participative approaches are expected to bring.

Doing 'incorrect' research: The importance of the subjective and the personal in researching poverty

9

Dina Abbott

It is not uncommon for both academics and practitioners involved with development research to feel uncomfortable with their choice of methodologies because of the limited interpretations that these allow in defending their research or in evaluating and monitoring groundwork. This may be because we are no longer convinced that poverty alleviation can be singularly achieved through economic growth, and that the quantitative information that necessarily goes with this is enough to give us a clear understanding of the complexities of social realities and the truths of the vulnerable lives of those individuals caught up in poverty. It can also be because we have come a long way in recognising that both developmental interventions and developmental fieldwork require a context specific understanding of power, morality, ethics and sensitivity.

Therefore, in recent years we have seen a growth in undergraduate textbooks (Scheyvens and Storey, 2003; Desai and Potter, 2006) and practitioner manuals (Law, Harper and Marcus, 2003; Mikkelsen, 2005) directing us to better ways of designing and analysing research into development issues. Yet there are contradictions between the ordered and systematic way this literature guides us into the research process, and the reality that we do not always shape our understanding of poverty-related issues in a consciously organised way. More often than not, it is difficult to 'prove' how we have 'found out' about a particular situation because our knowledge has been built up through a process involving random observations, trials and errors, unsystematic approaches and generally 'untraditional' and untidy ways of 'finding out'. By its nature, this indiscriminate method of acquiring knowledge is necessarily subjective, value-laden and very very personal. Any analysis and interpretation of data (whether for academic research or for monitoring and evaluation purposes) is therefore bound to be tricky, particularly as this requires a major shift from the 'informal' processes of information gathering to the 'formal' one of information dissemination. It is therefore not surprising that academics and practitioners continue to struggle around what is acceptable as 'proof' and what others will reject as 'unproven'.

This chapter argues that, rather than seeking out proofs that fit in with 'traditional' notions of research, we reflect on the processes that have shaped our understanding of particular situations and context. This especially includes the subjective, value-laden and personal interpretations that have enabled us to build relationships and, in turn, widen our understanding of their specific situations. Unlike positivists who regard research as value free, restrained by a need to be 'objective', this chapter draws on a feminist discourse on methodology and suggests that values play a fundamental role in enhancing understanding of development issues. If as academics and practitioners we begin to understand what these values are, where they are coming from, and how and to what extent they contribute to our knowledge of particular situations, we may be able to deal with some of the contradictions and dilemmas of researching poverty related development issues. In this way, we also have the potential to contribute to the development of new epistemologies such as that of action research that many practitioners are currently involved with (for example McNiff and Whitehead, 2006).

I will illustrate this argument from my own study on how poor women, supported by a women's organisation called the *Annapurna Mahila Mandal* (AMM), struggle to make a living through home-based cooking activities in the vast slums of Mumbai. This was an academic study that formed the basis of a PhD. It began in 1989 with the evidence gathering, data analysis and writing altogether taking up to five years. In drawing my conclusions, I will also refer to recent research that I did with others (Abbott, Brown and Wilson, 2007) on development practitioner perceptions of poverty. This study suggests that it is not just academics, but also those doing everyday ground work in poverty alleviation, who struggle to locate their own understanding of poverty within that of organisational needs for rigid evaluation and monitoring methods. From this, I will suggest that:

- Information gathered in what appears to be a haphazard way can be organised systematically for analytical purposes, and that
- Instead of being regarded as methodologically 'incorrect', the subjective and the personal have the potential to enhance knowledge of the specific context of the research as well as general issues of development.

9.1 The academic research: The AMM and the *khannawallis* (mealmakers) of Mumbai • • •

To begin with, something about my academic research. This was about a group of women known as *khannawallis* – women who supply meals for migrant workers. (For the complete version, see Abbott, 1993.) Simply told, their story began in colonial times when Mumbai started to develop rapidly as an important port and an industrial base. The city's labour requirements were at the time, and still are, largely met by rural migrants. Early census figures suggest that migration was predominantly that of single males from neighbouring states, mostly of men who retained their ties with the land and continued to return seasonally to their fields (Burnet-Hurst, 1925).

There are several reasons why this pattern of single male migration emerged in Mumbai. Firstly, poor rainfall, drought and crop failure, together with British demand for agricultural taxes, brought abysmal poverty to rural families who were forced to seek cash opportunities in the towns. At the same time, they could not afford to let go of the land or neglect it. Migration was thus selective and seasonal so that agricultural activity could continue. Secondly, while there were plenty of opportunities in Mumbai's thriving ports, docks and textile mills, the shortage of housing was so chronic that even if they wanted to, it would not have been feasible for whole families to migrate. The men, married or otherwise, thus migrated singly to Mumbai.

When they arrived in Mumbai, inadequate housing plus the compelling necessity to save forced the migrants to share single room tenements (known as *kholis*), often between thirty to forty of them. Besides a place to sleep, the *kholis* did not provide much. The rooms were bare, and had hardly any cooking, washing or other basic facilities. In fact, large numbers meant that even the space for a sleeping mat had to be negotiated on the basis of shift and work timings. At the same time, the working conditions of the textile mills and other industries were horrendous. The men had to cope with long hours of intense labouring in Victorian circumstances. (See Morris, 1965, and Upadhyay, 1990, for further detail.) Whilst sheer exhaustion forced them to sleep wherever possible, an overwhelming necessity was that of cooked food. 'Outside' food was not really a suitable alternative for home-cooked food for various economic reasons such as expense, and social reasons, such as caste as well as religious food taboos.

Some of the women who did manage to join their husbands in Mumbai saw an opportunity to make an income in this, and for an agreed sum began to cook two meals a day for the *kholi* dwellers. The men could have their meals packed and delivered to either their *kholis* or their workplaces in lunch boxes consisting of three or four containers (*tiffins*). Or they could come to the woman's house to eat their food. Women who provided cooked food (*khanna*) thus became known as *khannawallis*.

Throughout Mumbai's history, there have of course been several attempts at rectifying the housing situation, particularly during those times when persistent congestion and lack of hygiene have resulted in an outbreak of disease. Thus, in the 1920s when Mumbai was engulfed by the bubonic plague for a second time, the municipality was forced to make improvements, particularly in the supply and control of basic water and sewerage facilities.

Mumbai, however, continues to suffer, and for millions of migrants, and the city's poor, housing still remains unacceptable. It is of little surprise, then, that in 1994 history repeated itself and brought national shame when the plague took hold of Mumbai once again.

The demand for the *khannawalli* service has therefore continued, and has provided a living for many generations as the 'trade' is passed on from mother to daughter. As in the past, even today, several mills and factories of Mumbai open their gates at midday to allow cartloads of *tiffins* to be brought in for the workers' lunch, and thousands of Mumbai's migrants still rely on the *khannawallis* to supply a home-cooked evening meal. Some of the *khannawallis* go even further and enter into 'boarding' arrangements for men who might not be able to access *kholi* accommodation (which essentially remains bare even today), although their own homes are themselves no more than slum huts or tenements.

Like the single male migrants, the *khannawallis* are poor, illiterate and live in slum localities, all of which ensures them a low social status. Thus, as one report put it:

> ... the very term *khannawalli* has a derogatory meaning. It insinuates a socially ignorant woman, plying for a trade, looked down upon ... Her work is not recognized. After all, what is so special about a woman cooking? Contributing to the family income? What a fancy idea! She is only feeding herself and her children. As a mother it is her moral duty to do so.

(AMM, 1990, p. 1)

Because of this image, my interest in the *khannawallis* was a puzzle to many people in Mumbai, including the women themselves. But my interest was based on at least three aspects:

1 The *khannawallis* were and are an essential part of Mumbai's industrial development and have historically enabled scores of migrants to live and work in conditions that would otherwise have been unacceptable.
2 The *khannawallis* contribute extensively to their family's income (in cash or kind) and enable survival for both their extended rural and urban families, even if this often remains unacknowledged.
3 In 1975, under the leadership of Prema Purao, a former trade union official and Communist Party cadre, the khannawallis, who normally work in isolation in their homes, founded a trade-union-like organisation known as the Annapurna Mahila Mandal (Abbott, 1992). The AMM functions on similar principles to other 'grassroots' organisations that have attempted to organise poor women in India, such as the Self-Employed Women's Association (SEWA) and Working Women's Forum (WWF). Its achievements are impressive and, like SEWA and WWF, it is often regarded as an exemplary model of self-organisation of women in self-employment in the informal sector (Abbott, 1997).

Self-organisation has brought isolated women together, and has allowed them to raise questions about the future of their activity (see Examples 1 and 2 below for some life stories). The AMM itself was initially interested in my research, particularly as it was in the process of promoting itself more broadly to women outside its initial membership. At the time, the AMM was also initiating micro-credit for women, something which is now mainstreamed in global poverty alleviation strategies. Bearing all this in mind, I wanted to find out more about the dynamics of the *khannawalli* activity and the detail of how the *khannawallis* organise and make a living from it.

9.2 Shaping methodology • • •

9.2.1 A process of rejection

As with any empirical work the first question that I needed to work out was 'Which method?' The answer was difficult. I, like other research students at the time, had my mind focussed on 'scientific' methods as being the most 'objective' and rational paths towards research, the most obvious of which is that of surveys. However, the specific context of Indian poverty and local social and political set-ups suggested otherwise.

Weiner (1982, pp. 277–320), for instance, has argued that in India most social science research (even that undertaken at universities) leans heavily in one direction, i.e. that of applied and policy-directed research, rather than academic or 'basic' research. In this, there is a high emphasis on large-scale, statistical types of study in order to provide ministers and decision-makers with data that they can easily comprehend. Weiner therefore suggests that often, if the research raises controversial issues or the ministers in question do not agree with it, it is disregarded or 'scrapped'. It is arguable to what extent this remains the case today, although even a cursory glance at Indian social science studies on poverty suggests a continued focus on large surveys which allow a speedy accumulation of data on numerous aspects of women's and child poverty (the two often not being seen as separate issues).

Besides this, there were also several questions on how suitable or ethical survey methodology is for the context and setting of the investigation. Surveys, for instance, usually involve structured questionnaires that require 'official' looking paraphernalia such as notebooks, forms, and tape recorders. What I realised was that 'officialdom' is regarded with hostility and suspicion because officials from banks constantly threaten slum dwellers. At the other extreme, they are also under threat from 'clean up' programmes where homes are demolished and people displaced. In a bid to beautify Mumbai, at the time of the research, several slums were wiped out overnight. In addition, the poor were the targets of Malthusian attempts to control population (as with Sanjay Ghandi's notorious forced sterilisation of slum dwellers in the 1970s).

My worry was that I would also become associated with this type of officialdom and therefore would not be trusted. My feelings were confirmed in an incident that occurred during my first visit when I was talking to a *khannawalli* and her husband. A neighbour came rushing in and screamed, 'These people are very poor, and you have come to make them even more poor – we know you are from the Government!' The questions I was asking and the notebook I was carrying made this man suspect that I was a government official with alternate motives. Luckily the incident was contained when the person who had accompanied me rescued me. From that day, I did not openly write in notebooks or record conversations. I quickly learnt that data gathering cannot be divorced from local political realities and histories. Therefore, research methods have to adapt to the specifics of that, and not the other way round.

Secondly, whilst survey based information gathering is necessary from time to time, by its very rigidity it can turn people into 'objects' if not thoughtfully conducted. In India, the manner in which poor people are subjected to survey investigations some-times leaves much to be desired. From what I observed, such surveys often rely on inex-perienced undergraduates who are sent to 'gather data' on poverty, sometimes in one sitting. They are given questionnaires which can be insensitive in themselves, and there is often little account taken of settings and ethical or gender considerations. Gulati (1991, p.15), for instance, cites a UN-sponsored study on returned migrants. The survey (which was conducted by a junior team member) asked:

> What were the effects on marital and family relations (on the migrant returning home)? Was the adjustment very good/good/bad/very bad? Did migration of one of the spouses lead to:
>
> 1 greater sharing of responsibility by both spouses?
> 2 strengthening of family bond?
> 3 loss of affection between spouse, respondent, and children?
> 4 infidelity or other marital problems caused by separation?
> 5 breakdown of family relations?

It would appear that, in full view of the small audience that generally gathers when-ever there is an outsider, and the returned husband, the wife was supposed to give hon-est responses to these leading questions, particularly the fourth! This kind of insensitive approach leaves one wondering whether such surveys are reserved only for the poor.

Finally, mine was a gender-focused study which had noted the feminist critique of dominant methods of sociological research, particularly the survey. While accounts of 'gender aware' survey method had begun to emerge at the time (Chandler, 1990, pp. 119–140), I nevertheless felt that a survey method would be too rigid, particularly in a study which focused on women in the 'informal' sector in a developing country.[1] In fact it would have been almost impossible (and counterproductive) to feign objectivity and rationality (for further discussion on this point, see Section 2.3 below).

Thus I rejected structured survey methods aimed at gathering quantitative data and searched for a methodology which would allow people to tell their stories as they wished, rather than those I wanted to hear. I decided to adopt a more flexible approach, that of an anthropological type of case-study research based on several semi-structured interviews and participation with a smaller number of people (about 50). In this I was guided by what I felt sure I wanted to reject rather than my being sure of what

---

[1]Literature that recognised survey methodologies for the developing world require a separate focus to that of those undertaken in the developed world only began to emerge in the 1990s, with Bulmer and Martin (1993) being one of the earliest. See also Devereux and Hoddinott (1992).

I wanted to keep! The process involved in this was important in enhancing my knowledge of the localities in which I was to base my research, but also in building up confidence in challenging methodologies which were inappropriate to local settings.

9.2.2 A question of representation

Having rejected the survey approach in favour of semi-structured interviews with a smaller number of people, I was left with another large question: 'Who and how many?' I had to choose whom to interview from a group of people I barely knew and who were spread out over a vast area of Mumbai. I found plenty of careful guidelines on selection and sampling methods to assist me in this. However, I also found such methods invariably focused on macro-studies and large surveys carried out in developed countries where communications and administrative systems are well established. And, whereas sampling may work well there, I could not imagine it working in the places I was going to.

Trying to find representative samples in congested Indian settings throws up numerous difficulties and frustrations. A good early example of this awkward fit is Elder's (1973) comparative study of educational achievements of 11-year-olds in Uttar Pradesh and Tamil Nadu, where he attempted random sampling. After obtaining some 400 names and addresses of 11-year-olds in Lucknow (and with a growing realisation that this represented a sample of higher castes and those who could afford to send their children to school), on checking the addresses Elder came across what he calls a 'serious deficiency'. He discovered that:

> ... the school register might carry something like 'Ram Lal, son of Roshan Singh, Aminabad Park'. Several thousand people live in Aminabad Park. How was one to find Ram Lal, son of Roshan Singh? In the end we were forced to abandon nearly three-fourths of the Lucknow sample frame because we could not trace the addresses.
>
> (Elder, 1973, p. 125)

Clearly, formalised registration, statistics and all such sources of information and secondary data cannot be approached in the same way in all countries. In fact, Elder ended up by concluding that 'no sampling frame existed for such a universe. Therefore I had to generate one' (Elder, 1973, p. 123). (See also Olsen, 1992, and Bulmer and Warwick, 1993, for further discussion on sampling in India).

Fortunately, micro-studies such as mine did not require sampling frames (as discussed in Woodhouse, Chapter 7). It is nevertheless important to think about selection, representation and cross-sectioning. In the 'universe' I set out to study, like Elder, I too faced shocks and difficulties that would defy anyone arguing for a representational sample, random or stratified. For instance, at a very early stage of my research, to my horror I discovered that some of the people I had contacted and intended to interview after my first visit were simply not there when I returned some nine months later. Their homes had been demolished and they had 'vanished'. This meant that, firstly, I wasted a lot of time in trying to trace them, lost out on relationships I had built with them, and, secondly, I quickly had to find others who might fit into a similar type.

At other times, in a desperate attempt to 'complete the picture', I made many efforts to talk with members of particular groups who I felt were essential in giving a fuller account of the *khannawalli* story. Sometimes, however, all my efforts were defeated. For instance, to my continued regret, I had to give up on seeking information from scheduled-caste[2] men whose food was supplied by the *khannawallis*. There were a number of reasons for this. Firstly, it became impossible to trace the men amongst several hundred others who slept and lived on footpaths and at railway stations, or to locate them at a workplace because they moved daily in order to take whatever work was going. Their only permanent daily contact was with their *khannawallis*, who would not allow me to speak to their clients for fear of 'frightening them away' or reprisals from higher-caste clients who consider contact (especially food contact) with the lower-castes as 'polluting'.

Secondly, even if a subsection of scheduled-caste men could be located in their workplaces because they had permanent jobs, it was impossible to interview them before or during work because they were usually employed by the municipality cleaning out the streets and lavatories of Mumbai. This meant that they left for work even before dawn and they shifted quickly and hastily between tasks and locations. Thirdly, interviewing after work was equally difficult because on finishing work (usually by midday) the men, who are usually homeless, head straight to a liquor supplier with a 'no-hope' attitude. By about 1 p.m., the effects of the liquor and the heat make the men uncommunicative and sometimes hostile, making it impossible to conduct sensible conversation (particularly in a situation where as a woman researcher I felt especially vulnerable). Therefore, I was only able to talk to a handful of clients, and like others who have had difficulties of a similar type, I was forced to abandon my plans (see Pettigrew, 1981, for a discussion of problems of accessibility for female researchers in India).

Any researcher or practitioner in the fields of poverty and social exclusion will no doubt have several such examples that confirm that neat social science methodology cannot fit easily into all circumstances. On the other hand, there may be no need to force a fit, because these very differences and limitations tell you a lot about the reality of the situation. My example above, for instance, taught me that, even amongst the very poor, social segregation of the scheduled castes is very strong. Perhaps my knowledge of how this operated would have remained superficial had I not been so keen to find a representational sample of different subgroups.

9.2.3 Shaping methodology: gender questions

Apart from the 'technicalities' of the research method discussed above, one very important question was how I could deal with gender issues, particularly given the importance of gender relations in the specific social context I was investigating. There was already a growing feminist critique of what is regarded as the male domination or

---

[2]Scheduled castes and tribes are those groups declared to be such by the President of India by public notification under article 341(i) and 341(ii) of the Indian Constitution. They are recognised as underprivileged groups, and often include those previously regarded as 'untouchables', e.g. New Buddhists and Harijans. Who falls into these categories is reviewed regularly in order to target positive action.

'androcentrism' of the research process (Mies, 1979, p. 2). Feminists argued that the whole of the research process was deeply ideologically biased. They challenged all aspects of the research process, for example, the direction of research policies, choice of areas for research and research methodology (Morgan, 1981), theoretical concepts (Beneria, 1982, p. 120), analysis, and eventually the selection process of publication itself (Spender, 1981) as being positivist and 'masculinist' led research. Thus feminists argued that much work on women's issues did not even make it on to the institutional research agenda, leaving huge gaps in our knowledge of gender relations in society.

Feminist critique thus called for a re-evaluation of the whole process, one aspect of which was the way fieldwork is done. In a challenge to positivist rationality which was so dominant in social science research at the time (Warren, 1988, p. 46), feminists argued that emotionality, subjectivity and a recognition of difficulties enables rather than hinders a deeper understanding of gender relations. In fact, subjectivity may even make women researchers more sensitive in the field and be of substantive and methodological interest in itself (Nadar, 1986, p. 114). This challenge to the then dominant methodology based on 'objectivity' and scientific truths began to be regarded by some feminists as crucial to broadening women's emancipation. For example, Mies (1979, pp. 6–7) argues that 'conscious partiality' leads to 'active participation in actions'; that is, by her research and her partiality the researcher is actually entering into activism that eventually brings about change. Since then, feminist discourse on methods and modes of research has blossomed into a subject in its own right and there is now a large literature on this.[3]

In India too feminists have also strongly argued for a marriage between academic research and activism which they believe is essential if academic work is to relate to reality and not remain abstract and theoretical. A good example of this type of activist action-based research is the pioneering *Report of the National Commission on Self-Employed Women in the Informal Sector* (Sharamshakti, 1988). Here, a team of activists and academics committed to women's struggles set out to investigate poor women's situations throughout India (a huge and daunting task) by subjective participation in group meetings and conversations with groups of women in several different working situations. There was no sampling, no issue of verifiability, no concealing of emotions and feelings, but simply the telling of the story of thousands of women who struggle to survive in poverty. The evidence gathered was so startling that the *Sharamshakti* report consequently led to massive changes in policy and the way the Indian Government views the struggles of millions of poor women in India.

Equally, in my investigation into the *khannawalli* story, it would have been impossible to have gained insights into the rich details of the *khannawallis*' lives had I been concerned about neutrality and credibility. In fact, it was direct identification rather than an objective stance that enabled this study. The point at which people began to relax with me or to

---

[3]Ramazanoglu and Holland (2004) provide a useful history of feminist methodological discourse. Also bearing in mind that feminists also had issues with qualitative research, see Ribbens and Edwards (1998).

accept me was when I brought out my identity as a trade unionist or my identity as a woman (and particularly my involvement with a battered women's refuge at home in the UK). It was only then that they began to ask me questions – and several of them.

Thus in my 'objective' role as a researcher I was just an outside observer, and quite frankly (as I was reminded a few times) a nuisance. In fact people did not understand what I was doing. However, in my 'subjective' role as a woman, a mother, a daughter and a wife, I could make friends and have proper conversations with *khannawallis*. Information thus obtained was information given in trust, and I learnt all kinds of 'secrets' about savings, affairs and quarrels to which I would have been denied access otherwise. Feminist critique thus gave me the confidence to admit subjectivity and to reflect on its advantages.

9.3 Conducting the fieldwork • • •

This section outlines how information was gathered mainly from the *khannawallis* and their clients. In doing so, it discusses various difficulties encountered in gathering information in 'informal' settings, and the ways in which some of these were resolved.

Like all research, this study also required information from those who were not the main actors, but nevertheless helped to complete the picture. Amongst others, I interviewed bank managers to understand credit arrangements for the poor, textile trade unionists to enable a clearer understanding of the textile history and how changes here have affected the *khannawallis*, and visited relevant women's organisations located in Mumbai and elsewhere. In addition, I talked to several academics and activists.

In comparison to *khannawallis* and their clients, there were no real problems encountered in gathering information from these actors as they were in one way or another associated in 'formal' institutional structures in some way. Below, therefore, I show the difficulties that arise when research is set within less formal set-ups.

9.3.1 Information-gathering from the *khannawallis*

Who and how many?
As discussed above, I did not aim for any statistically significant sample with the *khannawallis*, but to broadly cover as wide a range of differing situations as possible. In that, I was hoping to talk to at least fifty women initially and choose some for more extensive study.

It was, however, necessary for the sample to draw out social differentiation between the *khannawallis* (because that was a primary objective in the study). I felt that two sets of criteria might enable a comparison between women from various groups: (a) differences in their caste/religion/marital status; and (b) differences in their association with the AMM, i.e. AMM membership, non-membership, and 'potential' membership. (Potential members were those waiting to join the AMM, usually for six months. For further discussion see Abbott, 1993, ch. 8; also Abbott, 1992.)

I was confident that I could gain access to these women through the AMM because initially the AMM assured me of their full co-operation, and I knew that the *khannawallis* would not talk to me without the approval of the AMM. Although, for reasons unknown to me, certain influential individuals in the leadership later withdrew co-operation, I was able to continue with help from a number of AMM 'area leaders', who were responsible for looking after the *khannawallis* living in their localities or areas. Altogether, I managed to interview 33 AMM members, 12 potential members, and 17 non-members (these figures include two group interviews, which occurred when a number of *khannawallis* lived very close to each other – for example, in a 'police building' I visited, where the *khannawallis* had sons or husbands in the police force and were eligible as a family for rented accommodation from the police).

Once the initial visits were made, people were chosen for second and repeated visits depending on which categories they fitted into, and how interesting their case study was. As far as the categorical choice was concerned, there was no hope of selecting on the basis of ratios or proportionality. There were, for instance, proportionately far higher numbers of upper-caste and married *khannawallis* simply because (a) until the founding of the AMM it was the upper-castes who dominated the *khannawalli* activity and (b) in general, most of the women are married, very often at a young age. Thus, it was decided to choose from the predominant categories based on the variety each case offered, while all those in secondary categories (such as single women and scheduled castes) were automatically put down for at least one repeat visit. Who was visited for the third or fourth time thereafter often depended on how forthcoming the women had been on the previous visits.

A similar format was followed for non-members, although it was far more difficult to trace these. However, despite AMM's warning that I would not be able to find any *khannawallis* who were not associated with them, initial introductions 'snowballed' and I managed to interview at least seventeen. These women were introduced to me by union representatives as well as by clients who worked in textile mills. All seventeen lived in the better-off localities and appeared to be in a stronger financial position than the AMM members interviewed. There was also a higher level of male employment in this group. Perhaps because non-AMM *khannawallis* lack an organisational structure, they were more suspicious than AMM members. Therefore, the initial interviews were problematic, and on one occasion had to be abandoned because of a distinctly hostile atmosphere. However, return visits were made to those who responded well. Here, there were two particular cases that were considered exceptional and interesting. Therefore much time was spent with (a) a household that consisted of three generations of *khannawallis*, and (b) a household which catered for at least 70 clients.

Carrying out the interview

As suggested earlier, during the first three or four interviews I carried a very small tape recorder with a built-in microphone, thinking that it could be used without causing much distraction. It was my intention to record and then transcribe the majority of interviews in this way.

However, taping simply did not work because (certainly during the first visits) in every location I attracted a small audience. Friends and neighbours crowded into small hutments and tenements to see what was going on, and took great delight in chorusing answers to anything that was asked. It thus became impossible to make sense of the tapes or to distinguish the remarks that were being made by the *khannawalli* herself.

My problem, therefore, was twofold: how could I control the interview so that I captured the *khannawallis'* responses only; and how could I record them because (for reasons described in Section 9.2.1 above) I was loath to carry a notebook. Also, of course there was the additional problem of language, when, initially at least, even those fully conversant in Hindi insisted on using Marathi, which needed to be translated. (As I was later to discover, this was for social and political reasons. Firstly, the *khannawallis* associated Hindi with class and power, which they felt they lacked. Secondly, they saw the use of Marathi and a rejection of Hindi as a part of their fight to gain state recognition of Marathi as the regional language of Mumbai. The use (or non-use) of language, then, is a complex issue!)

I was aware of studies that had experienced similar problems in the Indian setting (Patel, 1986) and, like these, the only answer seemed to lie in memorising both the questions and the answers. But, in actuality, this proved to be a highly difficult task, particularly when translating is also taken into account. I discovered that I had often forgotten to ask questions or forgotten the replies given.

In order to help me memorise the questions, give some structure to the conversations, and control the constant interference, I therefore devised a 'questionnaire' (a semi-structured interview schedule in terms of Woodhouse, Chapter 7) that was divided into subsections. The headings and the gist of each subsection were memorised, and thus, during conversations, I was able to concentrate on a particular subsection and generally recall the questions that went with it. In this way, the conversations became more structured and if I had forgotten anything, a friend and translator (Anita), who accompanied me to most places, usually reminded me.

When I devised the questionnaire, I left many spaces in order to record the answers – spaces that were never filled out in front of the respondent. The answers were recalled as quickly as possible and, at the end of each interview, Anita and I would head for the nearest cafe where we would sit down to fill the blank questionnaire. Between us, we recalled statements and checked details. In this way, I was also able to query translation as well as work out what was missing and what remarks needed to be explored in the following session.

The question of interference from onlookers was never entirely solved, but, as my visits increased, the curiosity dwindled. With each repeat visit, therefore, the chance of the *khannawalli* responding openly and singly became stronger. What is also important to note is that, as the visits increased, the nature of our relationship (and therefore methods of information-gathering) changed. I was invited to participate in activities within the *khannawalli's* house (such as meals, celebrations), and outside it (such as accompanying *khannawallis* to hospitals, lawyers, their children's school – in fact anywhere

where I could be of use to them in filling out forms or meeting officialdom). This meant that, although information-gathering became less formalised, it nevertheless opened up areas which otherwise would have been closed.

In addition to interviewing, I accompanied a *khannawalli* to her native village, which gave me a concentrated case study in exploring the link between rural migrants and urban suppliers as well as networking in greater depth.

9.3.2 Information-gathering from the clients

In Section 2.2 I indicated one area of difficulty in obtaining information from this group, particularly from the scheduled caste clients. There were at least two other major problems: (a) the *khannawallis'* resistance to interviews with any of their clients; and (b) entry to a male domain by a female researcher.

With the first problem, whereas I did manage to interview at least 16 clients of the *khannawallis* in the study, the other 34 ate with *khannawallis* who did not take any part in the study. The disadvantage of this was that the 'mismatch' perhaps misses out on some of the detail about the *khannawalli*–client relationship that may have otherwise been highlighted. For instance, from the 16 'matched' clients (some of whom were boarders) I learnt the *khannawalli*–client relationship could be far more complex than that of a customer and a supplier. On the other hand, the advantage of interviewing the clients away from the *khannawallis'* presence was that they gave more honest answers (even more relevant when the *khannawallis* came from the same village or were relatives). Thus, I found that clients talked more easily about food tastes, quantity, and their general opinions about the service.

Locating other clients at their rooms (*kholis*) was not a problem, but gaining access to rooms which are never visited by women was. However, this was overcome when I met Vilas, a young man whose mother is one of the *khannawallis*. Vilas took a keen interest in my work and negotiated my entry to the *kholis* as well as acting as my 'escort'. Additionally, I received help from members of the Communist Party, which continues to retain a high profile in Mumbai's slum localities to this day.

The *kholi* interviews were slightly problematic in that the timing was always wrong. There were always some men heavily asleep and others too tired out from work to respond well. However, these interviews were important to me because, prior to seeing the full extent of the stressful conditions that these men lived in, I do not think that I fully appreciated the overwhelming demand for the *khannawalli* service. And, although the clients who lived here did not 'match' with my *khannawalli* sample, this group gave me invaluable insight into networking and how their relationship with the *khannawallis* began – not in the urban setting, but in its rural origin. The format was to interview groups of men numbering between 10 and 15 and this was done in four different locations. A third place where interviews were carried out was the clients' place of work, with a focus on textile mills because the study was located in the textile mill areas of Mumbai. These interviews were fairly easy to conduct in comparison with others because, in both a private and a government-owned mill, management provided full access to those workers who received *tiffins* from the *khannawallis.*

Therefore, while I am aware that my client sample was not neat, and that it was based on an opportunistic approach, I would argue that the mix that resulted proved very valuable. To the best of my knowledge, this is the only study that has even attempted to analyse the client–*khannawalli* relationship and explore its differentiation, rather than obtain survey data on specific variables such as those relating to credit facilitation.

9.4 Lessons • • •

The chapter closes by looking briefly at the results and asks some ethical questions related to poverty research, particularly in developing countries.

9.4.1 Alternate ways of conceptualising women's survival strategies

The study contrasted significantly with the tendency to regard women's home-based activities as micro-enterprises which was current at the time. I used my results to argue that poor women's income generating could be conceptualised in an alternate way. It appeared to me that the *khannawalli* activity made better sense if it was conceived as a part of an urban livelihood system or survival strategy rather than as a micro-enterprise. My study showed me that, for each individual, the *khannawalli* activity is just one part of a continuous struggle to mobilise resources for survival on a day-to-day basis. Equally, the relationships with clients are part and parcel of general relations of obligation and reciprocity in which caste, kinship and urban–rural relations mould how people interact. The idea that the *khannawalli* activity forms a separate 'business' part of a woman's life and her relations with clients are mediated mainly through 'the market' is less helpful for understanding what appears to go on.

Examples 9.1 and 9.2 below that draw on the lives of two of the *khannawallis* demonstrate this more complex picture. The first exemplifies some common patterns that affect the activity: strong caste and kinship ties with clients; payment for services overlapping with other aspects of reciprocal relations; changes over time relating to changes in other parts of a household's livelihood system (e.g. male employment or unemployment). The second example is an unusual case but reinforces some of the points about the mechanisms of the activity and its interrelationship with other parts of a survival strategy.

Example 9.1   A married higher-caste woman (Urmila)

Urmila's case history brings out at least two immediate points: the importance of the *khannawalli* activity to family survival in relation to male unemployment and the importance of kinship networks which enable the activity. Urmila is a 36-year-old Hindu Maratha woman who originates from the neighbouring Konkan. She married at 15 and has three children (a male aged 12 and two females aged 20 and 15). Like Sumiti (Example 9.2) she is illiterate and cannot even write her name. What is immediately apparent on meeting Urmila is that she is suffering from poor health. She has very bad eyesight, constantly suffers dizzy spells and has been receiving electric shock treatment to cope with depression. The result is that Urmila looks far older than she is.

The family live in a municipal-owned *chawl* (a single room tenement) where they qualify for minimal rent which is some Rs15 per month. Urmila's husband gained access to this housing when he was employed at a Government textile mill, a job he lost some six years ago. Since then he had had one short spell of employment as a 'compounder' with a pharmacist for which he was paid a monthly salary of Rs500. There has been no or very little direct cash income into the house for a long time. Some two months ago, Urmila's eldest daughter managed to find employment as a typist and she now brings home Rs400 per month.

From what she can remember, the family owes some Rs6000 to relatives, Rs2000 to one *marwari* (moneylender), Rs5000 to a second *marwari* and has received four loans of Rs2000 each from the AMM. Recently, Urmila has had to borrow another Rs1500 from a *pathan* for medical costs and thinks there may well be other loans that her husband deals with. (People in the slums live in dread that they might have to resort to borrowing from a *pathan*. Because a *marwari* lends on the basis of collateral – usually pieces of gold or silver jewellery, brass utensils and so forth – which he keeps until both the loan and interest are paid off; the pressure is on the borrower to pay up if they wish to reacquire their property. A *pathan*, on the other hand, may lend without collateral but will charge extremely high rates of interest and/or collect small instalments on a daily basis. Those who fail to meet the payments are often subjected to violence and terrorism by the *pathan* and his henchmen.)

It would appear that the family has sought income generation from the *khannawalli* trade over a period of time. Urmila's mother-in-law was a *khannawalli* and ever since her marriage she has participated one way or another in the activity. However, the crisis created by male unemployment has intensified the dependence on that form of income generation which has so far been regarded by the family as a sideline.

Although it might be argued that Urmila's connections with the activity may have made it easier for her to intensify and expand the activity, there were two major problems: (a) a loss of clientele due to external circumstances affecting the textile industry; and (b) in this particular case, the *khannawalli*'s inability to cope with increased workloads due to her poor state of health. Thus, when her husband became

(Continued)

(Continued)

unemployed, Urmila increased her client numbers from two to eight, but this has now levelled out to four men. All the four are closely related to Urmila (two brothers, one of her nephews, and one of her husband's nephews), and are allowed to board with the family. (The use of the term 'board' here has to be contextualised within its overall setting. Within highly congested situations, boarding simply means that the men can expect a space to sleep in.)

In arranging to provide board and cooked food for these close relatives, Urmila and her family benefit in at least two ways. Firstly, the relatives (as with any other clients) are expected to pay for services provided. This includes board, a morning cup of tea, and two cooked meals a day, for which they pay Rs250 each per month; any other requirements (such as washing of clothes) are expected to be met by the clients themselves. Secondly, the clients, in their obligatory role as close relations, help the family to stretch their resources. Thus Urmila's brothers buy her and her children clothes, bring her a constant food supply of whatever is grown in the village, and, twice a year, allow Urmila and her children to join them in the village for anything from two to four months at a time. There is no proper charge made for keeping Urmila and her children for this length of time (as in an urban area), but they are expected to work on the family land in return. The extent of mutual dependency between the client relatives and that of Urmila's family is reflected in the following reply Urmila gave when asked if she ever considered increasing the price charged:

> No, I have never thought about that. They have helped me in my difficult times. My eldest brother eats only once, but he still pays Rs250 ... they take care of my children's schooling and lend me money when I need it.

Urmila does not wish to expand the client numbers. She feels that with her ill health she will not be able to cook for 'outsiders':

> For them, I have to cook no matter what happens. At present, if I am ill, my relatives manage somehow ... they cook for themselves.

But, she knows that she will probably have to continue with the *khannawalli* work until (or even if) her husband finds employment, and this will probably be for a long time.

Example 9.2   A deserted scheduled-caste woman (Sumiti)

Sumiti's is an upsetting story about a single woman trying to bring up two children in the daily threat of male violence. In a struggle to survive, Sumiti has tried her hand at several income-generating activities, but she feels that the *khannawalli* activity is good because it ensures a daily meal for her children.

(Continued)

(Continued)

Sumiti is about 30 years old, a Harijan (an 'untouchable' caste) born in Nainital. She comes from a very poor family of agricultural labourers. When she was 13, her family accepted a brideprice of Rs1400 from a 20-year-old man. She was legally married to him and lived with him for about a year during which time she received constant harassment and beatings from her husband's family. Sumiti thinks that this might have been because she could not work as hard as she was expected to in the fields.

After a year, in the face of financial hardship, her father-in-law arranged for Sumiti to be sold into Mumbai's prostitution market. The agent who took Sumiti to Mumbai raped her and then decided to make her his mistress. Thus Sumiti escaped prostitution but was forced to live with this man. She was about 14 or 15 at the time when he was nearing 45. Sumiti managed to escape one day and eventually found a job as a live-in domestic servant. The man, however, succeeded in tracing her and 'persuaded' her to return to him. She became his mistress and lived with him until three years ago, having two children by him (8 and 9 years of age). During this time, the man bought a room in the slums of Siddarth Nagar Worli in Sumiti's name and, despite its locality, the room would now raise a large amount of money (anything between Rs50,000 and Rs60,000).

After years of cohabiting with Sumiti, the man decided to return to his wife and their children some three years ago and now wants to sell the room. He has not given Sumiti any money since he left and, in order to drive her out of the room, continuously and daily harasses her and the children through extreme forms of physical violence.

Sumiti feels that her neighbours are encouraging him. They do not like her caste, think she is a 'loose' woman, and are jealous that she has been sending her children to an 'English-medium' school.

Sumiti is in deep debt. She has pawned whatever she could to the *marwari* and has further borrowed money from the AMM. In order to survive, she combines a number of income-generating activities. She works as a part-time domestic servant, and buys saris at a wholesale price and sells them in the neighbourhood for (higher) payments by instalments (although she has now stopped doing this because there is no money left to make the initial purchase). Five to six months before the interview she became a *khannawalli* by letting out the partitioned top half of the room to four boarders. Sumiti is very hesitant in relating exactly how she has acquired these clients and the only information she imparts is that they are from the same village as her. She provides one daily meal of chappattis and vegetables for them. In return she receives Rs200 a month each from them. Various incidents and data discrepancies led me to believe that Sumiti had both acquired and retained clients by also providing sexual services.

At the time of the interviews, Sumiti was worried that she was going to lose her clients, who were thinking of returning to their native village, and was desperate to fill out a passport application in order to migrate to Dubai, where she has heard that domestic servants are paid Rs800 a month.

These examples highlight the social realities where each individual *khannawalli* has to negotiate the constraints of several boundries defined by complex caste, gender and other social power relations. These can only be deciphered through personal accounts of these individuals that require alternative mixes of methodology.[4]

I will argue that taking an 'alternative' methodological approach has, therfore, allowed me to develop an alternative conceptualisation of the *khannawalli* activity. In turn, this has very different implications for policy or public action. For instance, any intervention aimed at poverty alleviation for home-based women's activities has to be guided in a differing way to those for micro-entrerprises. In terms of provision of credit, for example, a micro-enterprise will have very different needs from a poor woman or family struggling to survive. The latter may not be helped at all by a policy that ties credit to meeting targets in business plans. To conclude, the discussion that thus arises from these types of alternate conceptualisations can contribute indirectly to a better understanding of urban informal economic activity.

9.4.2 Ethical questions

Throughout this research, the most pressing questions for me were those of ethics. Two main areas of concern were: (a) that of being a foreign-based researcher; and (b) that of commenting on poverty from a position of clear privilege.

To start with the first question, there is severe criticism levelled at foreign researchers in India. And this is understandably so. There is a long history of colonial sociological and anthropological research that has always given distorted and biased interpretations of Indian society. (See for instance Srivastava's (1991) follow-up of Elwin's (1939) work on the Bagia tribe.) As a result of this history, foreign-based researchers are often seen as reinforcing their higher educational status, and government research and teaching appointments frequently go to Indians who are trained in British or American universities. Sociological research is therefore seen as a political arena where 'western' ideology and power need to be challenged. This challenge has resulted in a strong critique of 'western' theories and 'western' models with the aim of replacing these by action-oriented research, where the researcher and the participant work together to enable change more suited to their country's need. (See, for example, Clinard and Elder, 1965, for a further discussion on defining characteristics of Indian sociology.)

Intellectual resentment of foreign methodology then spills over in a personal resentment of the researcher who is perceived as having more advantages than the Indian researcher. This includes the foreigners' ability to buy space and time because they have more money (even if this is simply due to unfair exchange rates) or better access to library computing and other facilities. Also, there is an awareness that if work is published in Britain or America it will be taken more seriously and gain quicker recognition

---

[4]See also Hulme (2003) for a further discussion on methodology and understanding of poverty.

than work published in India. Added to this is the question of how accurate studies carried out on flying visits might be.

I cannot say that this type of resentment has not bothered me in my role as a researcher, even if I understand the reasoning behind it. The only way I could cope with this dilemma was to be aware of it but go ahead in spite of it, realising that I could only narrate the story from a foreign point of view. And I determined to make an effort to understand the criticism levelled at this type of research.

To a certain extent, therefore, I have been able to deal with these issues by recognising the limitations of what can be changed and what cannot. But the question of being a foreign researcher has, in fact, posed a lesser dilemma for me than that of my ability to comment on poverty. How can I, who will never experience the type of poverty that the *khannawallis* face, write about it? And haven't poor people been research objects for long enough? Also, I found it difficult to answer the question 'What will you do for me?' – particularly when it was I who was going to benefit personally (with my degree, at least) from the research. Even where research is more directly policy related, it is not likely that those being researched will benefit immediately – policy change is more likely to have an indirect effect on others like them.

Nothing in social science had prepared me for dilemmas like this, or taught me how to react to poverty. My privileged status was a constant intrusion, and in their friendliness and hospitality the *khannawallis* continued to remind me of it. So they rushed to borrow a chair from the neighbours when I visited, even though I insisted on sitting on the floor; they sent children out to buy soft drinks and milk for my tea even when I knew that these would never be bought for the children themselves; and they insisted on 'honouring me' by cooking a mutton curry even though I am a vegetarian, because this is a rare treat for them!

Through their actions, the *khannawallis* made it quite clear that there was a vast gap between us and I would never be able to understand poverty except from a privileged position. Therefore, this is what I did, and my understanding of poverty came through my own reactions to it, an understanding which shocked me out of any assumptions that I held about being poor and which in turn generated numerous other moral dilemmas.

To give an example, social science has taught me that, when conducting fieldwork, expect the respondents to ask questions about yourself and be prepared to give truthful replies. So, when women asked how many children I had, I replied that I had two. What came to me as a shock was their next question 'How many have died?' The matter-of-fact tones of this question (which recurred several times), and my own startled response to something I would never have dreamt of asking anyone at home, told me more about poverty (and my privilege) than any amount of quantitative data on the subject of infant mortality.

In another instance, on a repeat visit to one of the *khannawallis*, I saw her seven-year old daughter lying on a mat. I stroked the child's head and asked her what the matter was. Her mother informed me that the child had typhoid. I had to prevent myself from jumping up and showing my panic at the thought that I had actually touched someone with typhoid. Having tried to control myself, I asked her if the child received any treatment. The mother nodded and showed me a packet of Boots® paracetamol!

In my supposedly objective role as a researcher, I faced many dilemmas in a matter of seconds. I cannot comment on how the mother must have felt because I had not come across that type of helplessness before. I could not inform the mother that the medicine on which she had spent (what was for her) a lot of money would do little for the child. I could not 'rescue' the girl because I knew that in poverty these things happen over and over again. Yet I could read into the mother's eyes that she wanted me to give her some money for the child, and I could not but empathise with her because I had a child of about the same age.

There are no sociological guidelines on how to deal with this, or the guilty feeling I developed, because, whereas I could walk away at any time, the people who had become my friends could not. I have never been comfortable in the role of a 'surveyor of poverty', and I could not remain objective when I felt angry and distressed at what I saw. Therefore, I could only deal with my privileged interpretation of poverty through a practical approach that was unwittingly suggested to me by one *khannawalli* when she said:

> I don't know why you want to write about me. I am illiterate and don't know much. But, you know how to write. It is your *job*, so write what you have to!

So this what I did. I wrote about what I saw, and was aware of my limitations. Working these out was a lengthy process in which personal reflection has played an essential and enriching role.

The decisions and dilemmas I faced in the piece of research described above are not singular to academic research. At the Open University a team of us (Abbott, Brown and Wilson, 2007) recently carried out research on the ways in which development practitioners reflect on the whole process of development intervention and development management. We did this by examining some 62 student Projects,[5] and although we attempted a form of discriminatory sampling (such as through alternate year presentations, differing north/south settings, differing sector and area types and so on), ours was by no means a representational sample of development managers. This was mainly due to the fact that these were practitioners who were all fee-paying students whether they were located in the north or the south. Nevertheless, we had rich first-hand data in the form of these projects telling us what development practitioners were facing in their everyday poverty-alleviation work, both in the private and voluntary sector. Also, we were aware that literature on development managers as people is as yet limited, so we decided to go ahead with our study in spite of the skewed nature of the sample.

---

[5] The Project refers to the Open University's distance-learning Development Management Project (Module TU874) which gives post-graduate (MSc) students a chance to integrate their personal experience of development management with what they have learnt on the programme. This consists of a report of some 10,000 words submitted in the final year of study.

This study revealed many aspects of how practitioners reflect on development management that I cannot go fully into here. (For a fuller discussion, see Abbott, Brown and Wilson, 2007.) For the purpose of this chapter, I will therefore focus on those aspects that suggest that practitioners too face methodological dilemmas that create tensions between everyday practice and fitting in with organisational requirements. For instance, the data suggested that practitioners favour more participatory approaches (see Chapters 7 and 8 in this volume) and methodologies that are inclusive. In fact they spend considerable time and reflection on how best to do this. If anything, they are encouraged daily by development agencies and development speak to engage with the need to ensure community involvement, participatory development, a right-based approach, action research, and so on.

Yet, at the end of the day, when it comes to evaluation and monitoring, it would appear that funders require a more rigid methodological approach and one which borrows from conventional management tools and techniques. These include log frames, decision-making frameworks, systems techniques, negotiating skills, mapping, conceptualisation, and so on (see, for example, Mikklesen, 2005). Maybe this is because the principles that guide these techniques continue to revolve around 'objectivity' and 'rationality' often denoted by phrases such as 'efficiency' and 'effectiveness'. As Dale (1998, p. 33–38) argues, this is in contradiction to 'substantive (value) rationality' which also assesses qualities such as the worthiness of projects and the value and end objectives of development!

It is little wonder, then, that many development practitioners feel uncomfortable and face ethical dilemmas of their own within the contradictions presented by the 'empowerment' dialogue of their everyday practice, and the tools and techniques of reporting on that practice which some may feel 'disempower' them.[6]

To end, both the case study of the AMM and the brief discussion on practitioners' methodological dilemmas suggest that, whilst we may be constrained by our obligations (to academic assessors or funders), we nevertheless need to reflect on the difficulties we have encountered in both the research and practice of development. Far from obstructing an understanding of poverty, the subjective and the personal are crucial both in researching poverty-related issues and in 'doing' development around them.[6]

---

[6]A quick reference to dilemmas and debates of development research can be found in Desai and Potter (2006).

PART IV

Bringing in data

Thinking with quantitative data

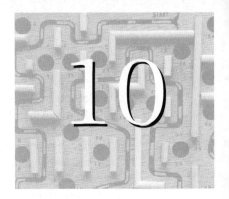

Chandan Mukherjee and Marc Wuyts

This chapter deals with the relationship between ideas and evidence and, in particular, with the role quantitative data play in substantiating ideas. Evidence matters because, as Perkins put it,

> ... you make a big deal of evidence because you know how easy it is for people to feel comfortable with an idea without evidence ... and how easy it is for people to think only of evidence that supports their viewpoint and not evidence that works against it.

(Perkins, 1995, p. 332)

These twin dangers of upholding ideas without evidence or, more commonly, defending ideas only with evidence which supports them, are undoubtedly prevalent in policy analysis where ideas in turn support the nature and direction of public action. In this chapter, we shall argue for a contrastive approach to data analysis which compares rival explanations (ideas) in the light of the evidence each brings to bear on the problem at hand. The purpose of such contrastive inference (Lipton, 1991) is to arrive at that explanation which is most plausible in the light of the overall evidence. Evidence consists of both quantitative and qualitative data. In this chapter, we shall deal particularly with the role quantitative data can play in choosing between rival ideas, although some of the points made below apply equally well to qualitative data.

Unfortunately, many policy analysts and policy makers suffer from data phobia and surrender without a fight when confronted by an army of numbers or formulae supporting a particular policy option. Yet, technical quantitative skills which are not backed up by a sharp conceptualization of the problem at hand may look impressive, but often rest upon shaky foundations. It is important, therefore, to acquire numerical literacy to make sense of numbers and be able to unpack quantitative arguments and subject them to scrutiny. This is not always easy: only careful study and a lot of experience will do the trick. But it is also true that quite a lot can be done with relatively simple techniques. This chapter gives you some examples and develops some principles which can help you in the task of questioning quantitative data.

Section 10.1 discusses the relation between ideas and evidence. To do this, we shall start by looking at how evidence is framed in quantitative analysis. Next we look at the nature of inference used in quantitative enquiry. In this respect, while many researchers hold the view that proper scientific analysis consists of testing an idea (hypothesis) against its evidence, we shall argue that empirical analysis is essentially contrastive in nature and consists of assessing rival ideas in the light of the evidence each brings to bear on the problem. This way, the relative strength of different ideas, their loose ends (that is, evidence which works against them), and their reliance on *ad hoc* justifications to guard against such loose ends, become more apparent. We shall further argue that data assume a dual role in analysis: testing ideas against data versus getting ideas from data. Both elements are important and tend to reinforce one another in the process of research.

Section 10.2 asks the question as to what extent data are "objective facts". With E. H. Carr, the historian, we shall argue that "a fact is like a sack – it won't stand up till you've put something in it" (Carr, 1990, p. 11). Data always yield a selective view of an aspect of reality and, therefore, what is considered to be a fact depends in part on the criterion which underlies the selection of data. Subsequently, we briefly discuss the difference between primary and secondary data and argue that this often shapes the attitude of researchers towards the "hardness" of their conclusions. Finally, we argue that certain types of data (in particular, official secondary data), once they appear on the scene, often acquire a life of their own and end up exerting great influence on the nature of policy debates.

Section 10.3 uses a concrete example to show how conceptualization and technical skill can work hand in hand in questioning secondary data so as to bring out patterns within the data which may help you assess rival arguments. The numerical skills involved in this exercise are deliberately kept minimal: adding, subtracting and calculating percentages is all that is needed. Finally, Section 10.4 draws the lessons from this example and emphasizes the main argument of this chapter by examining the respective roles of conceptualization and of numerical skills in quantitative analysis.

10.1 Ideas and evidence • • •

10.1.1 numbers and variables

It is often said that quantitative analysis deals with numbers while qualitative analysis deals with words. This is not surprising: numbers as evidence feature prominently in any piece of quantitative analysis. The implication is, of course, that acquiring minimal numerical literacy is a must if a researcher wants to engage in quantitative enquiry. The fact that quantitative analysis deals with numbers, however, should not leave you to conclude – as their labels unfortunately imply – that quantitative analysis only deals with quantity and qualitative analysis only with quality. This is incorrect: the dichotomy between numbers and words is not identical with – nor does it bear a one-to-one relation to – the dichotomy between quantity and quality.

To see this point, just think about how *often* you use words such as "typically", "generally", "frequently", "commonly", "rarely", "often", "seldom", "plenty", "far" or "near", "many" or "few", "long" or "short", and many others, all of which convey quantity. Conversely, think about the shape of a graph depicting a set of numbers, for example, relating to land holdings in a peasant community. Does this merely give you a quantitative dimension of the phenomenon under study, or does it also not convey qualitative features such as, for example, the prevalence of landlessness as a condition of life? In fact, neither qualitative nor quantitative analysts can ignore taking account of both these dimensions of social reality – quality and quantity – since, not only are they each important in their own right, but they also tend to interact. Imagine, for example, two rural societies, in one of which wage labour occurs only very sporadically, while in the other it is the dominant mode of employment. Don't you think that this is more than just a matter of quantitative difference, but also has qualitative implications?

But there is more to it. It is important not to confuse numbers with quantities. A number can stand alone, but a quantity always comes with units attached to it. In other words, a quantity is always a quantity *of something* – be it money (say, pounds sterling) or kilograms, or age in years, etc. Consequently, a quantity involves measurement and, hence, we should always be aware of what it is that is being *measured*. But numbers can also depict *counts* of something and that something being counted generally refers to a qualitative feature of our object of enquiry (for example, being male or female). If you say, for example, that the Board of Directors of a company is exclusively male, are you just making a quantitative statement? Or would you ever refer to "the quantity of women" because it is expressed as a number? To confuse numbers with quantities, therefore, ignores that numbers cut across the quantity/quality divide depending on whether they refer to measurements or counts. In sum, in quantitative analysis we work with numbers, but these numbers can refer to either quantitative or qualitative aspects of the objects of our enquiry.

This brings us to a further point about the way evidence is framed (and, hence, also collected) in quantitative data analysis – and in statistical enquiry in particular. If you compare qualitative with quantitative research publications you will undoubtedly have noted that qualitative analysts generally, but not always, work with one or a few cases, while quantitative analysts work with a large number of cases. Why is this? The reason is that qualitative analysts tend to adopt a more holistic case-oriented approach in which each case is looked upon within its own terms – its history, its context, and its complexity – against the background of which cases can then be compared by taking account of specificity and diversity of their different contexts. In contrast, quantitative analysts cut across cases rather than remaining within them. The key feature of a quantitative approach is the definition and use of *variables*, each of which highlights a specific attribute of the data – like, for example, income, gender, educational achievement, etc. – to be collected in the same manner for each of the cases in the sample

(Ragin, 1987). Note that a variable can refer to either a quantity (like income) or a quality (like gender). In the former case, the variable itself is numerical in nature; in the latter it features qualitative categories (say, male/female). As shown further on in this chapter, numbers can be applied to qualitative variables by using counts (frequencies of occurrence of each category).

The distinctive feature of a variable – as the name implies – is that *it varies across cases*. Quantitative enquiry – or, more accurately, statistical theory and practice – consists of the study of the variation in variables and of the co-variation between them. Quantitative analysts, therefore, look for patterns in the data and seek to make generalizations from them. In doing so, they are aware that chance is an ever-present rival explanation. In other words, they are aware that the patterns they discern in the data may be just due to chance variation – a fluke: a product of a particular sample. Statistical methods, therefore, do not only seek to obtain indications from the data, but also assess the extent of the uncertainty involved in making inferences from a sample to its population. It is this concern with dealing with this uncertainty of inference in making generalizations from a sample to a population that explains the probabilistic foundations of quantitative analysis – a point we shall not further elaborate upon here.

Let us end with two more general points about this variable-oriented approach inherent in statistical enquiry. First, the fact that quantitative analysis is focused on making generalizations across cases does not necessarily mean that case-specificity is ignored altogether. On the contrary, as shown further on in this chapter, good practice requires quantitative analysts to look for the exceptions or outliers: cases that do not fit the general patterns and thus warrant special attention. But, unlike in qualitative analysis, case-specificity is always looked at from the perspective of patterns first identified across cases. Second, not all quantitative analysis is variable-oriented rather than case-oriented. For example, an accountant who is looking at the financial data of an NGO will adopt a method of enquiry more akin to that of the qualitative researcher: case-oriented, context-specific and with an eye for past history (and performance). A good accountant will try to get the story right. Lessons of wider relevance may be drawn from this, but this is done in much the same as any qualitative researcher would do. Numbers here will refer mainly to quantities, but the analytical approach used is quite different from that of a statistician. Similarly, some qualitative analysts also work with larger samples – by interviewing a larger number of people – and thus make use of research methods more akin (but not identical) to those of quantitative analysts, by cutting across cases (using key words and/or coding) while looking for overall patterns within the data (see, for example, Richie and Spencer, 2002).

10.1.2 The case for a contrastive approach in analysis

Policy analysis seeks to understand reality, with the explicit purpose of informing public action aimed at changing this reality. Analysis has to be focused to come to grips with the essence of the problem at hand. Ideas help you to do this in so far as they offer tentative explanations for the problem. They are powerful since the understanding they yield can inform public action, which can change the conditions in which people live or work. It matters a great deal how you analyze a problem since it will shape the way you perceive the role of public action.

As a policy analyst, therefore, you should always be aware that your analysis could be seriously defective or plainly wrong. The problem, however, is that the stronger you hold on to a particular idea, the less open you are inclined to be to rival ideas. Indeed, the strength of an idea – that it allows you to see things in a certain light – also entails its weakness – it often prevents you from seeing them in any other way. So, unless you distance yourself somewhat from an idea you firmly hold, you will be unable to assess the strengths of rival ideas. Perkins gives the following example to illustrate this point:

> You enter a rather crowded lounge. You spy a comfortable chair and go over but see that someone has spilled a drink on the cushion. You look around but find nothing to wipe up the mess with, and anyway the cushion would still be damp. So you resign yourself to sitting on a nearby coffee table. Two minutes later someone comes along, takes a look at the same cushion, turns it over, and sits down. Why didn't you think of that?
>
> (Perkins, 1995, p. 161)

Does this mean that you should be suspicious of holding firmly to any idea whatsoever? Quite the contrary, because doing so would lead to inaction. An idea is needed to guide you in a certain direction. What this simple example teaches you, however, is that, as with many other things in life, it is often the case that, in order to advance, you first need to retreat. To check the firmness of the idea you hold and to be able to correct for errors, it is best to confront it with rival ideas and see how well it stands up to the insights they bring to bear on the problem.

This is where evidence enters the scene: evidence allows you to judge how to choose between rival notions. A contrastive approach to policy analysis compares ideas in the light of the evidence each brings to bear on the problem. You will have seen such a contrastive approach throughout this book, and it applies equally to data analysis as, for example, to a literature study. In Chapter 4, Stephanie Barrientos argued that you should not only look at arguments in isolation, but compare them through analysis. In a similar fashion, it is not sufficient merely to look at an idea and its evidence in isolation; you should also compare ideas in the light of the joint evidence they provide. In this way, the loose ends and the awkward corners of an idea come to the fore as well as the things it omits to consider.

A contrastive approach to data analysis also guards you against the common danger of merely collecting evidence in favour of your pet idea under the pretence that you are subjecting your hypothesis to severe testing. In fact, if your idea is at all plausible, it is generally not very difficult to find some evidence to substantiate it. There are two points to remember. First, it is important never to dismiss evidence which goes counter to a notion you hold firmly. This kind of counter-evidence may point you towards a stronger notion. Second, the fact that an idea is supported by some evidence does not mean that the same evidence may not support other ideas equally well. It is indeed not difficult to see that a piece of evidence which supports every idea under consideration is no evidence at all. It is worthless because it does not allow you to discriminate between ideas. So, evidence only really matters when it strengthens a particular notion, while at the same time going against a rival notion (Miller, 1987, p. 176).

Let us illustrate these points with two examples. The first example deals with a piece of counter-evidence. Suppose you firmly hold the view that famines are due to severe shortfalls in the availability (or the supply) of food and that you are now confronted with the evidence that food was being exported from a famine area when people were starving. This is a puzzling fact in the light of the hypothesis that famines result from an absolute shortfall in the supply of food. In other words, this piece of evidence goes counter to the notion held by the researcher. How strong is the evidence? Historically, the export of food from a famine area is not a rarity, but happens to be "… the widely observed phenomenon of what has been called a 'food counter-movement' by which food moves *out* of famine-stricken areas to more prosperous lands" (Sen, 1990, p. 380). In fact, "… this has occurred in many famines, such as the Irish famines of the 1840s, the Ethiopian famine in Wollo in 1973, and the Bangladesh famine of 1974" (*ibid.*). So how should you deal with this evidence?

One strategy is to ignore this evidence altogether and discard it as a nuisance. But this does not resolve the issue that this evidence goes counter to the hypothesis that the supply of food is all that matters in explaining famines. A more fruitful approach is to examine this evidence in the light of rival ideas. An alternative notion, for example, is that it is not the availability of food, but access to food, which matters in explaining famines. Using the latter idea, Sen explains how food comes to be exported from a famine area as follows: "… there is nothing terribly puzzling about this, since non-famine regions (England in the case of the Irish famines, Addis Ababa and Asmara in the case of the Wollo famine, India in the case of the Bangladesh famine) often have greater purchasing power and greater pull in comparison with the famine-stricken regions, and as a result food can easily be attracted away through the market mechanism from the famine regions to non-famine areas" (Sen, 1990, p. 380). In this case, therefore, the evidence points towards this rival explanation: the importance of access to food.

This does not mean that you should now conclude that the variations in the supply of food are irrelevant to the understanding of famines. On the contrary. There may well be some truth hidden within the notion that the supply of food matters. The argument that supply is all that matters, however, is clearly insufficient. But it may well be true that changes in the availability of food (due to, for example, a drought or a flood) matter a great deal in so far as they dramatically affect the access to food. In other words, grave failures of access to food may well be triggered off by the effects of sharp changes in its supply on the way markets operate. But this would lead you to pay greater attention to market mechanisms and the way they affect access to food, and not just to the changes in the aggregate supply of food.

TABLE 10.1 *Average farm size versus household size*

Average land size (acres)	Mean household size	% of households
0.8	3.5	6.6
1.8	3.5	12.3
2.7	4.4	20.5
3.7	5.1	15.0
5.2	5.6	22.5
7.1	6.7	10.9
10.0	7.6	9.4
16.7	9.9	2.8

Source: Collier et al. (1986, p. 50)

There is a further point. Few researchers abandon a theory because some evidence goes against it. In fact, few theories are foolproof. There are always some awkward loose ends sticking out of any explanation on offer. What makes researchers decide to abandon an idea is that a better idea is available, and not that some piece of evidence contradicts it. This is the reason why you should look at evidence in the light of competing ideas.

Let us now move to our second example, which deals with a case where the evidence supports rival notions equally well. Table 10.1 shows the relation between the average size of land holdings (in acres) and household size for a sample of 600 Tanzanian peasant households in 20 villages (as shown in Collier, Radwan and Wangwe, 1986, p. 50). The authors argue that in Tanzania "...other than their own labour, Tanzanian peasant households have only a limited range of assets", of which "undoubtedly, the major assets are land and livestock", but "in most of Tanzania land is abundant and so we would expect its distribution to be determined predominantly by the availability of household labour" (*ibid.*). The data in Table 10.1 are subsequently listed as evidence for this hypothesis that land size is determined mainly by household size. Take a good look at the table as presented by the authors. Note that its construction is somewhat awkward since it clearly refers to grouped data without, however, specifying class intervals. The table only lists group averages for each (unspecified) interval. Do you agree with the authors that the evidence supports their claim?

Undoubtedly, you will agree that the authors' hypothesis is indeed plausible in the light of this evidence; that is, the evidence does not go counter to the hypothesis. The point, however, is whether this is the only hypothesis that the data support. The authors did not explore alternative plausible explanations but merely gave the evidence in support of their hypothesis. Can you think of any other plausible hypothesis which fits the data just as well? Think about this for a moment before reading on.

A plausible alternative explanation could be based on the following argument. The authors assumed that household size is given and, hence, land size adapts to the number of hands available and mouths to feed. But is it correct to see household size as given? Perhaps the authors reasoned that household size depends on the number of children a couple chooses (or happens) to have, and, therefore, in this sense is given. But, even so, children may leave a household for a variety of reasons and, similarly, others (mainly, close relatives) may join the household. That is, some households fragment easily; others remain cohesive. So what then determines household size itself? Is it just a matter of chance or, perhaps, does it depend on the *assets* a household holds? For example, a poor household may be more subject to fragmentation: children leave home in search of better fortunes or are sent to live with better-off relatives. Similarly, a rich household may not only be more cohesive (i.e. less subject to fragmentation) but may also be able to draw upon the labour of poorer relatives. It is plausible, therefore, that assets (including, but not only, land) matter, even if, on average, Tanzanian peasants have few assets at their disposal. Differences in ownership of assets among households may well be a determining factor which explains differences in household size.

There may be further reasons why household size may not be unrelated to the socio-economic condition of the household in question. Take, for instance, the question of infant mortality. The survival of children into adulthood may differ between poorer and richer households. Furthermore, little is known about any differences in fertility behaviour between peasant households of different socio-economic status.

The point is that household size, therefore, is not necessarily given, but may depend on the assets a household holds. The implication of this argument is that household size may not be a determinant of land size, but that household size, and (possibly) land size as well, may depend on the assets (including land where it is scarce) a household has at its disposal. The data in Table 10.1 support this hypothesis equally well and, hence, do not allow you to discriminate between these rival explanations. To do so, you would need additional data, possibly including qualitative evidence about individual cases (see Chapter 13).

The important lesson here is that when a piece of evidence supports an idea, it does not mean that this is the only idea it supports. A piece of evidence which renders your idea plausible is not much use if it renders other ideas equally plausible. The only mileage you get is that it does not contradict your idea, but the same is true of rival notions which are equally supported by this evidence. Evidence really matters when it allows you to discard certain ideas in favour of others. Once more, this example points towards the importance of using the principle of contrastive inference to guide your research.

10.1.3 Testing ideas against data versus getting ideas from data

This leads us to the third theme of this section. Data assume a dual role in this contrastive perspective: at times, you test ideas against data, and, at times, you get ideas from data. Data allow you to test an idea, but you must also always be on the lookout for clues and hints which point in a different direction or which require you to deepen your analysis. Data analysis, therefore, is akin to an open-ended dialogue. Never impose a story on the data, but equally do not expect the data to tell a story by themselves. As with an interview, if you do not ask relevant questions, you are unlikely to get interesting answers, but make sure that your questions are not worded as your own pet answers which you merely seek to confirm with a simple yes or no.

An example may illustrate this point. Most people know from casual observation that, in general, women outlive men. But is this everywhere the case? How would you go about testing this proposition more broadly against empirical evidence?

One way to do this is to compare the life expectancies (at birth) of women and men across countries. The life expectancy at birth is a demographic indicator of mortality which shows the number of years a person would live on average if the present mortality rates for different age groups applied to this person's life. Note, however, that if, for example, life expectancy is 45 years (as in some African countries), this does not mean that most people die around 45 years of age. Rather, despite increased adult deaths from AIDS, it principally indicates that infant mortality is still very high and that many people do not reach adulthood, thereby pulling the average life span downwards.

So how can you test whether the life expectancy of women exceeds that of men? Statisticians do this through formal statistical testing which requires knowledge of probability theory and statistical inference. To keep matters simple, however, we shall use a straightforward graphical test which, in this case, does the trick equally well. To do this we shall make use of a scatter diagram which plots life expectancy of women (on the vertical axis) against that of men (on the horizontal axis) for each country in a sample of 99 countries taken from the World Bank tables for 1990. We use data from 1990 since, as pointed out below, this question about contrasting differences between male and female life-expectancy was particularly debated around that time. Figure 10.1 shows the scatter diagram: each point in the plot corresponds to a particular country and measures its female life expectancy on the vertical axis and its male life expectancy on the horizontal axis.

As you can see, there is quite a bit of variation in this plot. Life expectancies of men and women range from 40 to 44 years up to 74 to 81 years. There are significant differences, therefore, between countries. Furthermore, as you would expect, the scatter of points slopes upwards within a fairly narrow range. That should not surprise you. In countries where male life expectancy is relatively low (or high), female life expectancy will be relatively low (or high) as well.

The plot features a 45° diagonal. Why is this? We drew this line for a very simple reason. As you can see from the graph, the diagonal traces the (hypothetical) loci of points where the life expectancies of women and men are equal. Thus, in general, if there were no differences between life expectancies of women and men, the actually observed points would fall on the 45° line. If, however, life expectancy of women generally exceeds that of men, most points will be situated above the line. In contrast, the points would be situated mostly below the line if the life expectancy of women were generally below that of men.

The scatter diagram shows clearly that for the great majority of countries the life expectancy of women exceeds that of men. This simple graph, therefore, presents

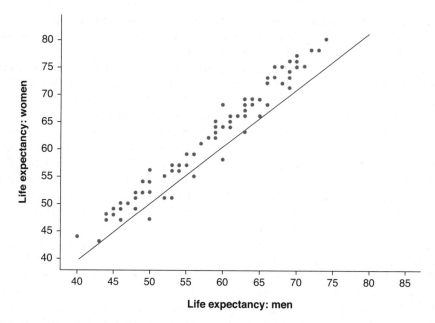

Figure 10.1 Female vs. male life expectancy: 99 countries (some circles represent more than one country with similar data)

strong evidence in favour of our initial proposition: namely, that, on average, women tend to outlive men. This is an example of testing an idea against the data.

But the fact that we confirmed the initial proposition against the data does not mean that our analysis should stop here. While we were pleased that the data confirmed the hypothesis, this result did not come as a great surprise: we more or less expected it. But perhaps the data can also give us some new ideas? Take another look at Figure 10.1 and, before reading on, note down any features of the scatter diagram which particularly strike you.

You undoubtedly noticed that there are five data points situated below the line. This means that, in these countries, women's life expectancy is less than that of men: a feature which contrasts sharply with general world-wide patterns. Did you ponder which countries these might be? A policy researcher needs to be inquisitive and keen to follow up clues and hints thrown up by the data. Reading from left to right, the countries corresponding to these points below the line are, respectively, Bhutan, Bangladesh, Nepal, Pakistan and India. Does it surprise you then that there is quite a debate in the literature whether or not there is a gender bias against women in these countries (see, for example, Harriss, 1990)? It is not our intention here to discuss this debate. The main point worth noting, however, is that such debates are often prompted by unexpected patterns discovered in the data. These exceptions cry out for an explanation and, hence, push the analysis further. This way, you can get ideas from data.

Did you further notice that, as you move your eyes from left to right along the graph, the scatter of points becomes more distanced from the 45° line? What this means is that the discrepancy between the life expectancies of women and men increases as life expectancy of both women and men increases. In fact, a bit more scrutiny of the data reveals that, in countries where life expectancy is low (low-income countries), the difference in life expectancy between women and men is about 3 years, while, in contrast, this difference rises to about 6 years in countries where life expectancy is high (mainly high-income countries). This is quite a significant pattern in the data which again throws up further questions. How to account for this rise in the difference in life expectancy between women and men as life expectancy increases? Are there specific risk factors (such as, for example, the greater risks of maternal mortality) which particularly affect women in poor countries? Or does women's biological advantage only come fully into play with ageing and, hence, under social conditions where infant and adult mortality is low? These are questions which came to mind when we looked at this plot. As we are not specialists in health matters, however, the best research strategy would be to confront a specialist with these patterns and enlist possible explanations.

In this example we used a simple device – a graph – to test ideas against data and to get ideas from data. In general, however, these two types of data analysis require different (but overlapping) skills. The former task is more akin to a court of law testing the hypothesis of not guilty according to the available evidence. The latter task is akin to detective work: looking for hints and clues which may guide you towards an explanation as to who committed a crime and how and why it was done. Confirmatory data analysis deals with the former; exploratory data analysis with the latter. Confirmatory data analysis generally involves the use of heavy artillery – probability theory and statistical inference – and its mathematical threshold tends to be fairly high, given its extensive reliance on formulae used in formal statistical testing. Exploratory data analysis is more playful in nature and makes extensive use of graphical tools to look at data.

Until recently, statistics texts dealt exclusively with confirmatory data analysis. The underlying idea was that scientific method should consist of testing ideas against data. Nowadays modern texts recognize the importance of getting ideas from data and devote attention to techniques which allow you to do this better. This greater emphasis on learning from data is undoubtedly due to the ground-breaking work of Tukey (1977), the innovative American statistician and founder of exploratory data analysis.

10.2 The factuality of data • • •

10.2.1 Data are theory inspired

Facts are not just given things; they are produced. That is, data are partial records which provide you with a selective visibility of a society and its economy (Hopwood, 1984, p. 170). This explains why Carr states that a fact is like a sack since it won't stand up unless you put something in it (Carr, 1990, p. 11). Facts, therefore, are always theory inspired: it is theory which renders a piece of information relevant and, hence, accounts for it to be selected as a fact. Evidence never exists in isolation; it is selected with reference to a particular idea which renders it relevant. That is the "something" which makes it stand up as a fact.

Thus, data are always theory inspired. But this should not lead you to think that the substance of data is entirely reducible to theories and concepts or is purely subjective in nature. For example, national income accounts are a product of (Keynesian) macro-economic theory but this does not mean that the national income of India is constructed of thin air. To say that national accounts data are theory inspired means that theory determines which data are deemed to be relevant and informs the way these data are collected and structured into meaningful policy-relevant macro-aggregates such as the gross domestic product, national income, consumption, investment, savings, and so on.

In policy analysis, factual evidence is obtained from primary and secondary data. The former are collected by the researcher (or research team), so it is the researcher who selects them, assesses their relevance, and shapes them as facts within analysis. This is a time-consuming process, but it allows the researcher greater flexibility in producing evidence for the research questions at hand. These primary data tend to be case and time specific because their collection depends on the efforts of a single researcher (or a single team) operating in a particular location during a specified period of time. Much depends on the skills of the researcher(s) in question and, given the case- and time-specific nature of the data collection and analysis, it is often impossible to verify data or to correct inherent biases in data collection. Good primary data analysts are quite aware of this and make sure to explain the nature of their data and the procedures which went into their collection.

Some primary data analysis involves fieldwork. Here, researchers generally develop strong local knowledge, acquire a feel of the specificity of the location in question and, as producers of data, tend to be quite aware of the complexity, variability and uncertainty of social data. They are, therefore, less inclined to generalize too quickly and are more tentative in their conclusions. Other primary data analysis is based on surveys carried out by the researchers themselves. For example, the above-mentioned study on rural households in Tanzania was based on survey data of 600 households in 20 villages. Such surveys are akin to, but generally smaller in size than, the large-scale surveys carried out by official institutions for the purpose of publishing secondary data. Survey analysts, unlike field workers, tend to be more distant from local circumstances and knowledge.

Secondary data are produced by specialized (predominantly official) institutions. Quite a lot of expertise goes into their production, which is generally repeated at regular intervals: national accounts, demographic data, trade data, social surveys, etc. These type of data are mostly aggregated using formal accounting frameworks which structure the data into predetermined categories. The production of such data, therefore, follows standard procedures and techniques which enhance their consistency over time as well as their comparability between, for example, countries or regions. The use of aggregation and accounting structures extends the reach of these data beyond local conditions. But, conversely, aggregation hides the internal variability of the data within each category, and accounting practices often resolve conflicts among data through formal procedures. This often leads researchers who work with secondary data and who are mostly consumers (rather than producers) of these data, to see them as hard facts because a lot of the variability and uncertainty within such data has been carefully removed through aggregation and formal accounting practices. Not uncommonly, therefore, these researchers (macro-economists, sociologists working with survey data, or demographers) tend to be more affirmative in their views of reality and see their conclusions as being more objective than those of researchers involved in fieldwork.

Streamlining the data through aggregation and accounting frameworks extends their reach at the expense of their flexibility in use. An example can best illustrate this point. Consider, once more, the case of life expectancy as an indicator of health. This is a very useful measure which allows you to make broad comparisons between countries, regions, town and country, or between women and men. The ability to make such comparisons and to draw interesting inferences from them illustrates the power of secondary data in extending the reach of analysis. But this attracts a cost as well. Most official published demographic surveys will give you life expectancy by nation (or region, or town and countryside) and by sex, but few give you life expectancy by, for example, class or social status. So if, say, your research leads you to question whether or not the mortality rates of urban manual wage labourers differ markedly from those of professionals, you will find it very hard to investigate this hypothesis with published secondary data. The data simply are not structured this way and, hence, prevent you from investigating this question. The question is nevertheless potentially interesting since, for example, research in Britain has shown that, even in a developed industrialized country, mortality rates can differ markedly between social classes (Townsend and Davidson, 1988; Whitehead, 1988).

As a researcher and policy analyst, therefore, you should always be aware that data never tell the full story. All data are partial records which yield selective visibility of a society or an economy. With secondary data, if this visibility is in line with the question you seek to explore, the data will help you do this. But, at times, the data remain mute because they are not structured to answer the type of questions you are interested in. That does not mean that your question is meaningless, but it does make it harder to get the evidence you need to prove your point. You saw this in Chapter 1 where official data assisted in the administration of policies which had been set for some time, but did not help to answer questions needed once new policies were under consideration. This explains why it is often important to combine the analysis of secondary data with targeted primary data collection, which is aimed to address questions that the secondary data do not allow you to address. At times, however, policy analysts and researchers may be able to convince decision-makers to extend the reach of official data though the inclusion of new questions within existing surveys or by commissioning new surveys. In Tanzania, for example, after the adoption of structural adjustment policies in 1986, there was increased interest in what was happening in the informal sector in response to such policies, but it was hard to arrive at any firm conclusions for lack of data. This led to a first official survey of informal sector activities being undertaken in 1991.

10.2.2 The 'domain of the factual'

In fact, the routine collection of official data forges a "domain of the factual" (Hopwood, 1984, p. 168) in that these data both reflect and, in turn, influence the emphases given in public debates (p. 169). For example, national income accounting emerged to aid the apparatus of a constrained wartime economy in Britain, but after the war, the desirability of economic growth rendered GDP, once a means to an end, into a desirable end in itself, a process which subsequently shaped the nature of government policies (Hopwood, 1984). In other words, once data enter the public domain they often assume a life of their own. They become the main indicators of success or failure and are used as such in public debates. The World Bank, for example, routinely classifies countries as high or low growth performers and uses such categories to advocate specific policies which the latter should follow to achieve the success of the former. In similar fashion, with the rise of monetarism all eyes turned towards the growth of the money supply and of the public sector deficit, which became new indicators of success or failure.

But official data also shape the way people perceive their position and role in society. Indeed, as the philosopher Hacking (1990, p. 3) pointed out:

> The systematic collection of data about people has affected the ways in which we conceive of a society, but also the ways in which we describe our neighbour. It has profoundly transformed what we choose to do, who we try to be, and what we think of ourselves. Marx read the minutiae of official statistics, the factory reports from the factory inspectorate and the like. One can ask: who had more effect on class consciousness, Marx or the authors of the official reports which created the classifications into which people came to recognize themselves? These are examples of questions about what *we* call "making up people".
>
> (Hacking, 1990, p. 3)

Official data, therefore, affect our consciousness in myriad ways. They enter public debates as indicators of failure or success and so acquire a quality of being ends in themselves, and they enter our lives by shaping how we see ourselves in relation to others. As Metz (1987, p. 224 and p. 338) pointed out, for example, the development of unemployment statistics in the nineteenth century gave rise to the concept of unemployment and became a subject of public debate in the later years of the century with the ascendancy of the working class movements. Similarly, the emergence of social statistics played a crucial role in the formation of public health policies.

This quality of (socially sanctioned) greater factuality is specific to official secondary data and sets them apart from the "soft" data of field workers. Policy analysts engaged in case-specific fieldwork often overlook this quality of official secondary data, and, while often better informed on certain subjects, find themselves stonewalled by a barrage of hard facts when engaged in policy debates. As a policy analyst, you should never ignore the story told by secondary data even if you are convinced that your case-related data are more insightful and support a different story. In such cases, it is important to analyze carefully why the secondary data fail to reveal the specific concerns you seek to address and how your own data can help to bring out a different story.

10.3 Questioning secondary data ● ● ●

In Section 10.1, we have shown how evidence is used to choose between rival explanations. To do so, we used a few simple examples which asked you to assess a question or rival questions in the light of a piece of evidence. In actual research, however, it is you as the researcher who needs to formulate such questions and select the relevant piece of evidence. Alternatively, you may come across a set of data (say, published statistics) and it is up to you to figure out whether these data help you to tackle the questions you are interested in. Many researchers find this quite difficult to do. The main reason is that the data do not come precisely in the form you want them, and it may take some time to see whether they are of relevance to your concerns. In this section we shall use one example to teach some basic principles on how you might go about questioning secondary data.

Suppose your interest is to analyze how the informal sector developed under structural adjustment in Tanzania. Indeed, since structural adjustment policies aim to give greater emphasis to private sector development (including informal sector activities), it is important to understand the specific nature of the development of the informal sector under structural adjustment, whether or not structural adjustment policies achieve their stated aims. You are looking for relevant data and you come across the informal sector survey of 1991.

Take a look at Table 10.2. It displays a table taken from this survey. The table is organized in matrix form and involves cross-tabulations of the number of small-scale enterprises with respect to their location (urban/rural), industrial sector and life span. Hence, the data in the table consist of counts, not measurements.

You now have to decide whether this table might help you to pursue specific questions concerning the possible effects of structural adjustment policies (initiated since 1986) on informal sector development. This is a typical research situation for quantitative data analysts.

However, in our experience, many researchers find it difficult to know what to do next. The reason why they find it difficult is that nobody tells them which question to

TABLE 10.2 *Number of informal sector enterprises by geographic location, by industry and by age of enterprise*

Geographical area/industry	Age (years)							Total
	Up to 1	1 and <3	3 and <5	5 and <10	10 and <20	20 or more	Not stated	
Dar es Salaam								
Agr. and fishing	3404	2658	1880	2067	1189	612	0	11 810
Mining/quarry	0	0	0	0	0	0	0	0
Manufacture	4579	7340	7922	5062	3373	3180	0	31 456
Construction	696	981	2654	2398	3128	905	0	10 762
Trade/rest/hot	31 863	43 333	27 927	27 045	7982	3544	347	142 041
Transport	382	595	462	525	197	153	0	2314
C. and P. services	1076	2489	2005	4054	2332	803	0	12 759
Total	42 000	57 396	42 850	41 151	18 201	9197	347	21 1142
Other urban								
Agr. and fishing	5905	13 782	12 159	6040	4957	9822	0	52 665
Mining/quarry	654	2173	3243	4773	2344	0	0	13 187
Manufacture	8978	13 041	9599	10 250	7149	4434	104	53 555
Construction	682	2006	4380	5125	4053	1842	48	18 136
Trade/rest/hot	69 943	77 147	58 099	33 989	14 466	9855	2645	266 144
Transport	614	1206	2152	1133	368	84	0	5557
C. and P. services	1838	9062	3617	4614	4356	3489	45	27 021
Total	88 614	118 417	93 249	65 924	37 693	29 526	2842	436 265
Rural								
Agr. and fishing	13 179	7440	13 852	22 387	11 330	9446	0	77 634
Mining/quarry	95	1517	190	1488	662	0	0	3952
Manufacture	20 950	54 691	62 001	83 943	59 368	69 572	4004	354 529
Construction	5943	14 302	18 368	19 432	13 836	15 258	459	87 598
Trade/rest/hot	93 467	132 959	114 591	95 206	53 848	30 941	4718	525 730
Transport	10 668	9129	11 877	6201	2237	743	653	41 508
C. and P. services	54 441	11 247	7169	14 727	13 960	9344	1297	63 185
Total	149 173	231 285	228 048	243 384	155 241	135 304	11 131	1 154 136

(Continued)

TABLE 10.2 *(Continued)*

Geographical area/industry	Age (years)							Total
	Up to 1	1 and <3	3 and <5	5 and <10	10 and <20	20 or more	Not stated	
Total								
Agr. and fishing	22 488	23 880	27 891	30 494	17 476	19 880	0	142 109
Mining/quarry	749	3690	3433	6261	3006	0	0	17 139
Manufacture	34 507	75 072	79 522	99 255	69 890	77 186	4108	439 540
Construction	7321	17 289	25 402	26 955	21 017	18 005	507	116 496
Trade/rest/hot	195 273	253 439	200 617	156 240	76 296	44 340	7710	933 915
Transport	11 664	10 930	14 491	7859	2802	980	653	49 379
C. and P. services	8355	22 798	12 791	23 395	20 648	13 636	1342	102 965
Total	280 357	407 098	364 147	350 459	211 135	174 027	14 320	1 801 543

Source: The Planning Commission and The Ministry of Labour and Youth Development (1991) Tanzania: The Informal Sector, pp. 2–5.

address or what technique to use. It is up to them to assess the relevance of these data. Some mainly stare at the table, and, possibly, end up by calculating some percentages or growth rates in a rather haphazard manner. They may decide the table is an important piece of evidence, but do not really know what to do with it, and end up reproducing the table in their research report without the data ever being put to work. We call this a strategy of hoarding data: the research report may look impressive because it is full of tables, but it is likely to be thin in analysis.

So how should you go about using this table more systematically and creatively? There are no hard and fast rules how to do this, but some simple principles can be formulated which may help your approach to data exploration. Let us use this example to illustrate some of these principles.

The first principle is very simple, yet unfortunately often forgotten. It consists of taking time to look carefully at the structure of the table, its various categories, and the way they are cross-tabulated. Having done this, reflect upon and note down any important conclusions you can draw about the limitations inherent in the data in terms of what they can possibly tell you of relevance to the questions you are interested in, in this case possible effects of structural adjustment, which might show themselves in terms of changes after 1986. Do this now for a few minutes and then read on.

In this case, we noted down that the survey covered enterprises existing in 1991 and, hence, information about the past was obtained through recall (that is, asking people when they started their enterprises). We concluded that, since mortality rates of informal sector enterprises at different periods in time are unknown, it is no use trying to calculate growth rates in the number of enterprises over time. Yet many people make this error. It is indeed tempting to try to use the table to show that the number of informal enterprises has been growing over time, but this would be wrong because you have no information how many enterprises actually existed in the past but ceased to exist before 1991.

With care, however, the data might be used to explore structural changes in the spread of the informal sector across activities before and after the implementation of structural adjustment policies and across the rural/urban divide. It would be useful if we knew how mortality rates of enterprises differ across different sectors or across the rural/urban divide, but unfortunately this information is not available. You might perhaps hypothesize that informal trading enterprises are easier to set up and perhaps also more easily abandoned than, say, craft or manufacturing enterprises which require more specific skills and more fixed investment. But the survival of enterprises does not only depend on production conditions, but also on the prevailing market conditions (for both inputs and outputs), which, in the case of Tanzania, changed dramatically over time (before and after structural adjustment). For example, goods shortages before structural adjustment – particularly also of intermediate inputs – hampered the development of productive activities. After structural adjustment, however, market competition became more severe as the economy was opened up to foreign competition (Wuyts, 2001; Wuyts, 2004). *A priori*, therefore, it is difficult to venture any guess about differential mortality rates.

With this caveat in mind, let us compare changes before and after structural adjustment in that, by 1991, structural adjustment policies initiated in 1986 had been in place for about 5 years; thus the breakdown of the table along columns allows you to look at the proportion of different types of enterprises which are less than 5 years old compared with those of 5 years or more.

The second principle is that, after studying the structure of the table, merely staring at the data does not help and, hence, to engage in a meaningful dialogue with data it is necessary to fire questions at the data. Each question approaches the data from a different angle. Some avenues may prove to be dead-end streets, while others yield valuable insights. One question which sprang to our mind here was whether or not there was an inherent bias in favour of trade among informal sector activities under structural adjustment.

This question was essentially theory-inspired and motivated by the fact that a key component of structural adjustment was import liberalization fuelled, furthermore, by its accompanying increased reliance on foreign aid as import support. It is reasonable to assume that this fuelled the revival of informal sector trade as well – particularly, trade based on imported goods in particular. What made us think of this question, therefore, was that, if structural adjustment mainly fuelled informal sector trading activities, there is a limit to the dynamism this sector could display in bringing about economic recovery and growth in Tanzania. Much depends also on the role the informal sector could play in reshaping production, particularly in a context of increased

TABLE 10.3   *Urban informal sector enterprises (numbers of enterprises)*

	Sector		
Age of enterprise	Trade	Non–trade	Total
<5 years	308 312	134 214	442 526
>5 years	96 881	104 811	201 692
Total	405 193	239 025	644 218

TABLE 10.4   *Rural informal sector enterprises (numbers of enterprises)*

	Sector		
Age of enterprise	Trade	Non–trade	Total
<5 years	341 017	268 059	609 076
>5 years	179 995	353 934	533 929
Total	521 012	621 993	1 143 005

competition from imported commodities (including, for example, second-hand cloth-ing). So, as a preliminary question we decided to check whether there was a bias in favour of trade.

This is only one of several questions which can be raised about the table. Each question gives you a different "handle" on the data. Each handle allows you to look at your data and gain specific insights. This is what selective visibility is all about: the question is the handle by which you make things visible. Exploratory analysis consists of trying out many different questions, exploring each of them in turn and following up those questions which appear more promising. Here we shall only pursue this particular question, but keep in mind that in actual research it is important to approach the data from different angles.

Third, it is useful to collapse the table so that it emphasizes the question we want to pursue. The point is not to carry around any extra baggage in terms of data overload. In this case, the table can be simplified along three dichotomous categories: trade/non-trade, enterprises with a lifetime of less than 5 years versus those of 5 years or more (since structural adjustment policies started in 1986 and the survey was held in 1991), and the rural/urban divide.

Tables 10.3 and 10.4 summarize respectively the urban and rural picture. Notice that what we have called "Trade" in Tables 10.3 and 10.4 corresponds to the rows labelled "Trade/rest/hot" in Table 10.2. We might have preferred figures on trading enterprises separate from restaurants and hotels, but as noted above, secondary data are generally not in precisely the forms one would prefer. We will have to assume that any change in the relative numbers of trading enterprises will be reflected in the change recorded for the "Trade/rest/hot" category, taking care to note this assumption and to check it later if possible. These tables do away with unnecessary clutter and focus your

TABLE 10.5 *Percentages of trading enterprises in total number of enterprises*

	Location	
Age of enterprise	Urban (%)	Rural (%)
<5 years	70	56
>5 years	48	34

attention on the question under review. This allows you to get a better grip on the data. Take a good look at both tables. You will note that the information is now structured in line with our specific question.

Fourth, the question now arises whether to continue working with the raw data (i.e. data in their original form) or to look for a suitable transformation of the data. Here the raw data are counts. The question now is whether we should continue to work with counts or perhaps switch to, say, percentage shares. Many ignore this question or, worse still, choose a particular transformation of the data without giving it much thought. This is highly unfortunate. Data transformations can either erect a smoke screen which prevents you from seeing any patterns in the data, or greatly enhance your analysis. It is worth giving this question some careful consideration. In this case, we decided to try out percentages as the appropriate data transformation since we are mainly interested in looking at structural changes. Table 10.5 gives the resulting cross-tabulation of percentage shares.

Did you notice that we have now compressed all the relevant information into a single table? Note also that we now have two variables at play, both categorical. The first is location (urban and rural) and the second a new variable we constructed referring to policy regime (before and after structural adjustment). The structure of the data in relation to our original question has now become much clearer. To take a better look at these data, however, it is useful to add an extra row and column to record the differences in the percentages. This simple technique is illustrated in Table 10.6. The number in the bottom right corner records the difference of differences, which, in statistical parlance measures the interaction effect between both categorical independent variables (policy regime and urban/rural location) on the categorical dependent variable (trade/non-trade).

This convenient set-up allows us to draw the following three conclusions:

1 The proportion of trading enterprises in the total number of enterprises is higher in the urban as compared with rural areas both before (48% vs. 34%) and after (70% vs. 56%) the start of structural adjustment policies.

2 After structural adjustment, the proportion of trading enterprises rose from 48% to 70% for urban areas, and from 34% to 56% in rural areas.

3 The change in favour of trading activities with structural adjustment is equally strong in urban and rural areas: the percentage shares increase by 22% in both cases. There does not appear, therefore, to be any urban (or rural) bias in this change towards greater emphasis on trading activities.

TABLE 10.6 *Percentages of trading enterprises in total number of enterprises (with added row and column differences)*

Age of enterprise	Location		Row differences (%)
	Urban (%)	Rural (%)	
<5 years	70	56	14
>5 years	48	34	14
Column differences	22	22	0

These conclusions may help us in evaluating alternative notions as to the effect of structural adjustment on informal sector activities. Of course, we should keep in mind that these changes in the structural composition of informal sector activities may *in part* have been due to (unknown) differential mortality rates across sectors or across the rural-urban divide. But, as argued above, changes in mortality rates, if they occurred (which we do not know), are more likely to have been driven by changing market conditions before and after structural adjustment.

We shall not pursue this analysis further here. The purpose of this example was to show how you can make data come alive if you care to fire a question at them and follow it up systematically by collapsing your data in line with the question, choosing an appropriate transformation, and selecting an appropriate technique. For didactic reasons we have kept the technical sophistication minimal: the calculation of percentages, addition and subtraction is all you need. More skilled data analysts might have used odds instead, or, better still, the logarithms of the odds (logits). These tools are more powerful and may yield insights where percentages fail to do so. Fortunately, in this case, percentages tell the same story.

Did you notice that, while our first and second conclusions might have been directly glimpsed (with difficulty) from the original table, the pattern revealed in the third conclusion would be very hard to spot if we had not gone about our analysis systematically? But this was to us by far the most interesting feature in the data. Why? Well, with our background knowledge of Tanzania, we more or less expected the first and second patterns to prevail, but the third conclusion came somewhat as a surprise to us. Our earlier hunch was that the change towards trade was more town-centred. The data tell a different story. But this is what a dialogue with data is all about.

Finally, would you call the foregoing exercise quantitative or qualitative in nature? The methods used clearly belong within the quantitative tradition, using numbers (percentages) to make sense of the data. But our variables referred to qualitative dimensions of the data. To see this, think back about the steps we followed in arriving at Table 10.6. With a specific question in mind, we collapsed the original table (10.2) by defining two categorical variables: location (rural/urban) and policy regime (before/after structural adjustment policies). In sum, we used numbers to deal with qualitative features of the data within a quantitative tradition (approach) to data analysis.

10.4 Matching conceptualization with skills in questioning data • • •

Let us now try to draw up some lessons about the type of problems you are likely to encounter when dealing with quantitative data in applied policy research.

Data do not tell you anything unless you fire questions at them. In fact, the search for data is itself driven by the type of questions you seek to explore. Conceptualizing your research question, therefore, is essential to determine your approach to the data. But good conceptualization is akin to an opening in a chess game: it sets the stage for the game but does not predetermine its final outcome.

Research almost invariably implies that you approach data from different angles. Angles allow you to define variables. Do not be afraid to try out different things. Some may turn out to be dead-end streets, but others will yield valuable insights. But there never are uninteresting results. Even if some result is unexpected or disappointing, it is worth your while to follow up the question of why the evidence fails to back up an idea you held. This may point you towards a rival idea which you might otherwise not have taken into consideration.

The angles you use do not only refer to quantitative features of the problem at hand. They can also refer to its qualitative dimensions, even when situated within a "quantitative" approach to data analysis. It is important, therefore, not to confuse the nature of the data (quality/quantity) with the distinction between words and numbers or that between quantitative and qualitative approaches to data analysis.

You approach data from different angles because you want to investigate rival notions in the light of the evidence each brings to bear on the problem at hand. Through contrastive inference you seek to arrive at that notion which appears more plausible in the light of the overall evidence. Your interest is not just to test a particular idea in isolation – or what Miller called a lonely encounter of a hypothesis with evidence (Miller, 1987, p. 173). What matters is to compare ideas. The implications are that you do not merely accept an idea because some evidence points towards it, because it may support other ideas equally well, and you pay particular attention to evidence which goes counter to an idea, because it may point towards a superior notion.

In policy analysis, you may make extensive use of secondary data relevant to your research question. It is important, therefore, to reflect carefully on the limitations inherent in the data. This is not just a question of checking the quality of the data. What matters as well is to ascertain the type of questions data allow you to answer and which questions cannot possibly be tackled with the data at hand. This point matters equally when you collect your own data (for example, through survey research). The design of a survey is predicated by the type of questions you seek to answer.

Analyzing data in relation to a specific question almost invariably implies further data manipulations. In the example above, we collapsed the table to be able to get a better grip on the data. In the process, however, new variables emerged. For example, we used the age of enterprises to define a proxy variable for policy regime, depending on whether the enterprise was started before or after the adoption of structural adjustment policies. In other cases, you might use an index of average nominal wages jointly with the consumer price index to construct an index of the evolution of real wages, or compute the real exchange rate using a set of domestic and foreign price indices and the nominal exchange rate, etc. Data manipulations are the "bread and butter" of good applied research. Good conceptualization of research often reveals itself first by the quality of data manipulations and, conversely, careless thinking often shows itself in the way data are organized or manipulated.

The question you seek to answer, the type of data at your disposal, and the way you manipulate and transform them, jointly set the stage for the kind of techniques best suited to address the question. This is not a one-way street. Often data are manipulated in certain ways so as to make them amenable to the use of a particular technique. Nor is it a one-shot effort. In the example above, we could have used odds ratios or logits, but percentages did the trick just as well and require less skill. We could also have used the cross-tabulation of raw data (a contingency table), but that did not give us additional mileage. In general, trying out different techniques using the same data to answer the same question is a good thing. This way you avoid turning a technique into a fetish: a tool to impress rather than to gain insights.

Numerical skills matter provided they are not used in a mechanical way. They should be used in combination with, and not as a substitute for, clear conceptualization of the problem. This is why we called this chapter 'Thinking with quantitative data'. Numerical skill in itself does not provide magical answers to problems. Good conceptualization of a problem determines whether numerical skills are used appropriately or foolishly. In the example above, we could have used the table to calculate apparent trends in the growth of the numbers of informal sector enterprises in different sectors. These results would have been meaningless, however, since the data are prepared at a given point of time and, hence, do not reveal how many enterprises ceased to exist in the past. The mechanical application of numerical skills, therefore, can be (and often is) quite misleading. But, conversely, to undertake good data analysis requires you to be numerically literate. Few patterns in the data can be seen by merely staring at them. It is through data manipulations, data transformations and the calculation of numerical summaries or the use of graphs, that conceptualization interacts with numerical skill to bring out patterns in data which either test or generate ideas. There is no easy shortcut, but fortunately much mileage can be obtained with relatively simple techniques and extensive practice.

Finally, good data analysis should be fun, although it may involve hard work. There is something very exciting about "finding out". This is why data analysis should never just consist of testing old ideas with new data, but new data should also generate new ideas (Heckman, 1992, p. 884). Do not hammer your data into submission in a mindless exercise of number crunching. Nor turn your back to them in an attack of data phobia. It is worth learning to converse with quantitative data in a genuine theory-driven dialogue.

Using evidence in advocacy

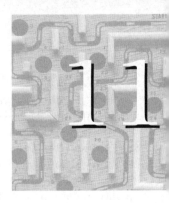

Sue Mayer

'Evidence-based policy making' has become the fashionable term for rational modern policy making by Governments and institutions worldwide. It has its origins in medicine (Gray, 1997), driven partly by demands for cost-effectiveness of treatments, but has now been much more widely adopted. Gray (1997) describes evidence-based policy making as moving away from opinion-based towards decision making more rooted in the findings of scientific research. The UK Government, for example, adopted this approach in their 'Modernising Government' White Paper in 1999 (HMG, 1999), saying that its aim must be: '... to produce policies that really deal with problems; that are forward-looking and shaped by the evidence rather than a response to short-term pressures; that tackle causes not symptoms; that are measured by results rather than activity; that are flexible and innovative rather than closed and bureaucratic; and that promote compliance rather than avoidance or fraud'. It is also being widely promoted in development policy and the Overseas Development Institute has a project dedicated to considering the use of research in policy (see: http://www.odi.org.uk/RAPID/).

Few would argue against the idea that policy making should draw on the best available information and knowledge. Research and the production of evidence has led to dramatic improvements in health care, and helped tackle many other problems. However, although the concept of 'evidence-based policy making' sounds logical and non-contentious, the implication that, by having the evidence the 'right' answer will emerge, can conceal many value judgements, political preferences and assumptions. This is because many questions about 'what evidence?' and 'what to do when evidence is lacking?', demand social, economic and political judgements to be made.

Similarly, gathering research for advocacy on the face of it seems rather straight forward, but it is often very messy and complex, involving serious issues of legitimacy and power relations. However, by thinking about the problems in advance and by critically evaluating what you are trying to do, you can better conceptualize the issues, the feasibility of the research and the data sources needed to provide evidence. This will improve the quality of your research and its effectiveness in changing public policy and public action.

When using evidence to try and change or support a particular policy it is tempting to think that it will be possible to 'prove' your position. You might feel that the evidence is indisputable and will inevitably convince all the stakeholders involved of the 'rightness' of your view. Such hopes are usually misplaced, however. The social and political acceptance of the relevance or interpretation of information and the highly disputable nature of 'scientific' evidence often become central issues in controversies. From studies of controversies involving technical or scientific advances, Dorothy Nelkin concludes: 'Nor is there much evidence that technical arguments change anyone's mind. No amount of data could resolve the premises underlying the conflict over animal experiments' (Nelkin, 1992, p. xxi). Whilst this should not be taken as meaning that evidence will never help, it does serve to underline some of the problems that may arise in situations where there is controversy over different possible actions. Although, as pointed out below, quantitative data have a special place in western policy structure, such problems will not be solved simply by finding or collecting more data. The notion that more empirical information is not the simple answer many people hope for will be explored further in this chapter.

Effectiveness in the use of evidence demands both a proper understanding of its limitations and measures to ensure their quality and appropriateness for use. Whilst evidence alone may not be the answer, good quality evidence used in the right context can help gain influence for a position and, most importantly, give it the necessary substance to gather support. By evaluating critically the data that support a particular approach, and data that support alternative approaches, evidence can be built up and support gained for your arguments.

The way in which the framing (or conceptualization) of an issue affects the outcome is a theme running throughout this chapter. An example of its importance in development is the conflict between 'expert' and 'local' knowledge, mentioned by Blackmore and Ison in Chapter 2 and taken up further here. In a world increasingly dominated by a western version of logic and rationality, and where the status of the expert in industrialized societies is growing (Krimsky, 1984), alternative approaches to understand or explain the world can be so different that they are discounted because they fall outside the accepted framework.

This chapter considers how to think about and make use of evidence to influence others to take action or to make changes in public policy. One of its main messages is that supplying what you may consider compelling evidence for a particular policy position may not be widely agreed, even in a climate where the rhetoric is one of 'evidence-based decision making'.

We will look first at the pitfalls associated with using evidence. Then we will explore how problems are defined since the way an issue is conceptualized is key to shaping public policy debates and agendas. Finally, we will consider practical steps to help you get the most out of your evidence.

11.1 Problems with using evidence • • •

11.1.1 Data cannot prove anything

When you gather evidence during a research project or conduct an overarching review of a range of studies, the temptation is to think there will be one straightforward conclusion that arises from it. However, the nature of data and their limitations means that any conclusions always carry an element of uncertainty. A range of possible conclusions can be drawn from examining even simple data, depending on your initial assumptions. Research findings may also raise more questions or may not give a complete picture. A collection of data about which nations received development aid, for example, is very likely to mask whether such aid is acting according to its aim to alleviate or eradicate poverty. And, although there is an increasing amount of evidence showing that poverty and lower social class is associated with poor health, there is very little research undertaken on the effectiveness of public health interventions according to social class (Macintyre, 2003). Therefore, debates about how to target action to reduce health inequalities continue both in the developed and developing world.

The boundaries implied by a question also make a difference to which conclusions can be drawn. Data may show that distributing money to women rather than men increases the production of food, from which you might draw the conclusion that this is the best way to spend money to improve nutrition. However, other differently 'boundaried' research may show that different sectors of society feel disempowered and long established social structures are becoming unsettled by such interventions and by the increased monetarization of local society, which could suggest a different conclusion from that formed originally.

And, of course, the very methodology you use will be open to challenge. If survey methods are used, did these involve use of a representative sample? Were the questions asked openly and how were the data analyzed?

Raw research data themselves are not knowledge and would not normally be presented as evidence without analysis and interpretation. Therefore, data need to be put into context before they become useful knowledge. For example, even though two data sets may be related, this does not mean they are *causally* related – just because children get taller as they get older and also progressively develop language skills does not mean that getting taller improves language skills or *vice versa*!

A striking example of how methodological arguments can lead to disputes is given in Example 11.1. It shows how choice of methodology can be shaped by your own worldview or particular priorities.

Example 11.1   What's in a method?

In the early 1990s a dispute arose in connection with the global warming debate between two non-governmental organizations (NGOs), the World Resources Institute (WRI) and the Centre for Science and the Environment (CSE).

The WRI, based in Washington DC, produced data detailing each country's emissions of carbon dioxide (CO_2) and other important greenhouse gases (Yearley, 1996, pp. 102–107). The WRI report calculated each country's emissions and then reduced the total by the amount that would be absorbed by natural processes. Calculating their emissions this way, the ranking of countries from highest downwards is, USA, USSR, Brazil, China, India, European Union, Indonesia, Canada and Mexico. What is surprising about this ranking is the suggestion that less-developed countries are major polluters.

These results were challenged by researchers at the CSE in India (Agarwal and Narain, 1992). On the face of it the calculations may seem straightforward, and the conclusions, although uncomfortable, apparently correct. But the CSE made two criticisms of the data analysis.

1   The natural processes which absorb CO_2 should not be apportioned by country but rather according to population size.
    Doing this gives recognition to the very low greenhouse impact of the average Indian compared to someone from the USA (0.3 compared to 4.2 on one index). Calculating things this way leads to India and China no longer being amongst the top five polluters, but replaced by Canada and Germany.
2   All types of emissions are treated as equal.
    Thus luxury emissions associated with driving to the shops are seen as no different from survival emissions of using fuel for cooking, for example.

The policy implications arising from both these criticisms are immense.

In the first, rather than pressure being placed on India to reduce its emissions urgently, as the WRI analysis would favour, using the CSE approach, India could have doubled its total carbon dioxide emissions without reaching 'its limit' (Agarwal, quoted in Pearce, 1992). Thus, the WRI could be accused of having collected and analyzed data in a way which was against the interests of less developed nations, even though their approach seemed superficially logical and unbiased.

The second has, if anything, a more fundamental effect, in that it could support a change in emphasis of the policy itself. The shape and effects of a policy to reduce CO_2 emissions would be very different if it was designed to cut luxury emissions as a priority.

(Continued)

(Continued)

For developed countries, under the WRI evaluation, the social adjustments may be small and incremental, but, under the CSE approach, they could lead to much more social equity in resource use (Jasanoff, 1993). Since then, other questions have also been raised about how to judge emissions, including whether a country's emissions today fairly represent its contribution to climate change – developed countries have been producing large amounts of CO_2 for very many years so their cumulative impact is greater than the newly industrializing countries. This has opened up further issues of equity and whether trading in CO_2 can be conducted fairly at all if consumption is not addressed (Lohmann, 2001). If cumulative emissions were considered the cuts required by developed countries could be immense.

Example 11.1 illustrates that decisions about what data to collect and how to analyze them are not simple matters. There can be serious political ramifications depending on which method or approach is chosen. This is because social, political and economic judgements are involved in decisions upon how an issue is to be framed and what knowledge is relevant.

All of these factors challenge the certainty of conclusions drawn from data. However, even if the framework of data analysis is agreed upon, there is also the issue of uncertainty in the raw data. In Example 11.1, the absolute levels of emissions in WRI's report were uncertain and the CSE could simply have challenged whether countries do emit what WRI claim. Such uncertainty exists whatever the nature of the data – be they qualitative data about people's wishes or their identification of problems, or the most tightly controlled scientific data. All methods suffer from data uncertainty.

Uncertainty in data and its interpretation has been the focus of many controversies (see Nelkin, 1992) and can be used by any side in a dispute. Uncertainty may be used, for example, to call for an end to nuclear power because the effects of radiation on human health are not fully understood but could be serious. On the other hand it can be argued that, since there is no proof of harm, preventing radioactive discharges may be unnecessary and the benefits of nuclear power lost without reason. Very often the call is for more research to try and resolve the uncertainty. In such situations, more research often only reveals more uncertainty and the demand for yet more research. In this highly critical model (Collingridge and Reeve, 1986), policy action is delayed and delayed until consensus is achieved even though uncertainty continues. For example, although it is widely agreed that smoking causes cancer and that lead causes brain damage in children, there are alternative causation theories which have not yet been discounted. In the cases of smoking and cancer and lead and brain damage in children, however, consensus about the link has been achieved in some countries and policy measures introduced to limit the risks. In contrast to these cases, the uncertainty surrounding arguments about whether a person's intelligence is determined by genetics or the environment, remains great enough that policy measures which, it might be claimed, would improve a person's environment and thus their intelligence, are more difficult to achieve.

To compound these issues of uncertainty surrounding the data and the uncertainty of conclusions that can be drawn from those data, there is also the issue of ignorance. It is a factor in disputes about data, and is often much more difficult to deal with than uncertainty. At least with uncertainty we know that a parameter exists. Even though we are unsure of its exact value, we have some idea of the extremes within which it might lie. However, with ignorance this cannot be so. To further complicate the problem, ignorance tends to be denied or discounted in policy circles – with a tendency to rely upon an exaggerated vision of the scope and power of scientific knowledge (Wynne, 1992, p. 115). This restricts debate by constraining the definition of what are relevant questions. Before the discovery in 1985 of the ozone hole above Antartica, it was considered rather eccentric to ask questions about the potential effects of ozone depletion on human health. The hole itself had been developing for some time, but we were ignorant of it. Questions on this subject before 1985 were therefore perceived as irrelevant.

One of the most innovative uses of data can be to expose the artificially narrowed boundaries of many policy debates. Posing new questions or looking at data in new ways may change our whole conception of a problem and policy responses to it (Myers, 1995). The international environmental NGO Greenpeace was the first to apply a research tool – gas chromatography mass spectrometry (GCMS) – to the measurement of chemicals in waste discharges in a policy context. Previously, GCMS had been used to look at the purity of samples or for the presence of one particular chemical. What was significant about the new data generated was that it exposed an area of ignorance which contemporary policy could not deal with. The regulation of industrial discharges was based on a chemical-by-chemical approach, with licenses being given which listed the levels of a list of chemicals which could be released. The GCMS study showed that there was often a complex cocktail of chemicals (sometimes over 100) in many industrial discharges and some of the chemicals could not even be identified (Johnston and Stringer, 1989). This new knowledge makes a chemical-by-chemical approach impracticable and has been used to support Greenpeace's policy alternative of clean production systems to give zero discharges.

Friends of the Earth, another environmental NGO, also used new data in a similar way in the early 1990s when they conducted a survey of tree health in the United Kingdom to demonstrate that acid rain generated in the UK was not only causing problems in continental Europe but was damaging trees in the UK. Because the UK was an important political player in the acid rain debate in Europe, and had been denying the seriousness of the impacts, the revelation that its own trees (symbols of 'a green and pleasant land') were being affected was important in changing the political climate (Hajer, 1995). This was the first time that such a tree survey had been conducted in this context, so Friends of the Earth exposed an area of significant importance of which the policy community had previously been ignorant.

But having *certainty* about the effects of acid rain or discharges of pollutants will remain elusive because of complexity. It has proved very difficult to unravel the cause-effect pathways arising from complex chemical mixtures and so controversy about what to do, if anything, continues. A whole chain of events has to be understood – from the origin of the chemicals; the interactions between them; the organisms they come into contact with and for how long; and the alternative causes of any effect seen. Multi-million dollar research projects continue 20 years after these issues were first raised.

Thus, for methodological reasons involving underlying assumptions, the boundaries of what is considered relevant, how data are collected and analyzed, and complexity and ignorance, no data, or the conclusions drawn from them, can ever be considered to be beyond dispute (see Chapter 2). Even where a consensus exists about a problem, this may suddenly be upset when new data on a previously unconsidered dimension of an issue are produced. The examples above illustrate that data collection for advocacy can achieve breakthroughs by reviewing the boundaries of an issue. Clearly, data by themselves cannot prove or disprove any argument or hypothesis. Data are the key, however, since their generation, analysis and exploration can suggest weaknesses within arguments, opinions and practices. Thus proficiency with data is important to your cause. Examining the evidence against your opinions is just as important as having evidence in your favour. As Mukherjee and Wuyts point out in Chapter 10, not only does it prepare you for policy debates, it can help you to rethink your arguments and point you towards a stronger case. Box 11.1 gives a useful checklist of some of the limitations of data as an 'objective' tool.

Box 11.1   Limitations of evidence as an 'objective' tool

- Evidence collection and interpretation will be influenced by social, political, economic and cultural factors.
- Uncertainty and ignorance limit our understanding of the world.
- Do not claim that your evidence proves something – this makes your use of data much easier to attack.
- Data cannot prove anything because of the variable and contingent nature of knowledge.
- Issues surrounding evidence can be politically significant and limit or extend policy options.
- Understanding how knowledge is being shaped in any particular debate is important to be effective in your use of evidence.

11.1.2 All evidence is not equal

As Box 11.1 reminds us, data and evidence are not homogenous masses of information, unconnected with where and how they are collected or derived. There are social, political and cultural forces affecting how data and the knowledge derived from them are perceived. For example, in some societies it might be difficult for a black, female, research student to have a new theoretical perspective accepted – even if it did fit the data available better than any other theory. In contrast, a white, middle-aged man with a track record in the subject might have the same revolutionary theory accepted much more readily. This section explores why social evaluation is not impartial when it comes to the type of data used and how expert knowledge has become automatically accepted as fact at the expense of other forms of knowledge.

'Hard' versus 'soft' data

Quantitative and qualitative data will be viewed and valued differently by different groups of people. Being able to count and measure phenomena is often seen as the 'best' approach since it is thought to allow attribution of cause and effect. This 'scientific tradition' seeks to provide 'objective' knowledge that is not shaped by people's beliefs or prejudices as qualitative data may be. This is similar to the idea that financial accounts provide the best information about organizations since they are quantitative and hence 'hard', 'objective' data. Of course, there is a great deal of contemporary work that challenges the assertion that the scientific method is impartial. The interests of the people doing the measuring, the questions they ask and the assumptions they make, have all been raised as issues that challenge the image of science as impartial. (See Webster (1991), for a useful introduction to the sociology of science; Irwin (1995) for an analysis of the complex relationship between science, the public and environmental threats; and Leach *et al.*, (2005), for a consideration of public engagement in science and technology in developed and developing countries).

However, despite this well established critique of 'the scientific tradition', the dominant atmosphere in policy circles is that quantitative data are invariably 'better' than qualitative data (see Chapter 10). Sometimes people talk about quantitative data being 'hard', as in the description of 'hard facts'. Qualitative data, on the other hand, are called 'soft' and portrayed as not dealing with facts. In many domains this leads to an emphasis on laboratory based rather than field research. In the search for hard data there can be a tendency to reductionism – to cut a subject down into smaller and smaller parts so that the variables can be controlled and altered and cause–effect relationships attributed. This approach has come from the natural sciences, and is seen as important in the construction of 'good science' which is so dominant in certain policy cultures, including the UK (Wynne and Mayer, 1993).

However, such approaches ignore complexity and can limit the possibility of alternative hypotheses being accepted. Policy makers may prefer the use of quantitative survey data of public attitudes because it provides simple figures and enough people can be surveyed to be able to claim the sample was representative. However, the complexity of *why* people hold the views they do is lost and can only be understood using qualitative methods, which are more time consuming and can not involve the same number of people as survey techniques can. Both types of data are important and using several methodologies to give confidence in your findings is strongly recommended. For example, a survey may suggest that a population of people do not support the development of GM crops to provide a source of anti-viral agents to be used in barrier creams to prevent infection with HIV during intercourse. Your assumption may be that they do not like GM crops but qualitative research may reveal different reasons that demand different policy responses. It may be that people do not trust the researchers involved and believe they are being used by a profit making enterprise that they will not benefit from. Or they may consider that barrier creams will not be used in high risk situations and research efforts would be better placed elsewhere.

While bias towards a particular notion of 'hard' science may also lead to laboratory-based data being regarded more highly than field observations, it can also lead to social sciences being seen as secondary to the natural sciences. For example, Weale (1992, p. 18) concluded that British governments across a wide range of policy sectors frequently play down sociological or other behavioural evidence in favour of economic or natural sciences evidence. The relative importance or credence given to different disciplines will vary in different countries. Nevertheless, the natural sciences claim truths that apply the world over (Yearley, 1996, p. 85), and remain dominant in explaining some of the problems of sustainable development such as resource utilization.

Therefore, the culture that defines what is 'good science' with the world-views contained in the definition, gives rise to a pervasive problem in ensuring that data lying outside the current perception of 'good science' are taken seriously.

It is therefore important to be aware of how different types of data will be viewed. As we discussed earlier, in policy debate there may be a bias towards quantitative data but, by their very nature, they cannot give the more subtle information you may need on how people feel or what works in practice. However, such qualitative data may be viewed as much more unreliable and open to debate and you have to be prepared for this when using your data.

Local knowledge versus 'expert' knowledge

Another problem is that disputed knowledge may be 'certified' by 'experts' – lending it greater credibility than it would otherwise have. The increasingly technical nature of society and its problems has meant that use of expert knowledge is of growing importance. One consequence of this is that it acts against wider (and more democratic) involvement in decision-making (Leach *et al.*, 2005; also Chapters 7 and 8 of this volume). The justification for the primacy of experts has been eloquently expressed by Stephen Yearley: 'The conviction that science speaks objectively and disinterestedly means that one need have no qualms about excluding other people from decision-making since they would, in any event, have arrived at the same conclusions as oneself' (Yearley, 1996, p. 118).

Because of this the 'high levels of mutual confidence that small élites in Britain have developed towards one another' (Weale, 1992, p. 212) is not seen as a problem – the same is probably true in other countries. However, this view is becoming increasingly difficult to defend as political and economic interests are more explicitly seen in science.

Not only are more experts employed by industry and other partial interests, but research agendas are increasingly driven by financial rather than purely knowledge-generating priorities. The UK public, for example, has become so cynical of certain types of expert advice, that they have more confidence in NGOs as sources of knowledge on the dangers associated with scientific and technological issues (Martin and Tait, 1992).

The dominance of experts in national and international policy debates has implications not only for who is allowed to be involved in decisions but also for the type of data or knowledge that is 'certified' by these experts. For example, the way in which Andean farmers classify potato varieties is complex and relevant to their farming systems, yet completely different from that of western taxonomy (Douwe van der Ploeg, 1993). During efforts to 'improve' Andean potato stock, only the 'superior' knowledge of the westernized system was used. This subsequently led to problems that could have been avoided, had local knowledge systems been taken into account. The potato classification system used by Andean farmers is just one example of the different knowledge systems that exist to make sense of the world.

Even academic studies of different knowledge systems have tended to take:

Western 'rationality' and 'scientificity' as the bench mark criteria by which other cultures' knowledge should be evaluated. So-called traditional knowledge systems of indigenous peoples have frequently been portrayed as closed, pragmatic, utilitarian, value laden, indexical, context dependent, and so on, implying they cannot have the same authority and credibility as science because their localness restricts them to the social and cultural circumstances of their production.

(Watson-Verran and Turnbull, 1995, pp. 115–116)

This raises particular dilemmas when using data and deriving knowledge from them. Western Judaeo-Christian belief is that man has dominion over nature, but this is not the only world-view. For example, the belief of many indigenous Americans is that of mother earth and a complex interdependence between all its inhabitants – human and non-human. Whereas useful knowledge in the western tradition will focus more on control and manipulation of nature, for native Americans knowledge is more useful if it reveals interactions and how to reduce impact on the natural environment.

So, although local knowledge may be most relevant to the design of sustainable social policies, this may have little impact in policy-making circles because of different presumptions and aspirations for society. This raises some interesting dilemmas. Should you find data that will fit in with the preferences of the policy-maker and possibly perpetuate the downgrading of local knowledge, or should you rely on local knowledge and risk lack of policy impact? In making a decision, it is also important to consider the extent to which citizen engagement will be affected. There is growing intellectual and political support for public engagement in policy development that is beneficial for empowerment, quality and trust in decision making (Stirling, 2005). Working in a way which is ultimately disempowering will not help this progressive movement. That decision making *processes* are important should not be forgotten in the drive for 'evidence-based' approaches.

Box 11.2 summarizes the main issues on the cultural contexts of data, data types and their impact.

Box 11.2   Cultural aspects of data impact

- There is a policy culture in the West that favours scientific measurement and this culture is becoming dominant across the world.
- Data which do not fit easily into the western tradition have less impact.
- There is bias towards data that demonstrate cause and effect and this can act against theories which take a more open view of society and the environment.
- There is a tendency to rely on experts to provide policy answers.
- Local knowledge is given little value
- Public engagement in technical or policy issues is often considered irrelevant or unhelpful.

11.1.3 Data that don't say what you want

While there may be considerable prejudice against certain types of data and knowledge, these are not the only problems that advocates can face. One of the biggest mistakes a campaigning organization can make is to announce publicly that it will be collecting data to prove this or that (setting itself up for charges that any data collected are biased towards that view or that the mere announcement will skew any data collected, because people know what is expected). Avoiding announcements about what you are going to prove is one important lesson.

Sometimes data do not validate your case. If you quietly collect and analyze data and they don't illustrate or validate what you expected, what has gone wrong? The first most obvious thing is that you may have been wrong in your initial assumptions. Data that don't fit should trigger a critical review of your aims and objectives, and a readiness to re-evaluate them. Evaluating alternative explanations and counter-evidence can, in many cases, point towards a stronger argument than that you developed initially. The example given by Mukherjee and Wuyts in Chapter 10 of alternative explanations of famine illustrates this. The second more complex explanation of famine, based on access to food, strengthens, not weakens, the case for increasing access to food in famine areas.

Thus, lack of support for your initial argument from the data you collected does not necessarily mean that your overall position is weakened, though it certainly points to a need for reflection and reconceptulization. You may have picked the wrong indicator, used the wrong methodology, or be trying to express your argument in the wrong terms. For example, finding that the number of deaths of cattle from a particular disease was low and so does not seem to support your call for more animal health provision, may not mean you should change your position. Other measures of cattle health, such as their condition, frequency with which they have calves, or the price they fetch at market, may be better indicators, and strengthen your argument. So rethinking your definition of the problem and the indicators of it will be an important response.

Another example could be your use of quantitative survey methods to try to examine whether women feel satisfied with their role in society. This may have been intended to support your position that women should have more control and be given support to gain control. Yet answers may show that women accept their current position with little evidence of dissatisfaction. But deeper qualitative questions may bring out the deeper feelings that women may hold and find difficult to express for a variety of reasons. Rather than abandoning the aim of empowering women, re-evaluation of the type of research methodology may be a better response.

There is a more pervasive problem, however, associated with some of the issues that have already been touched upon in earlier parts of this chapter. This is how the problem is 'officially' defined and therefore the context in which data are interpreted. For example, in policy debates you may be advocating that local people should be given responsibility for managing the land and its conflicts. But if the policy definition of the problem is that there is a conflict between conservation interests, tourism and local people's access to land to produce food, which needs managing, you may become drawn into producing data so you can argue in this particular debate. Data which you may present to show how local people are most affected by the conflict may come across, inside the terms of the debate, as indicating that they need 'managing'. The terms of the debate will not have allowed the issue of who should manage land to be discussed. Rather it is about how land should be managed (by those currently in control). Making sure your position is clear when you use data is crucial if it is not to be mis- or re-interpreted.

Box 11.3 summarizes some of the issues raised here.

Box 11.3 Where data do not support your arguments

- Don't announce in advance what your research will show or prove.
- In the light of your data, critically evaluate your policy position.
- Reassess whether you have used the correct methodology and analyzed the data properly.
- Question whether you have collected the most appropriate data.
- Ask whether your data is relevant to the policy debate.

11.2 **Defining the problem** • • •

As discussed already, the types of argument and data that will influence people's views will depend upon their social, political and cultural background. Different cultures will value things differently. Political commitments will shape the way in which people look at the problem and the breadth of responses which they consider plausible. For example, if power lies with a group of large landowners, they are unlikely to be convinced by data which show better yields from small-scale rather than large-scale farms. Aid agencies will also have their own particular organizational cultures which influence how they perceive problems and whether they think they are relevant to them. Governments use strategies such as the creation of new departments and the establishment of expert committees as ways of dealing with difficult social problems. In that way they try to gain control over the definition of the problem and thereby the policy responses to it (Weale, 1992). Being able to define the problem and have control over its definition gives considerable power to shape who and what is included or excluded.

As you begin to think about what evidence you are going to use, it is important to understand clearly what information is considered relevant to an issue. The context will have evolved over time and been shaped by the actors involved. For example, the task of providing water to a community may have been addressed from a technical analysis of what was possible, while social issues, such as where the supply should be sited, the differing needs of users, and who should be involved in the decisions, were regarded as marginal. This will affect how evidence can influence decisions.

The definition of a problem can affect whether your real feelings and thoughts about an issue are going to be allowed inside the debate. If they are not and you do not make your challenge to the framework clear at an early stage, this can inadvertently draw you into arguing and using evidence on someone else's terms, which can eventually be damaging in surprising ways.

For example, in the battle over the Brent Spar oil platform in the North Sea in 1996, Greenpeace was opposed to ocean dumping on principle, and believed that the Brent Spar would set a precedent for dumping of other unwanted oil installations. Even though their primary concern was not with the actual effect of the Brent Spar itself on the ocean floor, but rather with the danger of ocean dumping in general, Greenpeace became drawn into an argument about this one case because the UK Government did their risk assessment on an individual case-by-case basis. Greenpeace calculated the amount of oil on board the Brent Spar and then claimed that dumping the Brent Spar would be dangerous, even though this was not the long term basis of their objection. Later, a sampling error in Greenpeace's calculation was discovered that showed an overestimate in the amount of oil. The error allowed those in favour of dumping Brent Spar to portray Greenpeace as having unsound judgement. Greenpeace later accepted that it had been wrong to be drawn into a debate around the one-off case of Brent Spar, the terms of which they fundamentally disagreed with.

One common problem encountered when trying to challenge policy is that the boundaries exclude considerations about whether the policy is feasible in practice or whether it places unacceptable constraints on people. For example, when determining the safety of pesticides, expert committees in the UK argued that their assessments were correct as long as the instructions were followed (Wynne, 1989, pp. 36–37). But in calculating exposures, they failed to take into account the practical difficulties of using pesticides, for example when working with animals, how hot weather may make wearing protective clothing difficult and so on, even though this has a significant impact on the degree of risk. Because an expert committee had determined these chemicals to be 'safe', the underlying assumptions about what was relevant to the assessment of safety were difficult to challenge.

Thus, it took a considerable amount of effort, the documentation of cases of chronic toxicity and the demonstration of the practical impossibility of following safety instructions to get the possibility of harmful effects of pesticides on farm workers taken seriously. It was important in this debate that campaigners stuck to producing data about the realities of farm work and people's experiences, rather than concentrating on laboratory data on toxicity. Laboratory data alone may have led to somewhat stricter standards, but would not have addressed the real shortcomings in the safety assessment system, which were that it ignored important parameters and thus drew the boundaries too tightly.

I believe one of the most creative ways in which people can advance policy is by breaking down the boundaries of the debate and thereby making other policy options possible. However, the power of these boundaries is such that forcing them open is difficult; a great deal of work may be required to demonstrate why they are inappropriate. However, this can be achieved on occasions to dramatic effect. The Jubilee 2000 coalition campaign succeeded in getting the G8 to agree to cancel $110bn of debt owed by 41 of the poorest countries. Although there is ongoing debate about the extent to which promises on debt cancellation have actually been kept, and the conditions imposed before debts are cancelled, the Jubilee 2000 campaign was certainly successful in changing the framing of the debate so that the activities of the creditors not the debtors became the focus.

Until then, how the debtor countries failed to repay had been the issue at stake. This complete reversal of who should be responsible for taking steps to tackle debt was achieved through the collection and presentation of evidence, which showed what money was lent for (such as arms) and the conditions of its use. This required an enormous amount of very careful analysis, not only of the data, but also of the political and policy context (Pettifor, 2003).

Box 11.4 highlights some of the issues surrounding problem definition and policy debate.

> ### Box 11.4 Problem definition and policy debate
>
> - It is important to understand the way in which a policy debate is framed.
> - Governments tend to restrict and boundary policy debates in ways that fit with their preferred policy options.
> - To have a clear understanding of the policy debate it is necessary to find out how all the actors define the problem.
> - Data that fit within the policy framework will more easily be taken seriously than data which open new issues.
> - Redefining the terms of debate can be one of the most productive ways of using new data, but takes considerable time and effort.

11.3 Making the most of data ● ● ●

Your evidence will inevitably be put up for public scrutiny. Scrutiny will be most stringent where the data conflict with dominant views or, as discussed above, the data are drawn from sources attracting little credibility. They might be qualitative, based upon people's personal observations, or drawn from a different discipline, such as sociology, that might not immediately be considered relevant to a problem of, say, pollution. Here we will look at practical ways of maximizing the impact of your data. There are three golden rules:

1 Understand the positions of all the actors in the debate and how they interact with each other.
2 Constantly reflect critically on your own position and the way to achieve your goal.
3 Seek new ways to influence the debate and define the problem in ways that integrate your views and the data.

11.3.1 Do you have the right data?

The first thing to do is to ensure you possess, or are going to get, the right evidence to support your case, and/or throw doubt on alternative cases. Who will collect such data is a question to be addressed later but the criteria for choice will influence the planning stage of research. What purpose is the evidence to serve? This is another important question that is part of the planning process. In making decisions about research, it is important to be careful to focus on where new information is most needed or will have most effect.

The kinds of questions you might ask are:

- What do you hope the research will show?
- What effect will they have on the debate?

- Is there a better, easier or cheaper way to achieve the same effect?
- Are you looking at the best parameters?
- What are the weak points?
- How will the new evidence lead the debate forward?

All of these questions are best addressed at the planning stage by the whole of the team working on the issue. Often, supporters and sympathizers will help you. What you are doing is finding out how the evidence you intend to gather fits into your overall strategy. At this planning stage it is good to think holistically about the boundaries of the issue and data needs. Whoever does the actual research (whether yourself or a consultant), it is very important to write a brief. This concentrates the mind, enhances critical reflection and gives a basis for evaluating the work as it progresses.

11.3.2 Different types of evidence in different situations

It is also important to think creatively when you consider what kind of research you need to do. One area which illustrates this well is the difficult situation where there seems no direct evidence that a certain policy or practice will be harmful, but if it is allowed and something goes wrong the implications could be very serious. One response to such situations is to advocate the use of the precautionary principle. The precautionary principle is most widely used in environmental policy making and evolved from the failure to anticipate and prevent harm from certain human practices, such as the impact of chemical pollutants on the marine environment. Often, a lack of clear evidence between cause and effect was used to delay measures to prevent the release of pollutants.

The Precautionary Principle was defined at the 1992 Rio Declaration on Environment and Development (UNCED, 1992):

> *Where there are threats of serious or irreversible environmental damage, lack of full scientific certainty shall not be used as a reason for postponing cost effective measures to prevent environmental degradation.*

Although originally associated with environmental harm, it has now been adopted in other areas such as human and animal health. However, the precautionary principle has been accused of being 'anti-science' and delaying the progress of science and innovation. It also raises questions of how the precautionary principle fits into the era of 'evidence-based' decision making and the inevitable issue of scientific uncertainty and lack of knowledge. One contemporary policy area where this has been most controversial has been in relation to genetically modified organisms (GMOs) and the risks of introducing them. It illustrates the importance of finding evidence and considering audiences for the evidence outside the community of stakeholders immediately involved in an issue. It also illustrates the recurrent theme of this chapter about framing and context.

There has been relatively limited experience with the use of GMOs in agriculture and food. In this situation, who determines whether there is enough evidence to allow the release of a GMO and whether concerns over possible health or environmental effects are important? In this area, as in many others, differences between the views of experts and the public have emerged. Experts tend to dismiss public concerns as being based on a lack of knowledge, even though evidence about the basis of public concerns shows that people are raising questions which are not considered relevant to the official risk assessment (Mayer and Stirling, 2004). This situation poses dilemmas for society and also for those wanting to take a precautionary approach, especially where this has a wide degree of public support. Because the introduction of GMOs and other technologies is seen as a technical matter in many government and scientific circles, public views on the acceptability of risk and the framing of the debate tend to be discounted. How can the evidence of public preferences be given weight in circumstances like this? The approach, which was adopted with a great degree of success in Europe, was to present the evidence to the food producers and supermarkets. For this part of the commercial sector, the views of consumers would affect whether they purchased a product of not. As a result, the majority of supermarkets and major food producers in Europe do not use GM ingredients (Levidow and Bijman, 2002). Although there have been many examples of citizen's juries and other participatory techniques in an effort to generate evidence to influence political decision making and democratize it in relation to GMOs (e.g. Rusike, 2005), these tend to have had more limited effect. The challenge to established power structures of democratizing science and technology policy seems too great, but public investment in GM crops has certainly declined, with more emphasis being placed on other forms of agriculture.

This example shows how important it is to think about all the actors who will have a role in shaping policy and practice. In a period where market economy is dominant and government intervention is often seen less favourably, using evidence to influence the policy of commercial interests opens opportunities but is likely to demand a different range of evidence – economic and consumer based – than for the political domain.

11.3.2 Who should do the research?

There will also be questions about who should conduct the research. Your new evidence may derive from your own research – desk or original. Desk research is second hand and reinterpreting data, which is often not in exactly the form you want, can be hard (see Chapter 10). Gaining access to the raw data, especially if it is not yet published, can also be difficult. However, doing original research can be both time-consuming and costly. Here the key question is:

• Do you need new research or can you use existing data in new ways?

Not only may the type of knowledge (local or expert) influence how evidence is received in debates and hearings, but so will the identity of the presenter. The 'independent expert' is the voice that seems to carry most weight these days. These are people with no long-term financial involvement with the people for whom they do research and who, therefore, presumably, carry credibility in their field. Well-respected academics often fall into this class. Critiques of objectivity in research will inevitably apply, but the influences will be more subtle and disguised, less easily open to challenges of partiality. Using an independent expert to give weight and credibility to data that might be seen as 'soft' (qualitative) local knowledge can be a useful strategy to make the maximum impact with groups of people who would normally be resistant to such data.

Managing outside experts is not easy, however. Although using 'independent' people who have undertaken the research to present the findings can be very persuasive, there can also be problems. For example, in public they may be less willing than they were in private to draw conclusions that challenge orthodoxy. One of the most important things is to ensure that there is a clear brief produced, agreed by both parties, and including details about payment, who has the publication rights and deadlines. These may seem like bureaucratic niceties, especially when you are working with people you know well, but in the long run they can help maintain good relations and avoid the risk of argument through misunderstandings from oral communications.

In deciding whether to use an expert the important questions to be asked here are:

- Am I, or is my organization, qualified to do the research?
- Is there an outside person who could do the work better?
- How will who does the research affect its impact?

Again these are a questions of tactics and need to be answered in the context of your overall strategy. They need to be considered by the same group which discussed the questions about how to collect the right data.

Example 11.2 is a short description of one NGO's collection and use of evidence, which gives useful lessons about how important these kinds of questions are for overall effectiveness.

Example 11.2   ITDG and community animal health workers in Kenya

Where evidence supporting policy change comes from, how it is presented and what established power structures are challenged by it, all affect whether it will have influence. All these factors are illustrated in the prolonged time it has taken to see community animal health workers (CAHWs) accepted in Kenya.

The idea of CAHWs was taken up following the success of barefoot doctors in China. Where access to veterinary services is restricted because of lack of financial

(Continued)

(Continued)

resources or geographical constraints, a locally based network of people, trained in the basic diagnosis and treatment or prevention of animal diseases, can provide an important and effective service.

The UK based NGO, ITDG (now Practical Action), first started to put the concept of CAHWs into action in Kenya in the mid-1980s. The provision of veterinary services in the 'hardship' areas of Kenya, where 75% of animals are kept, had been difficult and limited for many years. When veterinary services were nationalized, and to an even greater extent following privatization, the remote and less-favoured areas of Kenya did not attract either veterinary surgeons or animal health technicians. Because the health of their animals is of such great importance to the livelihoods of many pastoralist communities, ITDG began a programme of active provision of CAHWs, training programmes and dissemination workshops from 1986 onwards.

ITDG gathered much on-the-ground evidence showing that CAHWs, both in Kenya and neighbouring countries, including Sudan, could provide good quality services without compromising animal health or welfare (as might be feared could arise through, for example, misdiagnosis). However, despite this, it is only now, some twenty years later, that CAHWs are starting to become accepted by the official veterinary establishment, although they are still not legally recognized in Kenya.

Several key factors have led to the clear and compelling evidence of the positive impact of CAHWs on communities in disadvantaged areas being less effective than it should have been:

- The veterinary profession in Kenya is modelled on the UK, where the provision of animal health care is tightly controlled and restricted to veterinary surgeons and people directly under their supervision. The veterinary profession in Kenya saw the introduction of CAHWs as a threat to this model of health care and their sphere of influence.
- The evidence was presented by NGOs and others who were considered to be biased. This only began to change following a review in the mid-1990s by a team which included two Kenyans who were well respected in official and veterinary circles.
- The focus of ITDG's work was on developing the practicalities of CAHWs through implementation, training and workshops. There was no strategy for informing or engaging with the official veterinary services and this engagement with the policy process was limited, restricting opportunities for influence.

This case shows how evidence will not simply 'speak for itself', unless there is careful thought about how to enable this. In the case of Kenyan CAHWs, knowing and engaging with the policy and political contexts and having a strategy for advocacy seemed to be missing (Young *et al.*, 2005).

11.3.3 How good is the evidence?

Once you have assembled your evidence it is important to ask whether it stands up to critical scrutiny. Try to be as critical as possible yourself. Get a sympathetic outsider who knows the area to evaluate it. Better still, ask a critic to give you an opinion. This helps prepare for criticism and gives you the opportunity to change tactics or re-evaluate your approach. It is time well spent.

The questions to ask here are:

- Has the evidence been collected and analyzed properly?
- Are the conclusions being drawn from it justifiable?
- What other interpretations of the data are there?
- What are the weak points?
- Should the issue be reconceptualized?

These questions are worth asking, both at the planning stage and when you have collected and used your evidence. They usually demand a different group of people from those planning the overall approach to what evidence is needed to support a policy position; technical expertise is most helpful here.

11.3.4 Did it work?

There should always be an evaluation of whether a piece of work was effective. This is an important part of the learning process. Here the questions to ask are:

- What was achieved by using the new evidence?
- How has the policy evolved?
- Did the research stand up to scrutiny?
- How could things have been done better?

It is often difficult to recognize when is the best time to ask such questions. The answer is probably that it is something to come back to repeatedly. Often the effect of a single piece of work will not be seen for some time, or, if it is part of a bigger campaign, the effect of an individual part may be difficult to detect. You will need both the strategists and technical specialists to help with evaluation.

11.4 Conclusions • • •

In this chapter, I have aimed to show that making the most of evidence for advocacy involves a range of conceptual issues and practical skills. I have emphasized that research data must be interpreted and displayed to reveal new knowledge and so advance your aims. Knowledge is not fixed so much as socially shaped by the questions people and groups ask and the ways they try to answer them. Different societies make sense of the world in different ways through their different knowledge systems. What is so striking at the moment is the way in which western scientific logic dominates debate and controversy over sensitive issues. Since so many issues, such as resource depletion, desertification and biodiversity are seen as global in nature, western knowledge systems are influencing decisions at all levels – national, regional and international.

'Relevance, credibility and providing useful solutions' (Court *et al.*, 2005) are considered three key features of evidence for policy. These also remind us of the issue of framing the problem and the limits that may be placed on what is considered a 'useful solution'. Even if well respected experts come up with a policy prescription which is outside the boundaries of the debate, it may be ignored. This doesn't mean that you should not consider radical new solutions and promote these if you think that this is the right approach, but that their acceptance is likely to take time and need a carefully thought through process of advocacy.

Although western science makes claims to impartiality and lack of bias, like all other forms of knowledge it is shaped by the cultures that make and use it. It will be influenced by the prejudices and interests of the communities involved in its generation and use. When western science comes to define a problem it necessarily encapsulates western values. Because the definition of a problem critically influences how the issue is finally addressed, understanding how an issue has been defined is fundamental in order to change it. Since great weight is placed on expertise, and experts tend to be chosen because they share the policy maker's position, breaking open the terms of the debate to represent your own can be difficult. Data have to be robust – open to critical analysis – for maximum effectiveness.

Independent experts can be enlisted to support a particular cause. There is increasing recognition of NGOs as experts in their own right (Weale, 1992). This raises other dilemmas. When using experts to counter other experts does this perpetuate the problem of public access and control of their environments? NGOs are not democratically elected and simply having their voice heard is an inadequate substitute for adequate democracy.

Issues of democracy may seem a long way from thinking about how to use data effectively. Day-to-day use of data may not, by itself, make a major impact on democratic processes and practices. But the use of data to influence public policy has historically been part of a social system grounded in the cult of the expert, accessed by the few. Finding innovative ways to give voice to concerns not usually heeded by those in power is one of the exciting and enjoyable things to do with evidence. Evidence production and use in advocacy has, for me, no merit on its own, but merely form part of a well designed campaign that allows the public to voice its concerns and understand the issues better, and improves the chance that all people will be able to influence events.

Organizational assessment and institutional footprints

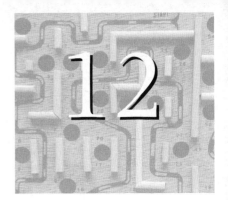

Chris Roche

This chapter concentrates on how one might investigate a variety of organizations in the public, private and non-profit sectors, for a variety of purposes. One might, for example, want to make a decision about whether to support an organization, or ally with it, or oppose it. One might want to know how to influence an organization, or what part the organization itself plays in public action to influence policy choice.

Following the definition used by Drèze and Sen (1989), I take public action to mean not only the activities of the state, but also actions by organizations of citizens, whether collaborative or adversarial in nature. This approach goes beyond recognizing that government policies are a result of the accumulated response to a variety of interests within government and from pressure groups and individuals outside government. It also recognizes that other organizations work alongside government agencies to produce policies and actions aimed at public benefit. So it is important to find out how their institutional structures, procedures and actors represent and further particular interests.

In general, the point of any policy-oriented investigation of an organization will be to promote change. This could be change in the organization itself resulting from an organizational assessment, or it could be public action on the part of an organization informed by an investigation of how another organization contributes to public action. These two cases form the substance of Sections 12.4 and 12.5 below. The second case involves the idea of 'institutional footprints'. An organization (or institution) leaves 'marks' where it has been active, which can be studied to give 'clues' both about the organization itself and the effect of its actions.

Before looking at these two cases of how investigating organizations can inform policy change, there are three more general sections. Section 12.1 introduces some different theoretical perspectives on how organizations can be understood. Some common questions emerge from these, which are outlined in Section 12.2. Section 12.3 then explores preliminary ways of answering these questions, using grey materials and informants both inside and outside the organization – to set up a framework for a more focused investigation aimed either at organizational change (Section 12.4) or at promoting change in the policy environment (Section 12.5).

12.1 Ways of looking at organizations • • •

This section refers to a selection of authors who describe different ways of looking at organizations. Their multiple perspectives help in developing a rounded understanding of public action and in identifying some common and fundamental questions.

Gareth Morgan, in his book *Images of Organization* (Morgan, 1997), explains that organizations are complex, contradictory and paradoxical. They are many things at once. Morgan draws on different disciplinary traditions and uses ideas such as 'organization as machine', 'organization as organism', 'organization as political system', 'organization as culture', etc. He suggests that looking at images and metaphors of organizations in this way allows us to take account more consciously of what we already know intuitively – that where you sit and who you are influences how you see an organization.

Building on this idea, I will explore three different frameworks you can use to analyze the role of organizations in public action:

1   the motivation of different stakeholders;
2   the organization's 'gender archaeology';
3   organizations and change.

TABLE 12.1   Stakeholder analysis

Category of stakeholder	Examples for an NGO such as Oxfam
Owner	the Board of Trustees
Financier	the public, Department for International Development (DfID), European Union
User	'beneficiaries', 'clients', 'partners'
Regulator	the (UK) Charity Commission
Political superior	governments (in the UK and in countries where operating)
Mafia	guerrilla groups active in particular area
Staff	paid and volunteer staff
Local communities	local populations, traditional authorities, local councils in areas where operating

12.1.1 Stakeholders, motivations and incentives

The motivation, incentives and rewards of different stakeholders within an organization, and also the pressures that are exerted on them from the broader environment, will shape the organization's actions. So organizations can be viewed 'less as products of culture, tradition, and history and more the result of the interactions of sets of rational actors pursuing material goals' (Moore *et al.*, 1994).

This raises the questions:

- What encourages staff to work towards making an organization perform?
- What are the sources of the pressures to do so?

Moore *et al.* (1994) suggest that there are perhaps up to seven sources of pressure in the broader environment, which influence outcomes for any organization. For some organizations, particular stakeholder roles might not exist, while for others they may be combined.

These roles, together with an eighth not mentioned by Moore *et al.*, are:

1 *Owner*: for private companies, the shareholders; for membership organizations, the paying members; less clear for non governmental organizations (NGOs) or government departments.
2 *Financier*: can take at least three forms:

- *investors* who expect a return;
- *grantors* who give funds for a particular purpose;
- *dispersed donors* who give amounts towards the organization as a whole.

3 *User*: a private company's customers; owner-users in membership organizations; those benefiting directly or indirectly from the services the organization provides.
4 *Regulator*: the agency responsible for ensuring that an organization is meeting standards laid down in law.
5 *Political superior*: national government in relation to regional government; more broadly, the power of states over the private sector.
6 *Mafia*: those who may be able to exert force on an organization to act differently, often illegally.
7 *Staff*: paid or unpaid workers in the organization, or perhaps owner-users.
8 *Local communities*: the whole population of areas where activities are undertaken, and their local institutions; likely to include more than just the targeted beneficiaries of the organization's activities.

Table 12.1 gives examples of how this framework could be used by a UK-based international NGO such as Oxfam. A national NGO or the country office of an international NGO could be much more specific in its use of the same framework.

This sort of stakeholder analysis can be extended. In this case we could add further columns showing the resources each stakeholder brings to the organization, what each expects to get out of the organization, and what power it has to prevent the organization's activities continuing successfully. This can be the starting point for understanding the degree to which the aims and incentives created by these groups diverge or cohere. It also helps us to understand how effective the different stakeholders are in 'pressurizing' the organization to perform, and to track how this changes over time.

12.1.2 Production and reproduction: the 'gender archaeology' of organizations

This approach is based on the following proposition:

An organization is both the product of the society in which it is situated and an actor in reproducing that society.

Gender, as an issue in organizations, can be explored fruitfully through this approach. Gender is also an interesting vehicle for understanding the two-way relationship between an organization and the society in which it is embedded. This provides us with an explanation of how one set of interests (in this case male interests) are institutionalized.

In looking at gender and institutions Anne Marie Goetz argues that it is often simpler to start by identifying the outcomes, or products, of an organization and how these affect men and women differently (Goetz, 1996). This often shows up internal reasons why a particular organization produced a specific product or outcome. For example, if we see that an agricultural extension agency only provides advice to male farmers we might then look at that agency to see why it does not recruit women extension agents or why it does not do research into crops which women in particular grow. This might in turn lead us into looking at the assumptions that organization makes about agriculture and who is making those assumptions. This helps us to understand how organizations are *gendered* (i.e. function in ways that reflect gender relations in society) and how they are *gendering* (i.e. reproducing those relations, which generally means reproducing inequalities).

Goetz then goes on to make the point that although structures and practices in organizations create incentives and disincentives for staff to behave and act in particular ways, those individuals help to create and recreate the structure and practice. Understanding the feedback loop between individual agents and these structures and practices can give important insights not only into how change might be effected in an organization, but also how policy directives can be blocked and subverted. Table 12.2 summarizes some of the questions that Goetz suggests can help uncover the 'gender archaeology' of organizations.

Goetz suggests that 'the key to understanding how such outcomes are produced is to trace the way institutional structures, practices and agents embody and promote gendered interests'. Figure 12.1 illustrates how these interact.

TABLE 12.2 *Towards a gender archaeology of organizations*

Institutional history	Who was involved in establishing the organization? Who was not? How was this done?
Ideology	What are the academic disciplines that animate the organization? What are the underlying assumptions those disciplines tend to make about gender roles?
Participants	Who makes up the organization? What is the gender division of labour? What is the gender profile of the different levels of the organization?
Space and time	Are working hours difficult for women employees? Are meetings or social activities held at times which might discourage women's participation? Is provision made for career breaks, childcare, etc.? Does the organization demand travel away from home as part of the job?
Authority structures	Can women command authority for their approaches and views in the organization? Do women have to take on 'male attributes' to be heard? What is valued in terms of achievements in the organization?
Incentives and accountability	On what do performance targets tend to focus; more on quantitative rather than qualitative targets? To whom and in what direction is accountability mainly oriented – upwards, downwards or horizontally?

(After Goetz, 1996)

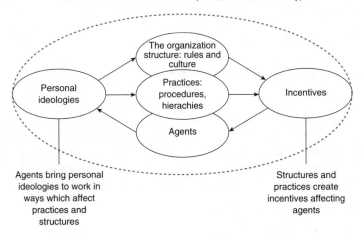

FIGURE 12.1   Organization structure, practices and agents (after Goetz, 1996, p. 4)

12.1.3 Organizations and change

Organizations are not static unchanging bodies. They are dynamic and change in line with changes in their environment and within their parts. In a world of growing inter-dependence and enhanced communications, rapid and unpredictable change is becoming more common. It is essential therefore to understand the nature of this change, what provoked it and how it occurred. Without this we only have a snapshot of where an organization is currently, not a moving picture of how it got there which might also provide clues to where it might go.

It is possible to focus purely on the organization itself, and to treat the environment within which it functions as a set of external forces that the organization has to cope with. But this gives us a rather limited view of how change happens. We can go further in understanding the nature and source of change if we treat the organization as an integral part of a wider system – interacting with its environment and able to shape and guide the forces that produce public action and hence to some extent change the nature of change itself.

This way of understanding change relates to a kind of 'acupuncture' approach to solving problems, whereby one is not looking necessarily to remove the causes of a problem, which is not always possible, but to alter the system through triggering changes that are already embedded in the logic of ongoing processes (Morgan, 1986). This means recognizing that most change is not linear and predictable but is based on interdependent relationships and feedback. Organizations do not behave like machines but are dependent on their contexts and the decisions and acts of a multi-tude of individuals.

The benefit of this sort of analysis is that, instead of seeing individuals, organizations and public action as separate, we start to see them as connected, overlapping and created by each other. The optimistic side of this is seeing the possibility of us as individuals effecting change in our own organizations and in doing so changing other institutions (Roche, 1994).

12.2 Towards some generic questions • • •

From the above it seems that there are perhaps four generic areas in which we could find out more about organizations. Of course, the way you choose to find out about organizations and the focus of the investigation will depend on your specific purpose. However, the following framework may be useful in thinking through investigation. I will be using these categories as a means of structuring some of the following sections, which look at different types of organizational investigation, for different purposes.

12.2.1 Historical analysis

The sections above on gender archaeology and on change in organizations both stress the importance of understanding institutional history and change over time. In order to understand public action at a particular moment, and what information is – or is not – available about that action, the historical dimension is critical.

Hans Singer's review of the lessons of post-war development experience provides several examples of how, for example, economic policies have developed over time and how this is related to which 'faction acquired ascendancy in and control over important institutions and governments' (Singer, 1989, p. 2). He cites in particular how 40 years ago there was an almost fundamentalist belief in planning, balanced growth and import substitution, whilst in the 1980s and beyond export orientation, market power and 'getting the prices right' provided the basis for a new orthodoxy.

He also shows how:

> Just as generals tend to fight the last-but-one-war, so the development actors, as well as the development thinkers, seem to base their action and thought on experiences of the last-but-one decade or a last-but-one phase.

> (Singer, 1989, p. 3; see also Hewitt, 2000)

This again suggests the importance of relating any analysis of action to the political, economic and academic climate, not only of the moment of any action being taken but also of the preceding period.

12.2.2 Internal division

Organizations are not monolithic entities. The importance of understanding the fragmented realities of organizations cannot be over-rated. There are diverging interests and power relations in any organization which may be based upon, amongst other things:

- informal divisions (e.g. between 'insiders' and 'outsiders', new employees and established employees, people who socialize after work and those who do not);
- functional divisions (e.g. between departments or divisions, between professional groupings);
- hierarchical divisions (e.g. between board members and employees, managers and workers, headquarters and other offices, home and 'overseas');
- gender, race or class divisions.

These divisions will reflect the cultural, political and economic context in which an organization is located, as well as being reproduced within the organization itself. It is therefore important to understand the divisions. One might want to exploit them (for example by a lobbying initiative seeking to influence an organization to adopt a particular position). It might be important to overcome divisions in order to improve performance. Or one might simply need to make sure that a particular project does not exacerbate existing tensions and cause conflict.

12.2.3 Performance, transparency and accountability

As Goetz (1996) and Moore *et al.* (1994) suggest, the relationship between the values and culture of an organization and the incentives placed upon it by its various stakeholders is important in determining performance and impact. Understanding how the identity, values, rules and norms of an organization have been constructed is therefore vital. It is equally important to analyze to whom the organization is accountable, and how multiple accountability is managed.

A number of observers note that organizations can have three main approaches to accountability. The first is perhaps the commonest approach and is based on the establishment of objectives, key performance indicators, etc. and the subsequent reporting, monitoring and evaluation of the degree to which these have been met. It is a variant of what is sometimes known as the 'principal-client' form of accountability, and is in essence often seen as part of a 'contractual' relationship – either between levels within organizations or between separate organizations. The legitimacy of this form of accountability resides largely in the legal domain.

The second and third approaches recognize that some forms of activity are difficult to specify in advance and are highly reliant on the discretion or judgement of a skilled decision maker, as they are hard to routinize. In addition, the outcomes of these activities may be inherently hard to monitor. The capacity to do this is limited by the degree of 'unboundedness' of the changes being sought. Change is 'unbounded' when it is hard for all parties to reach agreement over the nature of the problem and the solution and there are 'no limits in terms of the time and resources it could absorb' (Chapman, in Eyben, 2005, p. 101). An example of this might be the work of career counsellors. Furthermore, they also recognize that outcomes of the same action in different contexts may produce different results, and/or that most activities – particularly in the development or political field – are likely to have unexpected impacts. These approaches are peer reviews and processes of 'bottom-up' accountability, where attempts are made for clients or citizens to voice their opinion about the performance of an organization in various ways. These approaches are sometimes described respectively as 'mutual' or 'political' forms of accountability. The legitimacy of these forms of accountability resides largely in the expert, moral, or political domains.

Understanding an organization's approach to accountability can provide valuable insights. What it then puts into the public domain and whose voices and analyses are privileged can provide valuable clues about the organization and its values.

12.2.4 Learning systems, change and adaptation

Understanding the internal divisions in an organization, its performance and its accountability mechanisms can give us a good picture of current reality. However, we will often want to know about an organization's potential for developing in the future. I have already (in Section 12.1.3) highlighted the need to understand the overall dynamics of change, of which the organization is only a part. This raises questions about the organization's ability to learn from experience – in adapting to and changing its environment.

As Booth and Lucas (2002) have suggested in a review of good practice in the development of PRSP monitoring systems, agencies seem to need 'dynamic' inputs and feedback that can provide relatively rapid feedback into decision-making in a timely enough manner if they are to learn and make changes as a result. NGO experiences with participatory impact assessments, focus-groups, exit-polls, stakeholder surveys, etc. are all relevant here and provide some further examples of these 'shortcuts in monitoring' (Booth and Lucas, 2002).

However, it is also increasingly recognized that the ability to learn and adapt is highly dependent on an organization's procedures, behaviours, culture and incentives. Much of the literature on, for example, monitoring and evaluation, suggests that some of the biggest challenges for any form of accountability – particularly when it comes from less vocal stakeholders – are whether the feedback provided actually changes anything in the institution(s) in question (TEC, 2006). Most organizations have effective means of ignoring findings which challenge them. This suggests that the challenge is as much to look at how open organizations are to dealing with difficult information about their performance, as it is to develop sophisticated methods which produce results that might subsequently be ignored.

12.3 Background investigation of an organization • • •

How exactly you investigate an organization will depend on your particular purpose. The four areas in Section 12.2 will help you to formulate some more precise questions, but first you will need to undertake some background analysis, using literature, websites and documents which are readily available, noting the organization's public behaviour and reputation, and perhaps asking some preliminary questions both inside and outside the organization.

12.3.1 What an organization says about itself

The first place to start is to get hold of what an organization says about itself. Websites, annual reports, and accounts, public relations material, strategic plans, publications, and recruitment material are all useful but need to be read critically (see Bridget O'Laughlin's Chapter 6). Some of the questions you might like to ask yourself during your reading of such material are included in Box 12.1.

Box 12.1   What an organization says about itself

History

- When was the organization established, and for what purpose?
- In whose interest was it established?
- What major changes have occurred over time?

Identity, values and strategy

- What sort of identity and values does the organization convey through its material?
- What is the organization's legal status?
- Is the organization's vision, and strategy for achieving that vision, clear?
- What statements does the organization make about its attitude to equal opportunities, gender and racial equality, staff development?
- How many staff are there? Who makes up the organization in terms of gender, race, age? What skills, disciplines and abilities are there?
- Who are the Board of Trustees, directors, or ministers who ultimately are legally responsible for the proper running of the organization? What interests do they represent?

Systems and structure

- How is the organization structured? How is that structure presented or described: as a hierarchy, on a functional basis, on a geographical basis?
- What sort of formal decision-making processes exist? Are there particular committee structures, annual meetings, general assemblies, board meetings? How often do they occur?

Finance

- How is the organization funded and by whom?
- How is the money spent? How much is devoted to different functions, especially research and development, monitoring and evaluation, training and administrative costs?
- What is the income and expenditure and by how much does one exceed the other? What is done with any 'profit'? What 'reserves' does the organization have? How long could it survive if it received no further income? What assets does the organization have?

(Continued)

(Continued)

Performance

- What does the organization say about its achievements and performance in terms of effectiveness, efficiency and impact?
- Who is assessing that performance and on what basis?
- To what extent are problems, weaknesses and ideas to overcome them evident in this material?
- Are diverging views of performance made transparent?

Relationships

- Who are the major stakeholders that can influence the organization, positively and negatively, to adopt different policies?
- What alliances does the organization have with other actors?

It should be remembered that this material represents the public face of an organization and even when that includes quantitative information, such as accounting figures, this needs to be interpreted. As Hopwood and Miller (1996) make clear in their book *Accounting as Social and Institutional Practice* 'accounting is no longer to be regarded as a neutral device that merely documents and reports "the facts" of economic activity'. Accounts too are based on arbitrary classifications, political interests and compromises and are the product of the institutional dynamics noted earlier. However, having this information to hand is a useful first step in the processes of finding out more and contrasting the public image of an organization with its more 'private' one. This material is probably most useful in answering some of the questions about the history of an organization and what it considers are its most important achievements to communicate, and may provide some indication of corporate plans for the future. It is usually less revealing about internal differences, its accountability to less vocal stakeholders, and any errors made, failures or problem areas.

It should be remembered that institutional websites these days are an increasingly important means of how organizations project their identity. The websites of some organizations may give quite a full picture of what that organization does and how it likes itself to be seen, whereas for others, particularly in developing countries, there may be no website or it be may be very poorly maintained. It is clear that, whilst websites may, or may not, be a good starting point to look at what an organization is saying about itself they do not tell the whole story. Indeed, as a review of the World Bank's knowledge initiative indicated, whilst the investments made in their website and knowledge platforms had been significant, there had been little corresponding change in the organization's core business in the same period (OED, 2003). Thus, what the website was projecting, for example, about the Bank's commitment to learning was not necessarily a good reflection of what was happening internally. To discover that would need some other sources of information.

12.3.2 What staff and ex-staff say about the organization

Meeting, observing, and listening to individuals from organizations, in public fora, at meetings, and in the normal course of professional interaction, can tell you a lot – particularly about the culture of the organization they work for or used to work for. The questions in Box 12.2 are a useful checklist for this sort of interaction. (And particularly useful if you want to make the most of any opportunities to talk to staff in an organization you are or will be investigating!)

Box 12.2   What staff say about the organization

- Do staff tend to say the same thing or different things? Is this to do with their role or not?
- Is there a consistency across the organization? About what?
- How critical of the organization are they? How open to ideas from others?
- What elements of their organization do they emphasize (i.e. achievements, failures, structural issues, staffing issues)?
- What change would they like to see in the organization? How do they think this might be achieved?

12.3.3 What others say about the organization

As we have noted above any organization is influenced and pressurized by a variety of interests. What are others saying? This might include peers, adversaries, pressure groups, the press, academics, users or other interest groups. Getting this information is likely to require a mixture of searching for articles and other 'grey material' that include something on the organization you are concerned with, and opportunistic conversations with individuals from the various groups whose opinions you want to collect. Box 12.3 gives some questions to guide this part of your investigation.

The cross-checking of information between these sources can help to verify or discount facts, opinions and rumours. It can also be the means by which more precise questions can be formulated to explore in more detail.

Exploring and putting together different interpretations from staff and others is a key part of exploring the potential internal divisions within an organization. In addition, as Joseph Hanlon in Chapter 3 notes, 'finding the woman who knows' can save a lot of time and energy.

> ### Box 12.3   What others say aboutthe organization
>
> - Who are these other informants? What are their particular interests? Who do they represent? Where or from whom do they get their information?
> - Is there some consistency in their views? What do they emphasize?
> - How would they rate the organization and what do they think is the general view of it according to other actors?
> - What change would they like to see in the organization for their purposes? How do they think this might be achieved?

2.4 Organizational assessment and organizational change • • •

In this section I will concentrate on how to investigate organizations and public action when working with people in those organizations, with a view to promoting organizational change. It draws heavily on my own experience of facilitating and being involved in participatory exercises with NGOs. Mayoux and Johnson point out in Chapter 8 the inherent contradictions of any participatory investigation. These apply equally to participatory investigations in organizations. However, organizational assessments need not overtly be labelled 'participatory' and may even be conducted from outside with a view to catalyzing change within the organization. Much of what follows would remain relevant in any case.

Helping an organization reflect on what it does, how it does it and what its strengths and weaknesses are, is not only a way of analyzing its involvement in public action but also a means of improving its ability to do so. Indeed, as suggested above, this capacity for self-reflection is a key element in an organization's ability to change in line with its external environment.

The rest of this section follows the four generic areas laid out in Section 12.2 above.

12.4.1 Historical analysis: time lines and matrices

Exercises in constructing the history of an organization are important for participants who often have varied if not conflicting understandings of an organization's origins and background. Confronting these different interpretations, confirming facts and identifying gaps in the historical understanding of staff, provides an important foundation for constructing a joint understanding of how an organization got to where it is.

For these reasons, the time line of the international NGO consortium ACORD (Agency for Cooperation and Research in Development) (see Figure 12.2) was constructed by its headquarters staff during a 'Participatory Organizational Appraisal' of the organization, facilitated by myself and Mick Howes of the Institute of Development Studies at the

	Primary policy thrust	Programmes
1975	Rehabilitation	Mali – Gao Region Southern Sudan
1979	Institution building	Tanzania (Kiu) Southern Sudan (Amadi)
1981	Production systems	Mali – Timbuktu Region Sudan – Qal-En-Nahal, Port Sudan Uganda – Gulu, Pakwach Benin – Materi Burkina – Dori Somalia – Sablaale
1985–8	Reinforcing local structures	Mali – Gourma Somalia (expansion) Sudan – Red Sea Hills Angola (Adra) Uganda (redesign) Guinea Tanzania Sudan – Juba Rwanda (Aramet)
1988	Women in development (WID)	Mali (redesign) Rwanda Mozambique
1990	Gender	Angola Tanzania
1992		Burundi Niger Namibia

FIGURE 12.2   Time line of ACORD's policy development up to 1994

University of Sussex (Howes and Roche, 1995). Although the primary function of such an exercise is to generate agreed understanding for the participants, the information gained is also useful for the facilitator as an outside investigator.

What is interesting about the process of constructing the time line was the way it revealed the origins and subsequent policy development of the organization. ACORD was set up in 1973 in response to the Sahel drought and the civil war in southern Sudan. Later it was influenced by the 'climate' of events and development thinking, yet the programmes that were developed in different policy epochs still carried the imprint of the organization's origins. For instance, those programmes established when one of the primary policy aims was production-oriented (1981) had great difficulty in adapting to some of the demands made upon them in later years, when gender concerns (1988) and local structure development (1985–88) became more central.

If staff are able to think through a time line in this way, it can not only lead to a better understanding of why things are as they are, but also help them work out how their current decisions may affect future possibilities and choices.

12.4.2 Understanding difference and internal division

One important element that emerged from the appraisal mentioned above at ACORD was the distinction people made between the official and unofficial hierarchy in the organization, the importance of personal communication networks and how some felt that those already in more powerful informal networks did not see the need for more formal communication channels. In this case, encouraging people to map their perceptions of perceived lines of responsibility and decision-making and to draw their personal communication networks proved a good means of exploring issues of power and difference and providing the basis for further discussion of the issue. In other cases bringing out such potential conflict may be dangerous, inappropriate or raise expectations which cannot be met.

In some organizations this sort of process may require working separately with particular groups, for example men and women, managers and non-managers, in order for them to feel free to express themselves.

It is likely that in analyzing organizations and public action different opinions will be given about the same issue. Dealing with this discordant information is an important element of analysis. It is important to capture this diversity rather than diluting it through aggregation.

One important way of capturing this diversity is to present differences of opinion in people's own words. This allows the reader to interpret what is going on for themselves (rather than be given your interpretation of it), and read between the lines. The following provides an example of this. It comes from research by Oxfam into the way the Zimbabwe Government introduced user fees for health care and how regulations regarding exemption were implemented. It shows how talking to particular groups, in this case users, can give conflicting views of how an organization works in practice.

The attitudes of staff to claimants can have a significant effect on access to welfare payments. Roda Ncune is a married woman with three children. She lives in Sigangatsha, South Matebeleland, while her husband works in South Africa. She earns a little money from selling beer, and qualifies for an exemption:

'I can take a letter to the clinic from my village development worker. The worker will give me the letter when I need it, after asking questions about my husband and my work. It doesn't cost anything.'

But Sophia Mutare's experience of the system was less positive:

'I visited the hospital and said that I had no money to pay, so they asked questions about my husband, looked at my clothes, and then asked other people what they knew about my family. It's bad that they decide like this but you cannot do anything.'

(Lennock, 1994, pp. 25–6)

Another way of capturing diversity of opinion is to ask different groups to rate their organization according to an agreed scale and then compare these scores in order to discover key areas of divergence and agreement. Norman Uphoff (1987), in his field methodology for participatory self-evaluation, suggests a simple four point scoring system where:

3   represents a most satisfactory situation with little room for improvement;
2   represents a satisfactory situation but with some room for improvement;
1   represents an unsatisfactory situation with considerable room for improvement; and
0   represents a very unsatisfactory situation with very great room for improvement.

If we see in an organization that senior managers, for example, are constantly rating women's participation in decision-making at 3 and junior females are rating this at 1 then it is clear that important differences exist.

12.4.3 Organizational diagnosis; performance, transparency and accountability

Another important element in any self-assessment is an honest appraisal of an organization's identity, values, and strengths and weaknesses. Box 12.4 is a synthesis of some of the major elements put forward about how to do this. However, it can be better to let staff construct their own categories for what they deem to be the most important elements on which an organizational diagnosis should focus.

The importance of this sort of participatory diagnosis is that it leaves the categorization and classification of organizational elements in the control of staff rather than imposing upon them a necessarily general theoretical framework. The result is therefore more likely to reflect their priorities and concerns. And, although the result may miss out some of the elements in Box 12.4, what is missed out is in itself an indication of where an organization is at in terms of its own self-analysis. Furthermore, this sort of analysis can lead to other elements being included which are often not referred to in the generalized checklist of Box 12.4. These might include issues particularly related to local circumstances and culture. Tracking what self-appraisal processes focus upon is therefore an important means of assessing organizational development and change.

In addition to participatory self-assessment, it is important to analyze the relationship between an organization's stakeholders and its performance. This is crucial in order to understand who is assessing performance and on the basis of what criteria.

In analyzing the design of policy and the impact of public action it is once again important to capture diverse opinions, to seek out those voices that are not usually heard, to juxtapose those views against the orthodoxy and to enrich public debate by doing so. Box 12.5 lists critical features that are useful in assessing the degree of different groups' involvement in the policy-making process. This type of methodology can be used in many contexts. This example is adapted from a study of the Bangladesh Flood Action Plan commissioned by Oxfam and other NGOs in Bangladesh (Adnan *et al.*, 1992). For further tools to explore the impact of advocacy work see Roche (1999), chapter 6.

Box 12.4   Organizational self-assessment checklist

Identity and values

To what degree are the organization's identity and values explicit, agreed and understood?

Vision and strategy

Does the organization have a clear vision of what it wants to achieve and a strategy to achieve it?

People and resources

How well does the organization maximize the contribution of its staff? Does the organization have the financial, human and technical resources it needs to achieve its vision? How effectively does it use these resources?

Structure, systems and procedures

Does the organization have the systems and procedures necessary to use the resources at its disposal to achieve its vision and strategy?

Organizational culture

Is the culture of the organization consistent with its values and its vision? How open and transparent is it both internally and externally? How are staff motivated and rewarded? How does the organization deal with difference and conflict?

Control and accountability

Who owns and controls the organization? Who is the organization designed to serve and how does the organization know if it is succeeding in doing so? How does it balance its multiple accountabilities?

Programmes and services

What does the organization do? Is what it does consistent with what it wants to achieve and its values?

Performance and results

How well does it perform in relation to its own vision and strategy and in relation to other organizations with similar goals?

(Continued)

(Continued)

Learning, innovation and change

How well does the organization learn from its experience and that of others and adapt in the light of that learning? How well does the organization cope with change?

Leadership, management and decision-making

How effective is the leadership and management of the organization?

Partnerships and alliances

To what degree is the organization externally oriented and to what degree does it enter into strategic collaboration with others in ways that add value?

(Adapted from Campbell's organizational effectiveness questions (1992), Fowler's Community Organization checklist (1988) and his work on participatory self-assessment of NGO capacity (1995), Drucker's questions for organizational self-assessment (1993), and dimensions for benchmarking coming out of a NOVIB partners meeting in 1996 (NOVIB, 1996). See also, Fowler (1997), the European Excellence Framework, http://www.efqm.org/Default.aspx?tabid=58, and Intrac's Capacity Building resources http://www.intrac.org/arena_org_cap.php)

Box 12.5   Critical features in assessing involvement in policy development

1 *Transparency*

To whom are the different stages of policy development visible, including the decision-making and implementation processes?

2 *Access to information*

Who has access to adequate and timely information on policy formulation, design and monitoring?

3 *Accountability*

To what degree are the agencies involved in policy development and implementation procedurally and periodically answerable to different groups in the impact areas, as well as the citizens of the country in general? What mechanisms are in place for grievances to be expressed and responded to?

4 *Meaningful choice*

Who can participate in policy development in a voluntary manner without being compelled, constrained or otherwise left with no other choice?

(Continued)

(Continued)

5 *Comprehensive*

Who has been consulted from the very outset in defining the nature of the problem, as contrasted to those consulted at other stages?

6 *Non-alienation*

Have people participated in a way that they do not feel distanced and alienated from policy actors, the implementation process and the eventual outcomes?

(Adapted from Adnan *et al.*, 1992; see Roche *et al.*, 2005)

12.4.4 Learning and adaptability

One of the quickest ways to gain an understanding of organizational change is to investigate how organizations learn and adapt. Learning audits and self-assessment questionnaires are now becoming increasingly common tools to involve staff in analyzing existing processes. Part of this is in recognition that the emphasis may need to shift from the more formal learning systems, for example monitoring and evaluation and the usual reporting systems, to more nimble, creative and less formal learning which allow the exchange of tacit knowledge. Box 12.6 suggests some of the questions that might be explored with staff.

Box 12.6   Questions related to organizational learning

- Who learns in the organization and how?
- What kind of learning is rewarded?
- To what degree are errors admitted and analyzed?
- What forms of knowledge are legitimated and how?
- What constraints are there to learning?
- How does information flow in the organization?
- How is institutional memory constructed, how accessible is it, and to whom?
- What changes occur through self-learning as opposed to other influences?
- How does the organization react to learning which challenges its assumptions?
- Is the organization better placed now to anticipate change in its environment and adapt accordingly?
- What changes are being made to the organization's learning systems?

(Adapted from Edwards, 1996; Roche, 1999; Development in Practice, 2002)

Recent exercises of this type undertaken in NGOs have revealed some common constraints on organizational learning which are perhaps not confined to NGOs, for example: learning being seen as an 'overhead' cost; weak or negative incentives for learning and admitting error; cumbersome systems for recording and disseminating; or the need for success stories skewing learning away from difficult or uncomfortable experiences (Edwards, 1996; Roche, 1999; see special edition of Development in Practice, 2002).

These studies also reveal that, when analyzing non-profit organizations, including government agencies, we need to bear in mind the differences between them and the profit-making organizations on which much of the 'learning organization' literature is based. These differences stem partly from the fact that NGOs and governments do not face the discipline of market forces in the same way as private companies, which can be wiped out if they do not learn and adapt 'efficiently'. This difference is compounded for NGOs by the fact that the ultimate 'customers' of their services do not guarantee the survival of their organizations. Furthermore, it needs to be recognized that much of the literature on knowledge management and organizational learning ignores the fact that issues of power within organizations are also critical in determining not only what is learnt but whose learning is deemed important.

However, if as I suggested in Section 12.4.3 finding a single framework for analyzing and presenting data on performance and accountability is difficult, then to do so for learning and adaptability is even more problematic.

One possibility is to explore and present different levels of learning in any organization – individual, team, departmental and organizational – on the basis of questions suggested in Box 12.6. Another is to look at functional divisions of learning, such as experiential learning, project-based learning, policy-related learning, advocacy-based learning and scientific research and visionary thinking (Edwards, 1996).

However, we also have to be aware of the links between any organization and those external to it but who nevertheless influence its development. Studies such as that by Judith Tendler and Sara Freedheim in northeast Brazil demonstrate how important this is. In their study they show how the high performance of government health workers is partially due to the trust and respect that they had from their clients in the community (of which they were a part), as well as their relative autonomy to respond to them in ways they felt appropriate (Tendler and Freedheim, 1994; World Bank, 2004). This throws up interesting issues relating to current western policies, which continue to be based on the mistrust of public sector workers and their supposed 'rent-seeking' behaviour.

From the point of view of investigating organizations, monitoring what happens at the interface of an organization with the outside world, in terms of its relationships with its primary stakeholders and how they shift over time, gives an interesting insight not only into how receptive an organization is to its stakeholders, but also into how well it learns and adapts as a result of that experience.

Some possible measures of how well an organization is learning and how adaptable it is are set out in Table 12.3. These were developed by the NGO ACORD building on the ideas of Tom Peters (1992).

TABLE 12.3   *Possible measures of learning and adaptability*

Listening better	Indicators
1 To improve quality	Is the organization open to continuous quality control by those it seeks to benefit and open to ideas from others? Do measures of quality exist?
2 Making contact	How and how often does the organization talk/listen to its clients and funders?
3 Listening	What is the percentage of time spent with 'front-line' staff on the ground and key decision makers in other organizations?

Efficiency of learning	
4 Greater responsiveness	How long does it take for the organization to respond to or deal with newly identified needs or new situations?
5 Constant innovation	How involved is the organization in action research, pilot initiatives, etc. and what lessons are being learnt from these?
6 Keeping a degree of specificity	What differentiates the organization from other agencies?
7 Learning from other agencies	How many ideas have been gained through discussion with or observation of other agencies?
8 Management support to innovation	Is the analysis of interesting past failures encouraged? What is the degree of acceptance of failure? Is the organization learning from past failure? Does it admit past failure? Does it undertake studies to understand errors?
9 What has changed as a result of learning	How much does the organization change from year to year? What adaptation or modification in procedures, structure, staffing, methodology, activities, objectives, indicators have occurred? Do reports reflect these changes?

Organizing to react to rapid change	
10 Decentralized marketing and fund-raising	How many funder visits to the organization, how many staff visits to funders?
11 Word of mouth marketing and fund-raising	How much time is spent selling ideas and programmes face-to-face with funders?
12 Developing multi- functional teams	Percentage of people/problems solved in multi-layered, multi-disciplinary team configurations
13 Training	Hours/pounds devoted to skill upgrading of 'front-line' staff as opposed to other staff
14 A changed middle management role	Number of acts of boundary bashing, degree of insistence on flexible bottom-up quality control measures, creation of supportive learning climate
15 De-bureaucratization	Number of unnecessary procedures, regulations, meetings, committees renounced per month
16 'Front-line' focus	Number of 'front-line' as opposed to middle-management staff at meetings

(After Peters, 1992)

The logic behind most of the measures in Table 12.3 relates to:

- *How closely and how well an organization listens to those it is trying to support and to those who fund it.* If organizations are constantly listening to those they support then they should be able to adapt more quickly, and if they are listening to donors/supporters then potential misunderstandings and delays can be more rapidly identified. (Items 1–3)
- *How quickly and efficiently the organization learns from listening and modifies its support accordingly.* Translating listening into action, being open to change, constantly testing new ideas, and learning from others and past mistakes, are all essential facets of being able to respond to turbulence and rapid change. (Items 4–9)
- *How well the organization structures itself to promote learning and innovation.* In order to react more effectively organizations need to structure themselves in a way that allows staff to take decisions where appropriate; to regroup different interest groups to solve problems on the spot; not to create bureaucratic hurdles which undermine horizontal learning; and to insist on the 'front-line' being the primary focus. (Items 10–16)

12.5 Institutional footprints and public action • • •

On occasion the aim of an investigation is to inform or influence public action on the part of your own or another organization, and you need to examine public action produced by yet another organization as part of that investigation. Then, as a researcher, you will need to look at the 'footprints' left behind in order to learn about the organization that made them. You may also find out about that organization more directly, but the methods used would then be interviews and interpretation of written documents with no specific use of participative techniques.

Investigating another organization from outside in this way can pose a number of challenges. It is often hard to decipher the power centres of organizations and for the investigator this means that it is difficult to judge how to conduct investigations and interpret reports. Some of the techniques and frameworks described above (e.g. the checklists in Boxes 12.4, 12.5 and 12.6), could be helpful in this type of investigation, although the technique and approach will clearly depend on the aim of the investigation.

A study commissioned by the European Union and relevant Polish ministries was designed to examine the funding of science and technology policy in Poland. The objective here was to understand how the system was operating, what impact it was having on the science and technology community, and whether or not the policy needed reform. What became apparent very early on in the investigations is that any attempt to understand the policy without extensive examination of the principal ministry involved would be grossly misleading. Historical analysis and understanding the divisions within the ministry were particularly important. For example, while policy statements indicated a concern for technology funding as well as more basic science, in practice the mechanisms for funding more basic work rather than technological applications were much more entrenched. In interviews it became clear that this situation was not the product of a policy shift, so much as the unintended consequence of institutional evolution and cultural bias. The ministry was very keen to protect its autonomy and to protect scientists from the type of interference that they had experienced during the previous era of central planning. This hindered the establishment of a peer review system and construction of a network of institutions which could have adequately addressed technologically oriented development as well as basic science. In this case, an understanding of explicit policy goals was complemented by an appreciation of cultural bias, historical factors and different interests within the Ministry.

Consultants carrying out the study based themselves in the Ministry and talked to a wide range of ministry officials. Interviews with other stakeholders not only gave important indications about the results of policy, but also provided consultants with 'pointers' as to the different power centres within the ministry. The consultants gained an understanding of how different stakeholders experienced policy, who they considered important, who they talked to or did not talk to. In the Ministry interviews helped investigators construct a 'map' of the Ministry itself.

On other occasions 'institutional footprints' may be all you have to go on. This is when organizations do not allow you in to analyze their organizational dynamics and the effects of their actions, but you still need to find out about them in order better to understand a situation. In such cases you may have no direct access into the organizations. What else can be done 'from the outside' over and above looking at their published and grey material? How can you 'find out fast' about public action in this situation in a way that will still be credible?

The following example from Zimbabwe tries to illustrate how this might be done and how understanding of organizational dynamics and the context in which they operate can be helpful in arguing for policy shifts. It comes from the same Oxfam investigation into the effect of introducing user-fees for health care in Zimbabwe quoted in Section 8.4.2. While occurring over ten years ago it is a good example for understanding the issue of 'footprints'.

Oxfam in Zimbabwe in the early 1990s became very concerned about the effect on low-income groups of the Zimbabwe Government and World Bank policy on cost-recovery through the raising of user-fees for health care. The Government's framework for Economic Reform (1991–5), drawn up in collaboration with World Bank and the International Monetary Fund (IMF), aimed to increase revenues from user fees from Z$15 million in 1989/90 to Z$60 million by the end of 1995. In 1991 households earning cash incomes of less than Z$150 a month were entitled to exemption from paying fees. This was increased to Z$400 a month in 1993.

This policy, pushed by the World Bank and willingly embraced by the Zimbabwe Government, can mainly be attributed to a caucus of US-trained health economists keen on pursuing models of health care privatization. The policy was based on the belief that price-based systems of rationing are the most efficient way to cope with growing demands for health care. People already paid for a proportion of their health care. The assumption was that they were willing to pay for health care and were therefore able to pay. Those charged with the implementation of the policy, including World Bank staff, were often less convinced as to the likely practical outcomes.

In order to investigate the potential differences between theory and practice Oxfam hired a consultant in 1993 to undertake a relatively rapid piece of research which would pull together existing material as well as complement this with primary research of a number of health service users.

The researcher pulled together secondary data on the effects of user fees on low-income groups as well as statistics regarding attendance at ante-natal clinics and trends in maternal and prenatal mortality – using Oxfam's existing network of partners and contacts as well as UNICEF, the Ministry of Public Service, Labour and Social Welfare, the Ministry of Health and Child Welfare, and Save the Children studies. In addition 16 interviews were conducted with rural women over a two week period in August 1993 in Manicaland, Masvingo, South Matebeleland, North Matebeleland, and North and East Matebeleland.

The resultant publication drew upon the secondary data but illustrated the human consequences of the policy with more qualitative data collected through the semi-structured interviews (including the examples quoted in Section 8.4.2; Lennock, 1994).

The findings of the report confirmed the growing body of research which indicated that:

- user-fees have the effect of pricing health services beyond the means of those most in need;
- exemption systems were too complex and too arbitrary and therefore did not effectively protect the access of poor people to health services;
- as in many poor countries, where a lot of users may be exempt, the costs of administering the system are greater than the revenue gained; and
- for poor people, user-fees set at even modest levels undermine access to basic health care.

In addition the report concluded that:

- as the revenue generated by user-fees is transferred to the general budget it is therefore not necessarily used on improving the health system;
- other revenue earning options which would be less damaging to the poor, such as a land tax or higher corporate taxes, were rejected for political reasons;
- that the government's claim that user-fees were needed to channel patients to the most appropriate point of entry to the health care system ignored the fact that patients often sought access to higher-level facilities because of the collapse of primary health care provision.

On the basis of the above evidence the report recommended that 'having initially endorsed the case for user-fees, the Bank has a responsibility to use its influence to press for their withdrawal. It could do so most effectively by demanding the phased withdrawal of user-fees over the lifetime of the adjustment programme'.

The report caused a furore in Zimbabwe, with Oxfam being accused amongst other things of having a political agenda by deliberately releasing the report during the run-up to the 1995 election; wanting to undermine the Zimbabwean state by undermining their position in negotiations with donors; wasting money destined for charitable purposes on spurious research and making up stories. Oxfam at one stage was threatened with expulsion from Zimbabwe. However, thanks to the experience and political expertise of the Oxfam representative in Harare, as well as backing from Oxfam headquarters in Oxford, instead of backing down Oxfam stood by the findings of the report, which ironically were borne out by the government's own research.

During this period and despite getting into processes that were unforeseen, Oxfam was able to point to the research which, despite its time scale, was rigorous enough to withstand much of the criticism as well as forming the basis for a detailed rebuttal of the accusations. Richard Jolly, the Deputy Director of UNICEF, stated that he was 'consistently impressed by.

- its careful analytical tone and style;
- its professionalism;
- the way its argument was based overwhelmingly on national data and general principles, with argument from particular districts, hospitals or individuals used only to illustrate more general points with specifics (in a way which matches closely UNICEF's own methods of advocacy);
- its relevant references, 11 about Zimbabwe'.

He went on to say that 'the evidence [is] well marshalled and convincing ... I see no reason for treating the study, though brief, as anything but a first rate piece of work ...'

In the end there was a relaxation by the World Bank of its policy on user-fees and the Zimbabwean Ministry of Health conceded that cost-recovery had resulted in adverse outcomes, especially for the rural poor. It suspended cost-recovery for rural health clinics in 1995, except for a nominal registration fee. In a post-drought phase this relaxation of policy was particularly important at a time when people were seeking to rebuild their asset base. The degree to which this is attributable to Oxfam and the report is debatable. Clearly, many factors combined to produce this outcome and it will never be clear whether such policy change would have happened anyway.

Although there were some particular circumstances that, together with the report, contributed to the policy change, and although that change was temporary, this example does illustrate how public action can be analyzed in a way that, along with other factors, leads to changes in policy.

Some of the success factors one can distil from this example include:

- Oxfam's understanding of differences of opinion within the World Bank indicated where there was room for change;
- the research explored a dimension where a professed policy of poverty-reduction by the World Bank was contradicted by the practice of introducing user-fees;
- the personal involvement of a senior World Bank official in visits to a mission hospital to see for himself the results of the introduction of user-fees;
- the ability of individuals in Oxfam to seize opportunities which unexpectedly presented themselves when the report provoked a wider debate in Zimbabwe, i.e. making the most of luck and coincidence;

- the support received from some partners with whom Oxfam had built up relationships of trust and mutual respect over many years, although most did not want to go public on the issue, as well as support from the Zimbabwe Congress of Trade Unions and from members of the public.

Overall this example illustrates again the importance of understanding the historical and organizational dynamics behind any policy, in this case the introduction of user fees. Combining this with detailed research on the performance and implementation of the policy and a good understanding of the kinds of incentives for change which had effected and would affect the World Bank and the Zimbabwe Government was critical. As Mayer points out in Chapter 11 good quality data on their own are not enough.

In addition the process involved a constant reassessment of Oxfam's relationship with the Zimbabwe Government and the World Bank, at times aligning with individuals within these organizations and at other times confronting them. Being capable of adapting in the light of changing circumstances was a necessary ability.

12.6 Conclusion • • •

At the heart of many of the ways of analyzing public action presented above is an implicit understanding that this analysis is used to help promote change. This can be about change within organizations through a better understanding of what they do. Alternatively, it can be about changes in broader public action, either change in the relationship between organizations through a better understanding of how they interact, or change in the policy environment through a better understanding of how it is made up and how it might be altered.

This chapter has attempted to explore different ways of analyzing public action through developing our understanding of where organizations are coming from, who makes them up, how they perform and who the decision makers are, and how they learn and adapt. Most of the examples that have been included come from my own experience of work within the NGO sector. In recent years the Fair Trade and Make Poverty History campaigns have indicated that mass public action can make a difference. Part of the reason that this has happened is that our knowledge has increased about how the ideas and beliefs of individuals change, and how this affects the policies and practices of institutions.

This chapter comes from a certain perspective; one that recognizes the crucial role of citizens in shaping, and being shaped by, public action. Those with more experience in the state sector might have looked at the issue from a different perspective.

However, although the chapter has an activist and NGO perspective, I feel that some of the ways of looking at the issue of organizational assessment and institutional footprints could be equally valid for someone working in local government or in private sector service delivery. Although there are key differences between public and private sector organizations there are also similarities, notably in terms of the ways bureaucracies tend to function and recreate themselves, and in the need for organizational learning and informed change.

Challenging cases

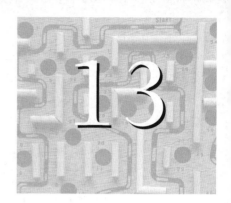

Alan Thomas

Case studies are often used as a form of investigation aimed at informing development policy and public action. Sometimes case studies form one part of an investigation alongside other parts such as a structured survey. Often, however, a piece of policy research consists entirely of one or more case studies. This chapter concentrates mostly on these occasions, but is relevant to case studies within combined methods as well.

Either way, the use of case studies is more like a framework for investigation than a specific method. Within that framework you can expect to use several methods, notably semi-structured interviews, but also including secondary data analysis, literature study including internet search and analysis of organizational data, and surveys, if appropriate. For example, a case study of a science park could include a survey of the businesses in the park, as well as overarching issues such as where the park is located and the history of how it was set up. Thus you would probably have to combine several of the skills discussed in previous chapters in order to undertake a case study investigation (see Section 13.3.1).

This chapter's title 'Challenging Cases' is chosen to have a double meaning. Case studies should be challenging; in fact, the cases you choose to investigate should challenge your ideas as fully and broadly as possible. The investigation itself should be undertaken by challenging the cases being studied, using your ideas to probe, ask difficult questions, and try to find satisfactory explanations.

13.1 Case studies for development policy and public action • • •

13.1.1 Case studies as a general research approach

Compared with other methods such as the analysis of generalized, secondary data (Chapter 10) or structured surveys (Chapter 7), case studies are used in specific circumstances and to answer different types of question (Stake, 1995; Gomm *et al.*, 2000). A case study is often 'an account and an analysis of particular events and decisions' (Curry, 1992, p. 1) and can be used to 'illuminate a decision or set of decisions, why they were taken, how they were implemented, and with what result' (Schramm, 1971, quoted in Yin, 1994, p. 12).

In terms of the distinction between 'intensive' and 'extensive' research used by Sayer (1992), and others, case studies are a form of intensive research in that 'the primary questions concern how some causal process works out in a particular case or limited number of cases' while structured surveys and other extensive methods are 'mainly concerned with discovering some of the common properties and general patterns in a population as a whole' (Sayer, 1992, p. 242).

Yin (1994, 2002) compares case study method with the use of experiments and with historical or archive analysis as well as with survey method. He suggests three factors are important in determining which approach is appropriate:

- the form of the research question;
- whether there is a contemporary event focus; and
- the degree of control available to the researcher.

Case studies ask 'How?' or 'Why?' questions (Chapter 1) about a contemporary set of events, over which the investigator has little or no control.

By contrast, survey methods (and data analysis based on secondary data) tend to answer questions of the 'What?', 'How many?', or 'How often?' types. Both survey and case study methods can attempt to answer 'Why?' questions, but they do so in very different ways. Survey or data analysis is used to look for consistent behaviours or generalizable 'laws' which can then be applied to sets of similar examples, while the case study approach is used to investigate causality directly by looking in detail at how the causal processes work within particular cases.

Yin's analysis also shows up the differences and similarities between case study methods and the use of experiments. In an experiment the researcher controls certain conditions in order to see if the processes which are observed occur in accordance with preconceived theoretical ideas or not. In choosing a case study the researcher cannot control the conditions precisely but can still try to find a case which will provide evidence for or against a particular theoretical idea. It is often more appropriate to think of case study research as a series of uncontrolled or 'natural' experiments (Lee, 1989), rather than as a survey with a very small sample.

13.1.2 Uses of case studies: classification and exploring causality

In what at first may seem to be a somewhat different characterization than Yin's, Langrish (1993) suggests that case studies can be used to differentiate between classes or types of phenomena. However, answering a 'What types?' question is actually closely related to answering 'How?' questions. Langrish argues 'If case studies can be compared with biological studies, then the purpose of case studies becomes clear, namely to assign the different examples into "classes" and to observe the different ways in which the different classes "survive" in either the same or different environments' (1993, p. 3).

Langrish continues by suggesting four aims for case study research:

1 to develop labels for a classification scheme;
2 to look for principles underlying a taxonomy;

3 to look for movement through time: for example, how things adapt, how control is exerted;
4 to unravel causation, especially relations between purposeful behaviour by several actors or agencies.

As you probably notice, the first two aims relate to classification but the last to causality. It is useful to understand how closely the two kinds of aim relate to each other.

Langrish suggests that cases grouped into classes are analogous to animals grouped into species. The way to understand how different cases differ is to observe in detail how they survive, in other words their internal workings and their relationship with their environment. Each different type is associated with a different answer to the 'How?' question and with a different pattern of causal relationships. This type of reasoning can be applied to many different contexts: how different firms succeed in different competitive environments, how households survive by adopting different livelihood strategies in response to policy changes, etc.

Research reported by Dina Abbott in Chapter 9 gave an example where individuals and their livelihoods were treated as case studies rather than as members of a group with basic similarities that could be surveyed. Abbott studied in detail the activities of *khannawalli* (women who provide meals for migrant workers on a regular basis). She did this in order to answer the question: 'How do *khannawallis* make a living from this?'. In doing so she found a number of types of survival strategy which varied according to 'internal' factors such as family labour and other resources available, as well as 'external' factors such as other income opportunities in the household, social relations (including links to rural kin), and indebtedness. Example 13.1 shows in another context (a study of worker co-operatives in the UK) how using case studies to answer a 'How?' question can lead to the generation of a typology or classification.

Example 13.1 'Developing successful worker co-operatives' in the UK

During the late 1980s I was part of a research team working on a project which started by asking how well worker co-operatives perform in the hope of suggesting ways of promoting more successful co-operatives (Cornforth *et al.*, 1988). There were several meanings of 'success' in effective use by different co-operators, ranging from the promotion of democratization in society and other radical social goals through simple survival to conventional measures of business performance.

The study combined a comparative data analysis element, in which we measured business and survival indicators for co-operatives in a number of sectors, with a number of case studies, which we then used to explore *how* co-operatives survived, *why* some failed, and *how* those that succeeded in various ways managed to do so.

(Continued)

(Continued)

We took a pragmatic view of what constituted success, including survival over a certain reasonable period, which required both a minimum business performance or better and at least some maintenance of other goals. We found a variety of strategies corresponding to different types of co-operatives, and for each type we were able to suggest likely future pathways, including different ways in which each type might fail as well as continue to succeed.

The 'preliminary typology' used to obtain a spread of types among the case studies was based on the origins and dominant motivation behind the formation of the co-operatives to be studied. Thus a number each of 'rescue', 'endowed', 'philanthropic new-start', 'alternative' and 'job-creation' co-operatives were included. However, looking at how co-operatives achieved success and their strategies for survival led us to concentrate on how they maintained commitment, both from their financial backers and from the members themselves. By the end of the study we were able to reconceptualize the meaning of success, and define a new typology based mainly on economic performance and 'orientation' in which each type maintained commitment in a different way. The four types we differentiated were:

1 *Marginals:* economically marginal, job and socially oriented co-operatives, consisting of peripheral workers with low or undervalued skills, working at low wages and low productivity, but maintaining commitment through providing social benefits and because of lack of alternatives.
2 *Radical marginals:* economically marginal but socially or politically radical co-operatives, often with potentially more highly skilled workers choosing to pursue social goals on a non-profit basis, with relatively low wages but maintained by combining shared political commitment and moral orientation with high labour turnover.
3 *Instrumentals:* more economically successful, job-oriented co-operatives, with higher-skill workers more like a cross-section of the general workforce, success seen in terms very similar to a conventional business, and maintenance of commitment requiring a combination of material rewards with opportunities for participation and non-material rewards for those taking on leadership roles.
4 *Pathfinders:* high economic performers with mixed orientations, still evolving, with continuing economic and organizational self-development, combining moral with instrumental orientations and material with non-material rewards, and trying to maintain a contradictory position of challenge to conventional capitalist working and management practices.

(Cornforth *et al.*, 1988, pp. 202-203)

13.1.3 When to use a case study rather than a structured survey

Case study approaches are different from – though not in any way inferior to or less rigorous than – other research methods. They are different not only in the types of questions addressed but in the contexts in which they are most practicable.

It is particularly important to understand when a case study approach is to be preferred to a structured survey. As noted in Chapter 7, to undertake a survey you have to be able to define the total 'population' about which you want to find out something. By studying a sample of the members of the population and analyzing the results, you make a statistical inference about the properties of the population as a whole. In order to consider case studies as an alternative method, it helps to generalize from the notion of 'members' of a 'population' to think in terms of 'units of analysis' within a 'universe' which you need to study. While 'members of a population' (e.g. firms within a sector; households in a village) are generally treated as constituting a group with basic similarities that could be surveyed separately, there could be several possible 'units of analysis' at different levels (workers, departments, networks of suppliers and subcontractors as well as simply 'firms'; individuals, gender relations, livelihood systems, 'patron-client' units and kinship groups as well as simply 'households') whose characteristics and inter-relationships could be analyzed within the 'universe' of a particular sector or village.

Consider the example in Chapter 10 about the effect of structural adjustment on firms in Tanzania. If you had to follow up the data analysis with a study about changes in the small scale informal trading sector in Tanzania as a result of structural adjustment, would it be better to do so with a survey of small trading enterprises or a number of case studies? A structured survey might do the job, but only *if*

- it is clear that the important unit of analysis is the enterprise; *and*
- you can answer your research questions from aggregate and comparative information about enterprises as individual units; *and*
- you have sufficient information about the population of enterprises within the sector; *and*
- you can get access to the statistical sample you require (see Section 13.2.1 on difficulties associated with sampling).

If, however, you have research questions about how and why enterprises react in different ways to the new policy regime, which require looking within them at how strategy is formulated, then you may prefer a number of more detailed case studies of enterprises and their inner workings. Or your questions may lead you to define a smaller unit of analysis than the individual trading enterprise, such as the decisions of individuals within them on their livelihoods, including the relationships between trading and other livelihood options, and how such decisions are made, and your research could focus on case studies of particular individuals or their decisions. Alternatively, again depending on the particular research questions being asked, you might want a larger unit of analysis, perhaps case studies of groups of enterprises or networks of informal trading relationships in particular localities, which would analyze how enterprises interrelate as well as how each enterprise within a network operates.

13.1.4 'Challenging cases' in policy research

So far we have been considering case studies as a general research approach alongside others such as structured survey. However, what about the use of case studies as an investigative method for development policy and public action? Are there ways in which case study method – and the notion of 'challenging cases' – is particularly appropriate for policy-oriented and action-oriented research?

Note that in a sense a particular policy or policy process *is* a case. Thus evaluating and monitoring a policy as it is implemented might be regarded as case study research in itself. There are many examples of the study of particular policies in this book, including the study of agricultural extension in northern Mozambique in Chapter 3, the work of the South African Labour Market Commission in Chapter 4, and science and technology policy in Poland in Chapter 12. These types of case studies are not exactly what I am looking at in this chapter. I am not concerned with the investigation or ongoing monitoring of a whole policy area, but with various scenarios where a development manager will choose to investigate a specific case study in order to inform policy choices. The case to be investigated could be much *smaller* in scope than the whole policy area; alternatively, it could be a similar case *elsewhere* (geographically or institutionally outside the development manager's own concerns) but nevertheless with potential to contribute something from which to learn (see below for examples of different relationships of case studies to the overall policy concern).

In keeping with the general approach of the book, the type of scenario I have in mind is where a development manager is considering a course of action and has a set of ideas which appears to justify (to himself or herself at least) that course of action. 'I think we should do so-and-so because X will lead to Y and the effect or result will be ... ', and so on. However, if challenged (that word again) there may not be sufficient or strong enough evidence to support (or disprove) the development manager's ideas. So more, or better, evidence, is required and the development manager must be open to evidence which suggests alternative ideas. If the evidence required is about the kind of questions which case studies are good at addressing ('How?' and 'Why?' questions particularly) and the type of phenomena which need investigating are such that the generation and analysis of survey data is inappropriate (as with events, processes or decisions), then the need may be to investigate a 'challenging case' or several 'challenging cases'.

This is not the only scenario. The investigator may well be distinct from the manager or the agency behind a particular policy – either commissioned to be independent or undertaking research from a separate, possibly critical, institutional position. Still, whether you are the investigator yourself or are commissioning research from others, you should develop your ideas before choosing a case or cases to study or writing the brief for a case study investigation. (How else can the case be challenging? As Yin (1994, 2002) says, case study design should be theory-led.) Your ideas will still be ideas about what to expect from the policy situation or process being investigated, and the above point stands about the need to conduct a case study investigation to get evidence that would challenge (or validate) the ideas.

Cases to be studied may have different positions in relation to development management and the policy process. Possibilities include:

1. cases of the 'object(s)' of policy interventions (cases of particular individuals, particular communities, villages, regions, firms, industries). Abbott's study of *khannawallis* in Chapter 9 and the case studies of particular co-operatives in Example 13.1 are of this type. If policies are already in place, such case studies could look at the impact of policies and the processes by which the particular 'object' has been affected by those policies. If it is a question of assessing potential policy interventions in advance of

implementation, the study might concentrate on existing 'coping' strategies or on inter-relationships, with a view to asking how these might be affected by the new policy.

2 cases of similar policies or interventions elsewhere (in another region or country, by another department or ministry, involving a different set of non-governmental orga-nization (NGO) partners, etc.). Although he did not undertake the study himself, Hanlon's example in Chapter 3 of using a case study about US sanctions against Cuba to inform work on how to make sanctions against apartheid South Africa more effec-tive is of this type. Here the focus could be on how far the policies there worked as it is envisaged the policy here should work, or on noting problem areas in order to check if they are likely to be problems here given the different circumstances.

3 cases of the policy development process itself (this could be a case of the process 'elsewhere', or of a previous process involving your agency). Examples include the case study in Chapter 1 of the National Policy on Education (NPE) in India. The cases in Example 13.2 are of a somewhat similar type, being studies of NGO influ-ence on environmental policy. Example 13.3 gives some detail of one of these stud-ies, on a campaign against a particular water development project in Botswana which forced a policy change. Such studies are likely to show how a multiplicity of agencies is involved over time and could inform the way the process of consultation and negotiation is managed in relation to policy development in the future.

4 a 'multi-level cut' (for example, the process of policy development, *plus* how implementa-tion occurred in a particular region or two, *plus* how it impacted on a small number of communities and individuals within them). An example here, in the context of an inves-tigation of how advice is given to small businesses in a country, would be a case study of the development of a particular policy, say towards state support for certain types of local advice agency, plus one or more case studies of the workings of particular advice agen-cies, plus several cases of individual firms and their relationships with those agencies.

Whatever the relationship between the cases to be studied and your policy concerns, it is important to have ideas to guide your case study investigation. For example 'a case study of Firm X' doesn't sound 'challenging' – it implies simply just finding out all you can about that firm rather than using the case for evidence in a focused way. It is better to conceive case stud-ies from the start in terms which reflect the ideas you want to challenge. For example, a case study of 'how Firm X has reacted to structural adjustment successfully enough to survive'.

13.2 Choosing cases which challenge ideas • • •

Having decided that a case study approach is appropriate, how should you decide on the case or cases to study? Since the boundaries of a case are never clear, this is a question of 'framing' (i.e. which aspects should be in the picture) as much as of choice.

Before looking at different strategies for using case studies, it is worth being very clear that it is *not* a question of finding a (small) representative sample. Sampling is a concept that belongs with structured survey method and requires that the 'universe' of investi-gation can be defined as a statistical population from which a sample can be taken. Choosing case studies is not like this.

13.2.1 Choosing case studies is not like sampling

Once we start thinking about case studies as focusing on units of analysis within a population or universe, there are several reasons why the idea of a representative sample is likely to be inappropriate or impossible.

1 There may in principle be no enumerable 'population' from which to sample.

   Studies of policy often hit this problem, particularly since it is well argued that the policies of many agencies depend as much on what does not get on to agendas as on what is actively debated and decided. How could one conceive of examples of 'non-decision-making' (Crenson, 1971) being 'representative'? Representative of what? To give another example, it would have been very relevant to the research in Example 13.1 to study attempts to set up co-operative businesses in order to see what distinguished successful attempts from unsuccessful ones. But there was no way of knowing the extent of the 'universe' or enumerating the 'population' of all such attempts. How far down the line would preliminary discussions have to go before being regarded as an 'attempt'? And there is probably no record of most unsuccessful attempts in any case. Thus, although case studies of attempts could be included in the research, once again they could not be chosen as a representative sample.

2 You may not know enough about the units of analysis in the 'universe' to be able to define a sample.

   There are often occasions when you want to focus on individuals or examples with particular characteristics, but available data does not tell you which they are. For example, Dina Abbott (Chapter 9) could not have defined a representative sample of *khannawallis* because there was no data on which women are *khannawallis*, and clearly a statistical survey of the membership of an organization such as the *Annapurna Mahila Mandal* (AMM) would not have given a representative sample of *khannawallis* as a whole since many *khannawallis* were not members of the AMM. This type of problem can also occur if you would like a stratified sample but data on the variable on which you would wish to stratify is not available. In effect you have to undertake the study in order to gain the knowledge that would enable you to define a sample. For example, to do a study of the effects of participative labour relations on firms you might want a sample stratified according to whether or not such participative relations are present, but this obviously could not be defined before some research to determine what does or does not count as participative. Any sample representative of firms in general might contain very few with what the study ends up defining as participative labour relations.

3 You may not have access to part of the population.

   If parts of the population cannot in practice be included in any sample, then this may effectively bias your eventual choice of cases so badly as to render the idea of sampling useless. Again, Chapter 9 provides examples of this problem, such as where Abbott was unable to interview scheduled caste men although they would have formed an important part of any sample of the clients of *khannawallis*, and this was one reason for her rejection of survey method. In Example 13.1 there was a slightly more subtle version of this problem, which can occur with any study aiming to uncover reasons for 'success'. Those co-operatives which regarded themselves as failing would be less likely to allow access to the study team than 'successful' co-operatives, for the understandable human reason of not wanting their failures exposed. Thus, any study undertaken by interviewing in a sample of co-operatives would be likely to be biased to an unknown extent in favour of success stories.

4   You may be specifically interested in rare or unique phenomena.

A recurring problem in policy research is how to study examples of 'good practice' where most examples are bad. Similarly, how can you investigate why certain courses of action, individuals or organizations are 'successful' when the majority are not? Yin (1994) gives the example of a study of the introduction of information technology into schools. A survey would have shown a depressing picture of failure and might even have failed to include any success stories at all. If there is even one example of success, it is surely more useful to study it in depth than to dismiss it as unrepresentative. Indeed, certain topics of investigation, such as innovation, by their nature occur rarely. Not surprisingly, a survey of NGOs in Zimbabwe showed very few of them engaging in innovative service delivery (Vivian, 1994). Vivian's conclusion that innovation by NGOs is unimportant seems too strong – since innovation in a few key NGOs might well show a substantial impact. Similarly, studying a phenomenon which is new requires studying cases which cannot yet be chosen as representative of anything.

5   There may be many independent variables that could occur in a very large number of possible combinations compared to relatively few actual examples in the 'population'.

In such cases a sample would have to be much larger than the available population before any significant inferences could be made about relationships between the variables. An example is a study of science parks in the UK (Massey, Quintas and Wield, 1992), where at the time of the study there were only 38 entities fulfilling the definition of science park used in the study. Although the study obtained data on the whole population which helped to describe the extent of the phenomenon, the small numbers meant that when it came to results like 'the parks in the south are more developed', the authors noted that 'no serious conclusions can be drawn from these figures' although they might 'point to an important line of enquiry'. Data that might have been obtained from a sample of parks would have been even harder to interpret except as data about particular cases.

The above points are all reasons why the logic of defining a sample in a survey method is not generally applicable to choosing and framing case studies. In fact, even when it might be feasible to define a representative sample, the logic of the case study approach is quite different, the choice of cases being based on the idea of challenge.

If cases are to be challenging, they must have a certain relation to the ideas behind existing or proposed policies and actions. There are different possible relationships between the cases chosen and the ideas, corresponding to different strategies for choosing case studies. These can be broadly grouped under three headings: exploratory, single case, and multiple case. The next sections look at each of these in turn. As we shall see, there are ways in which it is possible to choose single or multiple cases in order to make a general argument without resort to the concept of representativeness.

Example 13.2 is a practical account of using a case study approach for research on NGO influence on environmental policy, including why the idea of a representative sample was rejected in favour of using multiple case studies in a particular combination.

Example 13.2   A study of NGO influence on environmental policy

Between 1993 and 1996 I was part of a research team studying NGO influence on environmental policy. We were concerned that the study should include the relationship between local policy and policy influence, in Asia and Africa as well as in the 'North', and the issues on global environmental agendas. After some debate we formulated the following research question:

Why are NGOs influential in affecting the development of certain policies related to global environmental problems?'

(Potter, 1996, p. 1)

This wording was chosen because we wanted to focus on the reasons for successful influence in certain cases without implying that NGOs are necessarily influential in general or in all circumstances. We then set about structuring the research in terms of a number of detailed case studies, which would allow us to concentrate on *how* NGOs achieved influence in those cases where they did so, and on *why* they were able to do so in some cases and not others.

Although we wanted a variety of examples in order to achieve a degree of general applicability for our results, it was soon clear that there was no question of representativeness being a criterion for the cases we chose to study. First, representative of what? It was impossible to conceive of a 'list' of all the examples of attempted NGO influence in order to derive a representative sample of such attempts. What exactly is 'an attempt at influence', anyway? Presumably a clearcut case of a change in policy acknowledged as being caused by an NGO campaign would count. What about a long-term change in the way an issue is conceived by the general public or by world political leaders which may have been partly the result of long-term consciousness-raising on the part of various NGOs and others? And what about unsuccessful attempts? Quite apart from not being able to define these precisely, or even find out when they had occurred, we were actually more interested in reasons for success where there was success than in any statistical notion of how frequently different campaign tactics succeeded.

Then, we could not achieve access to all the campaigns we wanted to study, even though we had local partners who undertook research with us in most of the 10 countries in which we worked. In some cases, the NGOs concerned feared a backlash if they were seen to be co-operating with an international research team. In others language or distance and expense were barriers.

(Continued)

(Continued)

You might suppose that, even though a representative sample of influence attempts could not be defined, we could have studied a sample of NGOs instead. However, there are plenty of problems with this approach. In most countries there is no authoritative listing of all NGOs. Those organizations registered under national legislation may leave out particularly interesting examples. Once a list was compiled that cut across national boundaries, we could not be sure that the criteria for inclusion were consistent between countries. NGOs active and successful at policy influence are also a minority among the mass of small service providing or mutual aid organizations, so, although we could focus on some of the large, policy-oriented NGOs, those studies would not be 'representative' in any clearly defined sense. Even at this level, NGOs differ in so many ways (size; focus on client, member or public benefit; local, national or international; southern or northern; cultural basis; etc.) that a sample that allowed comparison between data on all these dimensions would be impossibly large and unwieldy.

Preliminary literature study and interviews with key NGO activists in each of the 10 countries gave us a list of potential cases and also allowed us to develop some theoretical ideas. In particular, we developed some criteria about how NGOs' influence would depend on a number of general factors: the political context (democratization – whether it was operating in a state with or without the several features of democracy which we identified); the nature of the target organization (how amenable to influence was the agency whose policies the NGO was trying to change); and international links and networking.

We were also able to differentiate between forms of NGO activity – what I have called the 'four Cs': collaboration; confrontation; complementary activities; and consciousness-raising (Thomas, 1996b, 2001). Finally, our preliminary analysis suggested that different circumstances and strategies would make each more likely to succeed, the circumstances being defined mostly in terms of political context and target, and strategies including crucially whether and how international links were used. Hence, we arrived at a number of ideas (or 'hypotheses') such as: 'Confrontation is most likely to succeed where there are multi-party elections and also a diversity of local power centres'; 'International networking generally makes NGO campaigns more likely to achieve influence by increasing the political "space" and providing extra resources' (plus others referring to the other 'Cs' and the target).

Our choice of case studies was then informed, on the one hand simply by what the key activists we interviewed said we would learn a lot from, and on the other by seeking cases which would give evidence for or against the 'hypotheses'. In doing this we included examples which were anything but representative in the countries concerned, including one in Nigeria where international networking played a prominent role, and the one depicted in Example 13.3 of the 1990 campaign against the Southern Okavango Integrated Water Development Project (SOIWDP) in Botswana, where multi-party elections were held and the government was confronted and forced to change its policy (Thomas and Selolwane, 2001; Thomas, 2003).

13.2.2 Exploratory strategies

This first strategy is aimed at finding as many different types as possible. It tends to lead to describing many cases but in not much detail. It corresponds to the first two of the four aims of case study research given by Langrish (see Section 13.1.2 above): developing labels for a classification scheme, and looking for principles behind a taxonomy. This kind of exploration is particularly appropriate when there is no prior way of defining a 'population' of which the cases are members, and it may be followed by studying one or a small number of cases in much more detail.

Searching for cases of different kinds has to start somewhere, so you will generally have to use some kind of preliminary typology (e.g. Langrish suggests looking at small, medium and large firms in different industrial sectors; in Example 13.1 we used different modes of start-up to look for different types of co-operative). However, you are actually looking for as many types as possible in a rather different sense – which will depend on how the research relates to policy and to the ideas behind the policies you are concerned with.

In Section 13.1.2 we also noted that different types of cases come from different answers to 'How?' questions. Thus you are probably looking for different types in terms of different answers to questions like 'How do firms succeed?', i.e. different strategies for succeeding or different ways of surviving. It often happens that your preliminary typology does not really correspond to differences defined in this way. With an exploratory strategy, you are basically looking for as many different answers to your 'How?' question as possible, but by the end of it you may have to reconceptualize and formulate a new typology, as we did in Example 13.1 with our marginals, radical marginals, etc. Sometimes, if it is a question of an exploratory phase followed by more detailed case studies, you may even reconceptualize in this way at a point well into the later phase of the case study research.

Given that the basic idea is to look for as many different types of case as possible, then you might start with cases which are easily accessible and then use a number of heuristic devices to extend your search.

1 Use obvious differences (age, size, geography, etc.) to form a preliminary typology.
    In Example 13.2 we chose a small number of different environmental issues and countries as a starting-point. In Abbott's *khannawalli* study (Chapter 9) she started by looking for cases of different caste and marital status. By this means you can soon be looking for at least one case to fit in each of the boxes of a small matrix (e.g. an example each of a small, medium and large firm in manufacturing and non-manufacturing would mean finding $3 \times 2 = 6$ examples).
2 Tell 'experts' about the cases you are already looking at and ask them to suggest other cases which might uncover different types.
    In Example 13.2, we started with a background literature study and a number of interviews in each country in the study with NGO activists, in order to gain a general understanding of the political context and the role of NGOs. Treating the

activists as experts, we asked each of them to suggest campaigns or other attempts at influence that they thought we might learn from.

3 Use multiple sources (e.g. if you obtained cases from a list of members affiliated to a certain group, or firms in a federation, look for a different group or federation or another source altogether to find non-members who may differ in unpredictable ways from the first set of cases you obtained).

Abbott (Chapter 9) originally obtained access to *khannawallis* who were members of the AMM; she later deliberately looked for *khannawallis* who were not members of that organization.

4 Ask people involved in one case about the existence of others, particularly if they can think of cases where the strategy or the way of trying to succeed is quite different.

A simple example of this was the way Abbott (Chapter 9) asked *khannawallis* who were AMM members for names of others outside the association.

5 Think of logical alternatives.

If all the cases you have found seem to do a particular thing in a certain way, look for examples where that thing is done in a different or even opposite way. In Example 13.2 we found a view in many African NGOs that they were obliged to collaborate with government because of political necessity and cultural expectations. So we deliberately sought cases where African NGOs had confronted government, even though they were few and far between.

6 Finally, look in different social and political environments.

Taking Langrish's analogy of case studies as animals, and thinking of how you would look for new kinds of animal on a newly discovered island, you might look on riverbanks, on the shoreline, in woods, in wetlands as well as in open country. Similarly one would look for different kinds of survival strategy among firms in sectors characterized by different competitive environments. In Example 13.2 we looked for NGO campaigns in countries with more or less democratic regimes, expecting the strategies for achieving influence to be very different.

13.2.3 Single case strategies

The point of choosing a single case to study is to explain how and why something happens by looking in some detail at the interrelationships involved and the inner workings of the case to be studied.

Yin (1994) suggests three main rationales for a single case design:

- the *critical* case (which may be a test of theory or a way of comparing theories or ideas);
- the *extreme* (sometimes unique) case; and
- the *revelatory* case (where the researcher gains access to a previously unavailable situation).

Critical cases may be set up rather like experiments, with conditions known to be favourable, or they may be chosen by repute. The latter method is similar to the idea of choosing a case of 'good practice', which is also one of the basic types of case study selection suggested by Langrish. In his types of selection he also includes two very pragmatic ones, namely 'the one next door' and the 'cor, look at that!' – though the latter is effectively the same as Yin's 'extreme' case.

Any of these methods can be used to choose a case to study in detail, and may be appropriate depending on the circumstances. If a small number of cases is required, similar rationales can be used for each, although the choice of a particular combination of cases will be subject to the strategies for multiple cases described in the next section. First, let us look in a little more detail at each of the suggested rationales for choosing single cases, starting with the pragmatic ones.

1   The one next door
    If you are interested in the detailed workings of a case, and there is no *a priori* reason to differentiate one from another, then there is no reason not to choose on a completely pragmatic basis. Why not study a case to which you have easy access? This might mean, for example, studying a case which involves an agency that is commissioning the research, although there are obvious dangers of bias to be avoided in such an example.

2   'Cor, look at that!' (the extreme case)
    Unusual or unique cases can be particularly useful for showing up causal mechanisms. For example, the research on NGOs and environmental influence (Example 13.2) included Botswana, where there is relatively little NGO activity and most NGOs work collaboratively with government but are rather uninfluential in policy. We deliberately chose to study one of the very few cases where NGOs had clearly opposed government and forced a policy change (Example 13.3 below).

3   The revelatory case
    Perhaps the most useful examples of a situation which suddenly becomes available for study relate to new phenomena. In the study of science parks mentioned in Section 13.2.1 (Massey, Quintas and Wield, 1992), these parks were in general a fairly new idea so that getting real data to explain how they evolved, as opposed to ideas on how they should evolve, required studying one or a small number of the few cases that had been going long enough to reveal how they worked in practice.

4   The critical case (1): a quasi-experiment
    This is the first of three ways of setting up a case study so as directly to challenge theory or ideas in order to explain how the cases work. In an experiment you control the starting conditions and see if the outcome expected by your theory does in fact occur. Here you cannot control the starting conditions but you can choose a case to match pre-determined characteristics and follow it to see if it reaches the theoretically predicted outcome. For example, in looking at the impact of a policy you might choose a case such that, according to the ideas behind the policy you are investigating, conditions are as favourable as possible for a good outcome.
    Another kind of example is given by Robinson's (1998) study of NGOs in health care reform in Tanzania. She suggested a way of conceptualizing NGOs, not purely as service providers or advocates, but in terms of public action, in which they would be

expected to play a role in defining what is to be regarded as 'public need' as well as help to meet that need alongside other types of agency. She chose a case study of the role of NGOs in community-based health care because it seemed to be an example where the conditions were such that the public action role of NGOs should be clear.

5 The critical case (2): chosen by repute

The second way of deliberately challenging theoretical ideas is to choose cases reputed to be cases of 'good practice' or where there has been a 'success'. Here you would be checking whether the reasons for 'success' or for the reputation of 'good practice' correspond to your ideas for what should be expected to lead to success. For example, in a follow-up to the study of co-operatives in Example 13.1, you could pick a well-known example of a radical bookshop (clearly a 'radical marginal') and look in detail at whether the mechanisms by which it maintained itself were indeed those suggested by the ideas behind the notion of 'radical marginal', including high labour turnover as well as moral motivations and political commitment.

6 The critical case (3): comparing two sets of ideas

This involves framing a case so that two competing sets of ideas or theories can challenge each other. This is perhaps the most testing of all single case designs, corresponding to the 'contrastive approach' to data analysis put forward by Mukherjee and Wuyts in Chapter 10. The investigation will look for evidence of which set of answers to the 'How?' and 'Why?' questions provides the best story or explanation. In Example 13.3 below there were two competing theoretical explanations for why the Botswana government backed down: one seeing it as a response of a democratic government to views of a section of its population which NGOs had helped to articulate; the other attributing it to the power of international networking among NGOs. As you will see when you look at the Example 13.3, neither explanation was exactly correct by itself, but having more than one 'handle' on the case allowed us to gain some very useful insights.

13.2.4 Multiple case strategies

It is an often repeated fallacy that you cannot generalize from case studies. It is quite possible for general conclusions to be reached from a relatively small number of case studies – or even from one case study. In fact, the main point of multiple case studies is to challenge the theoretical ideas which have been developed so that the ensuing generalization can be that much stronger. Either the case studies will confirm your ideas so that you are more confident about generalizing on their basis, or else the case studies will throw doubt on the applicability of your ideas in different circumstances, in which case you should be able to reconceptualize and generalize on the basis of changed or new ideas.

What you can *not* do on the basis of case studies is *statistical* generalization. Since you are not working from a statistical sample you cannot make general descriptive statements about the whole of a population. Abbott's study of *khannawallis* (Chapter 9) could not be used to say what proportion of them used loans for purposes of consumption rather than investing in their productive activities of home cooking. We could not generalize from the cases of worker co-operatives we studied (Example 13.1) to estimate the proportion of co-operatives of each of the types we identified or what proportion of each type failed within, say, five years.

What you *can* do with case studies is *theoretical* generalization. If you have a theoretical idea about how success is the outcome of the interrelationship of certain factors or influences for example, and if this idea succeeds in explaining your case studies, then you can make general explanatory statements that apply to all cases where the interrelationships are similar. Any challenge to your general explanation must be either a claim that the case studies were misinterpreted, which would need to be carefully answered, or else of the form 'Here's a case where that doesn't apply'. The latter should lead to a useful debate about why that case is different from the ones you studied and might lead to further reconceptualization, but in principle does not invalidate your theoretical generalization.

We have seen that, in choosing more than one case so that the combination challenges your ideas, you are *not* sampling. Instead, the logic to use is similar to that of multiple experiments. Each successive experiment is designed to reinforce the theory, to extend its application, or to force a rethink or modification. As Yin (1994, 2002) points out, to be done in a similar way case study design has to be theory-led; in other words ideas have to be worked out *before* you can decide which cases to study. Yin suggests borrowing the principle of *replication* from experimental method. He discusses two main forms of replication:

- literal replication; and
- theoretical replication.

In *literal replication* the cases are chosen to be as similar as possible to each other, according to your idea of what conditions are important. You check whether similar processes and outcomes do in fact occur. For maximum impact, and to avoid the possibility that your evidence would support more than one idea, you may want to choose cases which differ considerably in ways which your idea expects to be *un*important. If, either from *a priori* reasoning or as an outcome of a preliminary exploratory stage (see above), there are several theoretical categories of case, then you may need a literal replication of each (i.e. at least two similar cases in each category).

Abbott's study of *khannawallis* included literal replication when she studied cases of more than one married woman to check that in each case the same type of consideration (caste and kinship links, contribution to mixed livelihood strategy, etc.) was behind the way the activity was organized. With the study of NGO influence, the case study of the campaign against the SOIWDP (mentioned in Example 13.2 and described in Example 13.3 below) could have been followed by a case study of another confrontational campaign in Botswana or a similar country where multi-party elections are also held, to see if both campaigns succeeded for similar reasons, as envisaged by our theoretical ideas.

Theoretical replication means choosing case studies which are different from each other in theoretically significant ways. They should be chosen such that different or opposite conditions apply, so that your ideas lead you to expect different or opposite outcomes. You then investigate whether these different or opposite outcomes in fact occur, how, and why.

An example of theoretical replication from Abbott's *khannawalli* study is the inclusion of women without male partners (deserted or widowed), or whose husbands were unemployed, as well as married women with employed partners. Assuming that the *khannawalli* activity is best interpreted as contributing to livelihood strategies, one would expect married women to rely less on the activity and for it to vary in importance over time in relation to other income possibilities, whereas for deserted or widowed women it is more likely to be of prime importance as a livelihood strategy. This theoretical replication allowed Abbott to check that the different outcomes did more or less correspond to the differences in circumstances and thus tended to confirm these ideas.

With respect to the NGO influence study, another of the cases studied was of how NGOs in Botswana related to the government policy of fencing communal lands. The NGOs concerned opposed this policy in principle but certainly did not pursue any confrontation with government and were completely ineffective in achieving any influence (Selolwane, 2001).

Note that all three versions of the 'critical case' can be used in replication. Perhaps the last is the most powerful. *Contrastive inference* (see also Section 13.3.2) – comparing two sets of competing ideas, in similar and then theoretically dissimilar cases, is a very good way of ensuring that your case studies remain challenging. This approach was being followed both in the *khannawalli* study (where the notion of the activity as a micro-enterprise was constantly being contrasted with the livelihood strategies idea) and, as we will see, in Example 13.3 below.

3.3 Challenging a case with your ideas • • •

This section is concerned with how to conduct a case study investigation. Just as data will not tell a story unless you 'fire questions' at them (Chapter 10), you cannot expect to get an explanation from a case study unless you challenge it with your ideas. Thus the approach suggested requires developing your own theoretical ideas in advance, so that you know what kind of story or explanation to expect, and then using these ideas to give a focus and edge to the investigation.

In what follows we look first at the methods which may be combined in carrying out a case study and then at ways of trying to achieve rigour so as to be able to defend your results. Example 13.3 is a practical illustration of many of the points made.

13.3.1 Methods to use in a case study investigation

As noted in Section 13.1.3, a case study investigation is really a framework for research rather than a specific 'method'. Within that framework you can use any combination of the methods which have been discussed in the other chapters of this book, including 'thinking with' documents, people, and both quantitative and organizational data.

What follows are brief notes about how you might use different methods within a single case study.

Background literature and interviews

It is important to hone your ideas about the 'How?' and 'Why?' questions you want to ask before getting in to the detailed investigation. You will need to do a small literature study as part of any case study and you should probably start this before making direct contact and requesting access. This applies particularly to collecting and analyzing the most easily available 'grey' literature (Chapter 6). If the case is about an organization, for example, you should obtain annual reports, publicity material, recent newsletters and other publicly available documents from the organization. These days most organizations have their own websites, and much of this material is likely to be available there. It is also worth a brief internet search to see what the media or other sources have to say about the case. However, for less well-endowed or more informal organizations, you may have to request hard copies to be sent to you, or make a visit to read and make notes on documents which are only available on site. Another useful preliminary is open-ended interviews with peripherally involved 'experts' – people you can talk to safely even before you know if this is a case to which you will be able to get good enough access. This is another example of Hanlon's' finding the woman who knows' from Chapter 3.

Access

Your study may well have been preceded by an exploratory phase of finding out at a much lower level of detail about a relatively large number of cases of different types. While contacting those involved you may have been able to arrange in principle that you could come back and do a more detailed study. Or the question of access to the particular case or cases you want to study in detail may be more tricky. Depending on the circumstances, you may need a 'gatekeeper' (Chapter 7). For example, studying cases of the 'objects' of a policy may require the policy-making agency (which may be your own, of course) to agree to facilitate access to those 'objects', as with Abbott gaining access to *khannawallis* through the AMM. Alternatively, if the case is one involving interactions between several individuals or organizations you may find access to some of them easy, others requiring a gatekeeper and yet others harder or impossible.

Following through in focused interviews

Much case study analysis involves detailed interviewing ('focused interviews' in the terms of Chapter 7). A key element of such interviews is not only to have some standard headings but also to follow through. When asking someone how or why certain things happened, it is likely that new elements and contradictory causes are suggested, in which case you should follow through on investigating chains of causality. This may mean new people to interview (whose importance to the case you hadn't realized) and whom you now have to trace. It also means asking different interviewees to explain answers given by others which seem at odds with their own accounts or which leave loose ends in the explanation you are building up. Following up reasons behind reasons given is much more important in this type of interviewing than covering the same topics in each interview.

Using data analysis or survey within the case study framework

Although focused interviews are usually the main method used, there is often a place for other methods within the case study framework. Particularly with large single cases, there may well be definable statistical populations within the boundaries of the case, on a sample of which a structured survey could usefully be carried out; or there may be official data available on such a population that could be analyzed. An example from the science parks research (Massey, Quintas and Wield, 1992) is data on the individual firms within the parks studied. You would have to avoid what Mukherjee and Wuyts (Chapter 10) call 'hoarding data' – padding the report on your case study with numbers and tables without using them. Be sure to 'fire questions' at such data in such a way that the answers throw light on the main ideas you are investigating in the case.

Building a story

The main point of a case study is to put together a coherent explanation, or story. In the first place, you are trying to build a story based on your original set of ideas. You identify the major actors and get their stories, to see if an overall version emerges in the form expected. You compare this with the story that emerges from other evidence such as quantitative data. Much of what Hanlon says in Chapter 3 applies directly to gathering evidence in a single case study, particularly the sequence of 'throw the net out wider', 'redefine the question and select the key issue' and finally 'discard and deepen'. In particular, this may mean reconceptualizing, and your original ideas may end up not only challenged but changed as a result.

Example 13.3   Combining methods to challenge the Southern Okavango Integrated Water Development Project

One of the case studies in the research on NGO influence outlined in Example 13.2 was a study of the 1990 campaign against the Southern Okavango Integrated Water Development Project, Botswana (Thomas and Selolwane, 2001). This was a government project which would have dredged part of one of the main channels of the Okavango Delta and built a number of dams in order to supply domestic piped water, as well as water for irrigation and a diamond mine. It caused controversy because, in a largely arid country, the Okavango is not only one of the few sources of water but its delta is also one of the world's largest wetlands, ecologically unique and a big resource for wildlife and international tourism, as well as providing the resource base

(Continued)

(Continued)

for some 100,000 local inhabitants. The project was shelved after opposition, both from local communities led by a local community-based NGO Tshomorelo Okavango Conservation Trust (TOCT), and from international conservationists and NGOs, including Greenpeace.

This case study was chosen because it potentially offered evidence on two of the ideas being developed by the research team. The first was that a confrontational approach by NGOs is more likely to work where genuine multi-party elections are held and where there are alternative local power centres. TOCT was unusual for an NGO in Botswana in its confrontational stance and indeed was formed by a split from a more longstanding national NGO, the Kalahari Conservation Society (KCS), which followed a collaborative strategy, including sitting on government commissions and quiet attempts at lobbying. We wanted to find out why TOCT's campaign had succeeded. Was it through utilizing the democratic processes of the Botswana state, including the government's wish to avoid an issue blowing up into an electoral weapon for its opponents? Did they exploit the existence of 'alternative power centres', such as local MPs and councils of the opposition party as well as the 'traditional authorities' and chiefs with important influence both locally and nationally? If so, our original idea would be considerably strengthened.

The other idea on which we wanted evidence was that NGOs improve their influence on policy through engaging in international NGO alliances. Some of the early grey materials which we collected were reports and pamphlets from South African conservationist sources, which claimed that TOCT had worked together with Greenpeace and forced the Botswana government to back down through a combination of Greenpeace threats (such as an international 'Diamonds are for Death' campaign or an EU boycott of Botswana beef) with mobilization of the local population by TOCT. Had TOCT actually been more effective because of an alliance with Greenpeace and other international NGOs?

In following up this case, we interviewed protagonists representing various interests. Here it was useful that I worked on the case jointly with a local colleague from Botswana. She was able to interview local and national politicians, high-ranking officials, including those who had held key positions at the time of this campaign but since moved or retired, and directors both of the state diamond corporation and NGOs such as KCS. In the UK I interviewed one of the Greenpeace team which had spent three weeks in Botswana in 1990 investigating the project, and I also visited the locality and spoke to conservationists, founding members of TOCT and someone who had been a 'whistle-blower' within the government's water department. We found many discrepancies in their accounts, notably one between the South African sources noted above and the claim from Greenpeace that they had never threatened any international campaigns against the Botswana government and their study tour

(Continued)

(Continued)

had been on that government's invitation, culminating in a joint communiqué and press conference.

We also used different types of evidence, including not only interviews and grey materials but also media reports from the time, consultants' reports on the design and environmental assessment of the project, internal memos from government departments which some of the interviewees were prepared to let us see, a video of a local community meeting which had attracted several hundred people, and at which government officials had been harangued for several hours, and Greenpeace archives. These allowed us to cross-check some of the discrepancies and in some cases we went back and asked interviewees supplementary questions or asked them to comment on a draft of our case study report. In the end, where accounts differed, we had to make informed judgements on what was likely to have actually occurred and why. Thus, although we found several media reports from the time repeating the story about Greenpeace threats, we concluded that probably they had never actually made such threats but certain local and South African conservationists may have 'placed' stories which talked of the 'possibility' of a Greenpeace campaign.

On the first of the ideas we were testing, it seemed to be a concern to appear democratic to international observers as much as the actual workings of democracy which led the Botswana government to back down. On the second, the case helped us develop the idea that it may be the internationalization of the issue rather than specific alliances which helps local NGOs to win a battle. Too much reliance on the involvement of NGOs from outside a country may lead to a potential backlash. Greenpeace was clearly unwelcome in Botswana for some time after the campaign. Thus in the end, the explanation we gave modified considerably both our original ideas, particularly that on international NGO alliances.

Postscript

I revisited the case a few years later and found a very different situation (Thomas, 2003). The NGOs concerned lacked continuing capacity, but nevertheless the issue continued to be framed as an international one. In 1997, after Namibia announced its intention to extract water from the Okavango as quickly as possible, as an emergency measure, Botswana became a contracting party of the international Ramsar Convention, making the Okavango Delta into the core of the world's largest protected Wetland of International Importance, in a move interpreted as an attempt to counteract Namibia's plans. Thus, the claim that the Okavango should be regarded as a global common has shifted from being an NGO strategy in opposition to the Botswana government's claim of sovereignty over natural resources within its state boundaries to being part of the government's own strategy for protecting the same resources from sovereignty claims by another state.

13.3.2 Achieving rigour in a case study investigation

Case study methods present a problem with respect to rigour. It is easy to be criticized for simply finding evidence to fit your preconceived ideas. Since you choose the case to study and start with a theoretical explanation already in mind, then finding evidence to fit your pre-prepared story may appear to be a self-fulfilling prophesy. Case study research can indeed be a matter of using a mixture of mainly qualitative methods and subjective judgement to tell a story which confirms what you expected. Yin (1994) argues that this is unavoidable but acceptable. The important point is to be open to the possibility that the story is wrong or needs changing.

If your ideas really are open to challenge then simply showing that, as more and more detail comes to light the same basic explanation remains consistent, is in itself a useful result. The postscript to Example 13.3 above shows how, in that case, although the situation changed as time went on, the conclusion that the internationalization of the issue was more important than particular NGO alliances still held good.

Some of the ways of showing that your ideas are open to challenge are similar to the ways rigour is achieved in semi-structured interviews more generally (not surprising since, as we have seen, such interviews usually form a big part of any case study investigation). From Chapter 7 you will recall that Philip Woodhouse suggests *triangulation* and *documentation* as the two key means of achieving rigour in semi-structured interviews, and these are important for case study research.

Triangulation is getting evidence on the same point from different points of view. It means both using different methods of investigation (analyzing archive records, secondary data or media reports as well as published literature and interviews) *and* getting evidence from several sources (interviewing several individuals; checking reports from several agencies). A simple example is Abbott's interviews with clients as well as *khannawallis* themselves (Chapter 9). Another, from Example 13.1, was checking co-operative members' accounts of the history and performance of their co-operative against records such as minutes of meetings and financial accounts.

Documentation: Since there is so much subjective judgement in carrying out a case study investigation, it is essential to keep good records of the progress of the study. This should enable you, either in response to criticism or for your own purposes, to go back and check what evidence actually led you to frame your explanation in the way you eventually did. Ideally these records should include the following: a diary; notes on interviews (including headings worked out in advance, additional lines of questioning, suggestions for further investigation and loose ends thrown up); documents obtained (with their source, notes on your skim reading – see Chapter 6, perhaps more detailed notes later, and again loose ends to be followed up elsewhere); other data (with how obtained and results of analysis); and other items as required in your particular enquiry.

An additional, and very important, way of avoiding the accusation of the self-fulfilling prophesy is to follow a *contrastive approach* similar to that taken in the case of data analysis using 'contrastive inference' by Mukherjee and Wuyts in Chapter 10.

This means, again in the words of Mukherjee and Wuyts, using more than one 'handle'. In other words, you start with more than one set of competing ideas; you have more than one type of explanation in mind and you use the evidence from the case study to decide which explanation stands up best. (This is like the third version of the 'critical case' in Section 13.2.4).

Yin gives the example of Allison's (1971) study of the Cuban missile crisis:

> Allison posits three competing theories or models to explain the course of events, including answers to three questions: why the Soviet Union placed offensive (and not merely defensive) missiles in Cuba in the first place, why the United States responded with a blockade (and not an air strike or invasion), and why the Soviet Union eventually withdrew the missiles. By comparing each theory with the actual course of events, Allison develops the best explanation for this type of crisis. Allison suggests that this explanation is applicable to other situations, thereby extending the usefulness of his single-case study.
>
> (Yin, 1994, p. 5)

Throughout the research on worker co-operatives (Example 13.1) we were using case studies to find evidence both for the suggestion that mode of start-up remained the greatest influence on a co-operative's performance and the contrasting notion that it is how commitment (personal and financial) is maintained that determines the ways that a co-operative could survive and flourish.

Example 13.3 also shows how contrastive inference worked in a rather different context. There we found different informants telling contrasting stories, some attributing the change of government policy to its democratic nature, others to the internationalization of the campaign.

The explanation we ended up with was rather more complex than either of the simple starting hypotheses.

13.3.3 Subjective judgement, validity and presentation

One can expect competing stories or explanations based on evidence from different sources. To some extent triangulation will eliminate some of the differences, but it is unlikely that there will be a single clear version agreed by all in every respect. There is a certain amount of professional judgement involved in putting together what others would accept as a rigorous and valid interpretation of a case – which could be used as evidence for or against your original ideas or in favour of a newly modified version.

3.4 **Presenting case studies as evidence** • • •

What are you to make of the evidence from case studies in order to present the results and try to make an impact on policy? It is useful to think in terms of a two-way interchange between you as investigator with your ideas, on the one hand, and the case study and the evidence it produces on the other.

There are two extreme types of possible result. First, your original ideas may stand up well but challenge the cases such that new insights arise which are something of a surprise to those involved in the cases themselves. This was more or less what happened in the *khannawalli* study, where Abbott's idea was that the notion of contributing to mixed livelihoods strategies would explain the activity and this idea stood up better than the alternative throughout, despite challenge from a variety of cases. This was to some extent a challenge in turn to the AMM, whose policies of lending to *khannawallis* as though to micro-enterprises looked less securely based as a result of the study.

At the other extreme, if the evidence from the cases investigated constitutes a sufficient challenge to your ideas there may be a need to stand back and completely reconceptualize. Example 13.1 explained how something like this occurred in the case of the research on worker co-operatives in the UK. In the science park research referred to in Sections 13.2.1 and 13.2.3 above there was a point where the original conceptualization which attempted to explain science parks as attempts to create synergy between university-based intellectuals and innovators and entrepreneurs had to be dropped. In the new version, property development and regional development considerations, which differed considerably between more central and more peripheral parts of the UK, came to the fore in explaining how and why different science parks prospered in different ways.

Between the two extremes are various possibilities: for example, one's ideas could lead to a slightly modified view of the cases while in turn they could be somewhat modified as a result of challenge from the cases. More than one set of ideas could have been pitted against each other, and unless one or other falls down completely this could mean a result with two competing overall explanations, each of which provides some evidence. Example 13.3 showed how the final explanation can well owe something to both of the originally competing ideas.

How results are to be presented in each of these situations is of course itself part of the policy process. If the evidence from your case studies is to have any impact you have to consider its presentation, how the case studies are used as evidence, which parties will be challenged by the findings, and so on. All the considerations in Chapter 4 on 'communicating results' will be important to ensure that the challenge of the cases you have chosen and analyzed is not limited to your own thinking but makes a real difference.

Conclusion: personal effectiveness and integrity

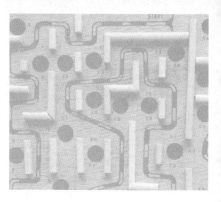

Alan Thomas and Joanna Chataway

The Introduction to this book started by noting that it is about 'research to inform policy and public action'. Hopefully the chapters of the book will have helped to make you more effective, whether as a policy researcher or as a user of policy-oriented research. It should also have become clear how important it is to maintain standards of personal integrity in the face of some difficult ethical issues which can arise in policy-oriented investigations. Indeed, we would maintain that in the long run integrity is the key to effectiveness.

But what exactly is 'effective' policy research? Does 'effective' mean getting a result in terms of action, policy implementation or change? If so, what if things don't work out as expected? Can the research still be regarded as effective because it led to action? On the other hand, what if research helps to clarify the consequences of a policy which works well and has well-understood negative consequences for some groups or interests? Is this effective simply because it has led to better understanding, irrespective of whether or how that understanding is then used? Or is such research to be judged in terms of more or less desirable outcomes: effective if it has helped less powerful groups to improve their position at the expense of the more powerful, but not effective if the research was at the service of those who exploit?

1 Differences between authors • • •

We noted in the Introduction the difference between those who think in terms of 'discovering reality' and those for whom there may be not one but several simultaneously valid versions of reality from different viewpoints. While both groups may want to see the results of their research used for policy or action, the former will judge the research ultimately by how clearly it uncovers how things really are, whereas for the latter the only way to judge research is by its 'utility'.

Indeed, different authors in the book do appear to take different positions in this respect. Some clearly hold to the idea that there is an underlying reality which research can find out more and more about, thus improving understanding and creating more and more certainty in knowing the results of policy change. For example, Mukherjee and Wuyts write:

> Policy analysis seeks to understand reality, with the explicit purpose of informing public action aimed at changing this reality.
>
> (Chapter 10, p. 234)

Other authors, however, point out how different accounts or pictures of reality are simultaneously possible based on different perspectives and interests. Blackmore and Ison, for example, show graphically in Figure 2.2 how different actors see different systems with different boundaries in the same situation. So how is one to choose between perspectives, except on a subjective basis of what seems most useful? Hanlon in Chapter 3 specifically suggests redefining the question one has been asked to investigate in such a way that the new conceptualization is more likely to bring about what the investigator sees as a useful result but is still acceptable to the agency commissioning the research.

This is not the only point of disagreement between authors. In Chapter 3 Hanlon also suggests using the short cut of 'finding the woman who knows', while O'Laughlin in Chapter 6 warns against following short-term consultants whose 'quick and dirty' methods include over-reliance on 'gossip'. In Chapter 11, Mayer bases her whole discussion on how to think about and use data when you are trying to convince others to do as you suggest, whereas in Chapter 10 Mukherjee and Wuyts argue that, even if your main purpose is advocacy of your particular point of view, you should nevertheless explicitly contrast rival ideas with yours to see which provide the better explanation of the data.

There are also differences over what is meant by uncertainty, about whether participation and empowerment should always be an aim of research, and about the desirability of the 'fast' in 'finding out fast'.

To what extent do these differences all relate to the basic difference noted in the Introduction between 'the realist notion of underlying truth which research aims progressively to discover by building up knowledge' and 'the social constructionist conception of the possible simultaneous validity of different accounts or constructions of human interaction based on different perspectives, interests and values'? Or are some of them differences in standards, and thus relate to the question of integrity? To what extent are these differences reconcilable?

2 Common ground • • •

We will return later to the question of reconciling the differences between the authors in this book. For the moment, let us note that, despite these differences, on the whole there is a lot of common ground between them. Much of this stems from a common interest in investigation to inform development policy and public action. In different ways, the authors follow the kind of approach outlined in Section 3 of the Introduction. Perhaps the strongest commonality is a recognition that policy and action has to be thought of in terms of process. The challenge for any policy investigation, then, is to fit into this process in an effective way.

Policy as process not prescription

'Policy as process' contrasts with 'policy as prescription'. This is why it is worth re-emphasizing the importance of thinking of policy as process. A 'policy as prescription' view would separate the policy-maker from the field of policy and see policy research as finding out about the field of policy in order to help the policy-maker prescribe what should be done. In terms of Table 1.1 on p. 28, it would concentrate only on the bottom right box in the matrix. An example might be agricultural research demonstrating the suitability of a particular drought-resistant crop in a certain area. Typically, such research would not pay specific attention to *who* would act or *how* the prescribed policy would be implemented. There might be an unstated assumption that the government should act or that people should simply adopt a new practice because the research had demonstrated its superiority.

The 'policy as process' view differs in that the process idea is felt in several ways. I will mention three here. Examples of all of them are found in various chapters of the book.

First, there is a constant process of change in the field of policy. Thus the suitability of a crop in a particular area will be changing, not only with climate changes but, perhaps more importantly in the short term, with changes in availability of labour, irrigation and other inputs, with changes in taste and marketability, with changes in combinations of other crops that are habitually grown, and with changes in sources of non-farm income and migration, land tenure patterns and so on. This implies that a policy investigation has to look for how and why people act as they do, and hence how changes occur. In other words it has to analyze social processes, rather than just describe the current situation. Hence, for example, it was suggested with respect to UK transport policy in Chapter 1 that investigation needs to find out why people make trips in order to understand changes in demand and also perhaps to be able to influence them.

Second, policy development is a process itself. It is not just a question of taking the recommendations from an investigation and implementing them. There are often several interests and considerable political interaction within just one agency. There will almost certainly be policy in the area already, to be reinforced or modified, rather than a new policy simply arriving fully formed. Thus the promotion of a new drought-resistant crop might have to be done by extension agents who already have views and practices involving promoting other crops. Any investigation will in practice be just one input into a continuing process of definition and redefinition of policy. Indeed, I don't think there is an example in any chapter of the results of an investigation being turned directly into a new prescription. The clearest examples of a process of interaction between an agency making and re-making policy and those doing research for it are perhaps in Chapters 3 and 4, but this aspect of process is found throughout the book.

The third area of process is the relation between action and those acted on, or between policy and the 'field' of policy in which action takes place. Rather than the policy-maker being the only active agent and those in the field being passive recipients of policy, in practice many agencies and individuals are actively pursuing their different policies and reacting to each other, all the time. An investigation is more than just one input to a process of policy-making within a particular agency. It is also an input into this process of interaction which might affect the actions and reactions of several actors. So, although farmers do not simply adopt a new crop because research says so, new training for extension agents based on new findings is a factor in their decisions, as is locally disseminated knowledge of agricultural trials carried out on neighbouring farms. Seed companies may begin to promote the new seeds and others may look for ways of marketing the produce. In Chapter 12 the Oxfam-commissioned report on the impact of user health care fees in Zimbabwe is described as causing a 'furore' and in the end both the World Bank and Government of Zimbabwe modified their policies. All policy investigation is subject to these considerations. However, it is research aimed at changing the way an issue is thought of by a wide range of actors, rather than at informing or pressurizing one or two specific policy-makers that fits with this aspect of process most closely. Examples from the book include several cited in Chapter 11 as well as the research on UK science parks mentioned in Chapter 13 and that on support to Zimbabwean co-operatives in Chapter 3.

Thus taking a 'policy as process' view means policy research can investigate policy itself as well as the field of policy. In other words, it can range over any or all of the boxes in the matrix of Table 1.1. In fact, it may be hard to fix boundaries between the boxes, to distinguish policy actors from those acted on, and it may be unhelpful to try to do so. Policy research means analyzing social processes, and seeing public action as resulting from existing structures and institutions but also acting upon them and thereby transforming them, thus changing the context of policy, sometimes in unexpected or unintended directions.

One investigation does not have to cover everything, however. Not every investigation can look at the whole policy process and all those involved. An investigation needs to be 'boundaried' so as to be effective in informing and providing an intervention into the policy process within the given constraints of resource and time. Although we may not be able to draw a clear line between policy itself and the field of policy, a particular investigation may focus more on one than the other.

Let us look briefly at a number of other points of commonality between the book authors. They all relate to aspects of the 'policy as process' view, and hence to how to turn a limited investigation into an effective intervention into such a process.

The two sides of public action

In considering investigation which is meant to inform public action, we should remember that public action has two complementary aspects. One side of public action is simply action to meet public (or collective private) needs. But since what are public needs is inevitably contested, the other side of public action is action that helps to define what are to be regarded as public needs.

To inform actions to meet needs requires fairly straightforward investigations: measuring the extent of needs, assessing the effectiveness of previous policies aimed at meeting those needs, and so on. But to provide evidence to help in defining areas of public need or issues where the public interest is at stake requires more open-ended investigations. In particular, you must be willing to reconceptualize, and to frame issues in a way that will bring them forcefully into the public arena.

Chapter 6 described contestation over how the problem of reducing rural poverty in Africa should be conceptualized, with some reports treating it as a matter of improving smallholder agriculture and others looking at the variety of income sources available to rural populations, including migration to find wage labour. Further useful research on poverty in particular African countries could well aim at defining the dimensions of the problem and hence exactly what the need is, rather than assuming a particular version of need and trying to measure it. These are also contested areas, where the way the problem is conceptualized (which partly derives from how it has been investigated) helps define how it is regarded as affecting the public interest. In these and similar cases, it is important to define research questions and carry out investigation with the need to make an impact strongly in mind. For example, 'grabbing attention', in Hanlon's terms, may mean *re*-defining the question so that the answers are more telling, while remaining in the realm of what is acceptable to those for whom the answers are intended.

An agency perspective

Consideration of *how* policy is to be carried out and *who* is to act leads one to treat all people and organizations involved in a situation as agents, not just 'objects' of policy. Hence the interest throughout the book in making inferences from what has been done in the name of previous policies by various agencies. Chapter 6 deals with analyzing institutional discourse and Chapter 12 with 'institutional footprints'. There is also the question of the implications of what might be done, maybe as a result of policy investigation, and how any change carried out will affect different people and organizations. Both policy and policy investigation generally take place in a multiple-actor field. There may be not just different views as to how social processes operate but different interests according to how people and organizations are likely to be affected by change. In other words, policy involves politics. Finding out fast is always done in a political context.

Viewing those involved in any situation as agents applies to those generally regarded as acted on as well as to those powerful agencies that have definite, worked out policies which they try to implement. A good example is provided by the study of the impact of health reforms in Zimbabwe carried out by Oxfam and described in Chapter 12. This study looked at what led the World Bank and the Government of Zimbabwe to implement reforms in a particular way and what might induce them to change as well as how people reacted to the reforms. The position of the researcher or research team is of prime importance. How do they relate to those they are investigating, to those who are usually regarded as 'objects' of policy and to the policy-makers? In the Oxfam study mentioned the researchers clearly had to establish 'rapport', both with the individual users of health services that they chose as case studies and with decision-makers in the Zimbabwean government and the World Bank. Remembering that Woodhouse in Chapter 7 points out that 'rapport can be manipulative', one might ask whether it was manipulation that allowed the Oxfam researchers to bring about a change in others' policy, and if so whether it was justified. Justified or not, such a result could not have been achieved without an agency view of both the users and the policy-makers.

The importance of theory

Policy-oriented research as the analysis of social processes implies coming to grips with theory, particularly social theory about how change takes place. This means recognizing that contesting theories play their part in the policy domain. Thus an important dimension of policy investigation resides in understanding the premises and theoretical underpinnings of different participants in policy debates and practice.

Despite the fact that some of the differences noted between authors are about the role of theory (discovering reality versus constructing realities), all of us recognize the importance of locating policy arguments within their theoretical traditions so as to get a better grip on the diversity of actions undertaken and the ways in which they are justified. This is covered explicitly by Barrientos in Chapter 5 on undertaking a literature study, but applies equally if one's way into a new topic or situation is through 'finding the woman who knows'. An initial map of a policy area has to include not only the main organizations and groups involved and how they relate, but also the bases of their actions, and that means their contrasting underlying theoretical views of the world.

When it comes to pursuing one's own analysis in order to provide an explanation and policy recommendations, we have seen the importance of theory emphasized again and again in the chapters of the book. That is to say, it is vital to come to a situation armed with clear ideas about what one expects to find. Whether they derive directly from recognized, named social theories or not, these ideas are the theories which one uses to interpret questionnaire survey results (Chapter 7), or to design questions to 'fire at the data' (Chapter 10) or to shape one's investigation of a case study (Chapter 13). At the same time, however, it is also vital to be aware of opposing theories and ideas, to allow one's own ideas deliberately to be challenged by them, and to be as open as possible to which gives the best interpretation. This is an important aspect of integrity as a researcher. But closing one's mind to opposing views and theories is not a particularly good way to be effective either.

3 Reconciling the differences • • •

Given such a lot of common ground, surely there is a basis for reconciling the differences between authors. We work towards this by first looking at the limitations of each of the two main positions identified, and then see how pursuing high standards of integrity may imply each taking account of the other.

Our discussion of some of the limitations of the realist and then the social constructionist positions is not a full philosophical treatment, but a brief consideration in the light of the use of research here to inform policy and public action. Then we look at rigour and accountability as two aspects of integrity in research practice which cut across any underlying difference of philosophical position.

Limits to realism

No one thinks that it is possible to understand reality completely, or even have complete knowledge of the particular small aspect of reality that relates to the policy issue one is dealing with. In Chapter 3 Hanlon writes: 'Not even historians have all the facts'. However, for those who hold to the notion of an underlying reality, while we can never have complete knowledge, so that everything is surrounded by more or less uncertainty, we can with effort and good technique approach closer and achieve greater precision in our understanding in any given area. The special problem for finding out fast is to be accurate enough to provide useful results with limited time and resources.

Most critiques of the idea that there is an underlying objective reality centre on the impossibility of determining that reality. One argument, mentioned in Chapter 11, concerns cases where causal interlinkages are so complex, so long term and so changing, that tracing them in detail cannot reasonably be done with any degree of certainty. A different argument concerns those cases where human purpose is involved. These include all cases of policy and thus this argument is of particular importance to us here and we will pursue it a little further.

As noted at several points in this book, investigation itself constitutes intervention, so that the very act of trying to find out why things were done or how policies had certain effects leads those questioned to construct different meanings for what they have done and to think of different ways in which they could react to those policies. Although mathematical and physical science analogies are often invoked in this discussion, with reference for example to Heisenberg's uncertainty principle, Gödel's theorem or chaos theory, we would argue that when human purpose is involved uncertainty is of a different order altogether, going well beyond physical or probabilistic uncertainty to the complete uncertainty of not knowing how a human being or human agency will react. (Perhaps, like Mayer, again in Chapter 11, it would be better to term this 'ignorance' rather than uncertainty.) The difficulty in getting a consistent answer from somebody about why they acted in a certain way in the past translates into the complete impossibility of inferring from past behaviour what they may do in new circumstances, because they always have choice and their purposes may change or be unclear. And there are many occasions in policy-oriented investigations where circumstances are unique.

Thus, situations involving human choice, and complex interactions between choices by different people, are in principle virtually impossible to know with any degree of accuracy. There are those who nevertheless hold to the view that there is an underlying objective reality, although it is extremely difficult to discover it. Perhaps unsurprisingly, such people tend to overemphasize those areas where it is possible to achieve greater apparent certainty. One such area is the regular production of secondary data by particular institutions through standardized mechanisms. Chapter 10 discusses the 'factuality of data' and how what is regarded as a 'fact' is actually socially constructed. Chapter 11 points out that, despite some well-known critiques of science that challenge the impartiality and assumptions of the people doing the measuring, 'hard' quantitative data are still thought of as somehow 'better' than qualitative data. Chapter 11 goes on to note how this attitude had led to the assumption of the superiority of western over other forms of knowledge and hence the discounting of traditional knowledge, in some cases with well-documented detrimental effects. Chapter 9 puts forward another critique of supposedly objective quantitative data, namely the need for involvement and hence subjectivity in order to become privy to personally sensitive information.

Problems with social constructionism

The alternative notion of research is that it is a question of bringing out and recording different accounts from different viewpoints, and then constructing what appears to be the best story.

Although many different and even contradictory constructions of reality may be valid in this way of thinking, not all accounts are equally so. There may be clear evidence against some versions of reality, as when warriors believing a certain oil gives them invincible protection are nevertheless mowed down by machine-gun fire. Most evidence, however, is not so incontrovertible. In that case, how does one decide what is the best story among several possibilities that all seem to fit the (ambiguous) 'facts'?

Sometimes, helping those generally silent or disregarded to formulate their accounts clearly may appear good in itself. As noted in Chapters 7 and 8, using participatory learning and action (PLA) or other techniques to allow a voice to women, to children and elderly people, and to members of poor communities, can be justified directly in the name of empowerment. These seldom heard stories may be full of new insights. However, they may also be trite, full of inconsistencies, or based on internalized versions of the stories of the powerful. Conversely, those in positions of power may also be in a good position to see and explain what is going on, even though their self-justifications are likely to be biased. No technique can automatically overcome power relations, and Chapters 7 and 8 also gave examples where PLA brings out not the stories of the downtrodden but the 'official' explanation of how things are in a community. Both Woodhouse in Chapter 7 and Mayoux and Johnson in Chapter 8 also point out that, despite its ideal portrayal of the sensitive outsider as 'convenor, catalyst and facilitator', the best insights from participatory investigation come when the researcher uses her or his judgement to make interpretations and to accept or reject what comes out of the various exercises used. They conclude that it is necessary to be explicit about a researcher's purpose in undertaking a participatory investigation.

We are left with the unavoidable need for subjective interpretation by the researcher in order to come up with 'the best story'. Inevitably, this means the explanation which is most useful for backing up the argument the researcher or those commissioning the research want to make. There is an obvious danger here that an investigation will simply find only what it is looking for, and prejudices and biases will be reinforced because contrary evidence will be overlooked or ignored. The idea that one can only choose between versions of reality on the basis of utility appears to allow those in powerful positions to manipulate reality in a way most useful to them. This may be acceptable if their power is legitimate, as when in Chapter 1 research is called for which will help transport authorities in 'changing people's behaviour in a way which is not occurring voluntarily but which would be intended to improve their quality of life'. As Hanlon notes in Chapter 3, framing different questions will give rise to different stories.

The integrity of the researcher may appear to be a poor defence against these dangers, but it is some defence. It is important to bolster it as much as possible, and rigour and accountability are two areas in which this can be done.

Rigour

In the Introduction rigour was defined as 'being able to show that one has enough evidence to justify one's conclusions, that the evidence has been obtained properly and that contrary evidence has been sought but either not found or found to be relatively unconvincing'. Woodhouse in Chapter 7 adds the question of how far research findings can be reproduced, corroborated or applied to other situations.

Woodhouse also points out that for structured survey methods there is a set statistical procedure for rigorously inferring characteristics of a population from a sample, but in other cases the key means of achieving rigour are triangulation and documentation. Thus, although subjective interpretation may have been to the fore, it will at least be apparent that evidence sought from different angles pointed to the same result (triangulation) and be possible to look up the record of what evidence was the basis for the interpretation (documentation).

The idea of contrastive inference, developed by Mukherjee and Wuyts in Chapter 10, was taken up by Thomas in Chapter 13 as a third element in an attempt at rigour. Here you deliberately start with more than one set of competing ideas, perhaps including those from your theoretical opponents as well as your own ideas, and look for evidence of both before deciding which is the best interpretation. Combined with triangulation and documentation, this offers some defence against accusations of bias or that one's research results are simply what Chapter 13 calls 'self-fulfilling prophesy'. But subjectivity remains and so no defence is complete.

Accountability

Chataway, Joffe and Mordaunt in Chapter 4 consider the question of to whom a researcher is accountable. One answer is: to her or his own organization, or to whoever commissioned the research. But this ignores the fact that research is only possible if it obtains information from a great many sources. To some extent a researcher is also accountable to those from whom information was obtained. They may have expectations of good resulting from their sharing of information. Certainly there could be accusations of false pretences if confidences are broken or information is used against those who provided it.

There is also an argument that research results should as far as possible be in the public domain, and that since policy research is aimed at informing public action then those who produce it should be publicly accountable. This position may be hard to uphold when more and more research is commissioned by those who wish to use its results privately. However, for research aimed at development policy and public action (that is, the kind of research where we hope this book helps you to find out fast) a claim of public accountability is another defence, this time against pressure to represent results in a predetermined way when you have found contrary but unwelcome evidence (what Mayer in Chapter 11 calls 'data that don't say what you want').

4 Challenge: 'Trying not to get it wrong' • • •

So the idea of searching for the truth is impractical, while telling the best story means making subjective judgements which are always subject to pressure and cannot be unbiased. Although the two philosophical positions may be in basic opposition, in practice one need not choose between them but can hang on to elements of each. Thus, since you can never get enough evidence to describe all aspects of reality in detail, you may as well choose to frame your research question to get the most useful answers; conversely, if you have a good idea of the story you want to tell you should try to find 'real' evidence that might disprove it so that if you fail you will be more certain that the story stands up.

The theme which has run throughout the book which is relevant here is that of challenge. Trying to find contrary evidence is a way of subjecting your ideas to challenge – one which several authors have proposed. Contrastive inference – contrasting one set of ideas with another so as to see which provides the best explanation of all the evidence – is another form of challenge. And if research results are to have any impact there is also the question of how to use them to challenge the people and organizations with power to act in a situation.

Whether or not you hold to a belief in an underlying reality, it is never possible to be sure you are right. If you want to be effective as a policy investigator, the best you can do is to adopt Hanlon's slogan of 'trying not to get it wrong'. In Chapter 3 this referred to trying not to reconceptualize in a way which those commissioning research would reject. This means choosing to tell a story which is acceptable as well as being what the researcher thinks is the best story. Hanlon's slogan can also be taken to refer to trying not to put forward an explanation which powerful evidence can be brought forward to contradict. This means looking for such evidence yourself and being prepared to change your story if you find it, rather than ignoring it and hoping others will not uncover it.

So, be challenging and be open to challenge, and – in both senses – try not to get it wrong!

References

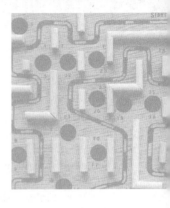

Abbott, D. (1992) 'Utilising bank loans as an organisational strategy: a case study of the Annapurna Mahila Mandal' in Prendergrast, R. and Ginger, H. (eds.) *Development Perspective for the 1990s*, London, Macmillan.

Abbott, D. (1993) *Women's Home-based Income Generation as a Strategy Towards Poverty Survival: dynamics of the 'khannawalli' (mealmaking) activity of Bombay*, PhD Thesis, The Open University, Milton Keynes.

Abbott, D. (1997) 'Who else will support us? How poor women organise the unorganisable in India', *Community Development Journal*, July.

Abbott, D., Brown, S., and Wilson, G. (2007) 'Development Management as Reflective Practice', *Journal of International Development* vol. 19, no. 2.

Adnan, S. *et al.* (1992) *People's participation NGOs and the Flood Action Plan: An independent review*, Dhaka, OXFAM Bangladesh.

Agarwal, A. and Narain, S. (1992) *Global Warming in an Unequal World: a Case of Environmental Colonialism*, Delhi, Centre for Science and Environment.

Allison, G. (1971) *Essence of Decision: Explaining the Cuban Missile Crisis*, Boston, Little Brown.

AMM (Annapurna Mahila Mandal) (1990) *AMM Annual Report*, Bombay, AMM.

Archer, D. (1998) 'The evolving conception of literacy in REFLECT', *PLA Notes* no. 32, London, International Institute for Environment and Development, pp. 100–108.

Archer, D. and Cottingham, S. (1996) *The REFLECT Mother Manual: a new approach to adult literacy*, London, ActionAid.

Armson, R., Ison, R. L., Short, L., Ramage, M. & Reynolds, M. (2001) 'Rapid institutional appraisal (RIA): a systemic approach to staff development' *Systems Practice & Action Research*, vol. 14, pp. 763–777.

Auret, D., and Barrientos, S. (2004) 'Participatory Social Auditing - a Practical Guide To Developing a Gender Sensitive Approach', *IDS Working Paper 237*, Brighton, Institute of Development Studies.

Baker, R. (1996) 'Participatory Rural Appraisal with street children in Nepal', *PLA Notes* no. 25, London, International Institute for Environment and Development, pp. 56–60.

Barrientos, S. (1997) 'Fruits of burden – the organisation of women temporary workers in Chilean agribusiness' in Afshar, H. (ed.) *Women and Empowerment*, Basingstoke, Macmillan.

Bebbington, A. J. (1994) 'Federations and food systems: organizations for enhancing rural livelihoods', in Scoones, I. and Thompson, J. (eds.), *Beyond Farmer First: Rural people's knowledge, agricultural research and extension practice*, London, Intermediate Technology.

Bebbington, A.J., Merrill-Sands, D. and Farrington, J. (1993) 'Farmers and community organisations in agricultural research and extension: functions, impacts, and questions', *Proc. Systems-Oriented Research in Agriculture and Rural Development*, Montpelier, pp. 699–705.

Beneria, L. (1982) 'Accounting for women's work', in Beneria, L. (ed.) *Women and Development: the sexual division of labour in rural societies*, New York, Praeger.

Biggs, S.D. (1995) 'Participatory technology development: a critique of the new orthodoxy', *Olive Information Service: AVOCADO Series* (ISSN 1025–0468), 06/95.

Bilgi, M. (1992) 'Entering women's worlds through men's eyes – a participatory rural appraisal at Boripitha, Netrang', paper presented to IIED Workshop on Gender and Participatory Rural Appraisal, Brighton.

Booth, D. and Lucas, H. (2002) 'Good Practice in the Development of PRSP Indicators and Monitoring Systems', *ODI Working Paper 172*, London, Overseas Development Institute.

Boserup, E. (1970) *Women's Role in Economic Development*, London, George Allen.

Brock, K., and Pettit, J. (eds.) (2007) *Springs of Participation: creating and evolving methods for participatory development*, London, Intermediate Technology Publications, forthcoming.

Brocklesby, M.A. and Holland, J. (1998) *Participatory Poverty Assessments and Public Services: Key Messages from the Poor*, London, DFID.

Bulmer, M. and Warwick, D. (eds.) (1993) *Social Research in Developing Countries: surveys and censuses in the Third World*, London, UCL Press.

Burnet-Hurst, A. (1925) *Labour and Housing in Bombay: a study in the economic conditions of the wage-earning classes in Bombay*, London, P. S. King and Sons Ltd.

Carr, E.H. (1990) *What is History?*, The George Macaulay Trevelyan lectures delivered in the University of Cambridge, January–March 1961, 2nd edition (first printed 1987), Harmondsworth, Penguin Books.

Chambers, R. (1980) 'Rapid rural appraisal: rationale and repertoire', *IDS Discussion Paper* no. 155, Brighton, Institute of Development Studies.

Chambers, R. (1992) 'Rural appraisal: rapid, relaxed and participatory', *IDS Discussion Paper* no. 311, Brighton, Institute of Development Studies.

Chambers, R. (1993) *Challenging the Professions. Frontiers for Rural Development*, London, Intermediate Technology Publications.

Chambers, R. (1994a) 'Participatory Rural Appraisal (PRA): Challenges, Potentials and Paradigm', *World Development*, vol. 22, no. 10, pp. 1347–1454.

Chambers, R. (1994b) 'The Origins and Practice of Participatory Rural Appraisal', *World Development*, vol. 22, no. 7, pp. 953–969.

Chambers, R. (1994c) 'Participatory Rural Appraisal (PRA): Analysis of Experience', *World Development*, vol. 22, no. 9, pp. 1253–1268.

Chambers, R. (1995) 'Making the best of going to scale', *PLA Notes* no. 24, London, International Institute for Environment and Development, pp. 57–61.

Chambers, R. (1997) *Whose Reality Counts? Putting the first last*, London, Intermediate Technology Publications.

Chandler, J. (1990) 'Researching and the relevance of gender', in Burgess, R. (ed.) *Studies in Qualitative Methodology: reflections on field experience*, vol. 2, London, Jai Press Inc.

Chapman, J. (2004) *System Failure: Why Governments Must Learn to Think Differently*, 2nd edition, London, DEMOS.

Checkland, P. (1981) *Systems Thinking. Systems Practice*, Chichester, John Wiley.

Checkland, P. (1999) 'Soft Systems Methodology: A Thirty Year Retrospective' in Checkland, P. and Scholes, J. *Soft Systems Methodology in Action*, Chichester, John Wiley.

Checkland, P.B. and Poulter, J. (2006) *Learning for action: A short definitive account of soft systems methodology and its use for practitioners, teachers and students*, Chichester, John Wiley.

Checkland, P.B. and Scholes, J. (1999) *Soft Systems Methodology in Action*, 2nd ed. Chichester, John Wiley.

Clinard, M. and Elder, J. (1965) 'Sociology in India: a study of the sociology of knowledge', *American Sociological Review*, vol. 30, no. 4, pp. 581–7.

Collier, P., Radwan, S. and Wangwe, S. (with Wagner, A.) (1986) *Labour and Poverty in Rural Tanzania: Ujamaa and rural development in the United Republic of Tanzania*, Oxford, Clarendon Press.

Collins, J. (2003) *Threads: Gender, Labor and Power in the Global Apparel Industry*, Chicago, University of Chicago Press.

Collingridge, D. and Reeve, C. (1986) *Science Speaks to Power. The role of experts in policy making*, London, Frances Pinter.

Cooke, B. (2001) 'The Social Psychological Limits of Participation?' in Cooke, B. and Kothari, U. (eds) *Participation: The New Tyranny?* New York and London, Zed Press.

Cooke, B. and Kothari, U. (eds) (2001) *Participation: The New Tyranny?* New York and London, Zed Press.

Cooperrider, D. L. and Whitney, D. (1999) *Appreciative Inquiry*, San Francisco, Berrett-Koehler.

Cornforth, C., Thomas, A., Lewis, J. and Spear, R. (1988) *Developing Successful Worker Co-operatives*, London, Sage.

Cornia, A., Jolly, R. and Stewart, F. (1987) *Adjustment with a Human Face*, 2 vols., Oxford, Clarendon Press.

Cornwall, A. (1992) 'Body Mapping in Health RRA/PRA', *RRA Notes* no. 16, Special Issue on Applications for Health, London, International Institute for Environment and Development, pp. 69–76.

Cornwall, A. and Fleming, S. (1995) 'Context and complexity: anthropological reflections on PRA', *PLA Notes* no. 24, London, International Institute for Environment and Development.

Cornwall, A., and Pratt, G. (eds) (2003) *Pathways to Participation: Reflections on PRA*, London, Intermediate Technology Publishing.

Court, J. and Young, J. (2003) 'Bridging Research and Policy: Insights from 50 Case Studies', *ODI Working Paper 213*, London, Overseas Development Institute.

Court, J. and Cotterrell, L. (2006) 'What political and institutional context issues matter for bridging research and policy? A literature review and discussion of data collection approaches', *ODI Working Paper 269*, London, Overseas Development Institute.

Court, J., Hovland, I. and Young, J. (2005) 'Crosscutting issues and implications: promoting more informed international development policy' in Court, J. Hovland, I. and Young, J. (eds) *Bridging Research and Policy in Development: Evidence and the Change Process*, London, Intermediate Technology Publishing.

Cowen, M. and Shenton, R. (1996) *Doctrines of Development*, London, Routledge.

Crenson, M. (1971) *The Un-Politics of Air Pollution: A Study of Non-Decision-Making in the Cities*, Baltimore, Johns Hopkins University Press.

Crewe, E. and Harrison, E. (1998) *Whose Development? An Ethnography of Aid*, London, Zed Books.

Crewe, E. and Young, J. (2002) 'Bridging Research and Policy: Context, evidence and links', *ODI Working Paper 173*, London, Overseas Development Institute.

Curry, S. (1992) 'Case Studies', Unit 7 of *Research Methods in Financial Economics* (ed. M.Wuyts), University of London, School of Oriental and African Studies, External Programme, MSc in Financial Economics.

Dale, R. (1998) *Evaluation Frameworks for Development Programmes and Projects*, New Delhi, Sage.

Dent, J. (1996) 'Stumbling towards gender-aware PRA training in Indonesia', *PLA Notes* no. 25, London, International Institute for Environment and Development, pp. 19–22.

Department for Transport (2004a) *The Future of Transport: a network for 2030*, Cm 6234, London, Department for Transport.

Department for Transport (2004b) *Feasibility study of road pricing in the UK: a report to the Secretary of State*, London, Department for Transport.

DETR (Department of the Environment, Transport, and the Regions) (1998):. *A New Deal for Transport - Better for Everyone*, White Paper on Transport Policy, London, The Stationery Office.

Department of Transport (1995) *Transport: the Way Forward*, Green Paper, London, Department of Transport.

Desai, V. and Potter, R. (eds) (2006) *Doing Development Research*, London, Sage.

DeStefano, L. and Ryan, K. (eds) (2004) *Evaluation as a Democratic Process: Promoting Inclusion, Dialogue, and Deliberation*, San Francisco, Jossey-Bass.

Development in Practice (2002) Special Edition on 'Development and the Learning Organization', vol. 12, nos. 3&4.

Devereux, S. and Hoddinott, J. (eds) (1992) *Fieldwork in Developing Countries*, Hemel Hempstead, Harvester Wheatsheaf,.

Douwe van der Ploeg, J. (1993) 'Potatoes and knowledge', in Hobart, M. (ed.) *An Anthropological Critique of Development*, London, Routledge.

Drèze, J. and Sen, A. (1989) *Hunger and Public Action*, Oxford, Clarenden Press.

Drucker, P. (1993) quoted in Fowler (1995) 'Participatory Self-Assessment of NGO capacity', *INTRAC Occasional Papers Series* no.10, Oxford, INTRAC.

Edwards, M. (1996) 'Becoming a learning organization, or the search for the holy grail?', paper presented at the Aga Khan Foundation Round Table on Systemic Learning: Promoting Support for Canadian Development Co-operation, Ottawa.

Eichler, M. (1988) *Nonsexist Research Methods*, Boston, Allen and Unwin.

Elder, J. (1973) 'Problems of cross-cultural methodology instrumentation and interviewing in India' in Armer, M. and Grimshaw, A. (eds.) *Comparative Social Research: methodological problems and strategies*, London, John Wiley and Sons.

Elson, D. and Pearson, R. (1981) 'Nimble Fingers Make Cheap Workers, An Analysis of Women's Employment in Third World Export Manufacturing', *Feminist Review*, Spring, pp. 87–107.

Elwin, V. (1939) *The Bhagias*, London, John Murry.

Eyben, R. (2005) 'Donors' learning difficulties: results, relationships and responsibilities' *IDS Bulletin* vol. 36, no. 3, Brighton, Institute of Development Studies, pp. 98–107.

Fals Borda, O. (1991) 'Some basic ingredients', in Fals Borda, O. and Rahman, M.A. (eds) *Action and Knowledge: Breaking the Monopoly with Participatory Action Research*, New York, Apex Press.

Feldstein, H.S. and Jiggins, J. (eds.) (1994) *Tools for the Field. Methodologies for Gender Analysis in Agriculture*, London, Intermediate Technology Publications.

Ferguson, J. (1990) *The Anti-politics Machine, 'Development', Depoliticization, and Bureaucratic Power in Lesotho*, Cambridge, Cambridge University Press.

Fetterman, D. (2005) *Empowerment Evaluation: Collaboration, Action Research, and a Case Example*, The Action Evaluation Research Institute, Stanford University. http://www.aepro.org/imprint/conference/fetterman.html

Fetterman, D.M., Kaftarian, S. and Wandersman, A. (1996) *Empowerment Evaluation: Knowledge and Tools for Self-Assessment and Accountability*, Thousand Oaks CA, Sage.

Floc'hlay, B. and Plottu, E. (1998) 'Democratic evaluation. From empowerment evaluation to public decision making', *Evaluation*, no. 4, pp. 261–277.

Fortmann, L. (1989) 'Peasant and official views of rangeland use in Botswana', *Land Use Policy*, July, pp. 197–202.

Fowler, A. (1988) *Guidelines and Field Checklist for Assessment of Community Organizations*, Nairobi, Ford Foundation.

Fowler, A. (1995) 'Participatory Self-Assessment of NGO capacity', *INTRAC Occasional Papers Series* no.10, Oxford, INTRAC.

Fowler, A. (1997) *Striking a Balance: A Guide to Enhancing the Effectiveness of Non-Governmental Organisations in International Development*, London, Earthscan.

Freire, P. (1972) *Pedagogy of the Oppressed*, London: Penguin.

Fry, R., F. Barrett, J. Seiling and D. Whitney (editors) (2002) *Appreciative Inquiry and Organizational Transformation: Reports from the Field*, Westport CT and London, Quorum Books.

Gereffi, G. and Kaplinsky, K. (eds) (2001) 'The Value of Value Chains: Spreading the Gains from Globalisation', *IDS Bulletin* vol. 32, no. 3, Brighton, Institute of Development Studies.

Gibson, T. (1994) 'Neighbourhood initiatives foundation. Showing what you mean (not just talking about it)', *RRA Notes* no. 21, Special Issue on The Application of Participatory Inquiry in Urban Areas, London, International Institute for Environment and Development, Sustainable Agriculture Programme.

Goetz, A.M. (1996) 'Understanding Gendered Institutional Structures and Practices', presentation for Oxfam meeting on Gender and Organizational Change.

Gomm, R., Hammersley, M. and Foster, P. (eds) (2000) *Case Study Method*, London, Sage.

Goodwin, P.B. (1994) *Traffic Growth and the Dynamics of Sustainable Transport Policies*, Oxford, Transport Studies Unit, Oxford University, October.

Goodwin, P.B. *et al.* (1991) *Transport: the new realism*, Oxford, Transport Studies Unit, Oxford University.

Government of India (1995) *Report of the International Conference on Women's Education and Empowerment*, Government of India and Royal Netherlands Embassy, New Delhi.

Government of Zimbabwe (1990) *Framework for Economic Reform (1991–5)*.

Gray, J.A.M. (1997) *Evidence-Based Health Care: How to Make Health Policy and Management Decisions*, New York and London, Churchill Livingstone.

Grimble, R. and Wellard, K. (1996) 'Stakeholder methodologies in natural resource management: A review of principles, contexts, experiences and opportunities', *Proc. ODA NRSP Socio-economic Methodologies Workshop*, ODI, London, 29–30 April.

Grimble, R., Chan, M.K., Aglionby, J. and Quan, J. (1995) 'Trees and Trade-offs: A Stakeholder Approach to Natural Resource Management', *IIED Gatekeeper series* no. 52, London, International Institute for Environment and Development.

Grindle, M. (ed.) (1980) *Politics and Policy Implementation in the Third World*, Princeton NJ, Princeton University Press.

Guba, E.G. and Lincoln, Y.S. (1989) *Fourth generation evaluation*, London, Sage Publications.

Guijt, I. and Shah, M.K. (eds) (1998) *The Myth of Community: Gender Issues in Participatory Development*, London, Intermediate Technology Publications.

Guijt, I., Fuglesang, A. and Kisadha, T. (1994) 'It is the young trees that make a thick forest', report on Redd Barna's learning experiences with participatory rural appraisal, Kyakatebe, Masaka District, Uganda, March 7–17, Kampala and London, Redd Barna and International Institute for Environment and Development.

Gulati, L. (1991) 'Understanding social forces through individual lives', *Manushi*, Jan-Feb, no. 62, pp. 14–18.

Hacking, I. (1990) *The Taming of Chance*, Cambridge, Cambridge University Press.

Hajer, M. (1995) *The Politics of Environmental Discourse*, Oxford, Clarendon Press.

Harriss, B. (1990) 'The intrafamily distribution of hunger in South Asia', in Drèze, J. and Sen, A. (eds.) *The Political Economy of Hunger. Volume 1: entitlement and well-being*, Oxford, Clarendon Press, pp. 351–424.

Heckman, J. J. (1992) 'Haavelmo and the birth of modern econometrics: a review of the history of econometric ideas by Mary Morgan', *Journal of Economic Literature*, no. 30, pp. 876–86.

Heron, J. (1989) *Facilitator's Handbook*, London, Kogan Page.

Hewitt, T. (2000) 'Half a century of development', in Thomas, T. and Allen, T. (eds.) *Poverty and Development into the twenty-First Century*, Oxford, Oxford University Press in association with The Open University.

Hickey, S. and Mohan, G. eds (2005) *Participation: From Tyranny to Transformation?* London and New York, Zed Press.

Hirschhorn, L. and Gilmore, T. (1992) 'The new boundaries of the 'boundaryless' company', *Harvard Business Review*, May-June, pp. 104–115.

HMG (1999) *Modernising Government*, Cm 4310, London, The Stationery Office.

Holland, J. with Campbell, J. (2005) Methods in Development Research   Combining qualitative and quantitative approaches, London: IT Publications.

Hopwood, A. (1984) 'Accounting and the pursuit of efficiency', in Hopwood, A. and Tomkins, C. (eds.) *Issues in Public Sector Accounting*, Oxford, Philip Allan, pp. 167–187.

Hopwood, A. and Miller, P. (1996) *Accounting as Social and Institutional Practice*, Cambridge, Cambridge University Press.

Houghton, J.Y. Jenkins, G.J. and Ephraums, J.J. (eds) (1990) *Climate Change: The IPCC Scientific Assessment*, Cambridge, Cambridge University Press.

House, E.R. and Howe, K.R. (2000) *Deliberative Democratic Evaluation Checklist*. http://www.wmich.edu/evalctr/checklists/dd_checklist.htm

Hovland, I. (2005) *Successful Communication: A Toolkit for Researchers and Civil Society Organisations*, London, Overseas Development Institute.

Howes, M. and Roche, C. (1995) 'A Participatory Appraisal of ACORD', *PLA Notes* no. 22, London, International Institute for Environment and Development, pp. 69–73.

Hulme, D. (2003) *Thinking 'Small' and the Understanding of Poverty: Maymana and Mofizul's Story, IDPM Working Paper 22*, Manchester, Institute of Development Policy and Management. Updated version (with K. Moore) to be published in *Bangladesh Development Studies* (forthcoming 2006).

IHT (1992) *Traffic Congestion in Urban Areas*, London, Institution of Highways and Transportation.

Irish Department of Foreign Affairs (1993) *Irish Aid: Consolidation and Growth – A Strategy Plan*, Dublin.

Irwin, A. (1996) interviewed in *South Africa Labour Bulletin*, vol. 20. no. 3, June.

Irwin, I. (1995) *Citizen Science: A Study of People, Expertise and Sustainable Development*, London, Routledge.

Ison, R.L. (1996) Seminar presented to the Systems Department, Open University, Milton Keynes, May 8th.

Ison, R.L. and Russell D.B. (eds) (2000) *Agricultural Extension and Rural Development: breaking out of traditions*, Cambridge, Cambridge University Press.

Ison, R.L. (2008) 'Systems thinking and practice for action research' in Bradbury, H. and Reason, P. (eds) *Handbook of Action Research*, 2nd edition, London, Sage (in press).

Jasanoff, S. (1993) 'India at the crossroads in global environmental policy', *Global Environmental Change*, no. 3, vol. 1, pp. 32–52.

Johnston, P. and Stringer, R. (1989) 'Complexity, entropy and environmental effect' in Wheeler, D., Richardson, M.L. and Bridges, J. (eds). *Watershed 89. The Future for Water Quality in Europe*, Proceedings of the IAWPRC Conference, Guildford, UK, 17–20 April 1989, Oxford, Pergamon Press, vol. 2, pp. 283–291.

Jones, P.W. (1992) *World Bank Financing of Education: lending, learning and development*, London, Routledge.

JSB (1996) *The Presenters Guide*, JSB Training, Dove House, Arcadia Avenue, London, N3 2JU.

Kabeer, N. (1994) *Reversed Realities: Gender Hierarchies in Development Thought*, London, Verso.

Kabeer, N. (2000) *The Power to Choose, Bangladesh women and labour market decisions in London and Dhaka*, London, Verso.

Kabeer, N. (2002) 'Reflections on the Measurement of Women's Empowerment' in Sevefjord, B. and Olsson, B. (eds) *Discussing Women's Empowerment - Theory and Practice*, Stockholm, SIDA.

Kanbur, R. (ed.) (2002) *Qualitative and Quantitative Poverty Appraisal: Complementarities, Tensions, and Way Forward*, New Delhi: Permanent Black Publishers.

Keeley, J. and Scoones, I. (2003) *Understanding Environmental Policy Processes: Cases from Africa*, London, Earthscan.

Kersten, S. (1995) *In Search of Dialogue: Vegetation Management in Western NSW, Australia*, PhD Thesis, University of Sydney.

Korten, D. (1980) 'Community organisation and rural development – a learning process approach', *Public Administration Review*, no. 40, pp. 480–511.

Korten, D. (1990) *Getting to the 21st Century: Voluntary Action and the Global Agenda*, West Haven, Connecticut, Kumarian Press.

Krimsky, S. (1984) 'Epistemic considerations on the value of folk-wisdom in science and technology', *Policy Studies Review*, no. 3, vol. 2, pp. 246–262.

Krueger, A.O. (1974) 'The political economy of the rent-seeking society', *American Economic Review*, vol. 64, no. 3.

Kumar, G. and Stewart, F. (1992) 'Tackling malnutrition: what can targeted nutritional interventions achieve?' in Harriss, B., Guhan, S. and Cassen, R.H. (eds.) *Poverty in India, Research and Policy*, Bombay, Oxford University Press, pp. 259–281.

Langrish, J. (1993) 'Case Studies as a Biological Research Process', *Research Paper* 67, Institute of Advanced Studies, Manchester Metropolitan University (version also published in *Design Studies*, October 1993).

Laws, S., Harper, C., and Marcus, R. (2003) *Research for Development: A Practical Guide*, London, Thousand Oaks CA, and New Delhi, Sage.

Leach, M., Scoones, I. and Wynne, B (eds) (2005) *Science and Citizens*, London, Zed Books.

Lee, A. (1989) 'Case Studies as Natural Experiments', *Human Relations*, vol. 42, no. 2, pp. 117–137.

Lennock, J. (1994) 'Paying for Health', *Oxfam Insight*, Oxford, Oxfam.

Levidow, L. and Bijman, J. (2002) 'Farm inputs under pressure from the European food industry', *Food Policy* vol. 27, pp. 31–45.

Lim, L. (1990) 'Women's Work in Export Factories: the politics of a cause' in Tinker, I. (ed.) *Persistent Inequalities: Women and World Development*, Oxford, Oxford University Press.

Lipton, P. (1991) *Inference to the Best Explanation*, London, Routledge.

Lohman, L. (2001) 'Democracy or Carbocracy? Intellectual Corruption and the Future of the Climate Change Debate', *Briefing Paper 24*, Sturminster Newton, The Corner House.

Lukes, S. (1974) *Power: A Radical View*, London and Basingstoke, Macmillan.

Macadam, R., Van Asch, R., Hedley, B., Pitt, E. and Carroll, P. (1995) 'A case study in development planning using a systems learning approach: generating a master plan for the livestock sector in Nepal', *Agricultural Systems*, no. 49, pp. 299–323.

Macintyre, S. (2003) 'Evidence based policy making', Editorial *BMJ* 326, pp. 5–6.

MacDonald, B. (1976) 'Evaluation and the Control of Education', in Tawney, D.A. (ed.) *Curriculum Evaluation Today: Trends and Implications*, Schools Council Research Studies, London, Macmillan.

Mackintosh, M. (1989) *Gender, Class and Rural Transition: Agribusiness and the Food Crisis in Senegal*, London, Zed Books.

Mackintosh, M. (1992) 'Introduction' in Wuyts, M., Mackintosh, M., and Hewitt, T. (eds) *Development Policy and Public Action*. Oxford, Oxford University Press in association with The Open University, pp. 1–9.

Malhotra, A., Schuler, S.R. and Boender, C. (2002), 'Measuring Women's Empowerment as a Variable in International Development', Paper prepared for the World Bank Workshop on *Poverty and Gender: New Perspectives*.

Martin, S. and Tait, J. (1992) 'Release of genetically modified organisms: public attitudes and understandings', Report to the laboratory of the Government Chemist, *Bioscience and Innovation*, June.

Massey, D., Quintas, P. and Wield, D. (1992) *High Tech Fantasies: Science Parks in Society, Science and Space*, London, Routledge.

Maxwell, S. (2005) 'The Washington Consensus is dead! Long live the meta-narrative' *ODI Working Paper 243*, London, Overseas Development Institute.

Mayer, S. and Stirling, A. (2004) 'GM crops: good or bad? Those who choose the questions determine the answers' *EMBO Reports*, vol. 5, no. 11, pp. 1021–1024.

Mayoux, L. (2003) 'Grassroots Action Learning: Impact Assessment for Pro-poor Accountability and Civil Society Development'. http://www.enterprise-impact.org.uk/word-files/GALContentsOverviewand1.1.doc

Mayoux, L. with ANANDI (2005) 'Participatory Action Learning System (PALS): Impact Assessment for Civil Society Development and Grassroots-Based Advocacy in Anandi, India', *Journal of International Development*, vol. 17, no. 2, pp. 211–242. [Original version: 'Participatory Action Learning in Practice: Experience of a Rapid Participatory Appraisal of Anandi, India', http:///www.enterprise-impact.org.uk/informationresources/toolbox/PALinpractice.shtml]

Mayoux, L. and Chambers, R. (2005) 'Reversing the Paradigm: Quantification, Participatory Methods and Pro-poor Growth', *Journal of International Development*, vol. 17, no. 2, pp. 271–298.

Mayoux, L. and Taraqee Foundation (2006) 'Women's Empowerment through Sustainable Micro-finance: Draft Report on Organisational Training'. http://www.genfinance.info/Trainingresources05/TaraqeeReportdraft.pdf

McClintock, D. and Ison, R.L. (1994) 'Responsible (response-able) design metaphors', *Proc. World Congress 3 on Action Learning, Action Research and Process Management*, Bath, UK.

McClintock, D., Ison, R.L. and Armson, R. (2003) 'Metaphors of research and researching with people' *Journal of Environmental Planning and Management*, vol. 46, no. 5, pp. 715–731.

McCormick, D. and Schmitz, H. (2001) *Manual for Value Chain Research on Homeworkers in the Garment Industry*, Institutes for Development Studies, University of Nairobi and University of Sussex. http://www.ids.ac.uk/ids/global/valchn.html

McGee, R. (2003) 'What has happened to poverty in Uganda? Contradiction, confusion and the quest for complementarity', Unpublished paper, Brighton, Institute of Development Studies.

McNiff, J. and Whitehead, J. (2006) *All You Need to Know About Action Research*, London, Sage.

Metz, K.H. (1987) 'Paupers and numbers: the statistical argument for social reform in Britain during the period of industrialization' in Kruger, L., Darron, L. J. and Heidelberger, M. (eds.) *The Probabilistic Revolution. Volume 1: ideas in history*, Cambridge (Massachusetts), A Bradford Book, MIT Press, pp. 337–350.

Mies, M. (1979) 'Towards a Methodology of Women's Studies', *ISS Occasional Papers* no. 77, The Hague, Institute of Social Studies.

Mikkelsen, B. (1995) *Methods for Development Work and Research: a guide for practitioners*, London, Sage.

Mikklesen, B. (2205) *Methods for Development Work and Research: A New Guide for Practitioners*, 2nd Ed, London, Sage.

Miller, R.W. (1987) *Fact and Method: explanation, confirmation and reality in the natural and the social sciences*, Princeton, Princeton University Press.

Mohan, G. (2001) 'Beyond Participation: strategies for deeper empowerment' in Cooke, B. and Kothari, U. (eds) *Participation: The new tyranny?* London, Zed Books.

Montgomery, R. (1995a) *Enhancing Stakeholder Participation in Aid Activities*, London, ODA.

Montgomery, R. (1995b) *Guidance note on stakeholder analysis for aid projects and programmes*, London, ODA.

Moore, M., Stewart, S. and Hudock, A. (1994) *Institution Building as a Development Assistance Method; A Review of the literature and Ideas*, report to Swedish International Development Authority (SIDA), Brighton, Institute of Development Studies.

Morgan, D. (1981) 'Men, masculinity and the process of sociological enquiry', in Roberts, H. (ed.) *Doing Feminist Research*, London, Routledge and Kegan Paul, pp. 83–113.

Morgan, G. (1997) *Images of Organization*, 2nd edtition, Newbury Park CA and London, Sage.

Morris, D. (1965) *The Emergence of an Industrial Labour Force in India: a study of Indian cotton mills 1854–1947*, Bombay, Oxford University Press.

Mosse, D. (1994) 'Authority, gender and knowledge: theoretical reflections on the practice of Participatory Rural Appraisal', *Development and Change*, vol. 25, no. 3, pp. 497–526.

Mosse, D. (1995) 'Social analysis in Participatory Rural Development', *PLA Notes*, no. 24, International Institute for Environment and Development, London, pp. 27–33.

Mosse, D. (2005) *Cultivating Development: An ethnography of aid policy and practice*, London, Pluto Press.

Murray, C. (1981) *Families Divided*, Cambridge, Cambridge, University Press.

Myers, N. (1995) 'Environmental unknowns', *Science*, no. 269, pp. 358–360.

MYRADA (1992) 'Analysis of Societal Roles and Problems from a Gender Perspective and Development of Gender-sensitive Tools in PRA-PALM', MYRADA, Bangalore, India.

Nadar, L. (1986) 'From anguish to exultation', in Golde, P. (ed.) *Women in the Field: anthropological experiences*, Berkeley, University of California Press, pp. 97–116.

Narayan, D. and Petesch, P. (2002) *Voices of the poor: from many lands*, New York, Oxford University Press.

Narayan, D. and Srinivasan, L. (1994) *Participatory Development Toolkit: Materials to Facilitate Community Empowerment*, Washington, World Bank.

Narayan, D., Chambers, R., Shah, M. and Petesch, P. (2000) *Voices of the Poor: Crying Out for Change*. New York, Oxford University Press.

Narayan-Parker, D. (1997) *Voices of the poor: poverty and social capital in Tanzania*, IBRD/World Bank Environmentally and socially sustainable development studies monographs series 20.

Nelkin, D. (1992) 'Science, technology, and political conflict. Analyzing the issues', in Nelkin, D. (ed.) *Controversy: Politics of Technical Decisions*, 3rd edition, Newbury Park CA, Newbury Sage.

Nelson, N. and Wright, S. (eds) (1995) *Power and Participatory Development: Theory and Practice*, London, Intermediate Technology Publications.

NOVIB (1996) *Notes from a Partners Conference on Organisational Self-Audit*, Penang, Malaysia, April 16–18 1996, mimeo.

Nutley, S.M., Smith, P.C., and Davies, H.T.O. (2000) *What Works? Evidence-Based Policy and Practice in Public Services*, Bristol, The Policy Press.

Oakley, A. (1981) 'Interviewing women: a contradiction in terms?' in Roberts, H. (ed.) *Doing Feminist Research*, London, Routledge.

Olsen, W. (1992) 'Random sampling and repeat surveys in South India', in Devereux, S. and Hoddinott, J. (eds) *Fieldwork in Developing Countries*, London, Harvester Wheatsheaf.

Open University (1996) *Working with Systems*, Milton Keynes, The Open University.

OED (Operations Evaluation Department) (2003) 'Sharing Knowledge: Innovations and Remaining Challenges', *OED Reach* 12, November. http://lnweb18.worldbank.org/oed/oeddoclib.nsf/DocPgNmViewForJavaSearch/KSReach/$file/KSReach.pdf

Patel, S. (1986) 'Contract labour in Ahmedabad textile industry', *Economic and Political Weekly of India*, vol. 21, no. 4, Oct 11, pp. 1813–20.

Pawson, R. (2002) 'Evidence-based Policy: In Search of a Method', *Evaluation*, vol. 8, no. 2, pp. 157–181.

Pearce, F. (1992) 'Ecology and the new colonialism', *New Scientist*, 1 February, pp. 55–56.

Pearson, R. (1998). 'Nimble fingers' revisited – Reflection on Women and Third World Industrialization in the Late Twentieth Century' in Jackson, C. and Pearson, R. *Feminist Visions of Development, Gender, Analysis and Policy*, London and New York: Routledge.

Perkins, D. (1995) *Outsmarting IQ: the emerging science of learnable intelligence*, New York, The Free Press.

Peters, T. (1992) *Liberation Management: Necessary Disorganisation for the Nanosecond Nineties*, New York, Alfred Knopf and London, Macmillan.

Pettifor, A. (2003) 'Policy Entrepreneurship', A transcript of a talk at ODI 11th June 2003. www.odi.org.uk/RAPID/Meetings/ Evidence/Presentation_15/Pettifor.html

Pettigrew, J. (1981) 'Reminiscences of fieldwork among the Sikhs', in Roberts, H. (ed.) *Doing Feminist Research*, London, Routledge and Kegan Paul, pp. 62–82.

Potter, D. (ed.) (1996) *NGOs and Environmental Policies: Asia and Africa*, London, Frank Cass.

Potter, S. and Parkhurst, G. (2005) 'Transport Policy and Transport Tax Reform', *Public Money and Management* vol 25, no 3, pp. 171–178.

Pretty, J., Subrahmanian, S., Kempu Chetty, N., Ananthakrishnan, D., Jayanthi, C., Muralikrishnasamy, S. and Renganayaki, K. (1992) 'Finding the poorest in a Tamil Nadu village: a sequence of mapping and wealth ranking', *RRA Notes* no. 15, Special Issue on Applications of Wealth Ranking, London, International Institute for Environment and Development, pp. 39–42.

Ragin, C. (1987) *The Comparative Method: Moving beyond Qualitative and Quantitative Strategies*, Berkeley: University of California Press.

Rahman, M.D.A. (1995) 'Participatory Development: Towards Liberation and Co-optation?' in Craig, G. and Mayo, M. (eds) *Community Empowerment: a reader in participation and development*, London: Zed Books, pp. 24–32.

Ramazanoglu, C. and Holland, J. (Reprint 2004) *Feminist Methodology: Challenges and Choices*, London, Sage.

Redclift, M. (1992) 'Sustainable Development and Popular Participation: a framework for analysis', in Ghai, D. and Vivian, J. (eds.) (1992) *Grassroots environmental action*, London, Routledge.

Ribbens, J. and Edwards, R. (eds) (1998) *Feminist Dilemmas in Qualitative Research*, London, Sage.

Richards, P. (1995) 'Participatory Rural Appraisal: A quick and dirty critique', *PLA Notes* no. 24, London, International Institute for Environment and Development, pp. 13–16.

Richie, J. and Spencer, L. (2002) 'Qualitative Data Analysis for Applied Policy Research' in Huberman, A.M. and Miles, M.B. (eds) *The Qualitative Researcher's Companion*, London, Sage, pp. 305–29.

Riddell, R. and Robinson, M. (1995) *Non-Governmental Organizations and Rural Poverty Alleviation*, Oxford, Clarendon Press.

Robinson, D. (1998) 'Rethinking the Public Sector: NGOs, Public Action Networks, and the Promotion of Community-Based Health Care in Tanzania', *DPP Working Paper* no. 38, Milton Keynes, Open University Development Policy and Practice research group.

Robson, C. (1993) *Real World Research: a resource for social scientists*, Oxford, Blackwell.

Roche, C. (1999) *Impact Assessment for Development Agencies: Learning to Value Change*, Oxford, Oxfam

Roche, C., Kasynathan, N. and Gowthaman, P. (2005) 'Bottom-up Accountability and the Tsunami' Paper prepared for the International Conference on Engaging Communities, Brisbane.

Roche, C. (1994) 'Operationality in Turbulence: the need for change', *Development in Practice*, vol. 4, no. 3, pp. 160–72.

Roe, D., Dalal Clayton, B. and Hughes, R. (1995) *A Directory of Impact Assessment Guidelines – an Output from the INTERAISE Project*, London, International Institute for Environment and Development.

Roth, S., Chasin, L., Chasin, R., Becker, C. and Herzig, M. (1992) 'From debate to dialogue. A facilitating role for family therapists in the public forum', *Dulwich Centre Newsletter*, no. 2, pp. 41–48.

Rowlands, J. (1995) 'Empowerment examined', *Development in Practice*, vol. 5, no. 2 pp. 101–107.

Ruskie, E. (2005) 'Exploring food and farming futures in Zimbabwe: a citizens' jury and scenario workshop experiment' in Leach, M., Scoones, I. and Wynne, B. (eds) *Science and Citizens*, London, Zed Books.

Russell, D.B. and Ison, R.L. (1993) 'The research-development relationship in rangelands: an opportunity for contextual science', Invited Plenary Paper, *Proc. IVth International Rangeland Congress*, Montpellier, vol. 3, pp. 1047–1054.

SACTRA (1994) *Trunk Roads and the Generation of Traffic*, London, HMSO, December.

Salmen, L. (1992) *Beneficiary Assessment: An Approach Described*, Washington DC, World Bank.

Sardar, F. Mumtaz, N. and Hussein, S. (2004) 'Women's and men's Views of Empowerment: Kashf Empowerment Diamonds'. http://www.genfinance.info/Documents/Kashf%20 Empowerment%20Diamonds.pdf

Sayer, A. (1992) *Method in Social Science: A Realist Approach*, 2nd edition, London, Routledge.

Scheyvens, R. and Storey, D. (2003) *Development Fieldwork: A Practical Guide*, London, Sage.

Schramm, W. (1971) 'Notes on case studies of instructional media projects', Working Paper, Academy for Educational Development, Washington DC.

Schrijvers, J. (1995) 'Participation and power: a transformative feminist research perspective', in Nelson, N. and Wright, S. (eds) *Power and Participatory Development: Theory and Practice*, London, Intermediate Technology Publications.

Schubert, B. (1993) *Social Assistance to Destitute Urban Households as Part of the Social Safety Net in Mozambique: An Evaluation of the GAPVU Cash-Transfer-Scheme*, Maputo, consultancy provided within the framework of the Social Dimensions of Adjustment (SDA) Initiative of the World Bank.

Segone, M. (1998) 'Democratic Evaluation: A proposal for Strengthening the Evaluation Function in International Development Agencies', *Democratic Evaluation Working Paper No 3*. UNICEF, Regional office for Latin America and the Caribbean. http://www.ird.ne/ partenariat/rense/democeval.pdf. http://www.avaliabrasil.org.br/democeval.pdf

Selolwane, O. (2001) 'Ineffectual NGO Influence on the Policy of Fencing Botswana's Communal Rangelands' in Thomas, A., Carr, S., and Humphreys, D. (eds.) *Environmental Policies and NGO Influence: Land Degradation and Sustainable Resource Management in Sub-Saharan Africa*, London, Routledge.

Sen, A. (1990) 'Food entitlement and economic chains', in Newman, L. F. (ed.) *Hunger in History: food shortage, poverty and deprivation*, Oxford, Blackwell, pp. 374–386.

Sen, A. (1999) *Development as Freedom*, Oxford University Press, Oxford.

Shah, P. and Shah, M.K. (1995) 'Participatory Methods: Precipitating or avoiding conflict?', *PLA Notes* no. 24, International Institute for Environment and Development, pp. 48–51.

Sharamshakti (1988) *A Report of the National Commission on Self-Employed Women in the Informal Sector*, New Delhi, Government of India, Ministry of Social Welfare, Dept. of Women and Child Development.

Singer, H. (1989) 'Lessons of Post War Development experience 1945–88', *IDS Discussion Paper* no. 260, Brighton, Institute of Development Studies.

SLIM (2004) 'Stakeholders and Stakeholding in Integrated Catchment Management and Sustainable Use of Water', SLIM PB2 (available at http://slim.open.ac.uk).

Slim, H. and Thompson, P. (1993) *Listening for a Change – Oral Testimony and Development*, London, Panos.

Spender, D. (1981) 'The gatekeepers: a feminist critique of academic publishing' in Roberts, H. (ed.) *Doing Feminist Research*, pp. 186–202, London, Routledge and Kegan Paul.

Srivastava, V. (1991) 'The ethnographer and the people: reflections on fieldwork', *Economic and Political Weekly of India*, June 1–8 (part 1), pp. 1475–81, and June 15 (part 2), pp. 1408–14.

Stake, R.E. (1995) *The Art of Case Study Research: Perspectives on Practice*, Thousand Oaks CA, Sage.

Stanton, N. (1986) *What Do You Mean 'Communication'? How People and Organizations Communicate*, London, Macmillan Education.

Start, D. and Hovland, I. (2004) *Tools for Policy Impact: A Handbook for Researchers*, London, Overseas Development Institute. *http*://www.odi.org.uk/publications/rapid/tools1.pdf

Staudt, K. (1991) *Managing Development: State, Society and International Contexts*, London, Sage Publications.

Stirling, A. (2005) 'Opening up or closing down? Analysis, participation and power in the social appraisal of technology' in Leach, M., Scoones, I. and Wynne, B. (eds) *Science and Citizens*, London, Zed Books.

Sutcliffe, S. and Court, J. (2005) 'Evidence-Based Policymaking: What is it? How does it work? What relevance for developing countries?', London, Overseas Development Institute.

TEC (2006) *Joint evaluation of the international response to the Indian Ocean tsunami: Synthesis Report*, Tsunami Evaluation Coalition (hosted by ALNAP, Overseas Development Institute, London). Available at: http://www.tsunami-evaluation.org/The+TEC+Synthesis+Report/Full+Report.htm

Tendler, J. and Freedheim, S. (1994) 'Trust in a rent-seeking world: Health and Government Transformed in North east Brazil', *World Development*, vol. 22, no. 12, pp. 1771–1791.

TfL (2004) 'Update on scheme impacts and operations', *Congestion Charging – February 2004 update*, London, Transport for London., Available at: http://www.tfl.gov.uk/tfl/cc_monitoring.shtml, [Accessed on 20 Feb 2004].

The Planning Commission and The Ministry of Labour and Youth Development (with assistance from UNDP/ILO URT/91/028) (1991) *Tanzania: the informal sector*, Dar Es Salaam, Tanzania, The Government Printer, pp. 2–5.

Thomas, P. (1982) Social Research and Social Policy in Loney, M., Boswell, D. and Clarke J (1983) *Social Policy and Social Welfare*, Milton Keynes, Open University Press.

Thomas, A. (1992) 'Non-governmental organizations and the limits to empowerment', in Wuyts, M., Mackintosh, M. and Hewitt, T. (eds) *Development Policy and Public Action*, Oxford, Oxford University Press in association with The Open University, pp. 117–146.

Thomas, A. (1996a) 'What is Development Management?', *Journal of International Development*, vol. 8, no. 1, pp. 95–110.

Thomas, A. (1996b) 'NGO Advocacy, Democracy and Policy Development: Some Examples Relating to Environmental Policies in Zimbabwe and Botswana', in Potter, D. (ed.) *NGOs and Environmental Policies: Asia and Africa*, London, Frank Cass, pp. 38–65.

Thomas, A. (1999) "What makes *good* development management?" *Development in Practice*, vol. 9, nos. 1&2, pp. 9–17.

Thomas, A. (2001) 'NGOs and their influence on environmental policies in Africa: a framework' in Thomas, A., Humphreys, D. & Carr, S. (eds) *Environmental Policies and NGO Influence: Land Degradation and Natural resource Management in Africa*, London: Routledge, pp. 1–22.

Thomas, A. (2003) 'NGOs' role in limiting national sovereignty over environmental resources of global significance: the 1990 campaign against the Southern Okavango Integrated Water Development Project', *Journal of International Development*, vol. 15, no. 2, pp. 215–219.

Thomas, A., Chataway, J. and Wuyts, M. (1998) *Finding out Fast: Investigative Skills for Policy and Development*, London: Sage.

Thomas, A. and Selolwane, O. (2001) 'The campaign against the Southern Okavango Integrated Water Development Project' in Thomas, A., Humphreys, D. & Carr, S. (eds) (2001) *Environmental Policies and NGO Influence: Land Degradation and Natural resource Management in Africa*, London: Routledge, pp. 109–129.

Townsend, P. and Davidson N. (eds.) (1988) 'The Black Report', in *Inequalities in Health*, London, Penguin Books, pp. 44–128.

Tukey, J. (1977) *Exploratory Data Analysis*, Reading, MA, Addison–Wesley.

Ulrich, W. (1987) 'Critical heuristics of social systems design,' *European Journal of Operational Research*, no. 31.

UNCED (1992) *Rio declaration on environment and development*, United Nations Conference on Environment and Development. Available at: http://www.unep.org/Documents/Default.asp?DocumentID=78&ArticleID=1163.

Upadhyay, S. (1990) 'Cotton mill workers in Bombay 1875–1918: conditions of work and life', *Economic and Political Weekly of India*, July 28, pp. 87–99.

Uphoff, N. (1986) *Local Institutional Development: an Analytical Sourcebook with Cases*, West Hartford CT, Kumarian Press.

Uphoff, N. (1987) 'Participatory evaluation of participatory development. A scheme of measuring and monitoring local capacity being introduced in Sri Lanka', People's Participation Project Workshop (Ghana) on participatory monitoring and evaluation, Rome, UN FAO.

Uphoff, N. (1992) 'Local institutions and participation for sustainable development', *IIED Gatekeeper Series*, no. 31, London, International Institute for Environment and Development.

UPPAP (2000) *Learning from the Poor*, Uganda Participatory Poverty Assessment Report, Ministry of Finance, Planning and Economic Development, Kampala.

UPPAP (2002) *National Report, December 2002*, Uganda Participatory Poverty Assessment Process, Ministry of Finance, Planning and Economic Development, Kampala.

VeneKlasen, L. and Miller, V. (2002) *A New Weave of Power, People and Politics: The Action Guide for Advocacy and Citizen Participation*, World Neighbours, Oklahoma. www.wn.org

Vivian, J. (1994) 'NGOs and sustainable development in Zimbabwe; no magic bullets', *Development and Change*, vol. 25, no. 1, pp. 167–93.

Warren, C. (1988) *Gender Issues in Field Research*, London, Sage Publications.

Watson, R.T. and the Core Writing Team (eds) (2001) *Climate Change 2001: Synthesis Report*, A contribution of Working Groups I, II and III to the Third Assessment Report of the Intergovernmental Panel on Climate Change (IPCC), Cambridge, Cambridge University Press.

Watson-Verran, H. and Turnbull, D. (1995) 'Science and other indigenous knowledge systems', in Jasanoff, S., Markle, G.E., Petersen, J.C. and Pinch, T. (eds.) *Handbook of Science and Technology Studies*, Thousand Oaks CA, Sage.

Weale, A. (1992) *The New Politics of Pollution*, Manchester, Manchester University Press.

Webster, A. (1991) *Science, Technology and Society*, Basingstoke and London, Macmillan.

Weiner, M. (1982) 'Social science research and public policy in India' in Steifel, D. *et al.* (eds) *Social Sciences and Public Policy in the Developing World*, Massachusetts, Lexington Books.

Weiss, C.H. (1979) 'The many meanings of research utilization', *Public Administration Review*, vol. 39, no. 5, pp. 426–431.

Welbourn, A. (1991) 'RRA and the analysis of difference', *RRA Notes* no. 14, London, International Institute for Environment and Development, pp. 14–23.

Welbourn, A. (1992) 'Rapid Rural Appraisal, Gender and Health – Alternative Ways of Listening to Needs', *IDS Bulletin*, vol. 23, no. 1, Brighton, Institute of Development Studies.

Whitehead, M. (1988) 'The health divide' in *Inequalities in Health,* London, Penguin Books, pp. 229–356.

Woodhouse, P. (2004) 'Local identities of poverty: poverty narratives in decentralised government and the role of poverty research in Uganda', *GPRG Working Paper 13*, Manchester, Global Poverty Research Group. http://www.gprg.org

Woodhouse, P., Trench, P. and Tessougué, M. (2000). 'A Very Decentralised Development' in Woodhouse, P., Bernstein, H. and Hulme, D. *African Enclosures? The Social Dynamics of Wetlands in Drylands.* Oxford, James Currey, pp. 29–72.

World Bank (1975) 'Lesotho: a development challenge', *World Bank Country Economic Reports*, Washington, World Bank.

World Bank (1989) *Mozambique food security study*, report no. 7963–MOZ, Washington, World Bank.

World Bank (1994) *Adjustment in Africa: Reforms, Results and the Road Ahead*, Oxford, Oxford University Press for the World Bank.

World Bank (2000) *Attacking Poverty*, World Development Report 2000/2001, New York, Oxford University Press.

World Bank (2002) *A Sourcebook for Poverty Reduction Strategies*, Washington DC, World Bank.

World Bank (2004) *Making Services Work for Poor People*, World Development Report 2004, New York, Oxford University Press.

Wuyts, M. (1981) *Camponeses e Economia Rural em Mocambique*, Maputo, INLD no. 0251.

Wuyts, M. (2001) 'Informal economy, wage goods and accumulation under structural adjustment: theoretical reflections based on the Tanzanian experience', *Cambridge Journal of Economics, vol. 25, no. 3.* pp. 417–438.

Wuyts, M. (2004) 'Macroeconomic Policy and trade integration. Tanzania in the world economy', in S. Bromley, M. Mackintosh, W. Brown & M. Wuyts (eds) *Making the International. Economic Interdependence and Political Order*, Milton Keynes, The Open University and London, Pluto Press, pp. 331–378.

Wuyts, M., Mackintosh, M., and Hewitt, T. (eds.) (1992) *Development Policy and Public Action*, Oxford, Oxford University Press in association with The Open University.

Wynne, B. (1989) 'Frameworks of rationality in risk management – towards the testing of naive sociology' in Brown, J. (ed.), *Environmental Threats: Perception, Analysis, and Management*, London, Belhaven.

Wynne, B. (1992) 'Uncertainty and environmental learning', *Global Environmental Change*, vol. 2, no. 22, pp. 111–127.

Wynne, B. and Mayer, S. (1993) 'How science fails the environment' *New Scientist*, 5 June, pp. 33–35.

Yates, J. and Moncreiffe, J. (2002) 'Synthesis of PPA2 Cycle 1 Findings' Uganda Participatory Poverty Assessment Process, Ministry of Finance, Planning and Economic Development, Kampala.

Yates, J. and Okello, L. (2002) 'Learning from Uganda's efforts to learn from the poor: Reflections and lessons from the Uganda Participatory Poverty Assessment Project', in Brock, K. & McGee, R. (eds) *Knowing Poverty. Critical Reflections on Participatory Research and Poverty*, London, Earthscan.

Yearley, S. (1996) *Sociology, Environmentalism, Globalisation*, London, Sage.

Yin, R. (1994) *Case Study Research: Design and Methods*, 2nd edition, Thousand Oaks CA, Sage.

Yin, R. (2002) *Case Study Research: Design and Methods*, 3rd edition, Newbury Park CA, Sage.

Young, J. Kajume, J. and Wanyama, J. (2005) 'Animal care in Kenya: the road to community-based animal health service delivery' in Court, J., Hovland, I. and Young, . (eds) *Bridging Research and Policy in Development: Evidence and the Change Process*, Rugby, Intermediate Technology Publishing.

Young, J. and Court, J. (2004) 'Bridging Research and Policy in International Development. An analytical and practical framework' *RAPID Briefing Paper*, London, Overseas Development Institute.

Index

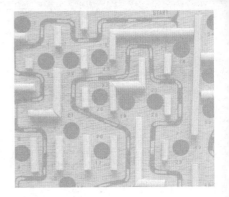

b refers to a box, f refers to a figure, t refers to a table